CW01646876

English Law and Language

Dedication

For Frances' Mother, Eileen.
For Kate and Anna.

English Law and Language

Frances Russell
Christine Locke

CASSELL

Cassell Publishers Ltd
Villiers House
41/47 Strand
London WC2N 5JE

© Cassell Publishers Ltd 1992

All rights reserved. This book is protected by copyright.
No part of it may be reproduced, stored in a retrieval system, or transmitted in any form or by any means, electronic, mechanical, photocopying or otherwise, without written permission from the Publishers.

First Published 1992

British Library Cataloguing in Publication Data
Russell, Frances
English law and language.
1. England. Law
I. Title II. Locke, Christine
344.2

ISBN 0–304–33011–6

Designed by Derek Lee
Typeset by Litho Link Limited, Welshpool, Powys.
Printed and bound in Great Britain by
Dotesios Ltd, Trowbridge, Wiltshire.

Contents

Preface

A knowledge of the English legal system and the associated mechanics of legal reasoning is becoming increasingly important for law students in countries other than the United Kingdom. This book provides an introduction to the English legal system and the means to develop the language and analytical skills which form an essential part of legal study. The two purposes of the book are therefore;

1 to provide factual knowledge;

2 to develop the necessary language and analytical skills.

It specifically addresses the needs of overseas students with no previous knowledge of the English legal system or law. These will include:

1 students whose first language is not English, attending a higher education institution overseas whose studies require a background knowledge of the English legal system;

2 overseas students with an Upper–Intermediate level of English, wishing to apply to a British institution of higher education to study law;

3 overseas students with an Intermediate level of English, studying law at pre-degree or undergraduate level at a British institution of higher education;

4 students studying without a teacher (see notes for self-study students at the end of the Preface).

The book begins by introducing some general features of the English legal system which will provide a background to the following topics. The legal system is then set within the constitutional framework with an examination of important constitutional concepts and with particular reference to the constitutional position of the judiciary.

The following four chapters are concerned with the institutions of the legal system: sources of law, the judiciary and the jury, the courts and the provision of legal services. The emphasis in these chapters is on procedural law rather than substantive law although cases are used to illustrate some of the concepts involved.

The study of cases is further developed in Chapters 7 and 8 which focus on two areas of substantive law – civil and criminal – and the process of legal analysis.

Discussion is then centred on the subject of law reform. The existing machinery of reform is examined together with an analysis of its weaknesses and proposed alternatives.

The final chapter considers the European dimension with reference to the European Convention on Human Rights and the law of the European Community.

Each topic is set within its social context by introducing relevant areas of debate and discussion.

It is important to note that, although for the purposes of convenience and structure each topic is dealt with under a separate title, the aim is to produce an overview of the English legal system and an awareness of the overlap between each subject.

There are sets of revision questions after Chapters 3 and 6. These provide an opportunity to consolidate existing legal knowledge and skills before moving onto the more advanced subjects in the following chapters.

Language work develops from the texts which were chosen for their relevance to the study of law and not as springboards for language exercises. Consequently, this book cannot provide comprehensive coverage of English grammar; the exercises provided concentrate on those reading, writing and study skills which are clearly necessary for academic study in the field of law.

Students and teachers should also be aware that the book is not intended to provide exhaustive coverage of legal topics. Inevitably many areas are not included, and those which are, are intended to provide only a firm foundation for further study. Further recommended reading is provided at the end of each chapter and students are encouraged to extend their knowledge and apply the skills gained by following up these references. The additional reading references will also be a valuable source of background information for teachers who are unfamiliar with the English legal system.

Form

The book comprises ten chapters each dealing with an individual subject. The broad subject-matter of each chapter is broken down into sections and sub-sections to provide a structured approach to the subject. These also provide a means of dividing a programme of study based on the book into suitable lessons.

The factual content is presented through extracts from authentic texts (books, cases, journals and newspapers) and commentary by the authors. Students are given more help through commentaries in the early chapters, whereas the proportion of authentic texts increases later in the book as the work becomes more challenging. Legal exercises aim to highlight the relevant legal concepts and areas of discussion and to train the student to think analytically. A proportion of these will be activity-based and require wider research. Guidance on how to do the legal exercises are provided through advice on essay technique, problem-solving and essay plans. This advice is quite detailed in the first part of the book and is gradually reduced as students acquire the necessary skills and confidence. Equally the complexity of the extracts and exercises increases throughout the book.

Language information and exercises are placed at relevant points within and between texts. Texts are annotated as follows:

1 *Text notes* designed to inform the reader, for example brief help with vocabulary or factual information which is essential to comprehension of the text; these notes are numbered consecutively within each chapter.

2 *Comprehension checks* designed to encourage the student to read actively by being aware of the writer's use of cohesive devices; this is done by short questions, e.g. 'What does "this" refer to?' Such questions together with those of a legal nature are also numbered consecutively within each chapter.

Information is given on advanced grammatical areas which arise from texts and on vocabulary (e.g. word formation and use of legal vocabulary). Exercises concentrate on reading, writing and study skills with some work on oral functions. Reading skills exercises focus on scanning, skimming, reading for detail and recognising main arguments. Writing exercises include the writing of paragraphs and short essays with guidance. Study skills exercises cover dictionary use, bibliographical references and notemaking, Vocabulary exercises deal with inferencing skills, word formation, prepositions and collocations.

The book also contains a very comprehensive and detailed Answer Section. This will be particularly valuable to teachers who are not legally qualified and students studying on their own. Those who are legally qualified but who are not English language teachers will find answers to all the language exercises.

Notes for self-study students

When writing this book the authors also had in mind those students who cannot attend classes. Although you need no legal training your English should be of at least intermediate standard. In addition to the textbook you will need only an English–English dictionary. All necessary reading material for the exercises is in the book and the answer key is very detailed. However, you should try and find sources of extra reading material (many suggestions for additional reading are included after each chapter). It is possible that a college or university in your region would allow you to use their library.

Acknowledgments

All the materials in this book appear with the permission of those who hold the copyright. The authors and publishers thank the following for their permission to reproduce copyright material:

The Controller of Her Majesty's Stationery Office for permission to include extracts from official publications; the Incorporated Council of Law Reporting for England and Wales for extracts from the *Law Reports* and the *Weekly Law Reports*; The Council of Europe for extracts of reports of the European Commission of Human Rights; Butterworths Law Publishers Ltd for extracts from the *All England Law Reports*, S. H. Bailey, D. J. Harris and B. L. Jones, *Civil Liberties: Cases and Materials*, M. Brazier (ed.), *Street on Torts*, Lord Denning, 'Misuse of power' in *What Next in the Law*, A. M. Dugdale, M. P. Furmston, S. P. Jones, C. H. Sharin and K. M. Stanton, *A Level Law*, P. James, *Introduction to English Law*, D. Lasok and J. W. Bridge, *Law and Institutions of the European Community*, G. Pearce, *Statutory Interpretation in Australia*, R. S. Sim and D. M. M. Scott, *A Level English Law*, J. C. Smith and B. Hogan, *Criminal Law*, R. J. Walker, *The English Legal System*, D. C. M. Yardley, *Principles of Administrative Law*; Sweet and Maxwell Ltd for extracts from the *Common Market Law Reports*, the *Law Quarterly Review*, the European Human Rights Reports, Lord Denning, 'The independence of the judiciary' in *The Lawyer and Justice*, D. W. Elliot and M. J. Allen, *Elliot and Wood's Casebook on Criminal Law*, J. Farrar and A. M. Dugdale, *Introduction to Legal Method*, Lord Hailsham, *Hamlyn Revisited*, B. Hogan, P. Seago and G. Bennett, *A Level Law*, G. H. Treitel, *The Law of Contract*, G. Williams, *Learning the Law*, G. Wilson, *Cases and Materials on the English Legal System*; C. Dyer for 'Barrister's rights go in strategic reform' in the *Guardian*, 8 December 1989; O. Hansen for 'A limiting franchise on giving legal aid' in the *Guardian*, 22 September 1989; Times Newspapers Limited for an extract from a lead article in *The Sunday Times* on 24 September 1972; Clarendon Press for extracts from R. Cross, *Precedent in English Law*; Harper Collins for extracts from J. G. Griffiths, *The Politics of the Judiciary*; The Penguin Group for extracts from T. Gifford, *Where's the Justice: A Manifesto of Law Reform*; Blackstone Press Ltd for extracts from T. Ingham, *The English Legal Process*, N. Johnson and A. Pannett, *SWOT A Level Law*, J. Steiner, *Textbook on EEC Law*; Longman Group UK for extracts from E. C. S. Wade and A. W. Bradley, *Constitutional and Administrative Law*; Basil Blackwell Ltd for extracts from the *Modern Law Review*, R. White, *The Administration of Justice*; Cambridge University Press for extracts from J. R. Spencer, *Jackson's Machinery of Justice*; Oxford Polytechnic for extracts from A. Pannett, *Criminal Law in Action*, N. Johnson, *Contract Law in Action*; Routledge & Kegan Paul Ltd for extracts from L. Scarman, *Law Reform: The New Pattern*.

While every attempt has been made to trace copyright owners, the publishers would be pleased to hear from any other parties who feel they hold rights to any of the material that has been included.

The authors would also like to thank David Bunn for reading the earlier drafts and providing helpful advice and comments, Ravid Paz for providing a student's point of view, Dr Malcolm Petyt for his encouragement and support, and our families for their forbearance and support.

List of abbreviations used in the book

AC	Appeal Cases (Law Reports)
ABWOR	assistance by way of representation
A-G	Attorney-General
All ER	All England Law Reports (Law Reports)
CA	Court of Appeal
CMLR	Common Market Law Reports
CPS	Crown Prosecution Service
DPP	Director of Public Prosecutions
ECHR	European Commission on Human Rights; when cited after a case means reports from the European Commission on Human Rights
ECJ	European Court of Justice
ECR	European Court Reports (Law Reports)
HL	House of Lords
KB	King's Bench (Law Reports)
J	Justice
JJ	Justices
LJ	Lord Justice
LL	Lords
LLJ	Lords Justices
LQR	Law Quarterly Review
MLR	Modern Law Review
MP	Member of Parliament
MR	Master of the Rolls
QB	Queen's Bench (Law Reports)
WLR	Weekly Law Reports

Table of cases

1

Central features of the English legal system

Summary

Legal content

1.1 The characteristics of English law
1.2 Common law and equity
  1.2.1 The development of common law
  1.2.2 The growth of equity
1.3 Classifications of law
  1.3.1 Criminal and civil law
  1.3.2 Substantive and procedural law
Additional reading

Aim

To provide an introduction to some of the central features of the English legal system and a background to your study of the subject. Much of the knowledge gained during the reading of this chapter will be applied throughout the book. Some of the topics will be examined more fully in later chapters.

Language content

Grammar: grammatical terms – noun, verb, adjective, adverb; identifying different grammatical forms of lexical items in texts; use of prepositions
Oral function: asking for meaning of words
Vocabulary: dictionary use – recognising dictionary order of words; finding appropriate (legal) meaning of words

1.1 The characteristics of English law

Pre-reading check

1 Before you read the text look at the statements below then read the text to decide whether they are true (T) or false (F). Do this as quickly as possible, remembering that at this stage it is not necessary to understand every word.

a The law in Scotland is the same as the law in England.
b English law has evolved[1] gradually.
c Most of English law has been codified.
d The common law was developed by the judges.
e The judiciary is not independent of the government.
f The court structure of the English legal system is the same throughout the country.
g All the courts in the system are of equal authority.
h English judges collect evidence in the cases before them.

Text note:
1 changed and developed

The United Kingdom does not have a single legal system. The law in Scotland was influenced by Roman law and is different from the law of England, Wales and Northern Ireland.

The English legal system is centralised through a court structure which is common to[2] the whole country. It is hierarchical,[3] with the higher courts and judges having more authority than the lower ones. Some important characteristics of English law are:[4]

1 English law is based on the **common law** tradition. By this we mean a system of 'judge made' law which has continuously developed over the years through the decisions of judges in the cases brought before them. These judicial **precedents**[5] are an important source of law in the English legal system. Common law systems are different from the civil law systems of Western Europe and Latin America. In these countries the law has been **codified**[6] or systematically collected to form a consistent body of legal rules.

2 English judges have an important role in developing case law and stating the meaning of Acts of Parliament.

3 The judges are independent of the government and the people appearing before them. This allows them to make impartial[7] decisions.

4 Court procedure is **accusatorial**. This means that judges do not investigate[8] the cases before them but reach a decision based only on the evidence presented to them by the parties to the dispute. This is called the **adversarial** system of justice. It can be compared to the **inquisitorial** procedure of some other European systems where it is the function of the judges to investigate the case and to collect evidence.

Text notes:
2 shared by
3 this word is explained by the rest of the sentence
4 notice how the colon (:) is used to introduce a list
5 this is explained in the previous sentence ('the decisions . . .')
6 also explained by the rest of the sentence
7 not favouring one side more than another
8 examine

Research

2 Find out whether the legal system in your country is adversarial or inquisitorial.

Legal exercises

The aim of the following questions is to help you to begin to understand the legal implications of the characteristics of English law. Read the text above again. Write short answers to each question below and use them as a basis of a discussion with your teacher and group. If you are working on your own compare your answers to those given in the Answer Section.

3 Would a codified system of law make the law more
  a certain, or
  b flexible?

4 Why is it important for judges to be independent?

5 What is the disadvantage of an adversarial system of justice?

Oral work

You may not understand all the key words in these discussion questions. How will you ask your teacher for an explanation? Here are some possible ways:

a 'Excuse me, can/could you tell me what "codified" means?'
b 'I'm afraid I don't know what "accusatorial" means.'
c 'I'm not sure what "flexible" means. Does it mean "adaptable"?'

6 Imagine that you do not understand the following terms. Ask each other for an explanation.

a evolve
b independent
c centralised
d hierarchical
e precedent
f impartial

If you are working on your own you should use your dictionary to look up any key words you do not understand.

1.2 Common law and equity

This is a complex subject and we will deal with it in outline only. Our main purpose is to draw a distinction between common law and equity and the way the courts apply the rules of these two areas of law. The differences arise from their historical development. First let us consider what we mean by the words 'common law'. You should be aware that they will carry a different meaning according to their context.

1 It is law which is **common** to the whole country – national law in contrast to local law.

2 It is law which is based on judicial decisions (**case law**) in contrast to the law which is made by Parliament (**statute law**).

3 It distinguishes the common law legal systems based on **precedents** from civil law jurisdictions based on **civil codes**.

4 It comprises the rules developed by the **common law courts** in contrast to the rules developed by the **courts of equity**.

It is definitions **1** and **4** which form the subject matter of this section. We will begin by briefly examining the development of a system of law which is common to the whole country.

1.2.1 The development of common law

Read the following passage and the language points in the margin then answer the questions which follow the passage.

Prior[9] to the Norman conquest in 1066, the legal system was decentralised. It consisted of local courts, the borough, shire and hundred courts, each applying its own local customary law. The Norman kings could have adopted this system by allowing the baron to whom a region had been given to run the court in that region. Indeed, by taking the office of sheriff and with it the administration of the shire court, some barons tried to do just[10] that. However, the fear that barons would become provincial princes rivalling the power of the King was one of the main reasons which led to a strategy of judicial centralisation under Henry II (1154–1189). His reign saw the creation of a permanent royal court of 'King's Bench' as it became known, sitting in London and manned by specialist judges. In addition, the King commissioned[11] officials, usually judges of the central court, to travel round a circuit of the regions hearing cases. These regional hearings were known as the 'Assizes' and dealt with both civil and criminal cases. Central control over the law was ensured by the procedure under which the legal issue in a case could first be decided by the royal courts in London, and then the legal ruling would be taken by the travelling judge to the region concerned where the facts would[12] be tried and the ruling applied to the facts found at the trial. This strategy enabled the royal judges to apply common legal principles to most parts of the land – hence[13] the term 'common law' which is still used to describe our judge-made system of law.

Dugdale *et al.*, *A Level Law* (Butterworths 1988), pp. 7–8.

Text notes:

9 before
10 precisely
11 ordered
12 this is not a conditional but shows that something happened frequently in the past
13 therefore

Comprehension check: detailed reading

In order to answer the following questions you will have to read the text very carefully:

7 a Line 1: What does 'it' refer to?
b Line 3: 'could have adopted this system'. Did they adopt it?
c Line 6: What did the barons try to do?
d Line 10: What was the 'King's Bench'?
e Where did the Assizes take place?
f Line 17: What does 'where' refer to?

1.2.2 The growth of equity

Before reading the following passage consider these questions:

a Why did the need for equity arise?
b Do the rules of equity remain different from the rules of common law?

Do not attempt to answer these questions at this stage but think about them as you are reading.

The student will learn quite early in his historical studies how equity came into being. He will learn how, in the Middle Ages, the courts of common law failed to give redress[14] in certain types of case where redress was needed, and how the disappointed litigants petitioned the King, who was the 'fountain of justice,' for extraordinary relief: how the King, through his Chancellor,[15] eventually set up a special court, the Court of Chancery, to deal with these petitions; and how the rules applied by the Court of Chancery hardened into law and became a regular part of the law of the land. The most important branch of equity is the law of trusts, but equitable remedies such as specific performance and injunction are also much used. The student will learn how, in case of 'conflict or variance' between the rules of common law and the rules of equity, equity came to prevail. This was by means of what was called a common injunction. Suppose that A brought an action against B in one of the common law courts, and in the view of the Court of Chancery the action was inequitable, B's proper course was to apply to the Court of Chancery for an order, called a common injunction, directed to A and ordering him not to continue his action. If A defied the injunction the Court of Chancery would put him in prison for contempt of court. Equity thus worked 'behind the scenes' of the common law action; the common law principles were theoretically left intact, but by means of this intricate mechanism they were superseded by equitable rules in all cases of 'conflict or variance.' The result justified the sarcasm of the critic who said that in England one[16] court was set up to do injustice and another[17] to stop it.[18]

This system went on until 1875, when as a result of the Judicature Act 1873 the old courts of common law and the Court of Chancery were abolished, and in their place was established a single Supreme Court of Judicature, each branch of which had full power to administer both law and equity. Also, common injunctions were abolished and instead it was enacted that, in cases of 'conflict or variance' between the rules of equity and the rules of common law, the rules of equity should prevail.

Williams, *Learning the Law* (Stevens 1982), pp. 26–7.

Text notes:
14 to make right
15 King's religious and legal adviser
16 see question **8a** below
17 see question **8b** below
18 see question **8c** below

Comprehension check

8 **a** Note 16: What does 'one' refer to?
b Note 17: What does 'another' refer to?
c Note 18: Do you think the writer agrees with the opinion of the critic?

Language notes: grammatical terms and vocabulary

We shall be using a few grammatical terms in this book. The following names of parts of speech will be found:

Noun: e.g. law, England
Verb: e.g. (to) study, (to) compare

Adjective: e.g. independent, legal
Adverb: e.g. independently, legally
Pronoun: e.g. it, she
Preposition: e.g. on, at

You will need to know these terms when using a dictionary but notice that abbreviations are used, for example n., vb., adj., adv., pron., prep.

9 using words from the text and, where necessary, from your dictionary, complete the table below:

Noun	*Verb*	*Adjective*
a	to petition	. . . .
history	×	**b** . . . .
equity	×	**c** . . . .
×	×	**d*** . . . .
e	**f**	specific
g	to abolish	×
litigant	**h**	×

* Give the opposite of **c**.

10 The previous extract contains some specialist vocabulary which you may not know. Check that you understand the following items, either by asking someone else or by using an English–English dictionary. (NB: It may sometimes be necessary to consult a specialised law dictionary. Several are suggested in the bibliography at the end of this book.)

a litigant
b equitable
c injunction (can you find the meaning in the text?)
d contempt of court
e to prevail
f to supersede
g to bring an action

If it took you a long time to find the words in a dictionary you should do the exercises which follow.

Dictionary exercise

11 Number the following words in the order you would expect to find them in a dictionary:

apply, unitary, federation, ascend, united, separate, systems, union, endure, appellor, commission, crime, appellant, committee, application, commit, criminal, ascertain.

If this exercise took you longer then three minutes or you had more than two mistakes, you should repeat the exercise with the following list of words:

resolution, procedural, discharge, proceeds, libel, liability, licence, appoint, profitable, process, profit, proceed, liable, repeal, procedure, respondent, represent, resolve.

Comprehension check

12 With reference to the Williams extract on p. 5 complete this brief summary. Gaps may need one or more words.

Equity came into being in the (**a**) . . . . because (**b**) . . . . was not always able to give (**c**) . . . . to all litigants. The Court of Chancery provided equitable (**d**) . . . . when it thought that the common law (**e**) . . . . was inequitable. Until 1875 there were two courts – the (**f**) . . . . and the (**g**) . . . . The (**h**) . . . . established a single court, the (**i**) . . . . When the common law and the laws of equity (**j**) . . . ., (**k**) . . . . should (**l**) . . . .

Refer back to the questions on p. 4 you were asked to think about before reading the passage from Williams. You should be able to answer the first question: equity developed because in many situations there was no legal remedy available at common law. Let us now consider the second question – do the rules of equity remain different from the rules of common law?

To answer this question we must remember the purpose of equity which is to achieve justice and fairness. To do this the courts have developed a set of rules to govern the application of equity. These are called the 'maxims' of equity. They are different from the rules which apply in the common law and these maxims are the reason why we continue to distinguish between common law and equity. There are many equitable maxims of which the following are just brief examples:

- **a** **Equity will not suffer a wrong to be without a remedy.** Equity will only intervene when there is no adequate common law remedy.
- **b** **Equity follows the law.** Equity recognises legal rights and does not take the place of the common law.
- **c** **He who comes to equity must come with clean hands.** A litigant who has behaved unfairly in the dispute will be denied an equitable remedy.
- **d** **Equitable remedies are discretionary.** Litigants do not have a right to an equitable remedy. The courts will decide whether to grant a remedy after considering the individual circumstances of each case.

These examples illustrate the wider principles and interests which the courts will consider before granting an equitable right or remedy. One of the most important features of equity which distinguishes it from common law is the maxim that equitable remedies are discretionary. We will examine this by way of a case study, but before doing so let us look at the way cases are reported.

As judicial decisions form an important part of the law it is necessary that they should be available to lawyers and the public. The judgments in the higher courts are published in a series of law reports the most common of which are:

All England Law Reports	Appeal Cases
Weekly Law Reports	Chancery
Queen's Bench	Criminal Law Reports
King's Bench	

There is a standard form of reference which tells the reader where the report of an individual case may be found. This reference contains the year in which the case was published, the name of the publication in abbreviated form and the page number at which the case can be found. In addition, when the case reports for a single year are contained in more than one volume of a publication the number of the volume will appear before the name of the publication. So, for example, a case reported at **[1979] 3 All ER 365** will be found in the third volume of the All England Law Reports for the year 1979 at page 365.

You will notice the use of square brackets; this signifies that knowing the year is essential to finding the case report. If the case is cited with the year only and not the reference, round brackets are used, for example *Donaghue* v. *Stevenson* (1932). A final point you should remember at this stage is that case names are always highlighted in some way. In most books this will be by italics but if you are writing by hand you should underline the case names. It is important that you get into the habit of doing this from the start of your legal studies. Now do the following exercise before moving on to the case study.

Case references

13 Where will the following cases be reported?

- **a** *Baker* v. *Willoughby* [1970] AC 467.
- **b** *Armstrong* v. *Jackson* [1917] 2 KB 822.
- **c** *Cox* v. *Green* [1966] 1 Ch 216.
- **d** *Day* v. *Grant* [1987] 3 All ER 678; [1987] QB 972; [1987] 3 WLR 537. (Note that some cases are reported in more than one publication.)
- **e** *R.* v. *Hudson* [1980] Crim LR 107.

1.2.3 Case study: *Miller* v. *Jackson* [1977] QB 966

The facts: The plaintiffs[19] owned a house adjoining a cricket ground. Cricket had been played on the ground for a long time before the house had been built. The plaintiffs complained of damage caused by cricket balls and loss of enjoyment of their property. They brought an action against the cricket club for private nuisance seeking damages (the common law remedy) and an injunction (an equitable remedy) to prevent cricket being played on the ground. The cricket club argued that it had done everything that was possible to stop the balls coming into the plaintiff's garden, including erecting a fifteen foot high fence.

Held: The cricket club were liable[20] to the plaintiffs for private nuisance. An award of damages[21] was made against them but a majority of the Court of Appeal refused to grant an injunction preventing the playing of cricket.

Per[22] Lord Denning MR:[23] 'The court when deciding whether to exercise its equitable jurisdiction and grant an injunction must have in mind that it is under a duty to consider the public interest. Where the effect of granting an injunction would be to prevent cricket being played on a ground where it had been played for seventy years or so, the special circumstances are such that the public interest must prevail over the hardship of the individual householders who were deprived of the ability to enjoy, in peace and quiet, their house and garden while cricket was being played.'

Can you see the difference in the court's approach to the common law remedy and the equitable remedy? In order to be awarded damages the plaintiffs only had to prove that the defendants were liable in nuisance. Having proved this the court had no power to withhold the common law remedy (although the judges will determine the **amount** to be paid by the defendants). In contrast, because equitable remedies are discretionary, the court could refuse to grant an injunction because it considered it would not be just and fair to do so.

Before concluding this introduction to equity you should be aware that although it was originally a flexible body of rules, the criticism that 'justice is as long as the Chancellor's foot'[24] can no longer be justified. Justice is a subjective[25] concept – what may appear just to one person would not be to another. Judicial decisions, and therefore the law, based on the individual judge's idea of justice creates uncertainty and in itself leads to injustice. Similar cases must be treated similarly if justice is to be achieved. Accordingly equity has developed over the years into a consistent body of rules which eliminates as far as possible a subjective and arbitrary[26] application of its principles.

Text notes
19 people bringing a legal action
20 responsible
21 money paid in compensation
22 as stated by
23 Master of the Rolls, the Head of the Court of Appeal
24 i.e. changed with each new Chancellor
25 explained in the rest of the sentence
26 based on opinion, not on reason

Structure of the text

14 The case study (*Miller* v. *Jackson*) follows several stages which are listed below. Try to identify each stage by giving line numbers:

Background line . . . .
Complaint line . . . .
Action line . . . .
Defence line . . . .
Judgment line . . . .
Reasons line . . . .

Vocabulary

15 Everyday words are often used in legal vocabulary but they convey a very specific meaning which may be different from the meaning you already know. For example, 'held' (see *Miller* v. *Jackson*) is used in legal terminology to introduce the judgment in a case. Look at the following words from the text:

a nuisance
b remedy
c interest

Can you find the legal meanings in your English–English dictionary?

Language note: prepositions

16 Using the right preposition can be a problem. Complete the short case study below by using some of the prepositions which were used in *Miller* v. *Jackson*.

The plaintiffs owned a house next door (**a**) . . . . the defendant's factory. Sometimes black smoke from the factory chimneys would blow across the plaintiffs' garden. The plaintiffs sued the owners of the factory complaining (**b**) . . . . damage caused (**c**) . . . . plants in their garden (**d**) . . . . the smoke and loss of enjoyment of their property. They sought (= past tense 'to seek') damages and an injunction to prevent the defendants using their premises as a factory.

Held: That the owners of the factory were liable (**e**) . . . . the plaintiffs (**f**) . . . . the tort of private nuisance. The plaintiffs were awarded damages (**g**) . . . . the loss of their plants and granted an injunction restricting the use of the defendants' property. It was reasonable that the defendants should use their premises as a factory but not (**h**) . . . . a way which would cause nuisance (**i**) . . . . adjoining property. The injunction would apply until the defendants were able to control the smoke (**j**) . . . . their chimneys.

Comprehension check: vocabulary

17 The following passage is a summary of the two extracts from Williams and Dudgale *et al.* Complete the passage by choosing the correct words from the list which follows it.

Before the Norman Conquest the law in England was (**a**) . . . . Fear of the power of local (**b**) . . . . led Henry II to create a (**c**) . . . . royal court in London called the (**d**) . . . . (**e**) . . . . from this court would travel the country hearing (**f**) . . . . and (**g**) . . . . cases. The central court in London (**h**) . . . . the legal issue in a case and this would be applied to the (**i**) . . . . in the regional courts. In this way a (**j**) . . . . system of law was developed which was (**k**) . . . . to most parts of the country.

Equity was developed by the Court of (**l**) . . . . It introduced new (**m**) . . . . to provide (**n**) . . . . for disappointed litigants. The common law courts were (**o**) . . . . from the Court of Chancery until a single court was established by the (**p**) . . . . Act 1873. Each branch of the (**q**) . . . . Court of Judicature can administer (**r**) . . . . law and (**s**) . . . . However, the difference between the two is still important because of the (**t**) . . . . of equity. These illustrate that equity is based on (**u**) . . . . and (**v**) . . . .

fairness, common, criminal, Supreme, separate, remedies, judge-made, decentralised, decided, facts, equity, Chancery, barons, redress, civil, permanent, justice, King's Bench, Judicature, common, maxims.

Legal analysis

18 Read the facts of the following case and prepare a short judgment based on your knowledge of the maxims of equity. You should do this by following the procedure outlined in the exercise on structure given in question 14 on p. 9. Discuss your decision with other members of your group and be prepared to justify it by reference to the maxims. You should then compare your arguments with the decision of the Court of Appeal summarised in the Answer Section. If you are working on your own prepare instead a written judgment, also by following the exercise on structure given in question 14 on p. 9.

D. & C. Builders v. *Rees* [1965] 3 All ER 837

The defendants owed the plaintiffs £482 for building work. The defendants consistently refused to pay the money until, knowing the plaintiffs were in financial difficulty, they offered to pay £300 to settle the debt. The plaintiffs reluctantly accepted. They then sued for the recovery of the outstanding debt of £182. Their action was based on the law of contract which allows a creditor to recover payment of a debt even after accepting part payment in full settlement. The defendants claimed the protection of the equitable doctrine of promissory estoppel which in some circumstances will prevent a person from going back on a promise – in this case the promise to accept £300 as full payment of the Rees's debt.

1.3 Classifications of law

There are many ways in which the law can be classified. Here we shall limit our discussion to the difference between **criminal** and **civil law** and **substantive** and **procedural law.**

1.3.1 Criminal and civil law

A simple distinction between the criminal law and the civil law is that the latter[27] regulates the relationships between individuals or bodies and the former[28] regulates the legal relationships between the state and individual people and bodies.

Text notes:
27 civil law
28 criminal law

The first practical difference is seen in the parties to the legal action. A civil case will involve two (or more) individual people or bodies whilst the parties to a criminal case will be the state and an individual person or body.

Later you will learn how this difference is reflected in the terminology and procedure of the law, but first let us look at an example of both criminal and civil law.

First, the civil law. Examples of this include the **law of contract**, **tort** (literally meaning 'wrong') and **property**. Consider the following situation.

You decide to buy a radio from a local shop. You pay the correct price and take the radio away. You have entered into a contract with the owner of the shop. After two days the radio fails to work.

This is a common situation and usually the shopkeeper will replace the radio or return your money. If not, you may wish to take legal action to recover your loss. As the law of contract is part of the civil law the parties to the action will be you (an individual) and the owner of the shop (an individual person or body).

Now let us look at some examples of the criminal law. This is the law by which the state regulates the conduct of its citizens. Criminal offences range from the petty[29] (e.g. parking offences) to the very serious (e.g. murder, rape). Look at the following situation.

You are driving your car at 70 m.p.h.[30] in an area which has a speed limit of 40 m.p.h. You are stopped by a police officer and subsequently a case is brought against you for dangerous driving.

Text notes:
29 small
30 miles per hour (70 m.p.h. = 112 kilometres per hour)

This is a **criminal offence**. The parties to the action will therefore be the state (in the form of the prosecuting authority) and you (an individual).

A further point to make is that although the division between civil and criminal law is very clear, there are many actions which will constitute a criminal offence and a civil wrong. Let us look again at the situation where you are driving your car too fast. Suppose that while you were doing this you knocked over and injured an elderly lady. You will have committed a **criminal offence** (dangerous driving) and a **civil wrong** (negligence).

Let us examine this more fully by reading the following extract.

> These examples show that the distinction between a crime and civil wrong cannot be stated as depending upon *what is done*, because what is done (or not done) may be the same in each case. The true distinction resides,[31] therefore, not in the nature of the wrongful act but in *the legal consequences that may follow it*. If the wrongful act (or omission) is capable of being followed by what are called criminal proceedings, that means that it is regarded as a crime (otherwise called an offence). If it is capable of being followed by civil proceedings, that means that it is regarded as a civil wrong. If it is capable of being followed by both, it is both a crime and a civil wrong. Criminal and civil proceedings are (in the normal case) easily distinguishable: the procedure is different, the outcome is different, and the terminology is different.
>
> In criminal proceedings the terminology is as follows. You have a *prosecutor prosecuting* a *defendant*, and the result of the prosecution if successful is a *conviction*, and the defendant may be *punished* by one of a variety of punishments ranging from life imprisonment to a fine, or else may be released on probation or discharged without punishment or dealt with in various other ways.

Turning to civil proceedings, the terminology generally is that a *plaintiff sues* (e.g. brings an *action* against) a *defendant*. The proceedings if successful result in *judgment for the plaintiff*, and the judgment may order the defendant to pay the plaintiff money, or to transfer property to him, or to do or not to do something (injunction), or to perform a contract (specific performance).

It is hardly necessary to point out that the terminology of the one type of proceedings should never be transferred to the other. "Criminal action," for example, is a misnomer; so is "civil offence" (the proper expression is "civil wrong"). One does not speak of a plaintiff prosecuting or of the criminal accused being sued. The common announcement "Trespassers will be prosecuted" has been called a "wooden[32] lie," for trespass has traditionally been a civil wrong, not (generally) a crime. (There are some statutory offences of trespass, such as trespass on a railway line; and a "squatter"[33] or other trespasser in a house that is occupied or required for occupation generally commits an offence if he fails to leave upon request.)

Again, the word "guilty" is used primarily of criminals. The corresponding word in civil cases is "liable"; but this word is also used in criminal contexts.

Civil and criminal courts are partly but not entirely distinct. The *Crown Court* has almost exclusively criminal jurisdiction. Magistrates are chiefly concerned with criminal cases, but they have important civil jurisdiction over licensing and family matters. On the other hand, the county court is only civil, and so is the *High Court* apart from appeals.

Williams, *Learning the Law* (Stevens 1982), pp. 3–4.

Text notes:
31 is
32 this refers to the notice board which is often made of wood
33 person occupying building without permission

You should be aware from studying this passage that, in our hypothetical situation, whilst the one act constituted both a criminal offence and a civil wrong, the legal consequences under the criminal and civil law will be different. You would be prosecuted by the state in the criminal courts for dangerous driving and sued by the elderly lady in the civil courts for negligence. The two actions will be totally separate. We will examine this more fully when we look at the court system in Chapter 4.

Comprehension check

19 In order to check your understanding of some of the important terms in the passage, on a separate sheet of paper complete the table below by placing the following words and phrases in the correct column:

civil wrong, crime, Crown Court, guilty, plaintiff, life imprisonment, to convict, defendant, to prosecute, conviction, liable, county court, judgment for the plaintiff, prosecutor, punishment, to punish, offence.

Civil	*Criminal*
civil wrong	crime
.	.
.	.
.	.

Vocabulary check

20 Find the correct word(s) in the passage to complete the following sentences. Try to remember the words from the previous exercise.

a A criminal case is brought by a . . . .
b The person charged with the criminal offence is the . . . .
c The party bringing a civil action is the . . . .
d A civil action is brought against the . . . .
e A court order not to do something is an . . . .
f The defendant in a civil case is . . . . by the plaintiff.
g A successful criminal prosecution will result in a . . . .
h If the plaintiff is successful the defendant will be found . . . .
i The distinction between crimes and civil wrongs relates to the . . . . of the act.

Comprehension check

21 Below, in note form, is an outline of criminal and civil proceedings. Some gaps have been left for you to complete. See how many you can fill without consulting the text.

Crim. Proc.:
Prosecutor (**a**) . . . . defendant → (if def. guilty) conviction → (**b**) . . . . or → (**c**) . . . . or → (**d**) . . . .

Civ. Proc.:
(**e**) . . . . (**f**) . . . . → (if pl. successful) liable → (**g**) . . . . or → (**h**) . . . . or → (**i**) . . . .

A further difference between civil and criminal law is the way that cases are cited.

It is helpful to know certain rules for the naming of cases. Trials on indictment[34] are in the name of the Queen (as representing the State); thus a criminal case is generally called *Reg*. v. whomever it is – *Reg*. being short for *Regina* (pronounced "Regyna"), and v. being short for *versus*. When there is a king on the throne, *Rex* is used instead of *Reg*. *Rex* and *Regina* both conveniently abbreviate to *R*., which saves having to remember which is which. Thus *Rex* v. *Sikes* or *Reg*. v. *Sikes* may both be written *R*. v. *Sikes*. Some textbooks on criminal law even print simply *Sikes*. This last is a convenient usage for the student of criminal law.

In some types of criminal case the title of the case will not contain *Rex* or *Reg*. before the "v.," but will contain the name of a private person. This happens when the case is tried summarily[35] before magistrates[36] (i.e. justices of the peace); here the name of the actual prosecutor (e.g. a policeman) appears instead of the nominal prosecutor, the Queen.

Civil cases will usually be cited by the names of the parties, thus: *Rylands* v. *Fletcher*. If the Queen (as representing the Government) is a party she is, in civil cases, usually called "The Queen," and similarly with the King, thus: *British Coal Corporation* v. *The King*; but *R*. may also be used.

There are peculiar conventions in pronouncing the names of cases. (1) A criminal case, such as *R*. v. *Sikes*, can be referred to informally as "R. v. Sikes" (pronounced as written), or "Rex" (or, "Regina") "v. Sikes" (again pronounced as written). In court, however, the proper method is to call it "The King" (or, "The Queen") "against Sikes." (2) In civil cases the "v." coupling the names of the parties is pronounced "and," both in court and out of it. Thus *Smith* v. *Hughes* is always pronounced (but never written) "Smith and Hughes," and similarly *British Coal Corporation* v. *The King* (which was a civil proceeding against the Crown) is pronounced with an "and." Lawyers thus write one thing and say another.

Williams, *Learning the Law* (Stevens 1982), pp. 17–18.

Text notes:
34 i.e. more serious crimes
35 i.e. less serious crimes
36 judges without legal qualifications

The language for naming cases given in the extract is very formal. In citing all cases in your daily studies it is usual to pronounce the 'v.' in both criminal and civil cases as 'and'.

Legal exercises

22 What is wrong in the following situation and why?

Bob has been charged with murder and is sued in the county court. The plaintiff is successful in the action and Bob is found liable. He is punished by being ordered to pay the plaintiff £10,000 in damages.

23 Are the following cases civil or criminal?

- **a** *Gibson* v. *Manchester City Council*;
- **b** *Leaf.* v. *International Galleries*;
- **c** *R.* v. *Bateman*;
- **d** *Leach* v. *R.*

1.3.2 Substantive and procedural law

Williams in *Learning the Law* defines **substantive law** in the following way: 'Substantive law lays down people's rights, duties, liberties and powers.' By this is meant the actual content or substance of the law. These are the rules on which the courts base their decisions. In Chapters 9 and 10 we will examine some introductory aspects of two areas of substantive law in more detail – the law of contract and the criminal law.

Procedural or **adjectival law** is also a set of rules. As you read the next passage think about these questions:

24 a Why was procedure so important in the past?
b Is procedure still important today?

Rules of procedure or "*adjective*" law, as it is sometimes called, are the rules which determine the course of an action; they govern such matters as how the case is to be presented, in what court it shall lie, or when it is to be tried. Procedural rules are, in other words, the rules which govern the machinery as opposed to the subject-matter of litigation. It is a striking fact, much remarked upon by historians, that in the earlier stages of legal development these[37] rules assume paramount importance: form is better understood than substance, and in early law formal requirements, rather than abstract principles, usually determined legal rights. Because the development of the common law has been continuous this early dominance of procedure has had a lasting influence upon many of the doctrines of the modern substantive law. Generally speaking, however, procedure, though it is of great importance to the practitioner, is today treated as the servant and not the master of substance, and the rules of procedure are now more flexible than once they were. They[38] derive from various sources. Most proceedings in the Supreme Court (that is, most of the more important civil proceedings) are now governed by a code of rules known as the Rules of the Supreme Court ("R.S.C.").

. . . These[39] rules, which were originally authorized by the Judicature Acts 1873–1875, are amended from time to time, under powers first conferred by those[40] Acts, by a committee known as the "Rule Committee" which is headed by the Lord Chancellor. The R.S.C. are set out in the *Annual Practice* (The "White book"). Similar rules are laid down for the County Courts: these appear in the *County Court Practice*. With some exceptions – such as the magistrates' courts rules – the rules of criminal procedure have not been codified; they[41] are to be found in works such as Archbold's *Criminal Pleading, Evidence and Practice* and Stone's *Justices' Manual*, which treats of the work of the magistrates' courts.

James, *Introduction to English Law* (Butterworths 1985), p. 62.

Comprehension check

25 a Note 37: To what does the word 'these' refer?
b Note 38: To what does the word 'they' refer?
c Note 39: To what does the word 'these' refer?
d Note 40: To what does the word 'those' refer?
e Note 41: To what does the word 'they' refer?

26 Are the following statements true (T) or false (F)?

a The rules of civil procedure are codified.
b None of the rules of criminal procedure have been codified.
c In the past legal rights depended mainly on abstract principles.
d Procedure is not important today.
e Lines 12–15 mean: 'nowadays the principles of law should control procedure'.

27 In the text the following words and phrases are used to discuss the distinction between substantive and procedural law. Use them to complete the table below:

Machinery, form, substance, abstract principles, subject matter, formal requirements, adjectival, substantive.

. . . . *law*	. . . . *law*
.	.
.	.
.	.
.	.

Legal exercise

28 Referring back to question **24b** consider the following situation.

> Thomas has been charged with murder. He is pleading 'not guilty' to the charge. His trial is taking place at Fenbury Crown Court. The leading prosecution witness is PC Boot. In his evidence he states that he saw Thomas running away from the scene of the crime. Thomas has evidence which suggests that PC Boot was at home at the time that he said he saw Thomas but the judge refuses to let Thomas's lawyer question PC Foot about this.
>
> When Thomas gives his evidence the judge allows the prosecuting lawyer to question him. During the questioning the prosecuting lawyer tells the court that Thomas has previously been found guilty of a serious criminal offence.

How has the procedure of the trial disadvantaged Thomas?

Additional reading

At this early stage in your studies you will probably not wish to read anything too complex. As well as the textbooks used in the chapter (which will provide you with more details of the topics), you will find a good account of the subject matter in *A Level Law* by Hogan, Seago and Bennett (Sweet and Maxwell). *Legal Institutions* by Stein (Butterworths) provides a more detailed introduction to the comparisons between English and continental legal systems. *How to Study Law* by Bradney, Fisher *et al.* (Sweet and Maxwell) is a very interesting and comprehensive introduction to legal study and legal methodology.

2
The constitution

Summary

Legal content

Aim

To examine the constitutional framework of the English legal system and to provide an introduction to the concepts which form the basis of the system of government in the United Kingdom. Particular emphasis will be placed on the constitutional role of the judiciary and some comparisons made with the role of the judiciary in other countries. The final section will consider some recent areas of debate arising from the nature of the British constitution.

Language content

Grammar: dealing with complex sentences (using signpost words); constructions of the type 'ought not to have taken . . .'
Vocabulary: inferencing meaning from context; forming antonyms (un-, in-, il-, im-)
Oral function: asking for repetition
Study skills: notemaking symbols

2.1 Definition and purpose

A **constitution** is a set of rules which define the relationship between the various organs of government and between the government and citizens of a country. Its purpose is to set the parameters of governmental power and the rights and duties of the citizens. Therefore, the constitution of any individual country will determine the system of government in that country.

Before we go on to examine the nature of the British constitution it is important that you have a clear understanding of what is meant by the 'organs' or 'institutions' of government. In this context we mean the

executive, the **legislature** and the **judiciary**. In addition, in the United Kingdom, the **monarch** has an important constitutional role as head of state.

Vocabulary

1 The four 'organs' of government mentioned are:

- **a** the monarch;
- **b** the executive;
- **c** the legislature;
- **d** the judiciary.

Use an English–English law dictionary to check the meaning of these terms.

Research

2 The executive is a broad term which includes the officials of government departments, but in the United Kingdom the collective name for the principal executive body is 'the Cabinet' which is made up of ministers of the Crown; for the legislature it[1] is 'Parliament'. Individual members of the legislature are called 'Members of Parliament'. What titles are given to these groups/individuals in the government of your country?

Text note:
1 i.e. the collective name

2.2 Characteristics of the British constitution

2.2.1 The nature of the constitution

The following text discusses some of the central characteristics of the British constitution. Before you read it look at the questions below and then look for the answers in the passage. Scan the passage for the relevant information, that is do not read every word.

Pre-reading check

3
- **a** When was the American constitution first written?
- **b** Can it be changed?
- **c** Does the United Kingdom have a written constitution as the USA does?
- **d** Who can alter the rules of the British constitution?

Because the rules of a constitution are laws of fundamental importance, it is not surprising that they are often embodied in a single written document. Thus, for example, the Constitution of the United States was reduced to writing in 1787 and the document which comprises it[2] (as subsequently amended) lays down the fundamental law of America today. Further[3] the U.S. Constitution, like many other written constitutions, cannot be altered easily; a constitutional amendment can only be carried if a very substantial majority, both in Congress and in the individual States, approve it.[4]

Our constitution is just as important to us as the U.S. Constitution is to the Americans. Nevertheless, it[5] is not 'written'; that is to say, it has never been wholly reduced to writing. Further, since Parliament is 'sovereign' it[6] can, without any special procedure, and by simple Act, alter any law at any time, however fundamental it[7] may seem to be. Although, therefore, our courts have always been astute[8] to safeguard the rights of the subject and although certain legal remedies, such as *habeas corpus*,[9] are designed to protect him,[10] yet, under our constitution, there are . . . no guaranteed rights similar to the fundamental liberties safeguarded by the U.S. Constitution.

The statement that our constitution is not 'written' does not mean that we possess no important constitutional documents; it merely means that the constitution is not embodied in any single document, or series of documents, containing our essential constitutional laws. Thus we have many enactments which either have been or still are, of great importance. One need only cite as examples Magna Carta (1215), the Bill of Rights (1688) – which sets out the principal rights gained by Parliament and the nation as the result of the seventeenth century constitutional struggles – the Act of Settlement (1700), and the Parliament Acts 1911 and 1949.

James, *Introduction to English Law* (Butterworths 1985), pp. 115–16.

Text notes:

2 see question **4a** below
3 in addition, also
4 see question **4b** below
5 see question **4c** below
6 see question **4d** below
7 see question **4e** below
8 careful
9 an order requiring a person who detains another to justify that detention before the courts
10 see question **4f** below

Comprehension check

4 **a** Note 2: To what does 'it' refer?
b Note 4: To what does 'it' refer?
c Note 5: To what does 'it' refer?
d Note 6: To what does 'it' refer?
e Note 7: To what does 'it' refer?
f Note 10: To whom does 'him' refer?

Language notes

5 Notice the use of inverted commas in 'written' (lines 10 and 18) and 'sovereign' (line 11). This indicates that the words do not have exactly the meaning you would expect. The explanation of 'written' is in lines 10–11 and 19–21. 'Sovereign' has probably been placed in inverted commas because the writer does not intend the more common meaning, i.e. king or queen. So what meaning is being used here?

Notice also the use of dashes (– . . . –) in lines 23–5 which function as brackets ( ).

6 Now read the statements below which also refer to the excerpt.

You should read the excerpt more closely in order to decide which statements are true (T) and which are false (F). Check your answers afterwards in the answer section before proceeding.

- **a** An unwritten constitution can be easily changed.
- **b** There are no legal remedies which the British courts can apply to protect the rights of the subjects.
- **c** Parliament has no power to make laws to protect individual rights.
- **d** Parliament must follow a special procedure to alter any constitutional laws.
- **e** There are no documents containing constitutional laws in the United Kingdom.
- **f** An unwritten constitution is more flexible[11] than a written constitution.

Text note:
11 adaptable

A number of issues in this text relate to our earlier definition of a constitution – the extent and control of government power and the protection of the rights of the citizens. Under a written constitution these are very clearly stated; for example, the constitution of the United States gives American citizens the right, *inter alia*,[12] to free speech, peaceful assembly and privacy. Any law passed in contravention of these and other constitutional rights, can be struck down by the American courts as unconstitutional and therefore void. Equally they[13] can enforce the provisions of the constitution. The courts in the United Kingdom do not have this[14] power. In the remainder of this chapter we will examine the reason for this[15] and the relationship between the judiciary and the other organs[16] of government.

Text notes:
12 among other things
13 see question **7a** below
14 see question **7b** below
15 see question **7c** below
16 see question **7d** below

Comprehension check

7 **a** Note 13: To what do 'they' refer?
b Note 14: To what does 'this' refer?
c Note 15: To what does 'this' refer?
d Note 16: Do you remember the other 'organs of government'?

Legal exercises

8 In countries with a liberal democratic system of government much emphasis is placed on the protection of individual freedom and rights. Can you think of six 'rights' which may be considered important in these countries?

9 Write a short essay of 150 words on the nature of the constitution in your own country. It should state whether the constitution is written or unwritten. If it is the latter what is the reason for this and how are individual rights protected? If the former, when did it come into existence and why? What are the provisions relating to the machinery of government and the protection of human rights?

Your essay should consist of four paragraphs each beginning as follows:

Paragraph 1: 'The constitution in (country) is written/unwritten . . . (follow on with historical reasons).'
Paragraph 2: 'The main features of (country's) constitution are . . .'
Paragraph 3: 'The constitution recognises a number of individual rights which include . . .'
Paragraph 4: 'The provisions in the constitution for protecting these rights are . . .'

2.2.2 The sources of the constitution

Having established that the constitution of the United Kingdom is not contained in any one single document we now need to look at the sources of the constitution. Other than the statutes mentioned in the preceding text, these can be found in custom, case law, books of authority, European Community law (since 1972) and, most important, **constitutional conventions**. These are informal or 'moral' rules – a code of practice for government which has evolved over the years. They are primarily concerned with the relationship between the Crown (or monarch) and the executive, and the executive and the legislature. The following text provides some examples of these conventions.

Many constitutional rules, such for example as the provisions of the Act of Settlement . . ., are "laws" in the ordinary sense, that is to say, they will be recognized and enforced by the courts. But there are certain other rules which govern the working of the constitution which are not laws in this sense. They are called "*conventions*". They arise from usage, or agreement, tacit or express, and they are adhered to, once they have developed, not because the courts will enforce them, but because political expedience and respect for tradition demand their observance.

Many of the rules which govern the functioning of the central government and the relationship of the Executive to the Legislature are thus conventional. The convention relating to ministerial responsibility . . . will be mentioned below; here it must suffice to give only a few general examples.

The cabinet came into being purely by convention: no statute created it. The Monarch's practice of abstaining from attending cabinet meetings started . . . as an historial accident and became a convention; no monarch would now claim the right to attend. By convention, when it becomes necessary to form a new Government, the monarch must invite the leader of the party or group commanding a majority in the House of Commons to form it; the Queen will not in practice invite any other person, though "legally" she could do so. The person so invited will become *Prime Minister* of the new Government; this, the most important of all political offices, grew up by convention, and it was not until the present century that it received recognition in any statute. The Queen *could* refuse her assent to an Act of Parliament, but there is now a long established convention that she will not do so.

By convention, a Ministry which is defeated on a major issue in the House of Commons should (though whether in fact a modern government *will* is quite another question) either resign or advise the Queen to grant a dissolution. If it advises a dissolution and is then defeated at the ensuing general election it should, by convention, resign either at once or upon its first defeat in the House of Commons. By convention Parliament must be summoned at least once a year, though *legally* it need only meet once in three years (Meeting of Parliament Act 1694 – generally known as the "Triennial Act"); this convention is, as we have seen, grounded firmly upon political expedience; for Parliament alone can grant the Government the funds it needs annually for the public administration. Finally, although it is not usually treated in works on constitutional law as such, the fact that the courts treat themselves as bound to apply Acts of Parliament is conventional, and so is the doctrine of judicial precedent itself.

Beside conventions, there are certain other important constitutional rules which are not "laws" in the sense that the courts will enforce them. These are the rules which regulate the internal affairs of Parliament, such as the rules governing the process of legislation and the conduct of debates. Many, but not all, of these "customs" of Parliament are now contained in the Standing Orders of the two Houses.

James, *Introduction to English Law* (Butterworths 1985), pp. 116–17.

By the convention of ministerial responsibility mentioned in the extract each individual cabinet minister is held responsible for all the actions of the civil servants in his or her ministry; it requires a minister to resign if those civil servants make an important mistake. One of the most significant examples of this convention in recent years was the resignation of the Minister for Trade and Industry after one of the civil servants in his department released a confidential document in order to embarrass another minister.

Vocabulary

There are several words in this passage which are important for the meaning of the text and which are commonly found in formal or academic writing. Some are listed below

Line 5: tacit
Line 6: express
Line 6: adhered
Line 7: enforce
Line 7: expedience
Line 12: suffice
Line 23: assent
Line 29: dissolution

If you do not know these words you could use a dictionary. However, it is always a good idea to consider whether enough information can be extracted from the 'unknown' word to enable you to carry on reading without using the dictionary. With each of these words that you do not know, ask yourself the following questions:

1 What part of speech is it?
2 Does it look (or sound) like any other word you know in English or another related language?
3 Is it next to or near a known word which can help you to understand?

Sometimes only question **1** will give you any information and you will want to use a dictionary (knowing the part of speech will be useful to you here). This self-questioning process takes much less time than you might think and will become quicker with practice. You probably already do something like this in your own language when you meet an unfamiliar word.

Let us apply this procedure to some of the words listed:

Line 5: 'tacit'

Question 1: You might think this word is a noun or an adjective.
Question 2: If you know Latin or the word 'taciturn' you will know that the idea of 'not speaking' is involved.
Question 3: It appears to be linked to 'express', but the meaning you probably know of 'express' as in 'express train' is not helpful.

At this point you will either have enough information from question 2 or you will go to your dictionary and discover that 'tacit' means 'understood without being stated'.

Line 6: 'express'

Question 1: It must be an adjective because it is linked by 'or' to an adjective ('tacit').
Question 2: The linking word 'or' could indicate that 'tacit' and 'express' have either similar or contrasting meanings. You will probably conclude that 'express' means the opposite of 'tacit'.
Question 3: We have decided that the usual meaning is not helpful, but you might consider the meaning of the verb 'to express', that is 'to state something'.

Sometimes it is not necessary to ask all the questions:

Line 12: 'suffice'

Question 1: Since it follows 'must' it is a verb.
Question 2: It looks like 'sufficient' so it probably means . . . .

10 Now, without looking back at the text, check that you remember some of the key words:

- **a** The opposite of 'tacit' is . . . .
- **b** A rule which is reached by agreement is called a . . . .
- **c** The head of state in the United Kingdom is called . . . . (several answers are possible).
- **d** Parliament consists of the House of Lords and . . . .
- **e** The leader of the government is the . . . .

Comprehension check

11 In line 12 of the passage from James you read: 'here it must suffice to give only a few general examples.' As briefly as possible, make a list of as many of these examples that you can find in the passage.

Legal exercises

12 Which conventions are involved in the following situations?

- **a** The government is defeated on a major issue in the House of

Commons. The Prime Minister advises the Queen to dissolve Parliament and a general election is called. The government wins a large majority in the general election but the Queen invites the leader of a minority party to form the next government.

b After a major defeat in the House of Commons the Prime Minister refuses to resign or ask the Queen to dissolve Parliament. A member of the opposition party applies to the High Court for an order forcing the Prime Minister to resign. The High Court grants the order.

c The Environment Party wins a general election on its promise to abolish all motor vehicles. The Abolition of Motor Vehicles Bill is subsequently passed by a large majority in Parliament but the Queen refuses to give the Royal Assent.

13 Conventions are not like 'real' laws in that there are no formal rules for their creation and they are not enforceable by the courts. Discuss the following questions with your group. You may find the additional reading references helpful in preparing your answers. If you do not have access to this material you can answer the questions by thinking about why informal rules of behaviour in general, such as social habits, are obeyed and the consequences of a breach[17] of these rules

a Why are conventions obeyed?
b Are all conventions of equal importance?
c What do you think would be the consequences of a breach of a convention?
d What is the main advantage of constitutional conventions compared to written constitutional rules?

If you are working on your own write an essay of 150 words on these topics. Use one paragraph to answer each part of the question as in the following essay plan:

Paragraph a: 'Constitutional conventions are . . . (follow with a definition). They are obeyed because . . .'
Paragraph b: 'Not all conventions are of equal importance . . . (follow with examples from the text).
Paragraph c: 'The consequences of a breach of a convention will depend upon . . . (relate your comments to paragraph b)'.
Paragraph d: 'Constitutional conventions have the advantage of being flexible because . . . (then compare to written constitutions)'.

Text note:
17 notice that this noun is the older form of 'break'; it is used in legal texts, e.g. 'breach of contract'

2.3 The constitutional role of the judiciary

2.3.1 Parliamentary sovereignty

The doctrine of **parliamentary sovereignty** governs the relationship between the legislature and the judiciary. It was described by A.V. Dicey as follows:

By the legislative supremacy of Parliament is meant that there are no legal limitations upon the legislative competence of Parliament. Parliament here does not refer to the two Houses of Parliament individually, for neither House has authority to legislate on its own, but to the constitutional phenomenon known as the Queen in Parliament: namely[18] the legislative process by which a Bill approved by Lords and Commons may receive the royal assent and thus become an Act of Parliament. Thus defined, Parliament,[19] said Dicey, has "under the English constitution, the right to make or unmake any law whatever; and further that no person or body is recognised by the law of England as having a right to override[20] or set aside the legislation of Parliament".

Wade and Bradley, *Constitutional and Administrative Law* (Longman 1985), p. 64.

Text notes:
18 that is, or i.e.
19 see question **14** below
20 refuse to accept

Comprehension check

14 Note 19: What does 'Parliament' refer to here?

Note that there are two aspects to the doctrine of parliamentary sovereignty:

1 that Parliament may enact any law it wishes, and
2 that no authority, including the courts, has the power to question the validity of the legislation.

The origins of the doctrine are historical arising from the political changes of 1688 which sought to limit the power of the monarchy. There is no law which states that Parliament is supreme but the doctrine is accepted and recognised by the courts. The only test for the validity of an Act of Parliament is that it has passed the necessary legislative procedures, that is it has been approved by a majority of both Houses of Parliament and received the Royal Assent. This procedure is known as **'The Queen in Parliament'**. It is the duty of the British judiciary to enforce the will of Parliament as expressed through its legislation.

Again we can contrast this with the role of the judiciary in the United States. The judges of the American courts are the upholders of the constitution. They determine the validity of legislation according to whether it conforms to the principles of the constitution. Compare the following cases.

In *Brown* v. *Board of Education* (1956), the Supreme Court of the United States judged that state legislation on racial segregation was contrary to the 14th Amendment of the Constitution which states, 'nor shall any state deny any person within its jurisdiction the equal protection of the law.'

By comparison, in *Cheney* v. *Conn* [1968] 1 All ER 779, an action brought by a taxpayer in the English courts challenging the validity of the Finance Act was dismissed:

> What the State itself enacts cannot be unlawful because [it] is the highest form of law in this country. It is the law which prevails over every other form of law, and it is not for the court to say that a parliamentary enactment . . . is illegal.

Similar statements have been made by many other British judges. The constitutional position can be summarised thus:

> It is often said that it would be unconstitutional for the UK Parliament to do certain things, meaning that the moral, political and other reasons against doing them are so strong that most people would regard it as highly improper if Parliament did these things. But that does not mean that it is beyond the power of Parliament to do such things. If Parliament chose to do any of them, the courts could not hold the Act of Parliament invalid.[21]
>
> *Madzimbamuto* v. *Lardner-Burke* [1969] 1 AC 645

Text note:

21 not having force in law, opposite to 'valid'; pronounced [ɪn'vælɪd] to distinguish it from 'invalid' (pronounced [ɪnvə'li:d]) meaning ill or disabled

---

An additional feature of the doctrine of parliamentary sovereignty is that each new Parliament is supreme. The traditional view is that no Parliament can limit the actions of a future Parliament. Much of the debate in this area centres on the issue of a Bill of Rights. Under the traditional view of parliamentary sovereignty a Bill of Rights enacted by one Parliament could be repealed by its successor. We will look at this subject in more detail in the final section of this chapter.

Another recent debate is the impact of Britain's membership of the European Community on the sovereignty of Parliament. We will also examine this in more detail in Chapter 10.

Legal exercises

15 To which relationship does the doctrine of parliamentary sovereignty apply?

16 What test do the courts apply to test the validity of legislation in the UK?

17 What legal authority is there for the rule that judges must obey Parliament?

18 Why was the Supreme Court of the United States able to strike down the legislation on racial discrimination in *Brown* v. *Board of Education*?

19 In 1995 the British government presents the Female Education Bill to Parliament. Section 1 of the Bill states: 'No blue-eyed female child shall receive a full-time education after reaching the age of ten years.' The legislation is approved by a majority of both Houses of Parliament and receives the Royal Assent.

- **a** Will the British courts be obliged to enforce this law?
- **b** Would your answer be different if Britain had a written constitution guaranteeing a right to full-time education up to the age of sixteen years?

2.3.2 Separation of powers

Another feature of the British constitution which is relevant to the constitutional role of the judiciary is the theory of the **separation of powers**. This theory was particularly developed by the French political scientist, Montesquieu:

> When the legislative and executive powers are united in the same person, or in the same body of magistrates, there can be no liberty . . . Again, there is no liberty, if the judiciary power be not separated from the legislative and executive. Were it joined with the legislative, the life and liberty of the subject would be exposed to arbitrary control; for the judge would then be the legislator. Were it joined to the executive however, the judge might behave with violence and oppression. There would be an end to everything, were the same man, or the same body, whether of the nobles or of the people, to exercise those three powers, that of enacting laws, that of executing the public resolutions, and of trying the causes of individuals.
>
> Montesquieu, *De l'Esprit des Lois* (Klincksieck 1982).

The theory has been criticised for being purist – that is, it is an impractical[22] model to which the British system of government does not conform. For example, members of the executive are also members of the legislature – the head of the judiciary, the Lord Chancellor, is a member of the Cabinet. Equally, the courts perform many administrative functions.

The constitution of the United States was expressly based on the separation of powers – the executive (President), the legislature (Senate/House of Representatives) and the judiciary (Supreme Court) are discrete[23] bodies. But even the United States government does not conform exactly to the theory. Each body exercises control over the functions of the others through a complex system of checks and balances. For example, the President appoints the judges to the Supreme Court but his nominations must be approved by the Senate, and we have already seen that the judiciary has the constitutional right to strike down legislation as unconstitutional.

By contrast, in France, the theory of separation of powers is the reason why the courts do not have the jurisdiction to question the legality of the acts of the executive and the legislature.

It is generally accepted that a precise separation of the functions of government is impracticable.[24] Montesquieu's theory should be seen as prescriptive[25] rather than descriptive, its essence being that no one person or body should have full control of all three functions of government. In particular, the courts should be independent of the executive and the legislature so that the judges can ensure that these bodies do not exercise their powers arbitrarily.

Text notes:

22 'practical' is the opposite of 'theoretical' or, as here, 'purist'
23 notice the dash on the previous line: the second part of the sentence explains the first part, so 'discrete' means 'separate'
24 'practicable' means 'can be used or done'
25 from the verb 'to prescribe', meaning 'to say what should be done'

Comprehension check

20 Fill in the missing words in the following passage from the list provided below.

There are (**a**) . . . . main functions of government. These are the (**b**) . . . ., the (**c**) . . . . and the (**d**) . . . . The theory of separation of powers states that these functions should be carried out by (**e**) . . . . bodies. The British constitution does not (**f**) . . . . to this theory. The same people are members of the (**g**) . . . . and the (**h**) . . . . and there are some (**i**) . . . . functions which are carried out by the courts. The distinction is clearer in the constitution of the (**j**) . . . . where the executive, legislative and judicial roles are performed by (**k**) . . . . bodies. The theory is (**l**) . . . . rather than (**m**) . . . . of the liberal system of government, an essential feature of which is that the (**n**) . . . . should be (**o**) . . . . of the (**p**) . . . . and the (**q**) . . . .

independent, legislature, United States, conform, executive, judicial, three, different, prescriptive, executive, judiciary, administrative, legislature, descriptive, legislative, different, executive.

Vocabulary

When forming and recognising opposites (**antonyms**) there are several prefixes which can be used, for example un- (as in '**un**known').

21 The following words, which have been used in Chapters 1 or 2, can be used with the prefixes un-, in-, il- or im- to form their opposites. Write them down using the correct prefix.

a lawful
b familiar
c practical
d legal
e fair
f valid
g dependence
h make
i justice
j partiality
k equitable
l written
m practicable
n constitutional
o licit*

* Not used in the book so far but often found in legal language.

NB: These prefixes often indicate an opposite meaning but the same letters (e.g. im-, in-) also occur in words where this is not the case, for example 'important', 'influence'.

Research

22 To what extent does the government of your country conform to the theory of separation of powers? To answer this question you should identify the three organs of government in your country and find out whether their functions are performed by different people or bodies.

Legal exercise

23 Write a short essay of 200 words on what you understand by the separation of powers and the reasons for maintaining it. You should include a discussion on whether the theory applies to the British constitution and make comparisons with other countries including your own. You may find the following essay plan helpful:

a Define the theory.
b The reasons for the theory.
c To what extent does it apply to the British constitution?
d Compare with the constitutions of other countries.

2.3.3. The rule of law

After reading sections 2.3.1 and 2.3.2 you should be aware of the two main characteristics of the British constitution. These are:

1 Parliament is the supreme organ of government, and
2 under a somewhat loose application of the theory of separation of powers, the courts are independent of Parliament and the executive.

We shall now develop the constitutional implications of these themes by examining the ways in which the courts can control the actions of the executive. In this context we are talking about the executive in its broad sense as the administrators of the system of government.

It is important to understand clearly that the courts have no power to review the **merits** of executive action; that is they are not concerned with the question: 'Is this action right or wrong?' The question they can ask is: 'Is this action lawful or unlawful?' At first the distinction may be difficult to recognise. The aim of these next two sections is to make the distinction clear and to demonstrate how it is reflected in the way the courts can control executive action. First, let us look at the principle of the **rule of law**:

> The rule of law means something more than rule in accordance with the law. The most terrifying dictatorship can rule in accordance with law by enacting laws to give effect to its policies, however inhuman these may be. The rule of law in the sense it is used here really involves certain presuppositions about law itself. The nature and extent of these presuppositions is open to argument but most would agree that the rule of law requires that all power and authority in the state be derived from law, and the notion of equality before the law.
>
> In a dictatorship judges might be understandably reluctant to question the legal basis upon which the dictator and his designates act. In a parliamentary democracy there is no such reluctance. Thus ministerial powers, however widely phrased, are generally subject to review by the courts and if a minister has acted *ultra vires* (beyond the powers of) his authority, his action is invalid even if done in complete good faith and in accordance with the public interest. If the police effect an arrest or search premises without the legal powers to do so, the arrest or search is illegal and it will not help the police to show that their action was reasonable or that it was done in good faith.
>
> Hogan, Seago and Bennett, *A Level Law* (Sweet and Maxwell 1988), pp. 15–16.

You will see from the extract that the principle of the rule of law embodies more than the requirement that government acts within its legal powers but also that it acts in accordance with the recognised principles of **liberal democracy**.

We shall now examine a recent situation involving the rule of law, using the facts to illustrate the distinction between 'right and wrong' and 'lawful and unlawful'.

Vocabulary

Before you read the extract, look at some of the key vocabulary below:

to intern = to force someone to stay in a special camp or prison. (Hence **internment**.)
to detain = similar to 'intern' but usually for a shorter period. (Hence **detention**.)
prejudicial = harmful. (In a dictionary look at the two quite different meanings of 'prejudice'.)
intelligence = new information.
to deprive someone **of** something.
to subject someone **to** something.
to suspect someone **of** something.
to amount to something. (Cf.[26] 'to constitute' which has a similar meaning.)

Text note:
26 compare with

Notice the prepositions which are used with the verbs above. It is essential to record any prepositions which are associated with a verb or adjective when you write down new vocabulary.

Comprehension check

24 On the basis of the information above give the meanings of:
a internee,
b detainee.

During 1971, the IRA[27] increased the ferocity of its campaign of violence in Northern Ireland, shooting soldiers and police and blowing up buildings. Early in August, the government of Northern Ireland, after consulting with the UK government, decided to exercise the power of internment available to it under the Civil Authorities (Special Powers) Act (Northern Ireland) 1922. This power could be used against persons suspected of having acted or being about to act in a manner prejudicial to the preservation of peace or the maintenance of order. On 9 August, 342 men were arrested. By November 1971, when the total arrested had risen to 980, 299 of those arrested were being interned indefinitely; the remainder were held under temporary detention orders or had already been released.

The security forces saw in internment an opportunity of obtaining fresh intelligence about the IRA. In August 1971 twelve detainees and in October two more were interrogated in depth. The procedures of interrogation included keeping the detainees' heads covered with black hoods; subjecting them to continuous and monotonous noise; depriving them of sleep; depriving them of food and water, except for one slice of bread and one pint[28] of water at six-hourly intervals; making them stand facing a wall with legs apart and hands raised. It was later held by a committee of inquiry that these procedures constituted physical ill-treatment . . . Subsequently the European Commission on Human Rights held that the interrogation procedures amounted to inhuman and degrading treatment and also torture, contrary to article 3 of the European Convention on Human Rights. When the Irish government referred the case to the European Court of Human Rights, the court held that the procedures were inhuman and degrading treatment but did not amount to torture.

Wade and Bradley, *Constitutional and Administrative Law* (Longman 1985), pp. 91–2.

Text notes:

27 Irish Republican Army (You need to know that the island of Ireland is divided into two parts: Northern Ireland, also called Ulster, which is part of the United Kingdom, and Ireland, also called Eire, which is an independent republic. The IRA is not an officially recognised army.)

28 1 pint = 0.57 litres

First let us separate the two aspects of the situation.

1 A number of suspected persons had been interned under the statutory powers of the Civil Authorities (Special Powers) Act (Northern Ireland) 1922.

2 During the period of internment fourteen internees had been subjected to ill-treatment during interrogation. There was no statutory authority for these interrogation procedures.

Now let us apply the two original questions to the separate issues:

1 a **Was the act of internment right or wrong?** Internment is a very controversial[29] procedure. It could be argued that to imprison people indefinitely without them being charged with and found guilty of any conduct which is illegal is an abuse[30] of human rights and therefore wrong. Alternatively it can be argued that such an action by the State is necessary to safeguard the national interest during war or other times of crisis. To examine these arguments is to examine the **merits** of the procedure and this is not the function of the British courts.

Text notes:

29 likely to cause an argument

30 notice this new (but unusual) 'opposite' prefix, ab-, meaning a wrong use

---

b **Was the act of internment lawful or unlawful?** There is no doubt that it was lawful under the powers of an Act of Parliament – the Civil Authorities (Special Powers) Act (Northern Ireland) 1922. If an action had been brought before the courts to challenge the validity of internment it would have been determined on this basis.

2 a **Were the interrogation procedures right or wrong?** Again to answer this question we would need to look at the merits of the procedures which are as controversial as internment. What arguments can you think of for and against such actions?

b **Were the interrogation procedures lawful or unlawful?** How would the British courts approach this question and what do you think their decision would be?

Oral work

In class or in discussions you will sometimes not hear or understand what somebody says. How will you ask them to repeat it?

Here are some possible ways. They are all polite and formal enough to be used with teachers but not too formal to be used with other students.

1 'I'm sorry, I didn't quite hear/catch what you said just now about [the rule of law].'
2 'Could you possibly repeat your answer to [the last question]?'
3 'Excuse me, but I still don't really understand what you said about [internment]; would you mind going over it again?'

25 Imagine that you did not hear or understand the following items. Ask each other for repetition.

- **a** examining the merits of the procedure;
- **b** question **2b**;
- **c** detainees;
- **d** the separation of powers;
- **e** how the courts can control executive action;
- **f** the distinction between 'right' and 'lawful'.

Legal exercises

26 How does the rule of law relate to the need to 'guarantee the courts their political independence'?

27 Discuss the following situation with your group using your knowledge of parliamentary sovereignty and the rule of law. Apply the same analytical procedure which is used in the discussion on internment above. If you are working on your own produce a written analysis in the same form.

The Prohibition of Dogs Act 1993 makes it a criminal offence for an individual to keep a dog as a household pet. William owns a dog contrary to the provisions of the Act. He is charged with the offence at the local police station and then locked in a cell for twenty-four hours. The Act does not give the police the power to detain people charged under its provisions.

28 In the recent case of *Malone* v. *Metropolitan Police Commissioner* [1979] Ch 344, an action was brought applying for a declaration that telephone tapping[31] authorised by the Secretary of State was illegal and unconstitutional. In dismissing the application Vice-Chancellor Megarry stated:

Text note:
31 listening to private telephone conversations without the speakers' permission

Finally, there is the contention[32] that as no power to tap telephones has been given by either statute or common law, the tapping is necessarily unlawful. The underlying assumption of this contention, of course, is that nothing is lawful that is not positively authorised by law. As I indicated, England is not a country where everything is forbidden except what is expressly permitted. One possible illustration is smoking. I inquired what positive authority was given by the law to permit people to smoke. Mr. Ross-Munro accepted that there was none: but tapping, he said, was different. It was in general disfavour, and it offended against usual and proper standards of behaviour, in that it was an invasion of privacy and an interference with the liberty of the individual and his right to be let alone when lawfully engaged on his own affairs.

I did not find this argument convincing. A stalwart non-smoker, whether life-long or redeemed,[33] might consider that most or all of what Mr. Ross-Munro said applied with equal force to the not inconsiderable numbers of non-smokers. In leading an ordinary life they often find themselves unable to avoid inhaling in an enclosed space the products of a combustion deliberately caused by a smoker who knows that the fumes that he is creating will spread, and will affect other people. But in any case the answer destroys the underlying assumption and mutilates the proposition. The notion that some express authorisation of law is required for acts which meet with "general disfavour," and "offend against proper standards of behaviour," and so on, would make the state of the law dependent on subjective views on indefinite concepts, and would be likely to produce some remarkable and contentious[34] results. Neither in principle nor in authority can I see any justification for this view, and I reject it. If the tapping of telephones by the Post Office at the request of the police can be carried out without any breach of the law, it does not require any statutory or common law power to justify it: it can lawfully be done simply because there is nothing to make it unlawful. The question, of course, is whether tapping can be carried out without infringing the law . . .

Text notes:

32 argument

33 try and infer the meaning – because of 'whether . . . or' it is probably in contrast to 'life-long'

34 likely to cause an argument

---

a In what way does this judgment differ from the principle 'that the rule of law requires all power and authority in the state be derived from law'?

b Do you consider the comparison drawn to cigarette smoking to be appropriate?

c How does the judgment relate to a lack of a written constitution in the United Kingdom?

Vocabulary

29 The extract from *Malone* above contains several words and phrases which mean 'legal' or 'illegal', 'allowed' or 'not allowed'. See how many you can find and list them in a table as follows:

legal/allowed	*illegal/not allowed*
. . . .	. . . .
.	.
.	.
.	.

30 Complete the table below, using a dictionary if necessary; all the words have been used in some form in Chapter 2.

Noun	*Verb*	*Adjective*
a	assume	×
b	contend	**c** . . . .
d	**e**	valid
f	prescribe	**g** . . . .
description	**h**	**i** . . . .
j	**k**	legal
l	compare	**m** . . . .
n	**o**	enforceable

2.3.4 Judicial review

The process of judicial review is a practical application of the rule of law. It forms the basis of a growing body of **administrative law** which regulates the relationship between the courts, public administrative bodies (including the executive) and individual citizens. Again, you should clearly understand that judicial review does not enable the courts to question the merits of administrative action or the validity of an Act of Parliament.

Pre-reading check

31 The passage below provides an explanation of the process of judicial review. After you have read it decide whether the statements which follow it are true (T) or false (F).

The primary ground upon which judicial review of administrative action may be based is that the jurisdiction of the authority concerned is defective . . . If a validly created power is exercised by the wrong authority, the latter will have acted *ultra vires*. Again, if the right authority exercises the power excessively or against the wrong person or in some other unlawful way, then a court may similarly condemn the illegality. And there are countless possible variations. Even though a power is apparently exercised by the right authority, that authority may not have been properly appointed or constituted, or some fact which is a condition precedent to[35] the possession of power may have been absent, or power may have been exercised in bad faith, unreasonably, for an improper purpose, or after taking irrelevant[36] considerations into account. Where an act is shown to be *ultra vires* the effect is that it is void. Judicial control of administrative action is not only the part of administrative law which most interests lawyers. It is also, and more importantly, the ultimate safeguard for the ordinary citizen against unlawful action by what would otherwise appear to be the more powerful administration.

Yardley, *Principles of Administrative Law* (Butterworths 1981), p. 42.

Text notes:
35 something which must be done before
36 not connected with the topic

---

a There is no legal basis for the powers exercised by administrative bodies.
b The *ultra vires* doctrine applies to administrative actions which exceed their legal authority.
c Failure to observe the correct legal procedure can be grounds for judicial review.
d The courts will not review an administrative decision on the grounds of unreasonableness.

The extract looks at some of the grounds for judicial review – illegality, irrationality and procedural impropriety.[37] These are all tests by which the courts have judged administrative actions to be *ultra vires* (i.e. in excess of power). The effect is to render the action void, that is it has no legal effect. It is treated as if it had never existed.

Let us now examine one of these grounds for review, **irrationality**, by means of a case study. Irrationality[38] is more commonly called unreasonableness. Unreasonable behaviour is very difficult to define – what may be reasonable in one set of circumstances will be unreasonable in another. In *Associated Provincial Picture Houses* v. *Wendesbury Corporation* [1948] 1 KB 223, Lord Greene MR outlined the factors which are relevant in determining whether an action was unreasonable:

Text notes:
37 from 'proper', meaning correct
38 notice this new negative prefix, 'ir-'

The court is entitled to investigate the action of a local authority with a view to seeing whether they have taken into account, or conversely, have refused to take into account or neglected to take into account matters which they ought to have taken into account. Once that question[39] is answered in favour of[40] the local authority, it may still be possible to say that, although the local authority have kept within the four corners of the matters which they ought to consider, they have nevertheless come to a conclusion so unreasonable that no reasonable authority could ever have come to it. In such a case again, I think the court can interfere. The power of the court to interfere in each case is not as an appellate authority to override a decision of the local authority, but as a judicial authority which is concerned, and concerned only, to see whether the local authority have contravened[41] the law by acting in excess of the powers which Parliament has confided in them.

Text notes:
39 see question **32a** below
40 see question **32b** below
41 notice that this verb could be added to the list of 'legal/illegal' words

---

Comprehension check

32 a Note 39: Which question is referred to here?
b Note 40: Has the local authority acted correctly so far?

Lord Greene's statement has been accepted as the standard test for unreasonableness in judicial review cases. It was used to unusual effect in the case of *Secretary of State for Education* v. *Thameside MBC* [1977] AC 1014. Under s.68 of the Education Act 1944 the Secretary of State was given powers to give direction to a local education authority which the Minister was satisfied was acting unreasonably. Thameside council proposed to modify its existing education scheme and the Secretary of State sought a court order enforcing the council to comply with his direction to adhere to the original scheme. He was satisfied that the council was acting unreasonably by seeking to change the scheme within a very short period of time.

The Court of Appeal and the House of Lords refused the order; the Secretary of State had misunderstood the meaning of the word 'unreasonable'. Although there were difficulties in setting up the new scheme within the prescribed time, the council's action was not so unreasonable that no reasonable council would do it. The House of Lords went further, declaring that it was the Secretary of State who was acting unreasonably in issuing the direction, primarily because his action was motivated by political considerations.

Language notes

The second sentence in the extract from Lord Greene MR (lines 4–9) is complex but very important. It consists of three parts:

1 'Once that question is answered *in favour of* the local authority . . .' **The local authority is right so far**.

2 '. . . it may *still* be possible to say that they have *nevertheless* come to a conclusion so unreasonable that no reasonable authority could ever have come to it.' **The local authority may be wrong**.

3 '. . . *although* the local authority have kept within the four corners of the matters which they ought to consider . . .' **The local authority has not taken into account any irrelevant considerations**.

In such long sentences it is helpful to read the whole sentence quickly, before and after examining the grammar and vocabulary, in order to understand the overall meaning.

Consider also the construction in lines 3–4: . . . they ought to have taken into account'. If this appears difficult to you, give yourself some practice with the exercise below along the lines of the following example:

Example: They took irrelevant considerations into account.
They ought not to have taken them into account.

33 a The council changed the scheme within a short period.
b The Secretary of State issued the direction.

c The police detained him for 24 hours.
d They used inhuman interrogation procedures.
e The police were in his house without permission.

Legal exercises

34 What is meant by the statement that 'judicial review is a practical application of the rule of law'?

35 What do you understand by the term *ultra vires*?

36 In what way does the process of judicial review regulate the relationship between administrative bodies and the individual citizen?

To answer the following two questions you will first need to identify the powers which have been given to the relevant authorities. Secondly, look at the actions which have been taken by the authorities, and thirdly compare these to their powers. Look to see if the authorities have done something which they have no power to do or if they have failed to do something which they are required to do.

37 Refer back to question 19 on p. 27. Consider the following situation in the light of what you now know about judicial review.

Marion has a nine-year-old daughter, Alison, who has grey eyes. Alison attends the local village school. One day Marion receives a letter from the local education authority advising her that under s.1 of the Female Education Act 1997 Alison's right to full-time education will cease on her tenth birthday.

Advise Alison on the validity of this action.

38 The Town Redevelopment Act 1994 gives local authorities the power compulsorily to purchase and clear land for 'the building of new housing estates'. It also imposes a duty to 'consult those people who will be affected by any such compulsory purchase'.

Newtown Council vote to compulsorily purchase and redevelop a group of houses which includes a house owned by Mr Stormy. The council issues orders for the immediate demolition of the houses and announces its intention to build a new housing estate and council offices on the site.

Advise Mr Stormy of his legal position.

2.4 Evaluation

In section 2.1 it was stated that the purpose of a constitution was to set the parameters of governmental power and the rights and duties of the citizens. In liberal democratic societies great emphasis is placed on maintaining the correct balance between public powers and the rights of the individual citizens: while it is necessary for governments to regulate the affairs of society this must not be achieved by restricting the basic rights and liberties of the individual. We have seen that in many countries these rights are guaranteed by a written constitution which is enforced by the courts.

Because there is no written constitution in the United Kingdom, the limitations on government power are largely self-imposed, relying on unenforceable conventions and a political culture based on the rule of law. Confidence in these traditional restraints has recently diminished and this has been reflected in an increasing demand for a more formal protection of human rights. Amongst others, Lord Scarman, an eminent member of the House of Lords, has argued in favour of the enactment of a Bill of Rights:

> This would[42] contain fundamental rights such as freedom of speech and assembly. It would be entrenched, i.e. it could not be repealed or altered without a special parliamentary majority. It would be enforced by the judiciary who would hold legislation or executive action to be invalid if it contradicted the Bill. Lord Scarman's main concern is that 'Parliament's sovereign power, more often than not exercised at the will of an executive sustained by an impregnable majority, has brought about a modern imbalance in the system'. He reinforces his argument by referring to the poor record of this country before[43] the European Court of Human Rights. The role of this court is discussed later . . . but it is true to say that over the years the Court has found a considerable number of our laws to conflict with the European Convention on Human Rights. The old laws on contempt of court, which in the 1970s were used to prevent the *Sunday Times* publishing material on the *Thalidomide* case, are a good example.[44] After the *Sunday Times* successfully complained to the Human Rights' Court, the laws were changed in an attempt to make them conform with the Convention. Lord Scarman's argument is that if we had a Bill of Rights, we would have held the old laws invalid ourselves without having to be taken before the Court. However, despite his campaign which has included attempts to introduce legislation into the House of Lords, the proposal has made little[45] headway. Opposition is deep.
>
> The arguments against a Bill were well put by Lord McCluskey when giving the 1987 Reith lectures. Firstly, it would 'draw judges into the political arena in a way alien to the best traditions of the judiciary'. Overriding the legislation of Parliament would certainly put the judiciary in the middle of the political arena, but whether as player or referee is another matter. Secondly, a Bill of Rights would necessarily entrench one set of values at the expense of another, i.e. a right of life could prejudice the rights of women to an abortion, a right to freedom of association[46] could prejudice the unions' right to operate a closed shop,[47] a right to free educational choice could prejudice the capacity of the community to distribute educational resources fairly. As Lord McCluskey put it, 'Rights are not to be regarded as if they were roses without thorns'. Of course, that may only mean that they should be cut carefully. Thirdly, the US experience of a Supreme Court enforcing constitutional rights has not been altogether happy. 'They legalised slavery, and when it was abolished, they legalised racial discrimination.' Only since the last war, have they adopted a basically 'liberal' approach. It is clear that a Bill of Rights of itself cannot guarantee rights. It must be supported by the spirit of the people and the judiciary. The question is whether a Bill makes rights more or less secure.
>
> Dugdale *et al.*, *A Level Law* (Butterworths 1988), pp. 28–9.

The European Convention on Human Rights is a subject which we will consider in more detail in Chapter 10. We will then also re-examine the debate surrounding the enactment of a Bill of Rights. At this stage you should be aware of the constitutional implications of such an enactment, particularly the impact that it would have on the role of the judiciary and the supremacy of Parliament.

Text notes:

42 see question **39a** below
43 does not relate to time here – it means 'in the opinion of'
44 see question **39b** below
45 see question **39c** below
46 to hold meetings
47 to allow only members of a particular union to work in a factory etc.

Comprehension check

39 **a** Note 42: Why is the conditional 'would' used here?
b Note 44: What are these a 'good example' of?
c Note 45: Can you explain the difference between 'little' and 'a little'?

Vocabulary

40 Try and find words or phrases in the excerpt above with an equivalent meaning to those below. (NB: They are listed in the order in which they appear in the text.)

a basic
b fixed
c most of the time
d caused
e strengthens
f in spite of
g damage
h alone

Notemaking

41 Use the outline below to make notes on the excerpt from Dugdale above. You will need to use abbreviations; many of them will be personal but below are some common abbreviations and symbols which you will find useful.

e.g.	for example
i.e.	that is, in other words
vs.	(versus) against
cf.	compare(d), with
+ (or &)	and
=	same as, like
≠	different from, unlike
→	cause, lead to, so
←	caused by
∴	therefore
∵	because
⁛	however
↗	rise, increase
↘	fall, decrease
>	more than
<	less than

NB: Personal abbreviations are not used in the outline so it is longer than usual. [Pers. abbrev. not used in outline → longer th. usual.]

1. Nature of proposed B. of R.:
   a)
   b)
   c)
2. L.S. sees need for B. of R. ∵
   a)
   b)
      e.g.
3. *But*
4. Arguments vs. B. of R.
   a)
   b)
   c)
5. Conclusion:

Legal exercises

42 What effect would a Bill of Rights have on the following constitutional maxims:

a parliamentary sovereignty,
b judicial review?

43 Use the answers to question 42 above as the basis for a debate on the following proposal:

'A Bill of Rights would increase the protection of human rights in the United Kingdom.'

Choose two teams of three people to present arguments for and against the proposition. The speakers should be allowed five minutes each to present their arguments and they should then answer questions from the rest of the group. A vote should then be taken on which team has presented the most convincing arguments.

To prepare for the debate you will need to reread this chapter very carefully, taking notes on the arguments which could support either side of the debate. The arguments should then be presented in a structured way with each member of the team addressing a particular issue. These should include:

a An examination of the features of the British constitution and how these affect the roles of the legislature, executive and judiciary.
b How are human rights protected under the present system? Are these safeguards adequate?
c What effect would a Bill of Rights have on the roles of the legislature, executive and judiciary? Would this provide greater protection of human rights?

If you are working on your own write an essay of 500 words analysing the arguments for and against the proposition using the preceding points.

44 Section 1 of the Protection of Citizens' Rights Act 1995 states: 'All citizens shall have the right to privacy and freedom from unwanted intrusion into their private lives.'

Detective Sergeant Squeeze is a senior police officer in the fraud squad. His work brings him into regular contact with a prominent businessman, Flash Harry, and on several occasions DS Squeeze has entertained Flash Harry at his home. A national newspaper, *The Investigator*, is publishing a series of articles on business fraud. It receives information that Flash Harry is not completely honest in his business dealings. During the course of investigating this information one of its reporters takes a photograph of DS Squeeze and Flash Harry having dinner together at a London restaurant. It publishes the photograph under the heading 'Senior Police Officer Dines with Suspected Criminal.'

How does this situation reflect Lord McCluskey's fears over the enactment of a Bill of Rights in the United Kingdom?

Additional reading

Constitutional and administrative law is a very complex subject. Many more issues are involved than we have been able to cover and the subject will not usually be studied in any depth in the early stages of legal study. If you wish to look at the issues in this chapter in more depth you should refer to the textbooks which deal exclusively with the subject rather than the more general textbooks which have been included. In addition, *Constitutional and Administrative Law* by de Smith (Penguin) is a very authoritative and detailed book whilst *Introduction to British Constitutional Law* by Yardley (Butterworths) provides a comprehensive and very readable introduction to the subject.

Lord McCluskey's 1987 Reith Lectures mentioned in section 2.4 are published in *Law, Justice and Democracy* (BBC), which also includes the transcript of a discussion between Lord McCluskey and Lord Scarman on a Bill of Rights. *Understanding Public Law* by Ganz (Fontana) provides further interesting comment on the British constitution.

Cases and Materials on Constitutional and Administrative Law by Allen, Thomson and Walsh (Blackstone Press) is an excellent and up-to-date collection of cases and commentary with exercises designed to make the reader think about the subject.

3

Sources of law

Summary

Legal content

3.1 Case law
- 3.1.1 The hierarchy of the courts
- 3.1.2 The binding element in precedents
- 3.1.3 Evaluation

3.2 Statute law
- 3.2.1 The purpose of statutory interpretation
- 3.2.2 Aids to interpretation
- 3.2.3 Reform

Additional reading

Aim

To provide an introduction to the law-making processes and to examine the ways in which the judges identify the law. The chapter concentrates on the primary sources of law – case law and statutes – through an analysis of judicial precedent and statutory interpretation. The advantages and disadvantages of these principles will be assessed and some comparisons made with other legal jurisdictions. A practical illustration of the system is provided by case and statute reading exercises.

Language content

Grammar: decoding long sentences (by identifying main clause); 'so' as a pro-form; unreal conditionals
Vocabulary: Latin plurals; adjectival suffixes
Study skills: bibliographical references

3.1 Case law

In Chapter 1 we looked at the different meanings of the phrase 'common law'. You will remember that one of those meanings is the law which is based on judicial decisions, otherwise known as **case law**. When we use the word 'case' in this context we mean the legal action or dispute which has been brought to the courts for resolution. The judges decision is the law – hence 'case law'. However, judges are not free to reach any decision they wish to; they are bound to follow certain rules and these rules form the system of **judicial precedent.**

> The strongly coercive[1] nature of the English doctrine of precedent is due to rules of practice, called 'rules of precedent', which are designed to give effect to the far more fundamental rule that English law is to a large extent based on case-law. 'Case-law' consists of the rules and principles stated and

acted upon by judges in giving decisions.[2] In a system based on case-law, a judge in a subsequent[3] case *must* have regard to these matters; they are not, as in some other legal systems, merely material which he *may* take into consideration in coming to his decision. The fact that English law is largely a system of case-law means that the judge's decision in a particular case constitutes a 'precedent'. If we place ourselves in the position of a judge in a later case, there may be said to be many different kinds of precedent. The judge may simply be obliged to consider the former decision as part of the material on which his present decision could be based, or he may be obliged to decide the case before him in the same way as that in which the previous case was decided unless he can give a good reason for not doing so. Finally, the judge in the instant[4] case may be obliged to decide it in the same way as that in which the previous case was decided, even if he can give a good reason for not doing so. In the last-mentioned situation the precedent is said to be 'binding' or of 'coercive effect' as contrasted with its merely 'persuasive' effect in the other situations in which the degree of persuasiveness may vary considerably.

Cross, *Precedent in English Law* (Clarendon Press 1977), pp. 4–5.

Text notes:

1 to coerce = to force
2 when they give decisions
3 coming later
4 see question **2** below

Comprehension check

1 Three situations are mentioned where the effect of precedent varies. Can you identify them?

2 Note 4: Can you work out what 'instant' means in this context? It obviously does not have its everyday meaning, but is contrasted with 'previous' later in the sentence.

You will see from the extract above that, when deciding a case before them, judges are bound by the legal rules in previous cases. This is called the principle of *stare decisis* which means 'stand by what has been decided'. Its purpose is to achieve certainty and consistency in the law, but it is also important that the system should be sufficiently flexible to allow the law to develop and adapt to changing social and economic conditions. Later we will examine the advantages and disadvantages of judicial precedent and assess whether it ensures the correct balance between certainty and flexibility. First, let us examine how the system works in practice.

3.1.1 The hierarchy of the courts

In the English legal system some courts have more authority than others. Judges in the lower courts are bound to follow the decisions of judges in the higher courts. The following text provides an outline of the hierarchy of the courts and the ways in which judges are bound by the decisions of other judges.

Pre-reading exercise

3 Before you read the following passage in detail **scan** the text in order to identify the seven courts which are mentioned, and list them separately.

The House of Lords[5] is the highest appeal court in the English legal system. Its decisions are binding on all other courts. Until 1966 the House of Lords was also bound by its own previous decisions. In that year the Lord Chancellor, Lord Gardiner, issued a Practice Statement which stated that 'while treating former decisions of this House as normally binding' their Lordships[6] would 'depart from a previous decision when it appears right to do so'.

The Court of Appeal is below the House of Lords in the hierarchy. It is bound by the decisions of the House of Lords and its decisions are binding on all lower courts. It is also bound to follow its[7] own previous decisions except when **a** a previous decision of the Court of Appeal conflicts with a decision of the House of Lords, **b** there are two conflicting Court of Appeal decisions when it must choose which one to follow, and **c** a previous decision was given *per incuriam* (through lack of care – generally when some relevant law was not taken into consideration). These exceptions to the rule that the Court of Appeal must abide by its own previous decisions are called the rules in *Young* v. *Bristol Aeroplane Company* (1944), the case in which the rules were laid down.

The court below the Court of Appeal is the High Court of Justice. It is bound to follow the decisions of the House of Lords and the Court of Appeal. Judges of the High Court will normally follow the decisions of fellow High Court judges but they are not absolutely bound to do so.

The court of first instance[8] for criminal cases, the Crown Court, is bound by the House of Lords and the Court of Appeal; the lowest courts in the hierarchy, the county court and the magistrates' courts are bound by the High Court, the Court of Appeal and the House of Lords. No court is bound by the decisions of these lower courts.

Since 1972 when Britain joined the European Community, the position of the European Court of Justice must also be considered. This will be examined in detail in Chapter 10 but you should be aware that it is a court of referral in relation to EC law and not a court of appeal, although its decisions on the interpretation of EC law are binding on British courts.

Text notes:

5 although this court has the same name as the second chamber in Parliament it is a separate body whose members are judges. These judges, known as Law Lords, are also members of the House of Lords in its legislative capacity but, by convention, do not take part in politically controversial debates.
6 judges who are members of the House of Lords
7 refers here to the Court of Appeal
8 the first place (i.e. where a case is heard for the first time)

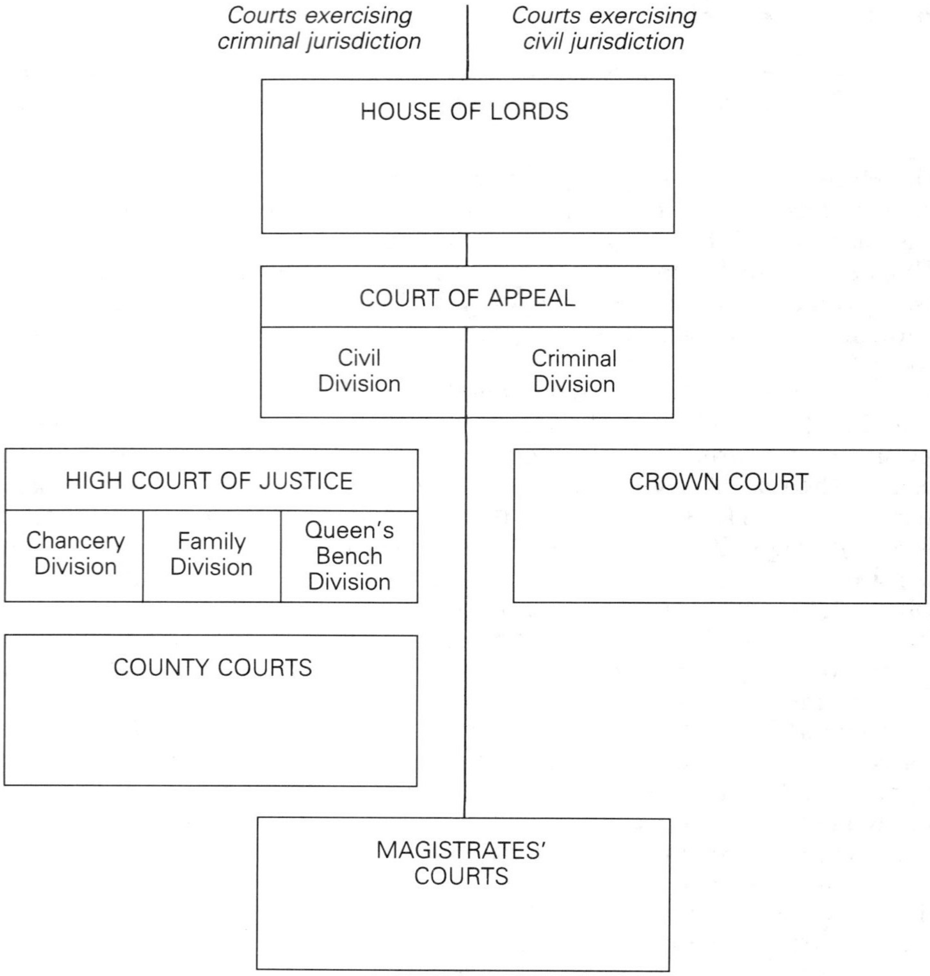

Figure 3.1 The hierarchy of the English courts. (*Source:* Hogan, Seago and Bennett, *A Level Law*, Sweet and Maxwell 1988, p. 21.)

The diagram given in Figure 3.1 should help you to remember this hierarchy of the English court system.

Comprehension check

4 Decide whether the following statements are true or false according to the passage above:

- **a** Only the High Court is bound by decisions of the Court of Appeal.
- **b** The House of Lords is bound by its own precedents.
- **c** The High Court must always follow the precedents set by the House of Lords.
- **d** English courts are not bound by the European Court of Justice.

Legal exercises

5 What is meant by the doctrine of *stare decisis*?

6 What was the significance of the 1966 Practice Statement?

7 When may the Court of Appeal depart from its own previous decisions?

8 What is the position of the European Court of Justice in the English legal system?

3.1.2 The binding element in precedents

In the course of a judgment a judge will say many things, not all of which are binding. For the purposes of judicial precedent a judgment comprises two parts: the *ratio decidendi* and *obiter dictum* (see the extract below for explanations of these terms). It is the *ratio decidendi* which is binding in later cases. The *obiter dictum* is merely persuasive, that is it may help future judges to reach a decision but they are not bound to follow it.

Before examining these concepts in more detail it is important that you understand the meaning of three words which are particularly relevant to the practice of judicial precedent. These are:

1 **Reversing** – in most cases the unsuccessful party may appeal to a higher court. The decision of the lower court is said to be reversed if the higher court reaches a decision in favour of the appellant.
2 **Overruling** – this occurs when a higher court in a later case refuses to endorse the statement of law in an earlier case.
3 **Distinguishing** – this occurs when the facts of a later case are sufficiently different to justify the court reaching a different decision from an earlier case involving the same legal principle.

You should be sure that you understand the meaning of these words before continuing. Check them in a law dictionary if you have any doubts about their meaning

Let us now look at the meaning of and the difference between *ratio decidendi* and *obiter dicta*.

> The decision or judgment of a judge may fall into two parts: the *ratio decidendi* and *obiter dictum*. When a judge delivers judgment in a case he outlines the facts which he finds have been proved on[9] the evidence. Then he applies the law to those facts and arrives at a decision, for which[10] he gives the reason (*ratio decidendi*[11]). More precisely, the *ratio decidendi* of a case is the principle of law on which the decision is based. The judge may go on to speculate[12] about what his decision would or might have been if the facts of the case had been different.[13] This is an *obiter dictum* ('something said by the way'). . .
>
> The binding part (if any) of a judicial decision is the *ratio decidendi*. An *obiter dictum* is not binding in later cases because it was not strictly relevant to the matter in issue in the original case. However, an *obiter dictum* may be of *persuasive* (as opposed to *binding*) authority in later cases. The *ratio* is not the decision itself. Only the litigating parties are bound by the actual decision in a case whereas the *ratio* of a case states the law for all persons and may be binding in later cases . . .

The traditional view was that the *ratio decidendi* of a case was what it was perceived to be by the judge who decided the case. But the difficulty with this approach is that the judge may have expressed the principle too widely or too narrowly for it to be useful in a later case. Moreover, in appellate courts each[14] judge may state the principle in different language and so it is not always easy to discover the *ratio* by a quotation from any one judgment.

The modern, generally accepted view is that the *ratio decidendi* of a case is what it is determined to be by a court in a later case and not what the judge in the original case considered it to be. This objective approach towards finding the *ratio* of a case makes it possible for a judge in a later case to relegate to[15] the status of *obiter dicta*[16] statements which had hitherto been thought to be *ratio*. It also means that, since the facts of two cases are unlikely to be identical, the judge in the later case usually has the task of either restricting or enlarging the *ratio* of the earlier case. If he decides that the *ratio* does not apply to the facts before him he is restricting its scope. If he decides that the *ratio* does apply to the different factual situation he is enlarging its scope . . .

Discovering the *ratio decidendi* of a case is often difficult but it may involve the separation of the relevant and irrelevant parts of a judgment. The *ratio* will hardly ever[17] be stated explicitly in the judgment but will be found buried among a mass of *dicta*. In some respects the old cases are easier to read because the reporter did not always trouble to report what he considered to be mere *obiter dicta*. The *ratio* may not be accurately encapsulated in the headnote[18] to the law report. The reporter may have misinterpreted the decision and attempted to state the *ratio* too widely or too narrowly. The decision in a case and, therefore, the *ratio decidendi* must always depend on the particular facts of the individual case. To discover the *ratio* of a case all the facts found by the judge to be material must be considered. Whatever words are not necessary for the decision must be *obiter*. However, a judge may give two or more reasons for his decision in which event they are both or all *rationes*[19] *decidendi* and not mere *obiter dicta*.

Ingham, *The English Legal Process* (Blackstone Press 1990), pp. 173–4, 193.

Text notes:

9 based on
10 see question **9a** below
11 see question **9b** below
12 form an opinion
13 see question **9c** below
14 note that each judge delivers an individual judgment
15 'to' suggests movement from one status to another. Since the *ratio* has a higher status than *dicta* 'relegate' means move to a lower position
16 plural of *dictum*
17 rarely, only very occasionally. Cf. 'I can hardly hear you' meaning 'I can hear you but only faintly and with difficulty'
18 summary of the judgment at the beginning of the law report
19 plural of *ratio*

Comprehension check

9 **a** Note 10: What does 'which' refer to here?
b Note 11: Can you now work out what *ratio decidendi* means?
c Note 13: Do you understand this conditional sentence?

10 Can you make out the main points in this extract? Each of the points below is contained in one of the five paragraphs of the extract.

Number them 1–5 to correspond to the appropriate paragraph.

- **a** It is not always easy to distinguish between *ratio* and *dicta*.
- **b** Nowadays it is usually the judges in subsequent cases who decide which part of the original case was *ratio*.
- **c** Only the *ratio decidendi* is binding in subsequent cases.
- **d** It used to be thought that the original judge best decided what was the *ratio* in his case.
- **e** There are usually two parts to a judge's decision.

Vocabulary

The Latin phrases *ratio decidendi* and *obiter dictum* are explained in the text but it is also useful to look at English words which are based on these Latin words.

ratio – rational, based on reason.
dictum – to dictate, e.g. to 'speak' a letter to a secretary, to 'tell' someone what to do.

Notice that plurals are formed in Latin in a different way from English, e.g.

ratio – (pl.) *rationes*
dictum – (pl.) *dicta*

If you have not learnt Latin you will need to note the different types of plurals each time you meet a new one.

The following case study will help to illustrate two important principles contained in the text – that the *ratio decidendi* of a case is determined by the courts in later cases and that a judge is only bound when the facts of a later case are sufficiently similar; they may restrict or enlarge the *ratio* in different factual situations.

Donoghue v. *Stevenson:* a case study in precedent

Donoghue v. *Stevenson* [1932] AC 562 is the case from which the modern law of negligence developed. The plaintiff's friend bought her a bottle of ginger beer which had been manufactured by the defendant. She became ill as a result of drinking the ginger beer which contained the remains of a decomposed[20] snail.[21] She sued the manufacturer for compensation for the damage she had suffered. The case was decided, on appeal, in the House of Lords. The leading judgment was given by Lord Atkin. There are two legal principles which can be drawn from the judgment. These can be found in the following extracts:

Text notes:
20 rotten (i.e. very old)
21 animal with soft body and shell

---

a

If your Lordships accept the view that the appellant's pleading discloses a relevant cause of action, you will be affirming the proposition that by Scots and English law alike a manufacturer of products which he sells in such a form as to show that he intends them to reach the ultimate consumer in the form in which they left him, with no reasonable possibility of intermediate examination, and with the knowledge that the absence of reasonable care in the preparation or putting up of the products will result in injury to the consumer's life or property, owes a duty to the consumer to take that reasonable care.

b

The liability for neglicence . . . is no doubt based upon a general public sentiment of moral wrongdoing for which the offender must pay. But acts or omissions which any moral code would censure cannot in a practical world be treated so as to[22] give a right to every person injured by them to demand relief. In this way rules of law arise which limit the range of complainants and the extent of their remedy. The rule that you are to love your neighbour becomes in law: You must not injure your neighbour,[23] and the lawyers' question: Who is my neighbour? receives a restricted reply. You must take reasonable care to avoid acts or omissions which you can reasonably foresee would be likely to injure your neighbour. Who then, in law, is my neighbour? The answer seems to be persons who are so closely and directly affected by my act that I ought reasonably to have them in contemplation[24] as being so[25] affected when I am directing my mind to the acts or omissions which are called in question.

Text notes:
22 in order to
23 this is a reference to one of the Ten Commandments in the Bible
24 in mind
25 here means 'in this way', i.e. 'closely and directly'

Language notes

Excerpt **a** consists of one very long sentence. This can more easily be understood if you can find the main part of the sentence and then look at the subsidiary clauses (more attention will be paid to this problem in later chapters). The main part here is contained in lines 2, 3, 8 and 9:

> . . . you will be affirming the proposition that . . . a manufacturer of products . . . owes a duty to the consumer to take that reasonable care.

11 Can you identify the three conditions which are mentioned in the subsidiary clauses?

The principle contained in extract **a** imposes a legal duty on manufacturers to take reasonable care to prevent injury to the life or property of the consumers of their products. The principle contained in **b** is much wider. It has become known as the 'neighbour principle', creating a general legal duty to avoid foreseeable harm in all areas of activity.

The House of Lords found for the plaintiff in this case. It was clear that the case established a precedent for future cases involving manufactured products which caused injury to the consumer's person or property. Some writers argue that this narrow legal principle was the *ratio decidendi* of the case and that the broader neighbour principle was *obiter dicta* and therefore not binding but merely persuasive. This is a debatable assertion – the neighbour principle has been the basis of many successful legal actions involving different factual situations.

A direct application of the principle can be found in the judgment of Denis Henry QC in the case of *Tutton & others* v. *A. D. Walter Ltd.* [1986] QB 61. The plaintiffs kept bees near land farmed by the defendants. The defendants sprayed their land and crop of oil seed rape with insecticide, killing the bees. The defendants knew the insecticide was dangerous to the bees but they failed to give the plaintiffs adequate warning of the spraying. The plaintiffs sued the defendants, basing their action on Lord Atkin's neighbour principle in *Donoghue* v. *Stevenson*. Note how the judge applies the principle to the specific facts of the case.

Per Denis Henry QC:

> I turn then to apply Lord Atkin's test in *Donoghue* v. *Stevenson* [1932] AC 562, 580. First: was spraying a noticeably yellow oil seed rape field with Hostathion likely to injure bees? Clearly the answer must be yes. Second: was this reasonably foreseeable? Again, yes, the defendants knew both of the dangers, and of the presence of the bee keepers within the area (the latter[26] from a previous spraying incident the year before). It is not a case where the defendants were ignorant of the presence of bee keepers. Third: ought then the defendants to have had the bee keepers in their contemplation? Again, the answer to that is not only yes, they ought to, but in the event they did; there is the instruction the defendants gave to Mr. Moon to warn the bee keepers. There is no suggestion that the defendants were ignorant of the existence of any of these plaintiffs.
>
> I therefore conclude that the plaintiffs were owed a duty of care.

Text note:
26 see question **12** below

Comprehension check

12 Note 26: What would 'the former' refer to in this instance?

This case is a good example of a simple application of the neighbour principle and clearly illustrates the point made in the extract on p. 48 that judges in later cases may apply a *ratio* in different factual situations. Of course, not all cases are so straightforward. The case of *Hedley, Byrne & Co. Ltd* v. *Heller & Partners Ltd* [1964] AC 465 provides a more complex example.

Apart from the basic facts there are two important ways in which this case can be distinguished from *Donoghue* v. *Stevenson*. Think about this as you read the following extract:

> The plaintiffs asked their bankers to inquire into the financial stability of a company with which they were having business dealings. Their bankers made inquiries of the company's bankers, who carelessly gave favourable references about the company. Reliance on these references caused the plaintiffs to lose £17,000. The plaintiffs sued the defendants for their careless statements. The action failed because the defendants had expressly disclaimed any responsibility.
>
> Nevertheless all five law lords proceeded to re-examine the authorities on liability for careless statements. They rightly limited the rule in *Derry* v. *Peek*

to its proper function of defining the limits of the tort of deceit and thus irrelevant to the issue of whether a duty of care arose in negligence . . .

But their Lordships were not prepared simply to recognise a duty of care in respect of statements on the basis of the *Donoghue* v. *Stevenson* neighbour principle alone. For liability for statements resulting in economic loss to be imposed some narrower test than the foreseeability of the loss must be satisfied. The House of Lords was not prepared to formulate rules which might expose a maker of careless statements to liability to a large indeterminate[27] class of plaintiffs. For instance, newspapers were not to be accountable to everybody who read their advice columns and suffered loss through relying on their negligent advice. The plaintiff to recover[28] for negligent misstatements must establish that the statement was made within a relationship where the plaintiff could reasonably rely on the skill and care of the defendant in making the statement. He must show some 'special relationship' with the defendant which properly resulted in the defendant undertaking responsibility for the accuracy of the statements made.

Brazier, *Street on Torts* (Butterworths 1988), pp. 186–7.

Text notes:

27 not fixed, vague

28 it will be easier to read this sentence if you insert commas after 'plaintiff' and 'misstatements'

Vocabulary

13 Find words in the excerpt which have similar meanings to those listed below:

a responsible
b careless
c clearly stated
d wrong reports.

Language and information check

14 In order to revise some prepositions and review information in the above excerpt, form six sentences, choosing one item from each column below:

a The bankers inquired	with	his advice.
b He had dealings	for	a large company.
c They relied	to	the loss.
d She sued him	on	its readers.
e A newspaper is not financially accountable	for	his negligence
f The bank was not responsible	into	the financial situation.

The distinguishing facts in *Hedley Byrne* v. *Heller* were:

1 the case involved negligent words or statements as opposed to negligent actions, and
2 the plaintiffs had suffered financial loss rather than physical injury.

You will see from the extract that these distinguishing facts led the House of Lords to restrict the neighbour principle which is based on foreseeability of harm. They added the further requirement of a 'special relationship' between the plaintiffs and the defendants. This has become the *ratio decidendi* of the case. As with the neighbour principle the nature of a 'special relationship' has been determined by subsequent cases involving financial loss suffered as a result of negligent words – and so the case law develops.

Legal exercises

15 Distinguish between *ratio decidendi* and *obiter dicta*. What is the significance of the distinction?

16 What is the difference between reversing and overruling?

17 Why do you think it was necessary for the House of Lords to distinguish between negligent words and negligent acts in *Hedley Byrne* v. *Heller?*

18 As a lawyer, you are consult by your client, Mrs Gamble, over the following problem. On which case precedent would you base your advice and why?

Mrs Gamble had inherited £10,000 when her rich uncle died. She consulted her bank manager, Miss Nugget, on the best way to invest the money. On the basis of her advice Mrs Gamble bought £5,000 worth of shares in Intoil plc. She invested the remaining £5,000 in a construction company called Kwikbuild plc after reading an article about the company in a national newspaper. Both companies were financially unsound at the times Mrs Gamble invested in them and six months later both Intoil plc and Kwikbuild plc have ceased trading and Mrs Gamble has lost all her money.

This last type of question is very common in legal study; it is called a 'problem' question. There is a special technique for answering these questions which is different from the usual essay technique. It can be quite simply stated although in practice it is more difficult:

- **i** Identify the area(s) of law involved – often there will be more than one.
- **ii** State what the law is in the relevant area(s) by an analysis of cases.
- **iii** Apply the law to the facts of the problem, particularly analysing any facts which distinguish the problem from the relevant case law.

Although you are in a way being asked to act as a judge in problem questions it is not important that you reach a decision – often the case law will be uncertain so that it will not be possible to do so. The questions are a test of your ability to recognise the legal issues involved and to analyse the law.

3.1.3 Evaluation

The common law will cease to grow. Like a coral reef, it will become a structure of fossils. If it is to avoid this fate, the law cannot afford to be a "lawless science" but should be a science of law. Just as the scientist seeks for truth, so the lawyer should seek for justice. Just as the scientist takes his instances and from them builds up his general propositions, so the lawyer should take his precedents and from them build up his general principles. Just as the propositions of the scientist fall to be modified when shown not to fit all instances, or even discarded when shown to be in error, so the principles of the lawyer should be modified when found to be unsuited to the times or discarded when found to work injustice.

Lord Denning, *The Discipline of the Law* (Butterworths 1979), p. 292.

This plea from one of Britain's best known and, indeed, controversial judges states the case for greater flexibility in the common law. He argues that the purpose of the law is to achieve justice and that at times, this may require a departure from the existing rules of judicial precedent. In particular he advocates that the Court of Appeal should be free to overrule its own previous decisions in the same way as the House of Lords is able to do.

Comprehension check

19 Notice that 'just as . . . so' introduce two items which Lord Denning feels are parallel. Complete the table below with parallel items from the excerpt. (NB: Some note forms have been used.)

Science	*Law*
Truth	**a** . . . .
Instances → gen props.	Precedents → **b** . . . .
If props. don't fit all instances → modify or **c**	If princ. out of date → **d** . . . .
	If princ. unjust → **e** . . . .

Pre-reading check

The next extract outlines some of the advantages and disadvantages of the doctrine of judicial precedent. Think about these questions as you read it.

20 a How does certainty in the law achieve justice?
b Why does justice also demand flexibility in the law?
c How does adherence to precedent assist impartiality in judicial decision-making?
d How does the process of distinguishing provide for flexibility in the law?
e How may 'bad decisions' be overruled?
f Would justice be more easily achieved if the Court of Appeal was free to depart from its own previous decisions?

Greater *certainty* in the law is perhaps the most important advantage claimed for the doctrine of judicial precedent. From this advantage other benefits flow. If case X was decided in a particular way in 1980 by the Court of Appeal or House of Lords, the doctrine of *stare decisis* would normally demand that a court in 1990 faced with the same problem as in case X should decide it the same way. The existence of a precedent may prevent a judge making a mistake which he might have made if he had been left on his own without any guidance. It may also allow persons generally to order their affairs and come to settlements with a certain amount of confidence. But the advantage of certainty is lost where there are too many cases or they are too confusing. This[29] can arise through the process of distinguishing cases and over-refining the principles embodied in them. Certainty in the law can only result from a large body of case law if the cases are uniform in outcome and not irreconcilable.[30]

The doctrine of precedent may serve the *interests of justice*. If the decision in a case between A and B was X, it would be unjust to reach decision Y the next day in a similar case between C and D . . .

The interests of justice also demand impartiality from the judge. This may be assured by the existence of a binding precedent which he must follow unless it is distinguishable. If he tries to distinguish an indistinguishable case his attempt will be obvious . . .

The making of law in decided cases offers opportunities for *growth and legal development* which could not be provided by Parliament. The courts can more quickly lay down new principles, or extend old principles, to meet novel[31] circumstances. There has built up over the centuries a mass of cases illustrative of a vast number of the principles of English law. The cases exemplify the law in the sort of detail that could not be achieved in a long code of the Continental[32] type. But therein[33] lies another weakness of case law.[34] Its very *bulk and complexity* make it increasingly difficult to find the law. There are at present some[35] 350,000 decided cases contained in several thousand volumes of law reports, and the number is being added to all the time . . .

The case-law method is sometimes said to be *flexible*, but this presupposes that a judge is free to lay down whatever rule he considers desirable in order to keep the law in step with changing social and economic conditions. But a judge is not thus[36] free where there is a binding precedent. Unless it can be distinguished he must follow it, even though he dislikes it or considers it bad law. His discretion is thereby[37] limited and the alleged flexibility of case law becomes *rigidity*. Judicial mistakes of the past are perpetuated unless bad decisions happen to come before the House of Lords for reconsideration. In any event, flexibility and certainty are incompatible[38] features of judge-made law. A system that was truly flexible could not at the same time be certain because no one can predict when and how legal development will take place.

Ingham, *The English Legal Process* (Blackstone Press 1990), pp. 241–2.

Text notes:

29 see question **21a** below
30 cannot be made to agree with each other
31 new
32 mainland Europe
33 in this fact – see also question **21b** below
34 see question **21c** below
35 approximately
36 in this way – see also question **21d** below
37 by this fact – see also question **21e** below
38 cannot coexist

Comprehension check

21 a Note 29: To what does 'this' refer here?
b Note 33 explains that 'therein' means 'in this fact'. To which fact does this refer.
c Note 34: If this is 'another weakness in case law', what was the earlier weakness?
d Note 36 explains that 'thus' means 'in this way'. Can you explain in what way?
e Note 37 explains that 'thereby' means 'by this fact'. To what fact does this refer?

22 Identify the advantages and disadvantages of judicial precedent which are mentioned in the excerpt and complete the table below.

Advantages	*Disadvantages*
a Certainty: **i** may prevent mistakes by judge; **ii**	**a** . . . .
b etc.	**b** etc.

Finally in this section we should consider, in outline, some comparisons with other legal jurisdictions – the USA and Continental systems of law.

Pre-reading check

23 Read the extract and then decide if the preceding statements are true (T) or false (F).

- **a** The USA has a centralised legal system.
- **b** The decisions in US Federal and District courts are binding in later cases.
- **c** The legal code is important in Continental legal systems.
- **d** Continental systems of law have been greatly infuenced by the writing of jurists.
- **e** In England, textbooks have greater authority than judicial decisions.

The following of precedent is easier in England than in many other countries because England has a centralised legal system with only a small number of courts. In the USA, where there are federal and state courts and legislatures, the number of reported cases runs into millions and this has led to a modification there of the doctrine of *stare decisis* (see Cross, *Precedent in English Law*, 3rd ed., 1977, pp. 17–19). Decisions of the US Supreme Court are binding on courts other than itself, but the Supreme Court tends to decide only constitutional issues. In all other cases, US Federal and District Courts are not bound by precedent. Previous decisions are of persuasive authority only and may be rejected. Particularly persuasive is an established *line* or *trend* of decisions rather than a single decision.

The English doctrine of *stare decisis* is based on the binding effect of a single decision, which must be followed even when manifestly unjust or wrong. Such an approach is alien to Continental systems of law wherein no single decision, even of the highest court, is absolutely binding (Cross, op. cit., pp. 12–17; Goodhart, 'Precedent in English and Continental law', (1934) 50 LQR 40). Continental law tends to be codified and the code is all-important so that cases decided on the interpretation of the code are of persuasive authority only. In practice, however, a long line or trend of decisions (what the French call *la jurisprudence constante*) is highly persuasive and will rarely be departed from. Another reason[39] for the relative unimportance of the single decision on the Continent is the great weight attached to *la doctrine*. The writings of jurists played a major part in the development of Roman law, which, in turn,[40] influenced modern Continental systems of law. In England, because judges commanded greater respect than jurists, lawyers looked to judicial decisions rather than to textbooks for authority.

Ingham, *The English Legal Process* (Blackstone Press), p. 242–3.

Text notes:
39 see question **23** below
40 then

Comprehension check

24 Note 39: What is the earlier reason for the relative unimportance of the single decision on the Continent?

Bibliographical references

The extract above contains three bibliographical references (or citations) which may need some explanation:

As with cases there is a standard way of referring to articles in legal journals. You will see that it is very similar to the way that cases are cited. There are a large number of law journals with most countries publishing their own. Full details of these journals and their abbreviated references can be found in most good law dictionaries.

(Lines 5–6)

(1) Cross, (2) *Precedent in English Law*, (3) 3rd ed., (4) 1977, (5) pp. 17–19

1. **Author's surname.**
2. **Title.** Italic letters indicate that this is a book not an article.
3. **3rd edition.** It is important to find the right edition because new information is included in later editions and, of course, page numbers may change.
4. **Year of publication.**
5. **From page 17 to page 19.**

(Lines 15–16)

Cross, (1) op.cit., pp. 12–17.

1 *opere citato* (Latin) means 'in the work cited', i.e. the book by Cross which has already been mentioned.

(Lines 16–17)

(1) (2) (3) (4) (5)

Goodhart, 'Precedent in English and Continental law', (1934) 50 LQR 40.

1 **Title.** Ordinary print and inverted commas indicate that this is not a book but a journal article.
2 **Year of journal.** 3 **Volume number.**
4 **Law Quarterly Review.** 5 **Page number**

3.2 Statute law

Statute law is the law enacted by Parliament. In section 2.3.1 on parliamentary sovereignty we examined the supreme legislative powers of Parliament and emphasised the constitutional fact that the judiciary have no authority to question the validity of an Act of Parliament. Nevertheless judges do have an important role in relation to legislation: Parliament passes the laws, and the courts apply them to individual cases. But before the law can be applied the judges must decide on its meaning. This process is called **statutory interpretation.**

Before examining this process in more detail you should study Figure 3.2 which shows the normal procedure of a Bill through Parliament. An individual piece of legislation is known as a Bill during its legislative process and called an Act after receiving the Royal Assent. Unless otherwise specified, an Act comes into force on the day it receives the Royal Assent. Figure 3.3. on pp. 61–3 shows a copy of an Act of Parliament. Look at the explanatory notes carefully as these indicate the different parts of the Act.

3.2.1. The purpose of statutory interpretation

When interpreting statutes the courts are said to be seeking the 'intention of Parliament'. This search is as difficult as that[41] for the *ratio decidendi* of a case. Parliament comprises[42] many individual members of Parliament who may have different views on any one subject. Seeking the common intention of such a disparate[43] group would be a speculative[44] and impossible task. In this sense the 'intention of Parliament' is a phrase with little meaning. It has been restated by Lord Reid in *Black-Clawson International Ltd* v. *Papierwerke Waldhoff-Aschaffenburg AG* [1975] AC 591, 613):

> We often say we are looking for the intention of Parliament, but this is not quite accurate. We are seeking the meaning of the words which Parliament used. We are seeking not what Parliament meant but the true meaning of what they said.

Text notes:
41 refers to search
42 is composed of/consists of – notice the different structure of each of these expressions

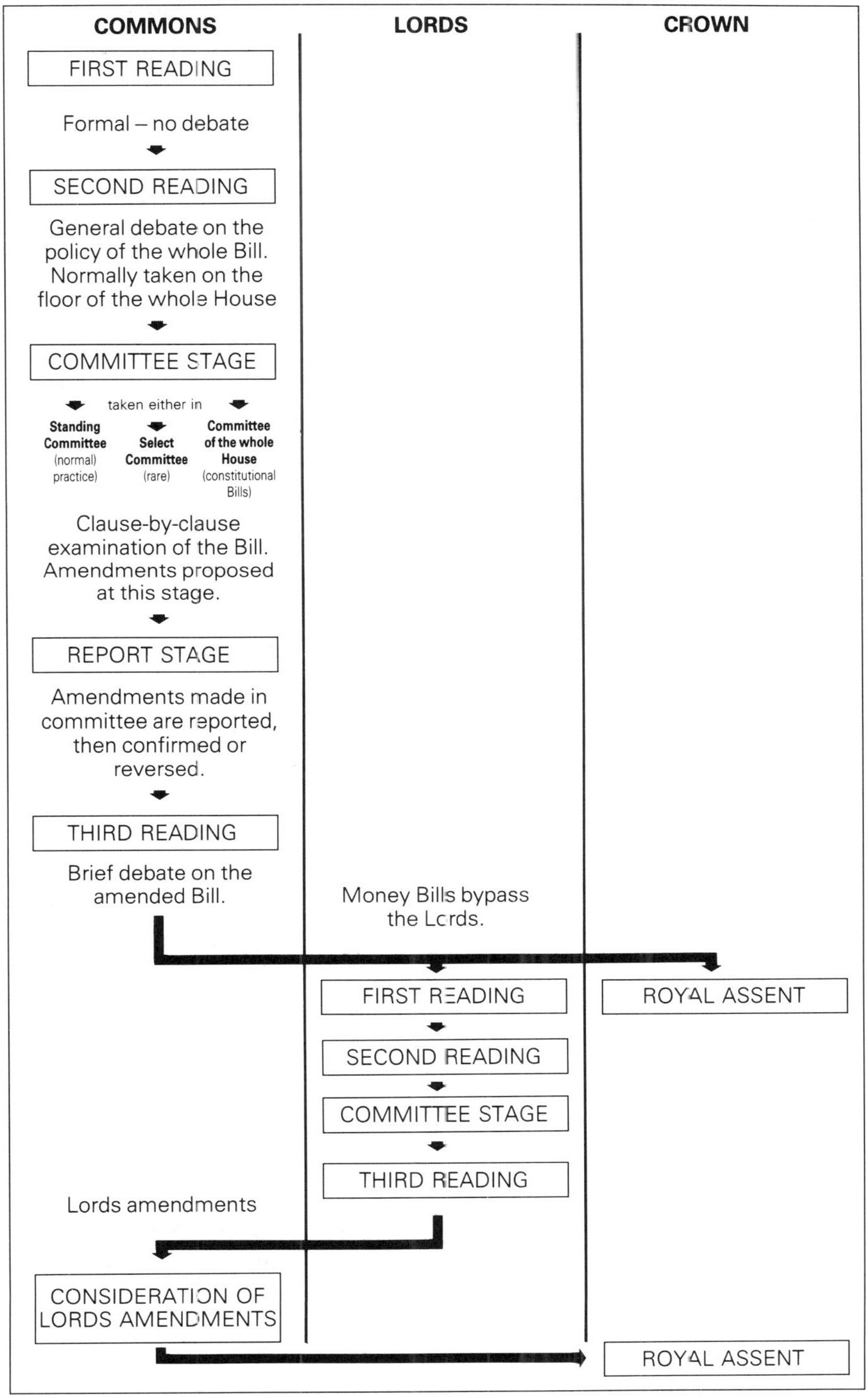

Figure 3.2 Typical passage of a Bill through Parliament. Note that the term 'reading' is a formal one for the legislative process – the Bill is not actually read out in Parliament. (*Source:* Johnson and Pannet, *SWOT A Level Law*, Blackstone Press 1988, p. 21.)

43 can you work out the meaning? It is contrasted with 'common', and the previous sentence tells you something about the members, so it means 'varied', 'without anything in common'
44 based on opinions and inadequate information

The purpose of statutory interpretation therefore is to find the meaning of the words used in the statute. As people studying in a foreign language you will be particularly aware that words are often complex and ambiguous and finding their meaning is not an easy task. The following passage outlines some of the inherent difficulties:

> It is never easy to express ideas in words and the more complex the idea the greater the difficulty. That which seems to have been clearly explained by the writer may not be so[45] found by the reader. There are many reasons for this.[46] All writing assumes a certain knowledge on the part of the reader, but the writer may have assumed that his reader knew more than was in fact the case and as a result the document may be stated too succinctly or abstrusely. The document may be concerned with something such as a mathematical calculation that does not readily lend[47] itself to a description in words. The idea may be so complex that it requires a very large number of statements, qualifications, exceptions and so on to set it out. Or the writer may not have foreseen all the subtle variations of human conduct relating to the topic dealt with in the document and thereby not have provided for some particular activity. These are but[48] some of the difficulties that confront both writer and reader of any document and they are all magnified in regard to legislation
>
> Pearce, *Statutory Interpretation in Australia* (Butterworths 1974), p. 1.

Text notes:
45 clearly – see language note
46 see question **25** below
47 is not suited to
48 only.

Comprehension check

25 Note 46: To what does 'this' refer here?

26 In this excerpt the writer suggests several reasons for difficulties experienced by readers; can you identify these reasons: (Sometimes a writer 'signposts' a list of items, for example 'the first reason', or 'first'; however, this has not been done in this excerpt.)

Language note

'So' often replaces a word or clause which has already been used in the same or previous sentence. It can be used formally in writing or informally in conversation.

Example: A: 'John *saw the Prime Minister yesterday.*'
B: 'Did he say so?' (so = that he saw the PM yesterday)

Example: Many people feel *that a Bill of Rights would increase the protection of personal liberties.*
The Labour party thinks so but the Conservative party does not. (so = that a Bill . . .)

Figure 3.3 Example of an Act of Parliament. (Courtesy HMSO.)
(See section 3.2 Statute Law on page 58.)

Short title –

Congenital Disabilities (Civil Liability) Act 1976

Official citation – 1976 CHAPTER 28

Long title – An Act to make provision as to civil liability in the case of children born disabled in consequence of some person's fault; and to extend the Nuclear Installations Act 1965, so that children so born in consequence of a breach of duty under that Act may claim compensation.

Date of Royal Assent – [22nd July 1976]

Enacting formula – BE IT ENACTED by the Queen's most Excellent Majesty, by and with the advice and consent of the Lords Spiritual and Temporal, and Commons, in this present Parliament assembled, and by the authority of the same, as follows:—

Section – 1.—(1) If a child is born disabled as the result of such an occurrence before its birth as is mentioned in subsection (2) below, and a person (other than the child's own mother) is under this section answerable to the child in respect of the occurrence, the child's disabilities are to be regarded as damage resulting from the wrongful act of that person and actionable accordingly at the suit of the child.

Civil liability to child born disabled.

Sub-section – (2) An occurrence to which this section applies is one which—

(*a*) affected either parent of the child in his or her ability to have a normal, healthy child; or

(*b*) affected the mother during her pregnancy, or affected her or the child in the course of its birth, so that the child is born with disabilities which would not otherwise have been present.

(3) Subject to the following subsections, a person (here referred to as "the defendant") is answerable to the child if he was liable in tort to the parent or would, if sued in due time, have been so; and it is no answer that there could not have been such liability because the parent suffered no actionable injury, if there was a breach of legal duty which, accompanied by injury, would have given rise to the liability

(4) In the case of an occurrence preceding the time of conception, the defendant is not answerable to the child if at that time either or both of the parents knew the risk of their child being born disabled (that is to say, the particular risk created by the occurrence); but should it be the child's father who is the defendant, this subsection does not apply if he knew of the risk and the mother did not.

(5) The defendant is not answerable to the child, for anything he did or omitted to do when responsible in a professional capacity for treating or advising the parent, if he took reasonable care having due regard to then received professional opinion applicable to the particular class of case; but this does not mean that he is answerable only because he departed from received opinion.

(6) Liability to the child under this section may be treated as having been excluded or limited by contract made with the parent affected, to the same extent and subject to the same restrictions as liability in the parent's own case; and a contract term which could have been set up by the defendant in an action

Figure 3.3 contd.

by the parent, so as to exclude or limit his liability to him or her, operates in the defendant's favour to the same, but no greater, extent in an action under this section by the child.

(7) If in the child's action under this section it is shown that the parent affected shared the responsibility for the child being born disabled, the damages are to be reduced to such extent as the court thinks just and equitable having regard to the extent of the parent's responsibility.

Marginal note

Liability of woman driving when pregnant.

2. A woman driving a motor vehicle when she knows (or ought reasonably to know) herself to be pregnant is to be regarded as being under the same duty to take care for the safety of her unborn child as the law imposes on her with respect to the safety of other people; and if in consequence of her breach of that duty her child is born with disabilities which would not otherwise have been present, those disabilities are to be regarded as damage resulting from her wrongful act and actionable accordingly at the suit of the child.

Disabled birth due to radiation.

1965 c. 57.

3.—(1) Section 1 of this Act does not affect the operation of the Nuclear Installations Act 1965 as to liability for, and compensation in respect of, injury or damage caused by occurrences involving nuclear matter or the emission of ionising radiations.

(2) For the avoidance of doubt anything which—

(*a*) affects a man in his ability to have a normal, healthy child; or

(*b*) affects a woman in that ability, or so affects her when she is pregnant that her child is born with disabilities which would not otherwise have been present,

is an injury for the purposes of that Act.

(3) If a child is born disabled as the result of an injury to either of its parents caused in breach of a duty imposed by any of sections 7 to 11 of that Act (nuclear site licensees and others to secure that nuclear incidents do not cause injury to persons, etc.), the child's disabilities are to be regarded under the subsequent provisions of that Act (compensation and other matters) as injuries caused on the same occasion, and by the same breach of duty, as was the injury to the parent.

(4) As respects compensation to the child, section 13 (6) of that Act (contributory fault of person injured by radiation) is to be applied as if the reference there to fault were to the fault of the parent.

(5) Compensation is not payable in the child's case if the injury to the parent preceded the time of the child's conception and at that time either or both of the parents knew the risk of their child being born disabled (that is to say, the particular risk created by the injury).

Interpretation and other supplementary provisions.

4.—(1) References in this Act to a child being born disabled or with disabilities are to its being born with any deformity, disease or abnormality, including predisposition (whether or not susceptible of immediate prognosis) to physical or mental defect in the future.

(2) In this Act—

(*a*) "born" means born alive (the moment of a child's birth being when it first has a life separate from its mother), and "birth" has a corresponding meaning; and

(*b*) "motor vehicle" means a mechanically propelled vehicle intended or adapted for use on roads.

(3) Liability to a child under section 1 or 2 of this Act is to be regarded—

(*a*) as respects all its incidents and any matters arising or to arise out of it; and

Figure 3.3 contd.

Congenital Disabilities (Civil Liability) Act 1976 c. 28

(*b*) subject to any contrary context or intention, for the purpose of construing references in enactments and documents to personal or bodily injuries and cognate matters,

as liability for personal injuries sustained by the child immediately after its birth.

(4) No damages shall be recoverable under either of those sections in respect of any loss of expectation of life, nor shall any such loss be taken into account in the compensation payable in respect of a child under the Nuclear Installations Act 1965 as extended by section 3, unless (in either case) the child lives for at least 48 hours. 1965 c. 57.

(5) This Act applies in respect of births after (but not before) its passing, and in respect of any such birth it replaces any law in force before its passing, whereby a person could be liable to a child in respect of disabilities with which it might be born; but in section 1(3) of this Act the expression "liable in tort" does not include any reference to liability by virtue of this Act, or to liability by virtue of any such law.

(6) References to the Nuclear Installations Act 1965 are to that Act as amended; and for the purposes of section 28 of that Act (power by Order in Council to extend the Act to territories outside the United Kingdom) section 3 of this Act is to be treated as if it were a provision of that Act.

5. This Act binds the Crown. Crown application.

6.—(1) This Act may be cited as the Congenital Disabilities (Civil Liability) Act 1976. Citation and extent.

(2) This Act extends to Northern Ireland but not to Scotland.

Legal exercises

27 There are four possible interpretations of the following simple sentence. What are they?

'John met Peter and he raised his hat.'

28 Which of the following would you consider to be a 'vehicle'?

a a car
b a pram
c a bicycle
d an aeroplane.

29 Which of the following would you consider to be a 'building'?

a a tent
b a house
c a garden shed
d a caravan.

3.2.2 Aids to interpretation

Given that words are an imperfect means of communication a number of aids have evolved to assist judges in the interpretation of statutes. The next extract provides an outline of some of these aids but be aware that statutory interpretation is not a scientific process and these 'rules' of interpretation are general principles rather than strict rules.

There are several *presumptions*[49] which guide a judge when he is called upon to interpret an Act. There are presumptions that the Act applies to the whole of the United Kingdom but no further, that the Crown is not bound, that the statute is not retrospective and that the common law is not altered . . .

In addition to the presumptions there are certain other *aids* to a judge. *Internal aids* such as the title of the Act, its preamble[50] (setting out its purpose), headings to sections and Schedules may be looked at in appropriate circumstances, but not marginal notes as these are not inserted by Parliament. Acts usually contain their own definition sections. *External* guidance such as text books in general may not be used. The *Oxford English Dictionary* may be referred to as a guide to the ordinary meaning possessed by words used in the Act . . . The Interpretation Act 1978 . . . gives a particular meaning to various words and expressions used in legislation unless a contrary intention appears. For example, the Act says that the masculine gender includes the feminine and the singular includes the plural (s.6[51]), references to the time of day are to Greenwich mean time (s.9) and Sch.I contains a five page list of 'words and expressions defined' . . .

Where a United Kingdom Act of Parliament incorporates an international treaty, *travaux préparatoires*[52] preceding it may be considered if they are publicly available and they unequivocally point to a particular legislative intention (see *Fothergill* v. *Monarch Airlines Ltd* (1980) HL).

. . . A particular rule of interest is the *ejusdem generis* (of the same kind) rule. Where two or more particular words are followed by general words the general words are to be read in relation to those particular words. For example, the Betting[53] Act 1853 prohibited the keeping of a 'house, office or other place' for betting with persons resorting thereto. The question arose as to whether Tattersall's Ring (an open air enclosure reserved for certain bookmakers[54]) fell within the statute. The court applied the *ejusdem generis* rule and said that 'or other place' referred to other covered accommodation and did not, therefore, include Tattersall's Ring.

Finally, a few words might be said about the so-called canons of construction. The 'Literal Rule' says that, where there is no ambiguity, the literal or usual meaning must be given to words even though hardship results. The remedy for the hardship lies in an amending Act of Parliament. . .

An extension to, or offshoot of this rule, is the 'Golden Rule' of interpretation which has been expressed thus:

> 'the grammatical and ordinary sense of the words is to be adhered to unless that would lead to an absurdity or repugnancy or inconsistency with the rest of the instrument, in which case the grammatical or ordinary sense of the words may be modified so as to avoid such absurdity, repugnancy or inconsistency and no further' (*per* Lord Wensleysale in *Grey* v *Pearson* (1857) HL) . . .

Another canon of construction is the 'Mischief Rule'. This provides that in cases of ambiguity the courts may look at the old law to discover the wrong (mischief) which the Act sought to remedy and then interpret the words of the Act in the light of this knowledge. This rule is also known as the rule in *Heydon's Case* (1584) . . .

Now that the United Kingdom is a member of the European Communities English courts are sometimes called upon to interpet the meaning of any Treaties of the Communities or a Community Instrument. The European Communities Act 1972 provides that such questions shall be treated as questions of law and, if they are not referred to the European Court, they shall be decided in accordance with the principles laid down by any relevant decision of the European Court. Thus it follows that in interpreting Community legislation the English courts are bound by the decisions of the European Court which is outside the area of jurisdiction of the English courts.

Sim and Scott, *A Level English Law* (Butterworths 1984), pp. 54–8.

Text notes:
49 'to presume' means suppose to be true
50 can you identify the preamble in the Congenital Disabilities Act?
51 what do you think this means?
52 French, meaning preparatory work and discussions
53 'to bet' means to risk money on a race
54 people who receive bets

Comprehension check

30 When you have read the passage above identify the main topics and complete the note outline which follows.

Note outline:
Para. 1:
1. Presumptions: (a) . . . .
(b) . . . .
(c) . . . .
(d) . . . .

Paras. 2–5:
2. . . . .: (a) . . . . e.g. title and preamble of Act
(b) . . . . e.g. (i) . . . .
(ii) . . . .
(iii) . . . .

Paras. 6–8:
3. . . . .: (a) . . . .
(b) . . . .
(c) . . . .

31 Line 29: How did the court know that 'or other place' referred to covered accommodation?

Let us now add some details to the outline information in the extract by examining some cases involving the canons of construction.

The Literal Rule: *London & North Eastern Railway Co.* v. *Berriman* [1946] AC 278 HL
The statute in this case imposed a duty on railway companies to provide an adequate warning system whenever railway workers were 'repairing or relaying'[55] the railway line. The plaintiff's husband was killed whilst oiling and cleaning the railway points. No warning system had been provided. The House of Lords, by a three to two majority, held that Mr Berriman had been engaged in **maintaining** the railway line at the time of his death and this was not the same as 'repairing and relaying' it.

It is interesting to note in this case that the Law Lords in seeking the 'literal and usual' meaning of the words 'repairing and relaying' reached different conclusions; that is the minority considered that Mr Berriman's actions did come within the meaning of 'repairing and relaying'. This gives a clear illustration of the difficulty in determining the meaning of what might appear to be very simple words.

The Golden Rule: *Adler* v. *George* [1964] 2 QB 7
The defendant was charged under section 3 of the Official Secrets Act 1920 which provides that no person shall 'in the vicinity of a prohibited place' obstruct any member of Her Majesty's forces. George was charged under section 3 after entering a Ministry of Defence airfield. He argued that he was not in the vicinity of, but actually in a prohibited place and had therefore not committed the offence according to the words of the statute. His argument was rejected – such an interpretation of the Act would lead to absurdity and nullify its purpose. The court interpreted the offence as 'in **or** in the vicinity of'.

The Mischief Rule: *Smith* v. *Hughes* [1960] 1 WLR 830
Section 1(1) of the Street Offences Act 1959 made it a criminal offence 'for a common prostitute to loiter[56] or solicit[57] in a street or public place for the purpose of prostitution'. The defendant was charged after soliciting from the balcony of her own home. She appealed against her conviction under the Act, claiming that she was not soliciting 'in the street or public place'. Lord Parker CJ approached the case by 'considering the mischief aimed at in the Act'. This was to 'enable people to walk the street without being molested or solicited by common prostitutes'. It did not matter that she had been standing on the balcony or in the street. Her appeal was rejected.

Text notes:
55 replacing, i.e. laying again
56 to stand around
57 to make a sexual offer for payment

Legal exercises

32 What is the constitutional reason for judges seeking to find the intention of Parliament when interpreting statutes?

33 Why does the need for statutory interpretation arise?

34 Distinguish between internal and external aids. Give examples of both.

35 Why do you think Parliament enacted the statute which was at issue in the *Berriman* case? Do you think the decision of the majority of the House of Lords in that case reflected the intention of Parliament?

There is a particular technique to use in answering questions which require you to apply legislation to a given situation:

- **i** Decide on the words which will require interpretation.
- **ii** Analyse the words on the basis of your knowledge of the rules of statutory interpretation.
- **iii** Apply your analysis to the situation.

Apply this technique to the following question.

36 Consider the following situations in the light of the relevant statutory provisions:

a Section 4 of the Offensive Weapons Act 1994 provides: 'Any person found carrying a gun, pistol, knife or any other offensive weapon shall be guilty of a criminal offence.' James is charged under the Act after being found carrying a piece of broken glass which he had picked up off the street.

b The Employers' Liability (Defective[58] Equipment) Act 1969 section 1(1) reads:

> 'Where, after the commencement of this Act – (a) an employee suffers a personal injury in the course of his employment in consequence of a defect in equipment provided by his employer for the purpose of his employer's business; and (b) the defect is attributable[59] wholly or partly to the fault of a third person (whether identified or not), the injury shall be deemed[60] to be attributable to negligence on the part of the employer . . .'

Section 1(3) reads: 'In this section – "equipment" includes any plant or machinery, vehicle, aircraft and clothing . . . "personal injury" includes loss of life . . .'

Bert is a sailor on board[61] the *Morning Star* (a supertanker). He was employed by Transpo plc who owned the vessel. The ship sinks on its first voyage as a result of a defect in its construction. Bert suffers serious injuries in the incident. Rose, who is also employed by Transpo plc, is on the ship for a free ride as a reward for thirty years' service to the company. Rose dies in the accident.

Text notes:
58 faulty
59 'to attribute' means to consider to result from
60 considered
61 on (for ships)

3.2.3 Reform

The case of *London & North Eastern Railway Co.* v. *Berriman* is an illustration of the way in which a strict adherence to the literal approach to statutory interpretation may fail to achieve the purpose of a statute – or the intention of Parliament. The argument in favour of such an approach is based on the doctrine of parliamentary sovereignty: the courts must accept the words used by Parliament and not seek to guess its intention or purpose if this cannot be readily supported by the words used. If this leads to injustice it is for Parliament to change the statute.

The most vocal critic of this approach was Lord Denning. He enthusiastically adopted what has become known as the 'purposive approach' to statutory interpretation. This is an extension of the Mischief Rule which looked beyond the words of the statute to its purpose. This approach received little judicial support. The conflicting statements of Lord Denning and Lord Simmonds in *Magor & St Mellors Rural District Council* v. *Newport Corporation* [1951] 2 All ER 839 highlight the judicial conflict.

Lord Denning:

> We do not sit here to pull the language of Parliament and of Ministers to

pieces and make nonsense of it. That is an easy thing to do, and it is a thing to which lawyers are too often prone.[62] We sit here to find out the intention of Parliament and of Ministers and carry it out, and we do this better by filling in the gaps and making sense of the enactment than by opening it up to destructive analysis.

Lord Simmonds:

. . . The court, having discovered the intention of Parliament and of Ministers too, must proceed to fill in the gaps. What the legislature has not written, the court must write. This proposition, which restates in a new form the view expressed by the Lord Justice in the earlier case of *Seaford Court Estates Ltd* v *Asher* (to which the Lord Justice himself refers), cannot be supported. It appears to me to be a naked usurpation[63] of the legislative function under the thin disguise of interpretation. And it is the less justifiable[64] when it is guess-work with what material the legislature would, if it had discovered the gap, have filled it in.[65] If a gap is disclosed, the remedy lies in an amending Act.

Text notes:
62 'to be prone to' means to have a tendency to
63 'to usurp' means to take wrongly
64 even less justifiable
65 notice this is an 'unreal' conditional – see text for more information

---

Comprehension check

Unreal conditionals (in the past) are formed as follows:

If + had + past participle, would/could/might have + past participle.

For example: 'If the legislature had discovered the gap, it would have filled it in.'

These conditionals are called 'unreal' because in fact both actions did not happen.

37 The second extract above is quite difficult. It may help you to understand it if you try and decide whether the following statements are true or false:

- **a** Lord Simmonds agrees with Lord Denning.
- **b** Lord Simmonds thinks that 'filling in the gaps' in an Act is part of the judges' role of interpretation.
- **c** Lord Simmonds thinks that 'filling in the gaps' is the job of the legislature.
- **d** Lord Simmonds thinks that judges should not try and guess how the legislature might fill a gap.

Apart from the constitutional implications of Lord Denning's approach it is argued that an excess of judicial creativity would lead to individual judges determining what is 'right and just'. This could result in accusations of bias and prejudice. Nevertheless there has been a general criticism of a strict adherence to the Literal Rule. The Law Commission report *The Interpretation of Statutes* (Law Comm. No. 21) approved the use of the Mischief Rule, preferring 'a construction which would promote the general legislative purpose over one which would not'. Lord Denning's campaign has undoubtedly led to a more flexible judicial approach to statutory interpretation.

Vocabulary

Adjectives can usually be recognised by their suffixes (endings) and this can help your understanding of a text.

38 Using the nouns and verbs below, choose appropriate suffixes to form adjectives. The following suffixes will be needed: -ive, -able, -al, -ory, -ary, -ing, -ent. (All the adjectives have already been used in the book.)

Noun	*Adjective*
defect	
reason	
law	
description	
continent	
statute	
convention	
excess	
equity	
hierarchy	
discretion	

Verb	*Adjective*
elude	
neglect	
foresee	
coerce	
precede	
attribute	
speculate	
reconcile	
distinguish	

39 Write an essay of 500 words on the following statement:

> Whenever the strict interpretation of a statute gives rise to an absurd and unjust situation, the judges can and should use good sense to remedy it – by reading words in, if necessary – so as to do what Parliament would have done, had they had the situation in mind.
>
> *Per* Lord Denning, *Northam* v. *Barnet Council* [1978] 1 WLR 220

Essay questions in the form of a quotation are very common. Before writing your essay think carefully about the meaning of the quotation and its particular emphasis in relation to the topic. You will rarely be asked to provide only factual information; you must also be prepared to comment critically on the subject and to analyse the relevant areas of debate or controversy. Read the following essay plan to help you structure your essay properly.

1. What is the aim of the judges when they are interpreting statutes? What is the constitutional reason for this aim?
2. What difficulties are involved in achieving this aim?
3. Why is statutory interpretation necessary? What aids are available to assist judges in the interpretation of statutes?
4. What is strict interpretation and how does it lead to absurd and unjust situations?
5. What approach to interpretation is Lord Denning advocating? Why is it controversial?

Additional reading

More detailed reading on the topics in this chapter can be found in all textbooks on the English legal system although some will be more detailed than others. *A Level Law* by Hogan, Seago and Bennett (Sweet and Maxwell) and *A Level Law* by Dugdale, Furmston *et al.* (Butterworths) provide a good comprehensive introduction. *The English Legal Process* by Ingham (Blackstone Press) contains a more detailed yet very readable account. *The Law Making Process* by Zander (Weidenfeld & Nicholson) is a collection of cases and materials on the English legal system with commentary by the author.

How to Do Things with Rules by Twining and Miers (Weidenfeld & Nicholson) and *Introduction to Legal Method* by Farrar and Dugdale (Sweet and Maxwell) provide an analysis of the process of legal reasoning.

Learning Legal Rules by Holland and Webb (Blackstone Press) offers a comprehensive introduction to judicial precedent and statutory interpretation together with exercises and analysis.

Revision 1: Legal knowledge and legal skills

Test your knowledge

Answer the following questions as briefly as possible.

1 Name the ways in which the term 'common law' is used.

2 Give an example of a country with a legal system based on a civil code.

3 Define the concepts 'criminal law' and 'civil law' Give examples of actions which fall into each category.

4 Outline the developments which led to the establishment of a common legal system.

5 Outline the reasons for the establishment of the original courts of equity.

6 Which court was the principal court for the administration of equity and who was its head?

7 What are the underlying principles of equity?

8 In a case of conflict between a rule of equity and a rule of common law, which will prevail?

9 Give three equitable maxims.

10 What is the significance of the Judicature Acts 1873–1875?

11 What are two classifications of English law?

12 Name the three organs of government.

13 What are the two elements of the doctrine of parliamentary sovereignty?

14 Outline the theory of the separation of powers.

15 Does the judiciary have any control over the actions of the executive?

16 Would a Bill of Rights change the role of the judiciary?

17 Why might statutes be ambiguous and uncertain?

18 What legal status do canons of statutory interpretation hold?

19 What is meant by the expression 'the intention of Parliament'?

20 Give an example of a case in which the literal rule was applied and a brief summary of its application.

21 What criticisms can be levelled at the literal rule?

22 Explain the basic recommendations of the Law Commission's report on the interpretation of statutes.

23 Give two examples of the presumptions used by the courts when interpreting statutes.

24 Define the following terms:

a distinguishing;
b *per incuriam*.

Test your legal skills

25 Read the following sections of the Theft Act 1968 and answer the questions which follow. To do this you will need to list the factors which make up the various crimes, e.g. 'trespasser' and 'intent' in section 1(a). Read the Act very carefully to make sure you identify all the relevant factors. You will need to do this at least three times. Then look at the situations which follow and decide whether all the necessary ingredients of the crime are present. You must justify your answers by reference to the relevant sections and subsections of the Act.

(1) A person is guilty of burglary if:
(a) he enters a building or part of a building as a trespasser and with the intent to commit any such offences as are mentioned in subsection (2) below; or
(b) having entered any building or part of a building as a trespasser he steals or attempts to steal anything in the building or that part of it or inflicts or attempts to inflict on any person therein any grievous bodily harm.
(2) The offences referred to in subsection (1) as above are offences of stealing anything in the building in question or part of the building in question, or inflicting on any person therein any grievous bodily harm or raping any woman therein, and doing unlawful damage to the building or anything therein.

a Reg is a homeless student. One night when the weather is particularly cold he enters Dave's house through an unlocked window. He falls asleep on the settee and in the morning leaves through the front door.
b Charles invites some of his friends to his house for dinner. During the evening an argument breaks out between Charles and his best friend, Peter. Peter hits Charles causing him serious injury.
c Bert, who is homeless, spends the night sleeping in John's garden shed. In the morning he uses John's ladder which is stored in the shed to pick some apples from a tree in the garden. In doing this he breaks the ladder.

Have Reg, Peter or Bert committed an offence under the Theft Act?

26 Read the following judgment from *Boardman* v. *Sanderson* [1964] 1 WLR 1317 and answer the questions **in your own words**.

The plaintiff and his 8-year-old son went to a garage with the defendant to collect the defendant's car. While reversing the car out of the garage the defendant negligently ran over the boy's foot. At the time of the accident the plaintiff was in the garage office paying the garage fee. He heard his son's screams and rushed out to help release him. He later suffered nervous shock and was awarded damages for this injury. The defendant appealed to the Court of Appeal.

ORMEROD LJ: . . . Mr Richardson, on behalf of the defendant submitted that this case must be considered on a similar basis with *Hay* (or *Bourhill*) v. *Young*, one of the leading cases on this question of injury by shock. In that case the plaintiff, who was a fish wife loading fish from a tramcar into her basket, did not see the accident happen and only saw the results of it when she was moved by the noise to go and see what had happened. In the present case, too, the father did not see the accident but was only moved to see what had happened when he heard the infant scream. Mr Richardson has endeavoured to submit that the line of distinction must be drawn somewhere and that must depend on whether the accident was witnessed by the plaintiff, and that if, in this case, the father did not witness the accident he cannot succeed. There has been no authority produced to the court to bear out that submission and, for my part, I must say I find it difficult to understand why the line should be drawn in that arbitrary fashion. It may be that, in some cases, that is a proper line to draw, as in *Hay* (or *Bourhill*) v. *Young*, and it may be that, in that case, as in many others, the proposed plaintiff does not come within the area of contemplated danger. On the other hand, clearly the facts in these cases are infinitely variable and it would be difficult, if not impossible, to draw any line of distinction and say in one case the plaintiff should succeed and in another case he should not.

In this particular case it does appear that all the necessary factors are present which should entitle the judge to come to the view that the father should succeed. The defendant knew that the infant was in the yard and that any carelessness in driving on his part might result in injury to the infant as, in fact, it did. He knew that the father was within earshot and he knew also that the father was in such a position that if he heard a scream from the infant he was bound to run out, human nature being what it is, to see what was happening to the infant; and that is, in fact what happened. In those circumstances it appears to me that the judge was right in coming to the conclusion which he did . . .

I think I need say no more than that if the facts of this particular case are fitted to the concept of negligence, it is clear that a duty was owed by the defendant not only to the infant but also to the near relatives of the infant who were, as he knew, on the premises, within earshot, and likely to come upon the scene if any injury or ill befell the infant.

In the circumstances, it appears to me to be clear that the father is entitled to succeed . . .

(DEVLIN and DANCKWERTS LJJ agreed with ORMEROD LJ.)

a What was the defendant's reason for relying on *Hay (Bourhill)* v. *Young* as a precedent for his case?

b Why did Ormerod LJ find it difficult to draw an arbitrary line of distinction between different cases?

c Mary was standing at the upstairs window of her house when she heard her 5-year-old son, Mark, scream. She ran out of the house and saw Bob backing his car over Mark's bicycle. She was 50 metres away from the incident and could not see her son. Mark had not been riding his bicycle at the time and he had suffered no injuries. Mary suffered nervous shock as a result of what she had seen and heard.

Do you think that Mary would recover damages for her injury on the basis of Lord Justice Ormerod's judgment in *Boardman* v. *Sanderson*? Follow this procedure to answer the question:

i Distinguish the facts in *Boardman* v. *Sanderson* from the facts in *Hay (Bourhill)* v. *Young*.
ii List the factors which led Ormerod LJ to reach a decision in favour of the plaintiff.
iii Are these factors present in Mary's situation?

Crossword

Across

3. law to protect personal liberty (Latin) (6,6);
6. 8 across;
8 and 6. to abide by precedents (Latin) (5,7);
9. see 1 down;
11. a bill which has been passed by Parliament;
12. see 13 down;
14. neither . . .;
15. . . . law is settled by precedent;
16. civil wrong;
19 and 25. through lack of care (Latin) (3,8);
21. see 22 across;
22 and 21. that is (Latin) (2,3);
25. see 19 across;
29. what a plaintiff does to a defendant;
30. judge's reason for a decision (Latin);
32. the CIA deals with this.

Down

1 and 9. in the work already mentioned (Latin) (2,3);
2. a system of laws;
3. the system of courts is an example of this;
4. and 23. the other part of a judge's decision (Latin) (6,5);
5. and 20. outside their powers (Latin);
7. to look at something quickly but not in detail;
10. only right;
13. and 12. among other things (Latin) (5,4);
17. either . . .;
18. allowed by law;
20. see 5 down;
23. see 4 down;
24. not completely;
26. regina, monarch;
27. agree(ment);
28. for this reason;
31. the . . . Court is below the Court of Appeal.

4
The courts

Summary

Legal content

Aim

To provide a factual account of the structure of the English courts based on the distinction between civil and criminal courts, and courts of first instance and appellate courts. A critical assessment of the functions and purpose of the system will be included together with an analysis of proposals for reform.

Language content

Grammar: long noun phrases
Vocabulary: dictionary use – using guidewords; verb + noun collocations; negative affixes (-less, dis-, mis-)

4.1 Classification of the courts

You will now be familar with the distinction between civil and criminal law; this distinction is reflected to some extent in the structure of the courts. Before you read the following extract you should also be aware of the difference between courts of first instance and appellate courts. The court in which a case is first heard is called the **court of first instance.** In almost all cases it is possible to appeal to a higher court for reconsideration of the decision of the original court. These courts are called **appellate courts.** It may be helpful to refer back to the diagrammatical representation of the courts in Chapter 3 (see Figure 3.1) before reading the following extract.

> There are, within the English legal system, a large number of courts of varying degrees of standing and jurisdiction. There are various ways of classifying courts . . . thus[1] it is possible to classify courts according to their functions. The obvious classification in this[2] respect would be into courts of civil and courts of criminal jurisdiction. This classification is not, however, a valid one since, although certain courts do exercise a purely civil or criminal

jurisdiction,[3] most English courts hear both civil and criminal cases. Thus the House of Lords, Court of Appeal, High Court, Crown Court and magistrates' courts exercise jurisdiction in both civil and criminal matters. A second classification would be into courts of original and courts of appellate jurisdiction. Nor is this division of general application. Although certain courts, such as the Court of Appeal and the House of Lords, exercise a purely appellate jurisdiction, while other courts, such as magistrates' courts, have no appellate jurisdiction, many courts, notably the High Court and the Crown Court, exercise both original and appellate jurisdiction.

The Court of Justice of the European Communities (the European Court) is, of course, *sui generis*[4] since, although not an English court, it exercises jurisdiction within the English legal system and the position of this Court within the system must be considered.

Walker, *Walker and Walker, The English Legal System* (Butterworths 1985), p. 179.

Text notes:
1 for example
2 see question **1** below
3 extent of legal authority
4 of its own kind, unique (Latin)

Comprehension check

1. Note 2: To what does 'this' refer?
2. What are the two suggested classifications of the English courts?
3. Why are both unsatisfactory?

Although there is no clear distinction between the civil and criminal courts or courts of first instance and appellate courts, it is usual to deal with the individual courts under those headings.

4.2 The civil courts

Before examining these courts in more detail let us consider their purpose. Civil actions take place between two or more individuals in dispute.[5] These disputes can take many forms, for example between neighbours, families, companies, consumers and manufacturers. It is the function of the civil courts to adjudicate[6] on these disputes. Different types of disputes will require different forms of adjudication; some disputes will be more serious and complex than others. These differences are reflected in the court system; the jurisdiction of the courts is limited by the type of case and, with the lower courts, by the geography and the amount of the claim. For example, the county courts are limited in tort and contract cases to incidents which occurred within their locality and to claims which do not exceed £5,000. Look for the differences as you read the extract below then answer the questions.

Text notes:
5 who disagree strongly with each other
6 to give judgment

Let us look more closely at the trial of civil cases. The courts with original civil jurisdiction are chiefly the High Court and county courts.

The High Court is divided into three Divisions: the *Queen's Bench Division*, the *Chancery Division*, and the *Family Division*. The first administers primarily the common law, the second primarily equity . . . The Family Division was created by an Act of 1970 in place of the previous Probate, Divorce and Admiralty Division – a curious miscellany[7] of jurisdictions (over wills,[8] wives and wrecks,[9] as Sir Alan Herbert put it[10]) which were lumped together for no better reason than they were all founded (to some extent) on Roman and canon law. In 1970, wills went to the Chancery Division and wrecks to the Queen's Bench Division.

A civil trial in the High Court is before a single judge, generally sitting without a jury. The judge may sit in London or the provinces . . .

There is almost always the possibility of an appeal from a court of trial (called a *court of first instance*). The party who appeals is the *appellant*; the other is the *respondent*. For the High Court the appropriate appellate court is the *Court of Appeal (Civil Division)*, consisting essentially of the Master of the Rolls and the Lords Justices of Appeal. The Court of Appeal generally sits with three members, and there will be several such courts in action at the same time.

Going down the ladder again, the less important civil cases are tried in the county courts, with appeals to the Court of Appeal. . . . magistrates also have some civil jurisdiction, chiefly in matrimonial matters, guardianship, adoption, and affiliation (maintenance of illegitimate children). There are lots of these courts (320 county courts, 700 magistrates' courts staffed by 24,000 lay magistrates and 52 stipendiaries) . . .

. . . Appeals from magistrates (by means of what is called a "case stated") go to a Divisional Court – in family matters it will be composed of judges of the Family Division . . .

When an appeal is taken to the Court of Appeal (either from the High Court or from a Divisional Court), a further appeal lies (with leave[11]) to the *House of Lords* . . .

. . . A civil case may go on appeal direct from the High Court to the House of Lords under the "leap-frogging"[12] procedure introduced by the Administration of Justice Act 1969. This can happen, with the consent of the parties and on certificate from the judge, if the case turns on[13] the construction of legislation or is governed by a previous decision of the Court of Appeal or House of Lords which one of the parties wishes to overturn.

Williams, *Learning the Law* (Stevens 1982), pp. 5–8.

Text notes:

7 variety
8 statement of how a person wants property to be distributed after death
9 destroyed ship
10 said
11 permission
12 game where one child jumps over the back of another
13 depends on

Comprehension check

4 Below is a diagrammatic representation of some of the information in paragraph two of the extract from Williams above. Use the following items to complete it.

Family Division, 'wives', Queen's Bench, 'wrecks', equity, admiralty affairs, divorce, 'wills', common law, Chancery Division.

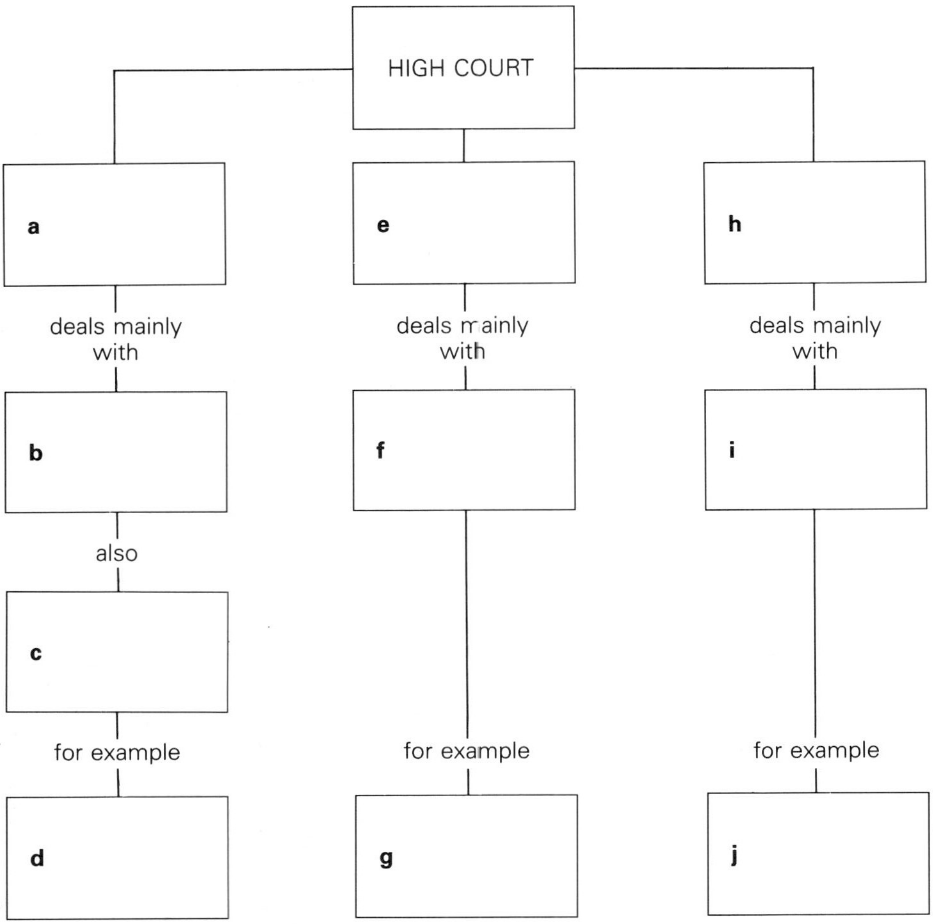

5 **a** What are the civil courts of first instance?
b Who will hear a case in the High Court?
c What is the term used for the party who appeals to a higher court?
d What is the most important civil court of first instance?
e From which courts will an appeal lie to the Court of Appeal?
f To which court will an appeal lie from the magistrates' court?
g What is the highest appellate court?
h What appeal procedure was introduced by the Administration of Justice Act 1969?

Dictionary use

Which page will the word be on? When looking for a word it is useful to look at the top of the page where the first and last entries on that page are printed. For example, if you are looking for **appellate** you will find it (in *The Cassell Concise English Dictionary*) on the page which begins with **apothecium** and ends with **appetence.** (NB. Other dictionaries will have alternative layouts.)

6 Match the words below with the correct pairs of entries. (NB: You will not need to use some pairs.) Do this as quickly as you can.

a jurisdiction, **b** original, **c** dispute, **d** consumer, **e** adjudication, **f** wreck, **g** will, **h** illegitimate, **i** matrimonial, **j** stipendiary.

A consummate – contend
B Stilton – stoccade
C wildebeest – wimple
D adherence – *ad libitum*
E adaxial – adhere
F stickle – stilt
G wicker – wild
H illegible – imagine
I dispossess – disseminate
J orgasm – ormolu
K junket – justify
L ignorantine – illegal
M materia medica – matting
N wrap – wring
O constitution – consummate

4.2.1 Small claims

We have accepted that cases will differ in seriousness and complexity and that the court system should take account of that fact – a straightforward action for the recovery of a £200 debt will require different practice and procedure from a dispute over a commercial contract involving a complex point of law and a claim for £500,000 damages. This is not to say that all cases involving small sums of money will be simple as regards the law and the definition of a small claim based on financial limits is necessarily arbitrary.[14] Nevertheless, the majority of cases are not complex and it is important that the system provides an efficient means of resolving these disputes. Within the formal court system this is done through the county court arbitration service. The following paragraphs provide an outline of this procedure.

The present county courts were set up in 1846 to provide a locally based service which was easily accessible to ordinary people. Figures provided by the Consumer Council in its 1970 report, *Justice out of Reach*, showed that the county courts had become primarily a debt-collection agency in which the majority of actions were taken out against the ordinary person: 'far from being the court of the ordinary person as plaintiff, it was the court in which the ordinary person was sued for debt' (White, *The Administration of Justice*, Blackwells, at p. 145). Equally, county court procedure had become too formal and expensive to fulfill its original purpose. In response the arbitration[15] scheme was introduced in 1973.

The original jurisdiction of the arbitration scheme was to hear claims involving less than £75. It is now mandatory[16] for all claims of less than £500, and may be used, if both parties agree, in disputes involving larger sums.

(There is a provision for certain cases involving complex legal issues to be referred to a higher court.) The case is heard by the Registrar of the county court (an 'assistant' judge who is employed by the court and whose role is administrative and judicial).

The first stage is the preliminary consideration; the Registrar will discuss the dispute with the parties and decide how the case is to be conducted. In very simple cases it may be possible to resolve the dispute at this stage. If the case goes to full arbitration the procedure is less formal than in the county court. This reflects the purpose of the scheme:

> The purpose of arbitration is to enable people to have small disputes resolved in an informal atmosphere, avoiding as far as possible the strict rules of procedure usually associated with court proceedings. This does not mean that rules are not observed because the object of all court procedure is to protect the interests of each party to the action and to ensure that the case is tried fairly. Nevertheless, the formalities are kept to the minimum . . .
>
> Birks, *Small claims in the county court – how to sue and defend actions without a solicitor* (Lord Chancellor's Department)

It is important to realise that 'arbitration' in the legal system does not have the lay meaning of conciliation and compromise, as, for example, in an industrial dispute. The county court arbitration scheme is adversarial in which one party 'wins' and the other 'loses'.

During the hearing the Registrar will hear both sides to the dispute and may call expert witnesses. Legal representation is permitted but no costs for this are awarded. This is to discourage the use of lawyers who have a tendency to complicate and formalise even a simple case! After considering the evidence the Registrar will give judgment. There is no right of appeal against the decision of the Registrar although the decision may be challenged on very limited grounds, e.g. evidence of misconduct by the Registrar.

The arbitration scheme has been relatively successful in increasing access to the courts for the ordinary people who make up 38 per cent of the plaintiffs. However, it has been criticised for still being too complex: in particular the adversarial style of enquiry, although modified, continues to disadvantage and intimidate[17] many ordinary people. There is general agreement that an inquisitorial form of hearing would be more appropriate in small claims actions, allowing the Registrar to play a more active role. Recent legislative reforms in this area will be considered in the next section.

Text notes:

14 based on random choice
15 settlement of a dispute
16 contrasted with 'may be used' later in the sentence so means 'obligatory'
17 frighten (cf. 'timid')

Comprehension check

7 Check your comprehension of the passage above by completing the summary below with words from the list which follows; you may use a word more than once.

in addition, because, excess, formal, nevertheless, agree, informal, informality, access, although, more, less, permitted, may, formality, must, discouraged, disagree, should.

The arbitration scheme was set up (**a**) . . . . county courts were no longer fulfilling their purpose of providing (**b**) . . . . to ordinary people in a fairly (**c**) . . . . situation and without excessive (**d**) . . . . or cost. Small claims of up to £500 (**e**) . . . . be heard by the scheme; larger claims (**f**) . . . . also be heard if both sides (**g**) . . . . Parties (**h**) . . . . be represented by lawyers but this is (**i**) . . . . Although rules are followed, the atmosphere is (**j**) . . . . formal than in the county courts; (**k**) . . . ., the procedure is said still to be very complex and to frighten many people.

Research

8 Find out the names of the civil courts in your country. Set them out in a diagram, noting which courts are courts of first instance and which are appellate courts.

Legal exercises

9 George had agreed to sell his car to Nigel for £200. George has delivered the car but Nigel refuses to pay the money. George wishes to take legal action to enforce the contract. He seeks your advice on the following:

a To which courts may he apply to enforce the payment?
b If he is dissatisfied with the result to which court(s) may he appeal?

10 Angela is seriously injured in a road accident caused by Percy's negligence. She estimates her damages to be £50,000.

a In which court would the legal action take place?
b If her action is unsuccessful, to which courts may she appeal?

4.2.2 Reform

Whilst it is the **function** of the civil court system to adjudicate on disputes, its **aim** should be to do so efficiently and fairly. The correct balance between these two requirements is not easy to assess or achieve. An efficient system which is quick and cheap may not provide an adequate opportunity for the litigants to prepare and present their case. Equally, delay and expense can lead to injustice. There was increasing criticism throughout the 1980s that existing civil procedure was neither efficient nor fair. Statistics seemed to support these criticisms. In personal injury cases the average period of time from accident to settlement in the High Court was five years; in 40 per cent of cases the costs involved in bringing the action were higher than the amount of damages awarded (Zander, *Cases and Materials on the English Legal System*, Weidenfeld & Nicholson, 1988). Costs and delays are less in the county courts but they leave no room for complacency.[18] The government responded to these criticisms by undertaking a major review of the civil justice system.

Text note:
18 one should not be satisfied with the situation

In 1985, Lord Hailsham of St Marylebone, the then[19] Lord Chancellor, announced the setting up of a civil justice review. The purpose of the review was to improve the machinery of civil justice in England and Wales by means of reforms in jurisdiction, procedure and court administration, and in particular to reduce delay, cost and complexity. Each of the five main classes of civil business, personal injury, small claims, housing, commercial and debt would be examined in three stages each. First research, secondly a consultation paper and thirdly, implementation by legislation. The Lord Chancellor would be assisted by an advisory committee which, besides lawyers, academics and consumer representatives, included a significant business element.

The research on each of the main areas has been imaginative. The civil justice process has been seen as a management system in which the efficiency of the system and the productivity of those within it was sorely[20] in need of improvement. The final consultation paper . . . was issued in March 1987 and it includes a number of radical proposals:

(a) Either an amalgamation of the County Court and the High Court into a single civil court, or a much closer integration of the two. The closer integration of the two could be achieved by a 'one court entry' system. All civil cases would start in the same way and be allocated to a particular court on the basis of their complexity. The Law Society[21] has said that it prefers a unified court system though the Bar[22] and the judiciary[23] are against it. The 'one court entry' system looks a likely compromise.

(b) Full pre-trial disclosure of evidence including witness statements.

(c) A new case flow management system giving a timetable for the progress of cases. This would reduce cost and delay.

(d) Increased judicial productivity. This would entail[24] reducing leave entitlements and an extra hour's sitting[25] per day. High Court judges would also go on circuit.[26] This proposal – which would effectively give 25 per cent more judging time – has not been popular with the judiciary!

(e) A new in-court arbitration system for cases involving claims between £1,000 and £5,000. The new small claims arbitration limit would be £1,000.

(f) A unified cost system.

(g) Greater incentives and competition in the remuneration of court-related work. Flat-rate[27] fees should be available for simpler forms of litigation and there could perhaps be incentives and penalties for speedy resolution or delay. It works with builders why not lawyers?!

Johnson and Pannett, *SWOT A Level Law* (Blackstone Press 1988), p. 41.

Text notes:
19 used as an adjective: 'at that time'
20 greatly
21 society of solicitors
22 barristers
23 judges
24 involve
25 i.e. sitting as judges in court
26 travel to provincial courts
27 fixed

Comprehension check

11 In point (g) of the extract above, can you work out from the context what are meant by 'incentives' and 'penalties'?

Language point – compound nouns

In formal and academic English you often find quite long phrases composed of several nouns. There are several in the extract above:

a Line 19: 'a one court entry system'
b Line 25: 'a new case flow management system'
c Lines 27–8: 'leave entitlements'
d Line 31: 'a new in-court arbitration system'
e Line 32: 'the new small claims arbitration limit'

If you have any difficulty understanding these phrases, try starting with the article (a/the) and the first adjective (e.g. 'new') and then the **last** noun; after that read the next to last noun and so on. For example, **b** becomes:

'a new system (of) management (of the) flow (of) case(s)'

English compound nouns are constructed 'backwards' in contrast to some other languages. If you look at **e** you will realise that the second adjective belongs to the first noun, thus:

'the new limit (for the) arbitration (of) small claims'

12 Now try **a**, **c** and **d**.

As a result of the civil justice review the Lord Chancellor, Lord McKay, introduced reforming legislation to Parliament – the Courts and Legal Services Bill. The Bill received the Royal Assent in late 1990. Most of its provisions relate to the deregularisation of the legal profession; these will be examined in Chapter 6. The Act gives the Lord Chancellor the power to redistribute business between the High Court and the county courts on the basis of the complexity of individual cases. The financial limit of £5,000 for cases heard by the county courts is therefore removed.

The proposal has been generally welcomed in theory but fears have been expressed over how the system will work in practice. The county courts are already overburdened and delay is a growing problem. Any increase in the workload of the county courts without compensating administrative reforms will defeat the purpose of the proposed changes.

The Courts and Legal Services Act also enacts the proposal in the civil justice review that the role of the Registrar in small claims actions should be more inquisitorial. It also gives a statutory right to litigants to be represented by a lay[28] person. This is part of the policy of the Lord Chancellor to break the legal profession's monopoly on rights of audience. This is discussed more fully in Chapter 6.

Text note:
28 here means without legal qualifications

4.3 The criminal courts

Whilst the purpose of the civil courts is to adjudicate on disputes between individuals and to provide a remedy for the wronged party, the purpose of the criminal courts is to determine whether the accused person has committed a crime and to punish the wrongdoer. The balance required is between the need to protect society and the need to ensure, as far as possible, that only the guilty are punished. Given the serious consequences which can result from being convicted of a criminal offence, it is necessary to provide safeguards against wrongful conviction. One way is that the burden of proof[29] is on the prosecution to prove 'beyond reasonable doubt' that the accused committed the offence charged. This can be compared with the burden of proof in civil actions where it is for the plaintiff to show that the defendant is liable 'on the balance of probabilities', that is the defendant is more likely to be liable than not. Also criminal court procedure seeks to ensure a fair hearing by imposing very strict and formal rules of evidence (compare the flexible procedures in the county court arbitration scheme). Many other safeguards relate to the powers of the police. Details of these will not be included in this book but references to relevant additional reading can be found at the end of this chapter.

Text note:
29 the obligation of proving

4.3.1. The decision to prosecute

Who can start criminal proceedings?

The general rule is that any private individual can bring a prosecution even if the individual has no particular interest in the case. This is usually referred to as a 'private prosecution'. . . A study done for the Royal Commission on Criminal Procedure (RCCP) showed that private prosecutions comprised 2.4 per cent of the overall number. Most of these were for domestic assaults although some were shoplifting[30] cases, as in some areas the police leave it up to the aggrieved shopkeeper to institute[31] proceedings (this is because shopkeepers frequently failed to turn up in court to give evidence) . . .

The greatest number of prosecutions, however, are brought as a result of action instigated[32] by the police . . .

Until recently the police made the final decision to prosecute in the cases they were dealing with. Moreover, the police effectively controlled the prosecution, and in some magistrates' courts police officers actually appeared as advocates. This practice was diminished by the appointment of prosecuting solicitors by many police forces, but even this arrangement was perceived to be far from ideal: solicitors had to act in accordance with the instructions of chief constables, even if the solicitors felt that a prosecution was unwise. In short, the system was criticised for its lack of independence. The police, having investigated the case and brought the prosecution, would have a strong interest to be successful in court – far stronger, it was alleged, than in the normal adversarial relationship found in civil cases. The police, for example, might be unwilling to reveal to the defence all the information they had obtained while investigating the charge.

The pressure group 'Justice' published a report in 1970 calling for an independent prosecution service which would separate the investigation of crime from its prosecution. The report pointed out that the system in England and Wales was different from that operated in many other countries, and particular reference was made to Scotland. In that country there is a long-established system whereby the police have to report crimes to local officials known as procurators-fiscal who study each case and make the decision to prosecute. In smaller cases they[33] conduct the prosecutions themselves.

The matter was considered by the RCCP. It concluded that the existing arrangements were unsatisfactory, giving rise to a possible conflict of interest on the part of the police between the collection of evidence and the prosecution of the case in court . . . The Crown Prosecution Service (CPS) was created by the Prosecution of Offences Act 1985 and came into effect nationally on 1 October 1986. It is under the control of the DPP.[34] The police still investigate criminal offences and initially prefer charges[35] but from then on the case is handed over to the CPS. It[36] may decide to amend or drop any or all of the charges . . .

. . . No detailed evaluation has yet been made of the working of the CPS but it has certainly experienced 'teething troubles'.[37] There have been arguments about salaries and consequential difficulties in recruitment,[38] especially in London . . .

. . . Nevertheless, there is some evidence in its first report that the CPS is already achieving one of its main objectives – the sifting out of weak or unnecessary prosecutions and the resulting easing of pressure on the overburdened criminal justice system.

Dugdale *et al.*, *A Level Law* (Butterworths 1988), pp. 98–9, 109–11.

Some of the points raised in this text have recently become the subject of intense debate over the adequacy of the criminal justice system. We will examine this at the end of the chapter.

Text notes:
30 stealing from a shop
31 start
32 encouraged, caused
33 see question **13a** below
34 Director of Public Prosecutions
35 bring before the court
36 see question **13b** below
37 see question **13c** below
38 see question **13d** below

Comprehension check

13 a Note 33: To whom do 'they' refer?
b Note 36: To what does 'it' refer?
c Note 37: Can you work out what is meant by 'teething troubles'?
d Note 38: Why were there recruitment difficulties?

14 On a separate sheet of paper complete the summary below of the main section of the extract:

A Pre-(**a**) . . . . police investigated cases + prosecuted/ instructed solicitor. → Problem: (**b**) . . . . e.g. (**c**) . . . .
B 1970 'Justice' group report: called for (**d**) . . . . as in (**e**) . . . .
C Report considered by (**f**) . . . .

D 1985 (**g**) . . . . created. Now (**h**) . . . . investigate + prefer charges but (**i**) . . . . takes over. → Positive result: (**j**) . . . .

Vocabulary

In the preceding extract there are several verb + noun groups (e.g. to investigate a case). These expressions are commonly used in legal texts and it is useful to learn each verb and noun as a pair. To help you to do this, try the following exercise.

15 Match the following verbs with appropriate nouns from the list which follows:

a to bring . . . .
b to instigate . . . .
c to institute . . . .
d to give . . . .
e to conduct . . . .
f to prefer . . . .
g to remedy . . . .
h to punish . . . .
i to commit . . . .

proceedings, the prosecution, a prosecution, a wrong, action, an offence, a criminal, charges, evidence.

Not all criminal offences are automatically followed by a prosecution. The CPS has discretion to prosecute; in some cases, for example, it may be considered more appropriate to administer an informal caution to the offender. Prior to the creation of the CPS this discretion rested with the local police force. This led to a lack of uniformity. Whether a criminal offence was followed by a prosecution could depend on where the offence was committed. This was a further criticism of the existing system.

The CPS was established as a national prosecution service in an attempt to ensure greater uniformity. The decision to prosecute should now be exercised according to the Code of Practice to Crown Prosecutors issued by the Director of Public Prosecutions. In deciding whether to start a prosecution the following factors should be considered:

1 Is there a realistic prospect of conviction? (This is known as the 51 per cent rule.)
2 Will the public interest be served by bringing a prosecution? Relevant considerations would be the age and physical or mental condition of the offender and the 'staleness'[39] of the offence.
3 Would it be more appropriate to issue a formal warning?

4.3.2 The classification of offences and the criminal courts

After the decision to prosecute has been taken the case will eventually[40] be heard in court. As with civil actions, criminal offences vary in seriousness and complexity. These differences are again reflected in the criminal court system. The following text outlines the way in which offences are classified and the courts of first instance and appeal.

Text notes:
39 opposite to 'fresh', e.g. stale bread = old bread
40 finally

Pre-reading exercise

16 Without reading the whole passage try scanning it quickly and answer briefly the following questions.

a What is a summary offence?
b Give an example.
c What is an indictable offence?
d Give an example.
e What are offences triable either way?
f Give examples.

There are three types of criminal offence: summary, indictable[41] and triable[42] either way. The nature of the offence will determine the mode of trial.

Summary offences are the less serious offences such as minor motoring offences. These offences are tried in the magistrates' court, without a jury, before a bench of three lay[43] magistrates or one stipendiary[44] magistrate. The magistrates will hear the evidence and reach a verdict. If the verdict is 'not guilty' the defendant will be acquitted; if 'guilty' the magistrates will pass sentence. The sentencing jurisdiction of the magistrates' courts is limited to imposing a fine of up to £1,000 or a maximum prison sentence of six months. A case requiring a heavier punishment must be referred to the Crown Court for sentencing. The defendant may appeal to the Crown Court for a retrial or to the Divisional Court of the Queen's Bench Division of the High Court 'by way of case stated'. This is on the basis that the magistrates were wrong in law or in excess of jurisdiction. The magistrates are required to 'state the case' (give reasons) for their verdict. This form of appeal is, unusually, available to the prosecution as well as the defence. A further appeal to the House of Lords is available in cases involving important questions of law.

Indictable offences are the most serious offences; examples are murder, manslaughter,[45] rape and arson.[46] The procedure for trying these offences begins in the magistrates' court with 'committal proceedings'. Here it is the role of the magistrates to conduct a preliminary enquiry into the prosecution's evidence and to decide whether it forms a prima facie[47] case against the accused. If not, the case will be discharged.[48] This is not the same as an acquittal as the prosecuting authorities can bring the case before the court again if further evidence becomes available; a person who has been acquitted of a charge cannot be tried for the same offence again. If a prima facie case is established, a full trial will take place in the Crown Court before a judge and a jury of twelve ordinary people. It is the role of the judge in this full trial to rule on points of law and, if the defendant is found guilty, to pass sentence. The jury assesses the facts and reaches a verdict. The defendant may appeal against conviction or sentence to the Criminal Division of the Court of Appeal. Under the Criminal Justice Act 1988, the prosecution may also appeal to the Court of Appeal for the sentence to be increased. A further appeal to the House of Lords may be allowed on an important point of law.

Offences triable either way are offences which can be committed in a serious or minor way. Burglary[49] and theft[50] are examples of these offences. They may be tried summarily in the magistrates' court or on indictment in the Crown Court. The magistrates will determine the mode of trial taking into account such factors as the seriousness of the offence and the possible appropriate sentence. The accused can insist on trial by jury in the Crown Court but not on summary trial, if the magistrates decide that the case should be tried on indictment. The trial procedure will then follow the summary or indictable form as discussed previously.

Text notes:

41 to indict = to charge with an offence
42 able to be tried
43 without legal qualifications
44 legally qualified, paid and full-time
45 unlawful killing without malice
46 burning of another person's property
47 a case supported by some evidence
48 'sent away' (NB: 'dis-' is a negative prefix, e.g. *dis*honest), or, as here, 'removed' (cf. dismiss, meaning to send away)
49 entering a building and stealing, causing damage, grievous bodily harm or rape
50 taking property from another person

Vocabulary

17 As in the last vocabulary exercise, match the following verbs with the appropriate nouns from the list below:

a to try . . . .
b to hear . . . .
c to reach . . . .
d to pass . . . .
e to impose . . . .
f to conduct . . . .
g to assess . . . .

a verdict, an enquiry, an offence, the facts, the evidence, a fine, sentence.

Research

18 Find out the names of the criminal courts in your country and make a diagram of them, noting which courts are courts of first instance and which ones are appellate courts.

19 Is there an independent body like the CPS in your country which is responsible for deciding which cases come to trial? If not, who is responsible for these decisions?

Legal exercises

20 Distinguish between the three types of criminal offence.

21 What is the role of the magistrates in trying each of these offences?

22 What are the respective[51] roles of the judge and the jury in trying indictable offences in the Crown Court?

23 What are the advantages of the Crown Prosecution Service?

24 Distinguish between 'discharge' and 'acquittal'.

25 Mr Smith is arrested by the police on the suspicion of murdering Mr Jones.

- **a** What factors will be taken into account when deciding whether to prosecute him?
- **b** What events will follow if the decision is taken to prosecute him?
- **c** If he is found guilty, may either Mr Smith or the prosecution appeal from the verdict?

26 Mrs Brown is charged with theft before the magistrates' court.

- **a** Before which courts may she be tried?
- **b** If she is found guilty, to which courts may she appeal?

Text note:
51 of each in turn

4.3.3 Review

In 1974 the Irish Republican Army (IRA) waged a bombing campaign on the mainland of Britain in which twenty-eight people were killed. A number of people were subsequently tried and found guilty of the offences. These people became known as the 'Guildford Four' and 'Birmingham Six' (after the names of the cities in which it was alleged they had planted the bombs). In addition, the seven members of a family named Maguire, the 'Maguire Seven', were gaoled for illegal possession of explosives. The 'Guildford Four' and the 'Birmingham Six' claimed that they had been beaten whilst in police custody in order to obtain confessions from them. The Maguire family questioned the validity of the forensic[52] evidence on which their conviction was based. All those convicted appealed through the formal appeal procedures; these were dismissed.

In 1989, as a result of receiving fresh evidence, the Home Secretary referred the case of the 'Guildford Four' back to the Court of Appeal. The Court of Appeal freed the men and the Home Secretary set up an enquiry into their case and that of the Maguire family, headed by Sir John May. The latter case has been referred to the Court of Appeal by the Home Secretary who has stated that their convictions are unsafe and can no longer stand. The case of the 'Birmingham Six' has also been referred back to the Court of Appeal.

The May enquiry revealed serious weaknesses in the system of criminal justice which has led to calls for the establishment of an independent tribunal to prepare evidence and to investigate appeals. Many of the weaknesses highlighted by the enquiry have to some extent been removed by changes which have taken place since the time of the original convictions; the CPS has taken over prosecutions from the police and the Criminal Evidence Act 1984 has placed stricter controls on detention and interrogation procedures, but most of these reforms are not applicable to suspected terrorists. Many people believe that the judges are too willing to accept prosecution evidence and the whole adversarial system of justice has been questioned. A change to an inquisitorial system would have an enormous impact on the whole system of justice; it is not something which can be undertaken lightly or speedily but the results of the May enquiry indicate that much could be done to improve the existing system without undertaking such a radical reform of trial procedure.

Text note:
52 medical evidence used in court

4.4 Tribunals and arbitration

The formal courts are not the only means of solving disputes; adjudication increasingly takes place outside the court system. This is a further reflection of the need to suit the form of dispute resolution to the nature of the dispute involved. The two main forms of extra[53]-court adjudication are tribunals and arbitration. Let us look first at **tribunals.**

Text note:
53 outside (Latin) – see also 2 lines above

Pre-reading check

27 Think about the following questions as you read the extract below:

- **a** What is the purpose of tribunals?
- **b** Why has there been a rapid growth in the use of tribunals over recent years?
- **c** Why do you think that the writer believes that tribunals are the most important courts in the country for the ordinary citizen?

There are over 50 different types of tribunal, each with its own limited jurisdiction over a particular type of claim. Both the tribunals and the claims they consider are the product of legislation. The interventionist philosophy which prevailed until recently, resulted in an ever increasing number of legislative schemes designed to regulate relations between social groups such as employers and employees or between the state and its citizens, as in the welfare system. Inevitably the administration of these schemes will produce disputes, e.g. an employee may claim that her dismissal was not legally justified under the terms of the employment legislation, a welfare claimant may claim that the reduction in his benefit was not legally justified under the terms of the welfare legislation. The legislation could provide that such disputes should be settled by ordinary courts and this has been done in some cases, e.g. cases under the Domestic Violence Act 1976, which was passed primarily to protect women from such violence, are heard by the county court. But in many situations it has been felt that the ordinary courts lack the necessary expertise or are too formal, slow and costly to hear claims arising under a particular scheme and hence the legislation has established a tribunal to do the job. Many tribunals have expert assessors sitting alongside a legally experienced chairman to make up the judging panel . . .

[Tribunals] vary enormously in the caseload[54] handled . . .

. . . There is no consistency in the nomenclature:[55] most tribunals are called tribunals but some are called 'commissions', others are called 'committees', . . . others still are called 'courts'. Their legal function also varies . . . Their appeal systems usually match their caseloads and function.

. . . One common feature of almost all tribunals however, is that they are subject to judicial review by the High Court. The Tribunals and Inquiries Act 1958 required most tribunals to give reasons for their decisions and this gives judicial review something on which to bite: it will often be clear from the reasons given that the tribunal has exceeded its statutory powers by taking a decision on the wrong grounds and in that case its decision can be 'quashed'[56] on review. The same 1958 legislation established a Council on Tribunals to act as a watchdog over tribunals, checking that their procedures are characterised by, 'openness, fairness and impartiality'. But it is a watchdog with bark and no bite.[57] It has no power and can only advise the government of problems. In the words of one leading commentator, its role is 'inconspicuous' . . .

One final comment on tribunals: from the point of view of the ordinary citizen they are among the most important courts in the country but from the point of view of the lawyer they are perhaps the least important element in the court system. Lawyers rarely appear before many of the tribunals and as a result are not familiar with the kind of law they apply or procedures they employ. The reasons for this are complex: in part it may be due to the 'trivial'[58] nature of the claims, in part to the lack of legal aid from the state to pay for lawyers' services in tribunal work, in part to an attitude that law and lawyers have little role to play in the tribunal system.

Dugdale *et al.*, *A Level Law* (Butterworths 1988), pp. 39–41.

Text notes:

54 load (i.e. number) of cases
55 system of naming
56 to set aside
57 explained in next sentence
58 the inverted commas suggest that the writer does not agree with the lawyers' view that the claims are unimportant, i.e. he is quoting them

---

Comprehension check: notemaking

28 Complete the following note outline which is based on the extract above.

A Tribs. set up ∵ of disad. of ordinary courts:
a . . . .
b . . . .
c . . . .
d . . . .

B $>$ 50 diff. types trib.

C Several names:
- **a** . . . .
- **b** . . . .
- **c** . . . .
- **d** . . . .

D All tribs. subj. to judic. review which examines . . . .

E Council on Tribs. set up to . . . .
but . . . .

F Tribs. v. important for ordinary citizen but unimp. for lawyers → they are unfamililar with law & procedures ∵
- **a** . . . .
- **b** . . . .
- **c** . . . .

You will see from the extract that 'administrative' tribunals are created by statute to resolve disputes arising from the relevant social legislation. In contrast, **arbitration** is a private means of adjudication, arranged and agreed between the parties involved. It is used in many different situations from the resolution of complex commercial disputes to those involving comparatively minor disagreements between the suppliers of goods and services and the consumer. An outline of the arbitration procedure is contained in the following extract:

> Arbitration. Here the parties agree to place their dispute in the hands of an independent third party and invest him with the power to decide the issue. Commercial contracts commonly contain arbitration clauses.[59] The arbitrator is likely to be someone with expertise[60] in the area and the arbitration is likely to take place in private. The arbitrator is bound to apply the law accurately but may, within the principles of natual justice, adopt whatever procedures he likes. The judgment of an arbitrator is known as an award and is subject to an appeal to the High Court on a question of law under the provisions of the Arbitration Act 1979.
>
> The best known use of the term arbitration is in the respect of the County Court Arbitration Service for small claims . . .
>
> The county court arbitration service is not the only way of dealing with small claims. Many trade associations include an arbitration scheme in their codes of practice. The best known is that of the Association of British Travel Agents (ABTA) for vexed[61] holiday-makers. If conciliation fails, the claimant pays a small deposit and the case is referred to arbitration. Oral hearings are rare; the arbitrator decides on the basis of written documents. About half the claims are successful.
>
> Johnson and Pannett, *SWOT A Level Law* (Blackstone Press 1988), pp. 38, 43.

Text notes:
59 parts of agreement containing special conditions
60 expert knowledge
61 annoyed, angry

The advantages of arbitration are similar to those of tribunals: speed, lower costs, flexibility, informality and adjudication by an expert. These advantages must of course be balanced against the disadvantages. There is the argument that cheaper, quicker and less formal hearings result in a poor quality service and a two-tier[62] system of adjudication, and that the legal training of judges and the formal rules of court procedure have been developed to ensure a fair trial. Nevertheless the increasing use of tribunals and arbitration seems to indicate that they are a popular way of resolving disputes. On a wider point, they also increase the points of access to justice for the ordinary person. This topic will be considered in more detail in Chapter 6.

Text note:
62 two levels, i.e. one higher and the other lower in quality

Vocabulary review

Below are three different exercises to help you remember some of the vocabulary in this chapter.

29 Complete the table below:

Verb	*Noun*	*Adjective*
arbitrate	**a**	×
	b	
c	claimant	×
	d	
e	**f**	×
	adjudication	
g	administrator	**i** . . . .
	h	
j	**k**	**l** . . . .
		intimidated

30 In Chapter 3 four common 'negative' prefixes were practised (un-, in-, il-, im-). Three other negative affixes are -less, e.g. hopeless, dis-, e.g. dissatisfied, and mis-, e.g. misread (= read inaccurately). Try and use the correct affix to form opposites of the words below. In some cases you will have to make other changes.

a useful
b conduct
c encourage
d agree
e colourful
f persuade

31 Complete the sentences below using one or two words:

a The claim __________ £5,000 (i.e. was for more than £5,000).
b A person who appeals is called __________.
c Money which is owed is called __________.
d __________ has a similar meaning to compulsory.
e A __________ is a person involved in a civil case.
f A __________ magistrate is paid, whereas a __________ magistrate is not.
g Minor motoring offences are __________ offences but murder is __________ offence.

Research

32 What facilities for the adjudication of disputes outside the formal court system are available in your country?

Legal exercises

33 Choose two teams from your group to debate the following proposition:

'The civil courts in the English legal system do not provide an adequate means of adjudication in the majority of disputes.'

Follow the instructions for the preparation and performance of the debate which are provided at the end of Chapter 2. You will need to reread carefully the sections in this chapter on the civil courts, tribunals and arbitration. The relevant issues are:

a The aims of the civil justice system.
b The existing machinery of the system.
c How adequate is it for the majority of disputes?
d Will the reforms contained in the Courts and Legal Services Act improve the system?

If you are working on your own, prepare a written argument for each side of the debate taking into account the preceding points.

Additional reading

The Administration of Justice by White (Blackwell) provides a detailed and critical account of the court system and tribunals set in the wider context of provision of legal services. The most recent publication is Ingham's *The English Legal Process* (Blackstone Press) which also contains an appendix on the Courts and Legal Services Bill. Chapter 1 of Zander's *Cases and Materials on the English Legal System* (Weidenfeld & Nicholson) contains analytical background and commentary.

Most textbooks on the English legal system will contain details of police powers but you should be careful to only read those which have been published since 1984 and the passing of the Police and Criminal Evidence Act. Good comprehensive accounts of police powers can be found in *A Level Law* by Hogan, Seago and Bennett (Sweet and Maxwell) and *A Level Law* by Dugdale *et al.* (Butterworths).

5
The judiciary and the jury

Summary

Legal content

Aim

To build on previous knowledge by providing an outline of the judicial hierarchy in relation to the hierarchy of the courts and a critical assessment of the judicial function in the context of earlier chapters. The section on the jury[1] will consider the reasons for the decline in trial by jury and possible alternatives.

Text note:
1 group of people who decide the truth of facts in a trial

Language content

Grammar: subject–verb inversion for emphasis after certain adverbs;
Vocabulary: dictionary use – choosing the right meaning
Study skills: interpreting non-linear data

5.1 The judicial hierarchy

There are some features of the court system which are naturally reflected in the nature of the English judiciary. First, it is **hierarchical** with judges in the higher courts having more authority than those in the lower courts. Secondly, most judges will hear both civil and criminal cases. Judges in the House of Lords and the Court of Appeal hear only appeal cases, whilst judges in the High Court and Crown Court have first instance and appellate jurisdiction.

A distinctive feature of the British system in comparison with many Continental systems is that it does not have a judicial career structure. Judges are chosen from lawyers who have gained considerable experience as legal practitioners before being appointed to the judiciary. In Continental systems law graduates can choose to be a judge at the outset of their careers and they gain their experience of the inquisitorial system as practising judges, something which is considered to be inappropriate to the common law adversarial system.

Let us now look at the different classes of the judiciary starting with those at the top of the hierarchy.

5.1.1 Lords of Appeal in Ordinary

These sit in the House of Lords and are therefore the judges with the most authority. They are appointed by the Prime Minister on the recommendation of the Lord Chancellor who is also the president of the House of Lords. There are eleven 'Law Lords', most of whom will[2] have been promoted from the Court of Appeal. A case must be heard by three Lords, although in practice five will[2] normally do so. The decision of the majority will[2] prevail.

5.1.2 Lords Justices of Appeal

These sit in the Court of Appeal and are also appointed by the Prime Minister on the recommendation of the Lord Chancellor. They will[2] usually be promoted from the High Court although it is possible for a barrister of fifteen years' experience to be appointed without previous judicial experience. The president of the civil division of the Court of Appeal is the Master of the Rolls; the president of the criminal division is the Lord Chief Justice. There is an average of twenty Court of Appeal judges. An appeal will[2] be heard by three Lords Justices.

Text note:

2 the use of future tenses here indicates that the judiciary is being thought of in an abstract way, and a hypothetical situation in the future is being considered.

5.1.3 High Court judges

These hear cases in the High Court and more serious cases in the Crown Court. They are appointed by the Queen[3] on the recommendation of the Lord Chancellor. High Court judges are sometimes referred to as 'puisne'[4] judges. To qualify, a person must be a barrister of at least ten years' standing.[5] There are a maximum of 80 High Court judges. The Lord Chief Justice heads the Queen's Bench Division, the President of the Family Division the Family Division and the Vice-Chancellor the Chancery Division. A single judge will hear a case at first instance; two or more may be required to sit in an appeal case.

Text notes:
3 note this is only a formality – the Queen does not actually take part in the selection procedure
4 pronounced [pjuni], from Old French
5 experience, duration

5.1.4 Circuit judges

These hear less important cases in the Crown Court and civil actions in the county court. They are appointed by the Queen on the recommendation of the Lord Chancellor, from barristers of seven years' standing or Recorders of five years' experience. There are about 400 circuit judges. It is very rare for a circuit judge to be promoted to higher judicial office.

5.1.5 Recorders

These are part-time judges in the Crown Court and they hear the less serious cases. They may also sit in the county court. Barristers or solicitors of ten years' standing may qualify; they are appointed by the Queen on the recommendation of the Lord Chancellor. There are around[6] 500 Recorders.

Text note:
6 approximately

5.1.6 Magistrates

Stipendiary magistrates
These are full-time paid appointments made by the Queen on the recommendation of the Lord Chancellor. Barristers or solicitors of seven years' standing qualify for appointment. There are about 100 stipendiary magistrates. They sit in the magistrates' courts in the larger cities, particularly London. A case will be heard by a single stipendiary magistrate.

Lay magistrates
These are part-time, unpaid magistrates often known as justices of the peace. They are appointed from ordinary members of society by the Lord Chancellor on the recommendation of local advisory committees. They are not legally qualified although they do receive some basic training. A case will be heard by a bench of three lay magistrates who are advised on the law by the clerk of the court. The justices' clerk is a barrister or solicitor of at least five years' standing. There are approximately 25,000 lay magistrates and they hear over 90 per cent of criminal cases.

5.1.7 Officers of the state

In addition to the above you should also be aware of the roles of the law officers of the state. These are:

The Lord Chancellor
The Lord Chancellor is the head of the judiciary and a Minister of the Crown. He is the Speaker[7] of the House of Lords (in its legislative capacity) and also the government's principal legal spokesman. We have seen that he has considerable influence over the appointment of judges. His position is somewhat[8] anomalous[9] within a constitution based on the separation of powers.

Text notes:
7 the 'chairperson'
8 rather, quite
9 not following the rule

The Attorney-General
The A-G is the chief legal advisor to the government. He is a Member of Parliament and a member of the government. He has overall responsibility for prosecution policy and his consent is required to bring a prosecution in certain cases involving state security. He is assisted by the Solicitor-General.

The Director of Public Prosecutions
The DPP is a civil servant[10] who is responsible for the running of the prosecution service. His consent is required to proceed in cases involving certain criminal offences. He may take over a private prosecution and conduct proceedings in difficult or important cases. He is responsible to the Attorney-General.

Text note:
10 member of the public service

Comprehension check

1 **a** How can a person become a judge in Britain?
b In what way is the Lord Chancellor's position anomalous?
c 'Separation of powers' is mentioned in the text above. What powers does this refer to?
d In some cases concerning state security who must give permission to prosecute?
e In some criminal cases who must give permission to prosecute?
f How does a person usually become a Lord Justice of Appeal?
g What is the role of the clerk of the court?

2 Can you find the following numerical data:

a the minimum number of Law Lords who must hear a case?
b the usual number of Law Lords who hear a case?
c the number of judges who hear a case?
d the average number of Court of Appeal judges?
e the number of circuit judges?
f the number of Recorders?
g the number of stipendiary magistrates?
h the number of lay magistrates?

- **i** the proportion of criminal cases heard by lay magistrates?
- **j** the number of stipendiary magistrates who hear a case?
- **k** the number of lay magistrates who hear a case?

3 Complete the following table using information from the previous text:

Judge	*Appointed by*	*Court* *Criminal*	*Civil*
Lord of Appeal	Lord Chancellor	**a**	**b** ....
Lord Justice of Appeal	**c**	Court of Appeal	
High Court judge	**d**	**e**	**f** ....
Circuit judge	**g**	**h**	County court
Stipendiary magistrate	**i**	**j**	**k** ....
Lay magistrate	**l**	**m**	**n** ....

Research

4 Find out the following information about the judiciary in your country:

- **a** Are the members of the judiciary appointed from practising lawyers or is there a career judiciary?
- **b** What are the titles of the different classes of the judiciary?
- **c** Do the same judges hear first instance cases and appeal cases?
- **d** Do the same judges hear civil and criminal cases?
- **e** Is there an equivalent group to the lay magistrates?

Vocabulary: choosing the right meaning from a dictionary

In some cases the dictionary will give only one or two meanings for a word; often, however, you will have to look at several or many possible meanings and make a choice. Look at the extract below (from *Cassell's Concise English Dictionary*). If you want to look up 'conduct' as used on p. 99. ('He may take over a private prosecution and **conduct** proceedings . . .'), you will need to know two things:

- **i** that 'conduct' in this context is a verb;
- **ii** that *v.t.* in the dictionary stands for transitive verb. (It is useful to know that a transitive verb is one which takes an object; here, the object is 'proceedings'.)

conduct[1] (kon′dŭct), *n.* the act of leading or guiding; the way in which anyone acts or lives, behaviour; management, direction, control: (*Painting*) manner of treatment; †a safe conduct: †a guide, a guard, a conductor. [partly directly from L *conductus*, p.p. of *condūcere* (CON-, *dūcere*. to lead), partly through OF *conduit* (L *conductus*) or OF *conduite* (cp. Sp. *conducta*, It. *condotta*). defence, escort]

conduct[2] (kəndukt′), *v.t.* to lead, to guide; to manage, to direct; (*Phys.*) to transmit (as heat etc.); to direct (as an orchestra); (*reflex.*) to behave, *v.i.* to act as a conductor. **conductance**, *n.* the reciprocal of electrical resistance. **conductible**, *a.* capable of conducting or of being conducted. **conductibility** (-bil′-), *n.* **conduction**, *n.* transmission by a conductor; conveyance (of liquids, etc.), **conductive**, *a.* **conductively**, *adv.* **conductivity** (konduktiv'-), *n.* the ease with which a substance transmits electricity. **conductor**, *n.* a leader, a guide; a director, a manager; the director of an orchestra; (*N Am.*) the guard of a train; the person in charge of a bus or tramcar; a body capable of transmitting heat, electricity, etc.; †a general. **conductorship**, *n.* **conductress**, *n. fem.*

You will then need to choose between the different meanings which in this dictionary are separated by semi-colons (;). You can exclude the meaning which is preceded by '(*Phys.*)', i.e. Physics, and the next one which refers to an orchestra. You will probably choose the second group of meanings (to manage, to direct).

Now look in the extract below for the meaning of 'standing' as it is used on p. 97: 'of at least ten years' **standing'**. In this dictionary many entries are listed under their 'root' word, in alphabetical order. You will need to know that:

i 'standing' in this context is a noun;
ii *n.* in the dictionary stands for noun.

Which meaning(s) will you choose?

appointment with. **to stand up for**, to maintain, to support, to take the part of. **to stand upon**, to stand on. **stand-by**, *n.* a thing or person to be confidently relied upon; a substitute or replacement kept esp. for use in an emergency. *a.* of a ticket not booked in advance, subject to availability. **on stand-by**, held in readiness for use in an emergency etc; of an airline passenger, awaiting an empty seat, not having booked in advance. **stand-in**, *n.* a minor actor who takes the place of a star in a scene until the cameras are ready; a substitute. **stand-off**, **stand-off half** FLY-HALF. **stand-offish**, *a.* distant, reserved. **stand-offishly**, *adv.* **stand-offishness**, *n.* **standpipe**, *n.* an upright pipe serving as a hydrant, to provide a head of water for pressure etc. **stand-point**, *n.* a point of view. **standstill**, *n.* a stoppage, a cessation of progress. **stand-up**, *a.* of a collar, upright; manfully fought, unflinching, thorough; of a comedian, telling jokes etc. directly to the audience in a solo performance. **stand-up fight** FIGHT. **stander**, *n.* **stander-by**, *n.* **standing**, *a,* erect; not cut down, fixed, established, permanent, not temporary or for a special occasion; stagnant, *n.* the act of one that stands; station; relative place or position; repute, estimation, esp. good estimation, duration, existence. **standing army**, *n.* a peacetime army of professional soldiers. **standing order**, *n.* an instruction to a bank by a customer to pay fixed sums at regular intervals in payment of bills etc; (*pl.*) orders made by a deliberate assembly as to the manner in which its business shall be conducted. **standing rigging**, *n.* the fixed ropes and chains by which the masts etc. on a ship, are secured. **standing room**, *n.* room for standing, esp. . . .

Sometimes, a students' dictionary can make a meaning clearer through examples; the extract below is from the *Oxford Student's Dictionary of Current English*. Notice that in this dictionary 'standing' is not listed under 'stand'.

stan·dard /'stændəd/ *n* [C] **1** distinctive flag, esp one to which loyalty is given or asked: *the royal* ~, eg as flown to show that the Queen is in residence. **2** (often as an *adjective*) something used as a test or measure for weights, lengths, qualities or for the required degree of excellence: ~ *weights and measures: set a high* ~ *for candidates in an examination; a high* ~ *of living*, one with plenty of material comforts, etc; ~ *authors*, accepted as good. ***be up to/below standard***, be equal to, not so good as, normal, etc: *Their work is not up to* ~. ⇨ gold standard. **3** (often used as an *adjective*) upright support; pole or column.

'**standard bearer**, (**a**) person carrying a standard(1)-(**b**) (*fig*) prominent leader.

'**standard lamp**, tall one with its base on the floor.

standard time, time officially adopted for (part of) a country.

stan·dard·ize (also **-ise**) /'stænd daiz/ *vt* make of one size, shape, quality, etc according to fixed standards.: *The parts of motor-vehicles are usually* ~ d.

stan·dard·iz·ation (also **'isation**) /'stænd daɪ'zeɪ *US*: -dɪ'z-/ *n*[U]

stand·ing /'stændɪŋ/ *n* **1**[U] duration: *a debt of long* ~. **2** [C,U] position or reputation; (if there is no *adjective*) established position: *men of high* ~: *a member in full* ~. *adj* established and permanent; ready for use: a ~ *committee*, a permanent one that meets regularly; *a* ~ *order for newspapers and periodicals*, to be delivered regularly.

stank /stæŋk/*pt* of stink.

stan·za /'stænzə/ *n* [C] (*pl* ~ s) group of rhymed lines forming a division in some forms of poem.

staple[1] /'steipl/ *n* [C] **1** U-shaped metal pin hammered into a surface, to hold something in position. **2** U-shaped part of a padlock. **3** piece of wire pushed through sheets of paper and bent to hold them together. □ *vt* fasten or fit with a staple.

5 Now choose the best meaning for the following highlighted words which occur later in this chapter.

a The jury system has been praised as being the '**bulwark** of our liberties' (see p. 116).

bulwark (bul'wək), *n.* a rampart or fortification:[1] mole, a breakwater; any shelter, protective screen; that part of the sides of a ship which rise above the upper deck. *v.t.* to furnish with or protect as with bulwarks. [formed like Dut. *bolwerk* and G *Bollwerk*, from words represented to BOLE[1], or the MHG v. *boln*, to throw, and WORK.

b '. . . by **redressing** the balance in favour of the accused' (see p. 117).

redress[1] (rēdres'), *v.t., v.i.* to dress again.

redress[2] (ridres'), *v.t.* to set straight or right again, to readjust, to rectify; to remedy, to amend, to make reparation for; †to repair, †to mend; †to re-erect, to set upright again. *n.* redressing of wrongs or oppression; reparation; rectification. **redressable**, *a.* capable of being redressed. **redresser**, *n.* †**redressive**, *a.* **redressment**, *n.*

c 'Juries are **ill-equipped** to deal with this' (see p. 117).

equip (ikwip'), *v.t.* (*past, p.p.* **equipped**) to furnish, accoutre, esp. to supply with arms and military apparatus; to fit out (as a ship), to prepare for any particular duty; to qualify. **equipage** (ek'wipij), *n.* that with which one is equipped; arms and general outfit of a body of troops, including baggage, provisions etc.; the outfit of a ship for a voyage; a carriage with horses and attendants; †retinue, attendance, train of followers. **camp-equipage**, (*Mil.*) tents, cooking-utensils etc. **field-equipage**, †(*Mil.*) saddle-horses, bat-horses, baggage-wagons and other things for the movements of an army. **siege-equipage**, the train of siege-guns, ammunition etc. **equipaged**, *a.* **equipment**, *n.* the act of equipping; the state of being equipped; that which is used in equipping or fitting out; outfit, furniture, apparatus required for work, intellectual and other qualifications. [F *équiper*, *esquiper* (A-F *eskiper*), prob. from Icel. *skipa*, to arrange, to man (a ship), from *skip*, ship]

ill (il), (*comp.* **worse** (woes), *superl.* **worst** (woest)) *a.* unwell, sick, diseased; bad morally, evil; malevolent, hostile, adverse, tending towards evil, noxious, mischievous, harmful; unfortunate, unfavourable, unlucky; not right, faulty, inferior, incorrect, improper; unskilful; awkward, cross (in temper); †unwholesome. *adv.* (*comp.* **worse**, *superl.* **worst**) not well, badly; not rightly; not easily; imperfectly, scarcely; unfavourably, in bad part or humour. *n.* evil; injury, harm; wickedness; *pl.* misfortuntes. **ill at ease**, uncomfortable, anxious. **to be taken ill**, to fall sick. **to speak ill**, to speak (of or about) unfavourably. **to take ill, to take in ill part**, to take offence at. **ill-advised**, *a.* imprudent; injudicious. **ill-advisedly**, *adv.* **ill-affected**, *a.* not friendly disposed; disaffected, †affected with bad impressions. **ill-assorted**, *a.* poorly matched; not compatible. **ill blood**, **ill feeling**, *n.* resentment, displeasure, enmity. †**ill-boding**, *a.* inauspicious. **ill-bred**, *a.* brought up badly; rude, unmannered, offensive. **ill breeding**, *n.* want of good breeding; rudeness. **ill-conditioned**, *a.* having a bad temper or disposition; in a bad physical condition. **ill-considered**, *a.* done without careful thought; misconceived. **ill-defined**, *a.* poorly defined; lacking a clear outline. **ill-disposed**, *a.* wickedly or maliciously inclined; unfavourably inclined (towards). **ill fame**, *n.* disrepute. **ill-fated**, *a.* unfortunate, unlucky. **ill-favoured**, (*Sc.*) **ill-faurd** (-fawd), *a.* ugly, deformed; forbidding, repulsive; unattractive, objectionable. †**ill-favouredly**, *adv.* **ill-favouredness**, *n.* **ill-feeling** ILL BLOOD. **ill-founded**, *a.* lacking any foundation in fact, not substantiated. **ill-got, ill-gotten**, *a.* obtained in an improper way. **ill humour**, *n.* bad temper. **ill-humoured**, *a.* **ill-humouredly**, *adv.* **ill-judged**, *a.* not well-judged; injudicious, unwise. **ill luck**, *n.* bad luck, misfortune. **ill-manned**, *a.* (*Naut.*) having an insufficient crew. **ill-mannered**, *a.* rude, boorish. **ill-matched**, *a.* not well-matched or suited. **ill-mated**, *a.* badly joined or mated. **ill nature**, *n.* evil disposition; lack of kindness or good feeling. **ill-natured**. *a.* of a churlish disposition, bad-tempered; expressive of or indicating ill nature; †not yielding to culture, intractable. **ill-naturedly**, *adv.* **ill-naturedness**, *n.* **ill-omened**, *a.* unlucky, inauspicious, of evil augury. **ill-starred**, *a.* born under the influence of an unlucky planet, hence unlucky. **ill temper**, *n.* **ill-tempered**, *a.* having a bad temper, sour, peevish. **ill-timed**, *a.* done, said, or attempted, at an unsuitable time. **ill-treat** ILL USE. **ill treatment** ILL USAGE. **ill turn**, *n.* an ill-natured act or treatment; †an attack of illness. **ill usage**, *n.* unkind treatment. **ill use**, *v.t.* to treat badly. **ill-versed**, *a.* uninstructed, lacking skill (in). **ill will**, *n.* malevolence, enmity. [ME, from Icel. *illr*]

5.2 The judicial function

It is often stated that the judicial function is to seek the facts of a case and apply the existing law to those facts. This statement is a simple one but it raises two important questions:

1 What is the judicial role in seeking the facts of a case?
2 In applying the law, do judges actually make the law?

The following extract addresses the first question:

> Most of the work of the judges is judicial in the sense that they have to adjudicate upon disputes. To do this they are required, dispassionately,[11] to find the facts upon[12] the evidence presented to the court, to apply the law to the facts as found and then to give the "right decision". Appellate courts have repeatedly pointed out that the judicial function in the conduct of litigation goes no further than that. Thus, in relation to finding the facts, the court must act on the evidence before it; it has no duty to seek out some 'independent truth' as LORD WILBERFORCE called it in the following interesting passage from his speech in a case concerning discovery of documents:

'In a contest purely between one litigant and another, such as the present, the task of the court is to do, and be seen to be doing, justice between the parties, a duty reflected by the word "fairly" in the rule. There is no higher or additional duty to ascertain some independent truth. It often happens, from the imperfection of evidence, or the withholding[13] of it, sometimes by the party in whose favour it would tell if presented, that an adjudication has to be made which is not, and is known not to be, the whole truth of the matter; yet, if the decision has been in accordance with the available evidence and with the law, justice will have been fairly done.'

Walker, *Walker and Walker, The English Legal System* (Butterworths 1985), p. 232.

Text notes:
11 impartially
12 based on
13 keeping back

So the answer to the first question is that the judges' role in seeking the facts is very limited. This you will remember is a central feature of an adversarial legal system. This is not to say that judges must be totally passive; they may, on occasion,[14] question the witnesses and they must control the proceedings according to the rules of procedure and evidence, but they must not intervene[15] excessively. Their role is that of the impartial adjudicator – reaching a conclusion only on the basis of the evidence presented to them.

Text notes:
14 occasionally, sometimes
15 interfere (literally 'come between')

Comprehension check

6 **a** What are the three parts to the judicial role?
b What reasons are mentioned for an adjudication which is not 'the whole truth of the matter'?

Let us now consider the second question. We have examined the issue of judicial creativity in the context of judicial precedent and statutory interpretation; you will be familar with the need for the law to balance the requirements of both certainty and justice and the restraints imposed by the doctrine of parliamentary sovereignty. These are very relevant to the question – do judges make law? The traditional view is that the judge applies existing law. This view is summarised by Lord Simon in *Jones* v. *Secretary of State for Social Services* [1972] 1 All ER 145:

In this country it was long considered that judges were not makers of the law but merely its discoverers and expounders.[16] The theory was that every case was governed by a relevant rule of law, existing somewhere and discoverable somehow, providing[17] sufficient learning and intellectual rigour was brought to bear.[18]

This theory is known as the **declaratory theory of law.** It reflects the importance placed on the literal rule of interpretation and strict adherence to the rules of judicial precedent. This traditional view is no longer widely accepted; legislation is often ambiguous and cases arise for which there is no precedent. In these situations judges create new law. Equally, in deciding whether to extend or restrict an existing legal principle, the judge is making law.

Text notes:
16 'to expound' means 'to interpret'
17 if, on condition that
18 'to bring to bear' means 'to apply'

Comprehension check

7 What are the three situations mentioned where a judge can be said to be 'making law'?

The proposition that judges do make law can be illustrated by reference to the case studies used in Chapter 3. The case of *Donoghue* v. *Stevenson* created the law that manufacturers of products will be liable for any damage to consumers caused by the manufacturer's negligence. Both this and the neighbour principle contained in Lord Atkin's judgment were new law; in addition, the latter was very broad. Later courts, in deciding whether to extend or restrict that principle, have also created new law. So we see that before the case of *Hedley, Byrne* v. *Heller* there was no legal liability for economic loss caused by negligent words. The House of Lords in that case created new law by extending the neighbour principle to such situations when there is a special relationship between the plaintiff and the defendant.

Conversely, in the case of *London & North Eastern Railway Co* v. *Berriman* the majority of the House of Lords restricted the scope of the law by giving judgment that the words 'repairing and relaying' did not include maintaining. This was therefore the law – the statute did not place a legal responsibility on an employer to provide an adequate warning system whenever railwaymen were maintaining the railway line.

So we can accept that judges do make law but within the constraints of parliamentary sovereignty and the rules of judicial precedent. To allow judges complete freedom would be to bring an unacceptable level of subjectivity[19] and uncertainty into the law. There are also some areas of law which are politically or morally controversial where judicial creativity is considered inappropriate to the apolitical[20] nature of the British judiciary. The situation was stated as follows by the then Lord Chancellor, Lord Hailsham, in the 1983 Hamlyn Lectures.

> The law has its discipline. It must never become the thing which seems right in the eye of the individual judge. It is not as long as the judge's foot,[21] and this limitation is as[22] much there, though of course less obviously so, in the case of customary or common law as in the case of obedience to an Act of Parliament. "Be you never so high[23] but the law is above you" is a rule for judges no less than[24] Ministers, and, if the independence of judges is to be preserved, the limitations on the judicial function must be clearly understood not only by the public and the media, but by the judiciary themselves, both collectively and individually.
>
> Lord Hailsham of Marylebone, *Hamlyn Revisted* (Stevens 1983), p. 49.

Text notes:
19 personal point of view
20 without political connections [ˌeɪpəˈlɪtɪkl]
21 i.e. the law must not vary from judge to judge
22 'as . . . as' (NB: the second 'as' is two lines below)
23 (archaic) however high you are
24 as well as

Legal exercises

8 What constraint does the adversarial system place upon the role of the judge?

9 Summarise the traditional view of the judge as lawmaker.

10 State the law relating to negligent misstatement before and after the case of *Hedley, Byrne* v. *Heller*.

11 How would the law be different if the majority of the House of Lords had found for the plaintiff in the case of *London & North Eastern Railway* v. *Berriman*?

12 Refer back to the case of *Boardman* v. *Sanderson* in question 26 of Revision 1 and remind yourself of the facts. In the later case of *McLoughlin* v. *O'Brian* [1982] 2 All ER 298, HL, the plaintiff's husband and children were involved in a car accident. One of her children was killed and her husband and other children were very seriously injured. The plaintiff was not with her family at the time of the accident but she was told about it two hours later and taken to the hospital. Here she was told of her child's death and she saw the appalling injuries which her family had sustained. The House of Lords allowed her to recover for[25] the nervous shock she suffered as a result.

a How do the facts of *McLoughlin* v. *O'Brian* differ from those of *Boardman* v. *Sanderson*?
b How did the House of Lords change the law by passing judgment in favour of Mrs McLoughlin?

Text note:
25 i.e. recover damages for

5.3 The independence of the judiciary

The discussion on the role of the judiciary can only be fully understood within its proper context – the independence of the judiciary. Much importance is placed on maintaining an independent judiciary, but, we must ask, independent of what? First, judges must be independent of the parties to a dispute. This ensures a fair and just trial. Secondly, they must be independent of the executive; this enables the judges to exercise control over government action. This latter freedom in particular is one which is fiercely defended by the judiciary. Lord Denning states the case clearly:

At one time the theorists said that there should be a complete separation between the legislative, the executive and the judicial powers. That theory in England has never been carried to its logical extent. There is here no rigid separation between the legislative and the executive powers. The Ministers who exercise the executive power also direct a great deal of the legislative power of Parliament, but they are subject to many checks.[26] And one of the most important checks is the independence of the judges. The power of the executive over the legislative power was strikingly shown in a recent debate in the House of Lords. Lord Simon said that "there is a greatly increased practice to regard individual members of Parliament, of whatever party, as automatons who would obey the call and authorise the Cabinet to do what it wanted." Lord Cecil said: "If they showed any disposition to take independent action, they were informed that they would not be the party candidates at the next election"; and Lord Salisbury said: "In recent years private members had been driven more and more into the party lobby, irrespective[27] of their personal views."

I am not concerned whether this is desirable or not. It may well be necessary in the interests of efficiency. All I would point out is that, if it is correct, it means that the personal views of Members of Parliament are no longer a check, or at any rate so strong a check, on the powers of the executive as they used to be. It is all the more important, therefore, to keep the only remaining check, the independence of the judges. And when I speak of Judges, I include also all the magistrates, and others who exercise judicial functions. No member of the Government, no Member of Parliament, and no official of any Government department has any right whatever to direct or influence or to interfere with the decisions of any of the judges. It is the sure knowledge of this that gives the people their confidence in the judges, and I would add also the Chairmen of Tribunals when they are independent of the executive, for then they too are judges. It does not depend on the name Judge or Chairman, but on the substance. The critical test which they must pass if they are to receive the confidence of the people is that they must be independent of the executive.

Lord Denning, 'The Independence of the Judiciary' (Haldsworth Club Lecture 1950), reported in *The Lawyer and Justice* (Sweet and Maxwell 1978), pp. 56–7.

Text notes:
26 controls
27 not taking into account

Lord Denning placed great faith in the judges as a check on the misuse of power. However, his words 'trust the judges' can be compared to those of others who ask 'can the judges be trusted?' We will examine these conflicting views later in this chapter.

5.3.1 Elements of judicial independence

There are a number of factors which contribute to the maintenance of an independent judiciary. These are summarised in the next extract. As you read the text think about the way in which each factor relates to the subject.

Constitutionally great stress is always laid on the independence of the judges, in particular independence from the executive. Although appointed on the recommendation of the executive, judges of the superior courts can only be removed by the Queen on an address of both Houses of Parliament. Their salaries are protected from annual scrutiny[28] by being charged on the Consolidated Fund instead of having to be voted specifically each year. They are protected from incidental[29] criticism in Parliament by the parliamentary rule that the judiciary may only be criticised on a substantive motion and various other rules which prevent the discussion of cases which are *sub judice*.[30] They themselves may not be Members of Parliament. On the other hand they are appointed in effect by the government of the day, and if the government of the day had a majority in the House of Lords as well as the House of Commons an address could be presented to the Queen for removal of any one of them. Their statutory protections are only secure as statutes themselves and from a legal point of view any statute can be changed by a simple majority in the House of Commons, provided the government either has a majority in the House of Lords or proceeds under the Parliament Acts 1911 and 1949. There are no special constitutional safeguards protecting the judges because there is no way in which such safeguards can be established.

Wilson, *Cases and Materials on the English Legal System* (Sweet and Maxwell 1973), pp. 160–1.

Text notes:
28 examination
29 casual
30 under consideration by a judge [ˌsʌb ˈdʒuːdɪsɪː]

In addition to the mechanisms outlined in the extract, members of the judiciary are also expected to present an independent image by refraining from controversial behaviour. Public statements on controversial issues could raise questions about impartiality. Public confidence in the judiciary could be undermined by the type of behaviour exemplified in the next extract.

Scarcely less damaging than when a judge gets convicted of a crime is the situation that arises when a judge behaves so badly when trying a case, or makes some public remark which is so outrageously biased, that the public or a section of it thereafter doubts his balance and impartiality; as when a High Court Judge threatened to lock a jury up all night if they did not reach a verdict in time to enable him to catch a train which would get him to a dinner engagement, or when another judge described the law which legalised homosexual behaviour in private as 'a buggers' charter which enabled perverts and homosexuals to pursue their perversions in private', or when another judge interrupted defence counsel's closing speech by saying 'Oh God!', putting his head on his hands, and groaning[31] aloud until he had finished.

Spencer, *Jackson's Machinery of Justice* (Cambridge University Press 1989), p. 370.

Text note
31 sound normally expressing pain

Notemaking

13 Complete the following notes which are based on the two extracts above:

Factors which contribute to judges' independence:

1. Removal of judges: can only be removed if . . . .
. . . .
. . . .
2. Js.' salaries: . . . .
. . . .
. . . .
3. Criticism of js.: . . . .
. . . .
. . . .
4. . . . .
. . . .
5. Js.' behaviour can affect image of independence, e.g.
   (a) . . . .
   . . . .
   (b) . . . .
   . . . .
   (c) . . . .
   . . . .

5.3.2 Should we trust the judges?

At the heart of the discussion on judicial independence is the perception of the judiciary as the upholders[32] of the rule of law. This is seen in the strongly held view of Lord Denning; his answer to the question is a firm 'yes':

> "May[33] not the Judges themselves sometimes abuse or misuse their power? It is their duty to administer and apply the law of the land. If they should divert it or depart from it – and do so[34] knowingly – they themselves would be guilty of a misuse of power. So we come up against Juvenal's[35] question, '*Sed quis custodiet ipsos custodes*?' (But who is to guard the guards themselves?) . . . Suppose a future Prime Minister should[36] seek to pack the Bench with judges of his own extreme political colour.[37] Would they be tools in his hand? To that I answer 'No.' Every judge on his appointment[38] discards[39] all politics and all prejudices. You need have no fear. The Judges of England have always in the past – and always will – be vigilant in guarding our freedoms. Someone must be trusted. Let it be the Judges."
>
> Lord Denning, "Misuse of Power" (The Richard Dimbleby Lecture 1980), reported in *What Next in the Law* (Butterworths 1982), p. 330.

Text notes:
32 supporters
33 expressing possibility
34 see question **14** below
35 Juvenal was a Roman poet and satirist
36 expresses a conditional
37 opinion
38 when he is appointed
39 throws away

Comprehension check

14 Note 34: To what does 'so' refer here?

Such absolute faith in judicial independence has been questioned by many.

An opposing view was powerfully argued by Professor John Griffiths in his book *The Politics of the Judiciary* (Fontana 1985). He took a broad view of the factors which influence judicial independence. In particular, he argued that the common[40] background of most judges led them to identify the public interest with the interests of those in authority.

Text note:
40 shared

[The appellate judges] "have by their education and training and the pursuit of their profession as barristers, acquired a strikingly homogenous[41] [*sic*] collection of attitudes, beliefs and principles, which to them represents the public interest. The judicial conception of the public interest . . . is threefold. It concerns first, the interests of the State (including its moral welfare) and the preservation of law and order broadly interpreted; secondly, the protection of property rights; and thirdly, the promotion of certain political views normally associated with the Conservative Party."[42]

Griffiths, *The Politics of the Judiciary* (Fontana 1985), p. 200.

Text note:
41 of the same kind
42 a moderate right-wing party, also known as the Tory Party

Critics of Professor Griffiths do not question the homogeneous nature of the judiciary in relation to education, social background, gender and age. The facts would make it difficult to do so:[43]

Database on the judiciary

Judge	Court	Salary (£)	Number (women in brackets)	Barristers	Solicitors	Average age	Public school[44]	Oxbridge[45]
Lord of Appeal in Ordinary	Appellate Committee of the House of Lords	74,750	11 (0)	11	0	70	10	10
Lord Justices of Appeal	Court of Appeal	71,750	22 (0)†	22	0	62	16	19
High Court (puisne) judge	High Court	65,000	79 (3)	79	0	60	61	60
Circuit judge	Crown Court or County Court	43,000	391 (14)	344*	29*	61*	246*	235*
Recorder	Crown Court	P/t	540 (19)	383*	37*	52*	265*	264*
Assistant Recorder	Crown Court	P/t	557 (25)*	505*	52*	–	–	–
Stipendiary magistrate	Magistrates' Courts	33,500	60 (5)*	40*	20*	54*	42*	24*
Justice of The Peace	Magistrates' Courts	unpaid	26,000 (approx.)	–	–	–	–	–

* 1985 figures given in Tony Gifford, *Where's the justice?*
† The first female Lord Justice of Appeal, Lord Justice Butler-Sloss has been appointed to the Court of Appeal with effect from 1 January 1988.

Johnson and Pannet, *SWOT A Level Law* (Blackstone Press 1988), p. 59.

Text notes:
43 i.e. to question the homogeneous nature of the judiciary
44 private secondary school
45 educated at Oxford or Cambridge Universities

Interpreting data

15 Using the information in the database above describe the 'homogeneous nature of the judiciary', giving relevant examples. Write between 100 and 200 words. You may like to use the following sentence to open:

'Where data are available, it can be seen that judges and magistrates share common characteristics in terms of education, social background, gender, salary and age.'

Some judges also accept that this does produce a common outlook:

> 'Since he is writing of men in their sixties and seventies whose working life has given them a common outlook on many questions, by no means[46] all political, I have very little doubt[47] that he is right. I have very little doubt either that the same might be written of most English institutions, certainly of all those which like the law are not of a nature to attract the crusading or rebellious spirit.'
>
> Lord Devlin (1978) 41 MLR 501.

Text notes:
46 certainly not
47 I am almost certain

Lord Devlin goes further by arguing that the conservative[48] nature of the judiciary is to be applauded: 'The oligarchs[49] who rise to the top of a democratic society are usually mature, safe and orthodox men – the silent majority[50] may see this as a good thing.'

Where there is disagreement with Professor Griffiths is over his assumption that the conservative nature of the judiciary leads to an inability and disinclination to control the abuse of power. Professor Griffiths is accused of political bias and the use of selective data. His critics point to the frequent division of opinion between the House of Lords and the Court of Appeal and between judges within those courts, as an indication that a common background does not automatically lead to common opinions. The growing body of administrative law demonstrates the willingness of the judiciary to examine government action through judicial review.

This debate illustrates the difficulties judges can experience; viewed from different perspectives they are either too conservative or too creative. Certainly the debate does highlight the sensitivity and importance of the judicial role within the English legal system.

Text notes:
48 cautious, opposed to sudden change (not referring to the political party as in note 40 above)
49 small number of people with power
50 see question **16** below

Comprehension check

16 Note 50: To whom are Lord Devlin referring by 'the silent majority'?

Summarising

17 Briefly, in note form, summarise the arguments put forward in section 5.2.2:

1. Lord Denning's view: ....
2. John Griffiths's view: ....
3. Supporting evidence for J.G.: ....
4. Lord Devlin's view: ....

Legal exercises

18 In what way do the following factors contribute to judicial independence?

a security of tenure
b protection of salaries
c freedom from criticism by Parliament
d exclusion of judges from membership of Parliament
e restraints on judges making controversial public statements

19 How might the common background of judges relate to their independence and impartiality?

5.4 The jury

The jury has a long history within the English legal system, although its role has changed significantly during that time. Originally, members of the jury were witnesses,[51] summoned[52] for their local knowledge. Today, they are a group of twelve ordinary people with no special knowledge, chosen at random to act as impartial judges of the facts of a case. In a jury trial, the jury is advised by the trial judge on the relevant law; its function is then to apply the law to the facts and then decide, in criminal cases, whether the defendant is guilty or not guilty and, in civil cases, whether the defendant is liable to the plaintiff. The decision of a jury is called a **verdict.** In civil cases the jury will also decide on the amount of damages to be awarded to the plaintiff.

Although the jury continues to have much symbolic importance in the English legal system, in practice its role has been greatly diminished over recent years. The extract below explains how this has happened.

> Before the Common Law Procedure Act 1854, most civil cases were tried by jury. By 1933, the number had declined to about half of all civil cases. The Administration of Justice (Miscellaneous Provisions) Act 1933, s. 6 (now Supreme Court Act 1981, s. 69) restricted the right to jury trial to cases of:
>
> (a) Libel and slander (right recommended for abolition by the Faulks Committee on Defamation, 1975).
> (b) Malicious prosecution.
> (c) False imprisonment.
> (d) Fraud.
> (e) Breach of promise of marriage or seduction (both actions now abolished).
>
> In all other cases the right to jury trial is at the discretion of the court.[53] In *Ward* v. *James* [1966] 1 QB 273, the Court of Appeal stated that in personal

injury cases (the vast majority of all civil actions) trial should be by judge alone in the absence of special considerations. In the High Court, jury trial occurs in considerably less than 1 per cent of all civil cases. In the county court, where a jury of eight may be empanelled,[54] only about 20 of the 34,000 cases per year involve a jury.

A surprisingly small proportion of criminal cases go for jury trial. About 85 per cent of all criminal cases are summary offences triable only in the magistrates' court. In a further 12 per cent of cases the cases are triable either way but summary trial is chosen. Thus only about 3 per cent of criminal cases go to the Crown Court. Taking into account the more than 60 per cent[55] who plead guilty[56] and the proportion of cases where a judge directs an acquittal[57] or where there is a change of plea,[58] *less than 1% of all criminal trials result in a jury verdict.*

Johnson and Pannet, *SWOT A Level Law* (Blackstone Press 1988), pp. 67–8.

Text notes:
51 a person who gives evidence (i.e. information) in court
52 told to appear in court
53 only the court may decide
54 enrolled, enlisted
55 see question **20** below
56 state, say that they are guilty
57 says that a person is not guilty
58 the noun from 'to plead'

Comprehension check

20 Note 55: '60%' of what?

21 Complete the following note outline, based on the extract above.

Trial by jury
. . . . cases
1. Pre-1854: . . . .
2. By 1933: . . . .
3. Now: only
   a) . . . .
   b) . . . . } tried by jury.
   c) . . . .
   d) . . . .
   In all other cases . . . .
   a) High Court: <1% . . . .
   b) County Court: . . . .

. . . . cases
85% . . . . = ...
12% . . . . = ...
3% → . . . . → 60% . . . . → (result) . . . .

Before we attempt to analyse the reasons for the decline in the role of the jury and the arguments for and against the system, it is necessary for you to be familar with the qualifications for jury service:

> Every person between the ages of 18 and 65 (there is a proposal in the Criminal Justice Bill[59] to raise the latter to 70 while allowing persons over 65 to excuse themselves from service if they so wish) is qualified for jury service

provided: (i) that person is registered as a parliamentary or local government elector; (ii) has been ordinarily resident within the United Kingdom for any period of at least five years since reaching the age of 13; and (iii) is not ineligible or disqualified for jury service.

Disqualification extends to any person who within the United Kingdom has (a) been sentenced to imprisonment for life (or to be detained during pleasure) or to a term of five years or more; or (b) served any part of a sentence of imprisonment of three months or more during the last 10 years, or has been detained in borstal.

Of those rendered ineligible by the Act the largest class comprises those who are connected with the administration of the law. For obvious reasons, judges, magistrates and police officers are ineligible but so too are many people (clerks and secretaries for example) who are employed (for instance by the Lord Chancellor's Office, the Director of Public Prosecutions, the police) in the day-to-day administration of justice. The other categories of ineligible persons extends to persons in holy orders and the mentally ill.

There is a further category of persons who, though eligible, may claim to be excused as of right. This category recognises that certain people (for example, Members of Parliament, doctors, nurses) may have more important duties than jury service and they may, if they wish, excuse themselves from it.

Hogan, Seago and Bennett, *A Level Law* (Sweet and Maxwell 1988), p. 129.

Text note:
59 now Criminal Justice Act 1988

Comprehension check

23 Which of the following are eligible for jury service?

- **a** A person who was in prison two years ago for one month.
- **b** A person who entered the UK six years ago at the age of ten years.
- **c** A Roman Catholic priest.
- **d** A doctor.

24 Which of the following may/may not/must do jury service?

- **a** A nurse.
- **b** A secretary in a police station.
- **c** A woman of 65 years.
- **d** A man of 70 years.

Let us now examine the mechanics of jury selection. In recent years this has raised several controversial issues which are explained in the following text.

A jury for a particular case will be selected from a panel of approximately 100 people who have been chosen at random from the electoral register[60] by an approved official of the court. This random selection procedure is a very important feature of the jury system; it seeks to ensure that any individual jury will be made up of an impartial cross-section[61] of the community. However, the random nature of the jury can be affected in two ways, both of which have aroused considerable controversy. The first is the process of **jury vetting**.[62] In some cases involving national security and terrorism, the police may be authorised by the DPP to check into the background of potential[63] jurors. This process first came to public attention in 1978 in what was known as the ABC trial – a prosecution under the Official Secrets Act

1911. Although the legality of the practice has been upheld by the Court of Appeal in *R* v. *Mason* [1981] QB 881, it has been criticised on the grounds that it interferes with the randomness of the jury and, because the resulting information is not normally made available to the defence, it benefits the prosecution. Lord Denning has called it unconstitutional on the grounds[64] that it has not been authorised by an Act of Parliament. The Attorney-General has issued guidelines governing the use of jury vetting ([1980] 3 All ER 786), but it is not known if these are adhered to.

The composition of a jury can also be affected by the process of **jury challenge.** Both the prosecution and the defence have an unlimited right to challenge a potential juror 'for cause'. A legitimate[65] cause would be something which would affect the individual's ability to act impartially or understand the proceedings. For example, a potential juror may be related to the defendant or have a limited command of English. In addition to the challenge for cause, the prosecution may also ask a potential juror to 'stand by for the Crown'. No reason need be given unless the number of the remaining members of the panel falls below that required to make up a jury. It is argued that this gives the prosecution an unlimited power of challenge which is not enjoyed by the defence. The right of the defence to three peremptory[66] challenges was removed by the Criminal Justice Act 1988 on the grounds that the process was often used to 'pack' a jury with people who would be more sympathetic to the defendant. This could be particularly effective in cases involving multiple defendants, each of whom had a right to three peremptory challenges. Examples cited include the Cyprus Secrets trial in 1986, where the defendants' peremptory challenges were used to secure a jury of men who were of a similar age to the defendants and arguably favourable to them. Nevertheless, the removal of the peremptory challenge has been criticised, particularly as the prosecution's 'stand-by' challenge remains, thereby creating an imbalance in favour of the prosecution.

Undoubtedly, jury vetting and jury challenging do[67] affect the randomness of the jury, but to what extent they affect the requirement of impartiality is less clear. It is possible to argue that this,[68] after all, is the most important requirement of trial by jury.

Text notes:
60 list of voters
61 representative sample
62 'to vet' means 'to examine closely'
63 possible
64 because
65 lawfully acceptable
66 without stating the cause
67 in a positive sentence as here 'do' emphasises the verb
68 refers to requirement of impartiality

Comprehension check

25 Decide whether the following statements are true or false; correct any false statements.

- **a** Jury 'vetting' is carried out by either the prosecution or the defence.
- **b** Twelve jury members are chosen at randon from 100 people.
- **c** Jury vetting is criticised because it is unlawful.
- **d** Only the prosecution can object to a potential jury member without legitimate cause.

26 Complete the following table of notes:

Way of influencing composition of jury	*Available to*
1. Jury vetting	Prosecution
2. Jury challenge	
a	. . . .
b	. . . .

Legal exercises

27 How does jury vetting influence the random nature of the jury? In what way does it relate to jury challenge?

28 How might the following characteristics of the jurors affect their impartiality?

- **a** The juror is married to the defendant's cousin.
- **b** The defendant is a young black female and the jury is composed of white, middle-aged men.
- **c** The juror is a mother of three young children and the defendant is accused of molesting a five-year-old child.
- **d** The juror has been convicted of several motoring offences and the defendant is accused of dangerous driving.

5.4.1 Evaluation and alternatives

Even the most enthusiastic supporters of the jury would agree that the system is not perfect. The decline in the role of the jury reflects its disadvantages. Some of these are outlined in the following text.

> Though the jury system is highly regarded in many quarters and has been praised by Lord Denning MR[69] as being the "bulwark of our liberties", it has not escaped criticism. The following are some of the criticisms which have been made:
>
> 1 Though s 2 of the 1974 Act governs the way in which jurors are summoned, it does not prescribe the criteria used to determine which particular voters are summoned. Although directions under s 5 of the Act lay down that selection should be on a "random" basis, rarely does[70] the composition of the jury reflect that of the community as a whole. This is a cause for concern in a multi-racial society when members of ethnic minorities are tried before predominantly white juries.
>
> 2 The rules for the disqualification of jurors are such that ex convicts may be eligible for jury service. The increase in "jury nobbling" (the practice of bribing or threatening jurors in order to secure a particular verdict), which is often aimed at ex convicts, has led to several attempts to extend the scope of disqualification . . .
>
> 3 As jurors are not selected on the basis of ability, cases involving complex facts may be beyond their competence.

4 Jurors' unfamiliarity with their role may lead them to be seduced by the eloquence of counsel and to acquit through misplaced sympathy.
5 The compulsory element in jury service is disliked by jurors, particularly when allied to the inadequate compensation for loss of earnings for the higher-paid.
6 Increasingly juries are being directed by judges that the meaning of so-called "ordinary" words in statutes, eg "dishonesty" in the Theft Act 1968, is a matter for them. This would seem to be a task for which juries were not designed and for which they are ill-equipped.

In view of the above, and the fact that in civil cases the jury has all but[71] disappeared, it might be thought surprising that the jury still plays such an important role in criminal trials. The argument in favour of retaining the jury in such trials is that it protects the accused. It does this, so it is claimed, by redressing the balance in favour of the accused in the face of prosecution-minded judges, by introducing the views of the man-in-the-street as a counterbalance to the narrow socio-economic background of the judiciary and by providing a safeguard against legislation[72] repugnant to the community.

Sim and Scott, *A Level English Law* (Butterworths 1984), p. 114.

Text notes:
69 abbreviation for Master of the Rolls
70 see language point below
71 almost
72 this is easier to understand if you insert 'which is' here

---

Language point

A few adverbs (e.g. seldom, scarcely, never) can be placed at the beginning of a sentence for emphasis (particularly in formal speech or writing); when this occurs the usual subject-verb order is reversed, as here. If the verb is in the simple present, as here, do/does will be used as in question forms.

Try the following exercise:

29 a I have never heard such a thing before.
Never . . . .
b The situation rarely arises.
Rarely . . . .
c This will never be seen again.
Never . . . .
d Such an opportunity seldom presents itself.
Seldom . . . .

Many studies of the jury system have been undertaken. In one of these, *Jury Trials* (1979) by Baldwin and McConville, the authors concluded that it was 'an arbitrary and unpredictable business'. Much of the research concentrates on acquittal rates and the levels of perverse[73] verdicts. Some studies have shown that judges and 'shadow juries'[74] agree with 75 per cent of jury verdicts. A recent Home Office publication by Moxon, *Managing Criminal Justice* (HMSO, 1985), suggested that juries are twice as likely to acquit as magistrates. Acquittal rates are, of course, only one way of assessing the adequacy of trial by jury; how do we judge whether an acquittal is wrong? For example, the Home Office research could suggest that magistrates are convicting innocent people rather than that juries are acquitting the guilty.

The debate is hampered[75] by the provisions of s. 8(1) of the Contempt of Court Act 1981 which makes it an offence to 'obtain, disclose[76] or solicit[77] any particulars of statements made, opinions expressed, arguments advanced or votes cast by members of a jury in the course of their deliberations in any legal proceedings'. Its main purpose is to prevent jury nobbling but it also prohibits legitimate research into how the jury system works in practice. This benefits neither the critics nor the supporters of trial by jury and prevents an objective assessment of its role in the English legal system.

The alternatives to the jury are also imperfect. These are trial by a single judge, trial by a bench of judges and trial by a composite tribunal of judges and laypersons. All presently feature in the legal system but none is seen as appropriate for those remaining trials which continue to be heard before a jury.

Text notes:

73 a verdict given by a jury which refuses to follow the judge on a point of law
74 mock 'jury' used by researchers to hear a case and reach a 'verdict'
75 obstructed, made difficult
76 give, reveal
77 try to obtain

Comprehension check

30 Match the six statements below with the six criticisms in the extract from Sim and Scott on pp.116–17.

- **a** Jurors who have committed crimes may be persuaded to make a wrong decision.
- **b** Juries are not capable of deciding the meaning of key words.
- **c** Some people lose a lot of money by doing jury service.
- **d** Juries are not a truly representative cross-section of society.
- **e** Some jurors are not intelligent enough.
- **f** Jurors may be over-influenced by the quality of barristers' speeches.

Language practice – prepositions

31 The gaps in the following sentences can be filled with prepositions, all of which have been used in this chapter:

- **a** High Court judges are appointed . . . . the Queen . . . . the recommendation of the Lord Chancellor.
- **b** There are many reasons . . . . the increase . . . . crime.
- **c** Lawyers . . . . considerable experience can be appointed . . . . the judiciary.
- **d** The constitution is based . . . . the separation of powers.

e The Attorney-General is responsible . . . . prosecution policy.
f The judge advises the jury . . . . the relevant law.
g In a civil case the jury must decide . . . . the amount of damages.
h Less than 1 per cent of all criminal cases result . . . . a jury verdict.
i People . . . . the age of 18 are qualified . . . . jury service.
j A nurse may excuse himself . . . . jury service.

Research

32 Is trial by jury available in your country? If so, find out which groups qualify for jury service and which cases are heard before a jury. Does the public have confidence in the system? Who tries the types of cases which are tried by a jury in the UK? If there is no trial by jury, find out the reasons for this and whether these reasons are accepted by the legal profession and the public

Legal exercises

33 If you were accused of an offence triable either way, would the fact that your case would be heard before a jury in the Crown Court influence your decision as to the form of trial?

34 Should s. 8(1) of the Contempt of Court Act 1981 be abolished?

35 Do you consider that any of the alternatives to trial by jury would be an adequate replacement for it?

36 Write an essay of 500 words on the question: 'Why is jury trial in decline?'

Question 36 is asking you to discuss a particular aspect of trial by jury – the reasons for its decline. With some questions, like this one, which are based on an assumption, you would be expected to dispute the assumption. For example, the question 'Why has the public lost confidence in jury trial?' assumes that the public **has** lost confidence in trial by jury. In your answer you would be required to argue both for and against the assumption, that is show that there are some reasons for a loss of public confidence, but also show that many people still retain considerable confidence in the system. This again illustrates how important it is always to think very carefully about what an essay question is asking you. Many students fail to achieve high grades because they do not read the question carefully and instead adopt a 'write all you know about the subject' approach. This demonstrates rote learning rather than understanding and should always be avoided.

This question on the jury does make an assumption that jury trial is in decline but it is an assumption based on fact and cannot really be disputed. Your answer must therefore look at the extent of the decline in trial by jury and the reasons for this. Reread the section on the jury very carefully, make notes on the relevant information and prepare an essay plan before you write the essay.

Additional reading

A collection of thought-provoking cases and materials on the role of the judge as law-maker can be found in Chapter 6 of Zander's *The Law-Making Process* (Weidenfeld & Nicholson). Lord Denning's series of autobiographical books, *The Discipline of the Law* (Butterworths) *What Next in the Law* (Butterworths), and *The Closing Chapter* (*Butterworths*), and Lord Devlin's *The Judge* (OUP) provide very readable insights into the authors' individual views of the judicial role.

Chapter 5 of *Cases and Materials on the English Legal System* by Zander (Weidenfeld & Nicholson) and Chapter 7 of Ingham's *The English Legal Process* (Blackstone Press) provide a more detailed evaluation of trial by jury. The results of the research carried out by Baldwin and McConville are published in *Jury Trials* (Clarendon Press).

6
The provision of legal services

Summary

Legal content

6.1 The legal profession
- 6.1.1 Reform: from Benson to Mackay
- 6.1.2 Legal services outside the profession

6.2 The state funding of legal services
6.3 The unmet need for legal services
Additional reading

Aim

To examine the adequacy of the provision of legal services against the background of the structure of the legal profession and the state funding of legal services. Recent legislative reforms are considered and the extent to which these correspond to the needs of the public.

Language content

Vocabulary: revision of prepositions
Oral function: presentation of arguments for and against
Study skills: use of signpost words to recognise arguments for and against

6.1 The legal profession

A distinctive feature of the legal profession in England and Wales is that it is divided into two groups: barristers and solicitors. This division has frequently been the focus of debate and criticism and there have been calls for the fusion[1] of the two branches of the profession. We will examine these and other proposals for reform in the next section. First you should read the following extract and table which outline the practical and administrative differences between barristers and solicitors.

> In the popular mind, the distinction between barristers and solicitors is that the former are concerned with advocacy[2] in court while the latter are concerned with legal work out of court. This is not quite[3] the case. Barristers are primarily concerned with advocacy and they have an exclusive right of audience[4] in the High Court, the Court of Appeal and the House of Lords; but they are not confined to advocacy and may devote a deal of their time to giving expert opinions on legal matters. Nor are solicitors exclusively concerned with out-of-court work for they have a right of audience in magistrates' courts, county courts and, in some instances, in the Crown Court.
>
> This division of the legal profession is a curious one and is unknown even

in many Commonwealth countries which might have been expected to adopt the English professional model along with their adoption of the common law. The education of both barristers and solicitors has common features. Both will normally complete the academic stage of their legal education by obtaining a law degree, though a law degree is not the only way to complete the academic stage. Both undergo a vocational[5] stage though here the differences are more marked.[6] The barrister takes the Bar Examination under the aegis[7] of the Inns of Court School of Law while the solicitor takes the Final Examination under the aegis of the Law Society and in these examinations the emphasis differs to take account of their different roles. Both must complete a period of apprenticeship; pupillage in the case of barristers served under a pupil master (an experienced barrister), and articles in the case of solicitors served under an experienced solicitor. Here, at this "practical" stage, the difference is perhaps most marked since the day-to-day work of the barrister is quite different to the office routine of the solicitor.

The difference, however, is one of function rather than purpose. It is the purpose of both to ensure that the citizen has available sound professional services and advice to enable him to order his business and social life. When a citizen consults a lawyer it is more likely to prevent matters going wrong (*e.g.* he wishes to form a company, or to organise his business affairs to attract the minimum of tax, or to make a will) than because matters have gone wrong (*e.g.* he is threatened with civil or criminal proceedings). Only exceptionally will the citizen require the specialist services of the barrister hence practising barristers number some 5,000 as against some 42,000 solicitors. But even a distinction between the "specialist" barrister and the "generalist" solicitor can be misleading; many barristers, particularly in their early years at the Bar, may take whatever cases come their way, and many solicitors, especially those in large firms, may specialise in a particular area of law.

That the fusion of the two professions is *possible* is demonstrated by experience in similar common law jurisdictions elsewhere. Whether it is *desirable* is another matter. The acid tests must be whether fusion would secure for the citizen an improved standard of legal services or whether it would significantly reduce their cost.

Hogan, Seago and Bennett, *A Level Law* (Sweet and Maxwell 1988), pp. 32–3.

Text notes:

1 'to fuse' means 'to join'
2 arguing a case
3 exactly
4 the right to be heard, i.e. to speak
5 training for a specific career
6 clear
7 i.e. organised by

Comprehension check

1 Complete the following table which is based on the extract above:

Preparation of lawyers

	Barristers	*Solicitors*
Academic:	**a**	**b** ....
Vocational exams:	**c**	**d** ....
Organised by:	**e**	**f** ....
Apprenticeship:	**g**	**h** ....

	Barristers	*Solicitors*
Number in practice	5,367 (13% women) including 535 QCs.	47,906 (19.5% women).
Mode of organisation	Independent practitioners practising from sets of chambers.	Sole practitioners or partnerships. Can be employed often by industry or local authorities.
Number of firms	London: 226 Chambers. Provinces: 112 Chambers.	7,833 (2,744 sole practitioners).
Professional body	Bar Council (restructured 1987).	The Law Society.
Professional discipline	Professional Conduct Committee.	Professional Purposes Department. The Lay Observer (the solicitors' ombudsman) also investigates complaints.
Relationship with client	Through solicitor, cab-rank principle.[8] Cannot sue for fees.	Contractual.
Professional liability	No liability in negligence in respect of advocacy in court (*Rondel* v. *Worsley* [1969] 1 AC 191). May be liable in negligence in respect of work outside court (*Saif Ali* v. *Sydney Mitchell & Co.* [1980] AC 198).	Liable in contract and tort to clients (*Midland Bank Trust Co. Ltd* v *Hett, Stubbs & Kemp* [1979] Ch 384). May be liable to others affected by their negligent professional actions (*Ross* v. *Caunters* [1980] Ch 297).
Professional etiquette[9]	No advertising. Wig[10] and gown[11] in court. Must join an Inn of Court.	Limited advertising (Publicity Code 1987). Gown in courts (except magistrates' court) but no wig.

Johnson and Pannett, *SWOT A Level Law* (Blackstone Press 1988), p. 55.

Text notes:
8 must take next client waiting as taxi (cab) drivers do
9 rules of behaviour
10 false hair
11 long, black robe

Comprehension check

2 Decide whether the following statements are true or false, based on the above table; correct the false statements.

- **a** There are more female solicitors than female barristers.
- **b** Solicitors are not allowed to advertise.
- **c** Solicitors always work in groups.
- **d** Barristers are only liable to clients out of court.
- **e** Both barristers and solicitors wear gowns in court.

Although at first the differences between the two branches of the profession may appear to be considerable, closer examination will show that these differences are more structural than practical, that is there is no **kind** of work which is not undertaken by both barristers and solicitors.

The monopolies and restrictive practices which have for so long regulated the legal profession have evolved to maintain professional standards and protect the public interest; it is argued that the nature of the work done by lawyers sets them apart from the competitive rules of the market-place and justifies the restrictions and controls. These arguments are summarised in the following extract.

> Professions place great value on their independence. The need to be independent of the state and of other institutions is seen as vital if the profession is to act in a disinterested and objective manner in its dealings with clients. The argument is that only in this way can it act in the best interests of the client. The profession's concern with the public interest is also seen as justifying monopolies and restrictive practices. Membership of the professional group entitles the lawyer to the exclusive right to deliver certain services, and justifies the governing body of the profession in applying restrictive practices in the manner in which the services are offered. This has tended to reduce competition among professionals, who all in theory offer the same service. This reinforces the exclusivity of the professions, whose systems of entry and training often involve a process of socialisation ensuring that members appreciate the importance of the customs, traditions, etiquette and rules of their profession before admission to it.
>
> White, *The Administration of Justice* (Blackwell 1985), p. 229.

Vocabulary

3 This extract stresses the separate nature of lawyers and their work. There are at least five adjectives in the extract which reflect this separateness. Complete the table below with the appropriate forms of these words. Use a dictionary if necessary.

Adjective	*Noun*
dis	. . . .
ex	. . . .
in	. . . .
ob	. . . .
res	×

The assertion that the public interest is best served by the present structure of the legal profession has been increasingly challenged. The debate originally centred on the fusion of the two bodies but it has more recently switched to the removal of restrictive practices and monopolies. We will follow the movement towards reform in the next section.

6.1.1 Reform: from Benson to Mackay

In the past the status quo[12] has been supported by the governing bodies of both branches of the profession. In 1975 the Bar Council and the Law Society issued a joint statement, known as the Declaration of Bath,[13] to the effect that the public interest was best served by a divided legal profession. The issue was considered by the Royal Commission on Legal Services, the Benson Commission[14] (1979), which undertook a large-scale inquiry into the provision of legal services. The well-rehearsed[15] arguments for and against fusion and the Commission's response are contained in the next extract.

The suggestion is sometimes advanced that the professions of barrister and solicitor should be amalgamated[16] in order to reduce costs. It is true that some types of legal work now being done by the employment of both a barrister and a solicitor could be carried out just as efficiently and more cheaply by employing only one man. For instance, undefended divorce petitions could well be presented in court by a solicitor instead of a barrister having the sole right of audience as at present. It is sometimes suggested that if fusion were to take place, larger firms would develop, overhead[17] expenses could be reduced, more office machinery bought and costs to the client consequently reduced. On the other hand, some types of work demand the attention of specialists. In large firms there would still be general practitioners and specialists such as specialist company lawyers and specialist advocates who would handle difficult cases referred to them from within their own firm. The major disadvantage in taking specialist members of the Bar into large firms is that they would then cease to be available to other firms and their clients throughout the country. At present a solicitor may choose any barrister to advise his client or to appear for the client in court. With the current tendency to increasing technicality in the law there is a greater need for more specialists readily available to the public seeking their advice through a solicitor whose job is to deal with such matters as he can, and in other cases seek counsel's opinion. Also, as an argument against fusion it may be said that one person who meets the client and prepares the evidence becomes so personally involved that he loses the detachment which is necessary to the conduct of cases, particularly lengthy or difficult ones, in court. A comparatively small Bar engenders[18] a trust between Bar and Bench[19] which in turn enables many cases to be accelerated and in most countries where the profession is fused this valuable confidence does not exist. Complete amalgamation would have the effect of making every lawyer competent to act as advocate in all courts. However, the strength of traditional ideas, both at the bar and among solicitors, makes amalgamation a remote possibility.

The Benson Report of 1979 (the Royal Commission on Legal Services) noted the following criticisms of a split profession: (i) inefficiency, in that it encourages failures in communication and inadequate instructions by solicitors to barristers; (ii) delay; (iii) lack of time for preparation if a barrister is unable to take a brief[20] and it has to be reallocated to another barrister; (iv) undermining of clients' confidence because of barristers' perceived "detachment"; and (v) the employment of two people instead of one increases the cost of legal representation. The Report concluded, however, that fusion was against the public interest, principally because it was felt that fusion would cause a serious fall in the quality of both advocacy and the consequent judicial decisions. It was also thought that fusion would lead to a concentration of large firms who would provide a comprehensive legal service in the wealthier neighbourhoods but as this would correspondingly diminish the provision of legal services in the poorer areas, smaller towns and rural areas, the public's freedom of choice would be adversely affected. It was further thought that fusion would disperse the available specialist service at a time when there is likely to be an increasing need for specialisation and that, on balance, fusion would not result in a saving in cost. Benson saw the objects of a two branch profession as being: (i) to ensure, through the barristers' right of audience rule, that advocacy in important matters is practised by specialists; and (ii) through the access via a solicitor rule, to free barristers from distraction and to encourage the sifting out by solicitors of irrelevant facts.

Sim and Scott, *A Level Law* (Butterworths 1984), pp. 111–12.

Text notes:

12 the existing situation
13 a town in Somerset
14 such commissions and the subsequent reports are named after the chairperson of the individual commission – in this case Lord Benson
15 often repeated
16 combined
17 expenses for running a business, e.g. rent, heating
18 creates
19 i.e. the judges
20 background and instructions for a case

Comprehension check and notemaking

4 List the arguments using the outline below for and against fusion and separation which are mentioned in the extract above. Notice 'signpost' phrases which show the direction a sentence is taking (e.g. 'for instance' (1.5) signposts an example, 'on the other hand' (1.10) indicates a contrast.

Declaration of Bath

Arguments for fusion:

1. It is true that . . . .
   e.g. . . . .
2. . . . .

Arguments against fusion:

1. On the other hand the major disadvantage is that . . . .
2. Also . . . .

Benson report

Arguments against separation:

1. . . . .
2. . . . .
3. . . . .
4. . . . .
5. . . . .

Arguments against fusion (i.e. for separation):

1. However . . . .
2. Also . . . .
3. Further . . . .
4. . . . .

Benson's arguments for separation:

1. . . . .
2. . . . .

Although the Benson Report was criticised by many it is unlikely that the fusion of the legal profession will take place in the foreseeable future.

However, two further issues[21] examined by the Commission have continued to receive widespread attention and these have lead to a break in the earlier consensus between the Bar Council and the Law Society. The first is the solicitors' monopoly on conveyancing. Conveyancing is the legal process of buying and selling property. Since 1804 it has been a criminal offence for any person other than a solicitor to undertake this work for gain. Conveyancing has become an important part of a solicitor's work providing over half the income of the average solicitor's practice.

The continuation of this monopoly was supported by a 10 to 5 majority of the Benson Committee. Given the serious financial consequences which could result from a faulty conveyancing transaction it was accepted that conveyancing should be carried out only by a fully qualified solicitor backed by insurance. There is no doubt that this guarantee of high professional standards is in the public interest, but equally it is in the public interest that the service should be available at the minimum cost. The argument against the solicitors' monopoly is that it limits competition and reduces the consumer's choice. This monopoly was removed by the Administration of Justice Act 1985. This Act allowed the work to be carried out by licensed conveyancers under the control of a Council of Licensed Conveyancers. The Council is responsible for the maintenance of standards whilst the availability of licensed conveyancers should increase choice and competition and benefit the consumer.

This prospective loss of business galvanised the Law Society into reassessing old practices and examining new ways of promoting the services of solicitors. The ban on solicitors advertising their services was partially lifted and the possibility of multi-disciplinary partnerships debated. This would enable solicitors to enter into partnership with other professionals such as accountants and estate agents. This quest for new avenues of business has led to the greatest point of controversy between barristers and solicitors – the barristers' monopoly of rights of audience. The Law Society argued that solicitors' rights of audience should be extended to the higher courts. This argument had been rejected by the Benson Commission but by a bare[22] 8 to 7 majority. The debate is outlined in the following extract.

Text notes:
21 try to identify these as you read on
22 only just adequate

In recent years, the Law Society has sought publicly to campaign for greater rights of audience. The irritation this has sparked off in the Bar has led to the dispute being termed 'the Bar Wars'. A significant increase in solicitors' rights of audience would call into question the whole status of the Bar as a separate profession . . . in 1986, the issue was considered by the courts in *Abse* v. *Smith* [1986] QB 536. A libel action had been settled out of court. A solicitor had drafted a statement for the court and an apology for the libel. The solicitor sought leave to read out the formal statement to the court rather than engage a barrister to do it. The issue went on appeal to the Court of Appeal. The Court of Appeal concluded that each senior court (i.e., High Court and above) has an inherent power to regulate its own proceedings. Thus each court can determine the extent to which it would derogate from the Bar's exclusive rights of audience. It was a question of weighing up the different public interests involved. On the one hand there is a public interest in having a small group of specialised advocates. On the other, there is the public interest in ensuring their availability and that their costs will not prevent anyone from obtaining their services. The Court of Appeal refused to alter the High Court's decision that the general practice was for barristers to be given exclusive rights of audience in the High Court even in respect of the reading out of formal statements to the court.

The arguments over rights of audience centre on the following issues:

(a) Quality. Both the Benson Commission and the Court of Appeal in *Abse* v. *Smith* laid stress on the need to maintain high standards of advocacy skill. They felt that the best guarantee of this was to maintain an exclusive group of advocates through the maintenance of a separate Bar. There are two arguments against this. Firstly, it is difficult to see why advocacy standards matter less in the lower courts since there appears to be no need to maintain the Bar's monopoly there. Secondly, if solicitors were given rights of audience, advocacy training would presumably become part of a solicitor's education programme.

(b) Detachment. Barristers cannot be approached by clients direct. A solicitor who has advised the client to go to court will prepare a brief for the barrister and negotiate a fee with his clerk. Two advantages are claimed for this system. First, the barrister is in a better position to appraise objectively the client's chances of success. Secondly, it makes it clear that a barrister's primary duty is to the court. Against this, it may be said that a barrister's detached objectivity can be seen by the client as lack of concern. The arguments in favour of the present system are somewhat undermined by the fact that the Bar has recently proposed allowing direct access to barristers in retaliation for the solicitors' campaign for greater rights of audience.

(c) Competition. The argument is that greater competition would give the consumer greater choice. Against this, it is said that the 'cab-rank' principle whereby a barrister has a duty to accept a client if he or she is available for work ensures a free choice for clients, even though of course they can only approach the barrister through a solicitor. In fact the issue is more complex than either of these positions. At present, most firms of solicitors obtain barristers from only two or three sets of chambers and do not normally range across the whole market. If solicitors were to be given greater rights of audience, many firms would increase their 'in-house' litigation departments, so that if a client's problems could not be resolved without recourse to the courts, the client would simply be represented by another solicitor of the same firm.

(d) Cost. Competition should act to bring costs down. It already seems to have had that effect on conveyancing charges. Benson, however, felt that solicitors might be unable to supply advocacy services as cheaply as barristers. Bar fees include about 30 per cent for overheads, whilst solicitors' overheads are roughly 70 per cent of their fees.

Johnson and Pannett, *SWOT A Level Law* (Blackstone Press 1988), pp. 57–9.

Oral work

5 Using the headings given in the extract above, write notes on the arguments for and against giving solicitors rights of audience in the senior courts. If you can, work with a partner and take it in turns to give an oral presentation of the pros and cons.

The latest stage in this debate came in the form of the Courts and Legal Services Bill (now the Courts and Legal Services Act 1990) published by the Lord Chancellor, Lord Mackay, in December 1989. The Bill was preceded by a Green Paper which put forward the government's proposals for reforming the legal profession. These proposals were:

1 Rights of audience in all courts would be open to both barristers and solicitors through a two-tier system of certification.
2 Solicitors holding a full advocacy certificate would qualify as judges in the higher courts.
3 Banks and building societies would be free to undertake conveyancing and so offer a 'one-stop' mortgage[23] and conveyancing service.
4 Restrictions would be lifted on lawyers taking cases on a 'no win, no fee' basis (contingency fees).

The Green Paper was generally welcomed by the Law Society and consumers' associations but vigorously attacked by the Bar and the judiciary. The latter[24] feared that the licensing system would give government control over the appointment of advocates and that the extension of rights of audience would lead to the demise[25] of the independent Bar.

The Courts and Legal Services Bill was modified to meet some of these criticisms. The article which follows provides an analysis of the Bill's main provisions. As you read it make a note of the ways in which you think the Bill will benefit the public interest under the following headings:

1 Will it increase access to legal services?
2 Will it reduce charges?
3 Will it improve the quality of legal services?

Text notes:
23 effectively the money lent to buy a house
24 refers to the judiciary
25 legal term for death

The bill to reform the legal profession and abolish barristers' monopoly rights in the higher courts will pave the way for solicitors to appear in any court, up to the House of Lords.

Lord Mackay, the Lord Chancellor, described the Courts and Legal Services Bill, which was published yesterday, as a "vital part of the government's overall strategy to improve the administration of justice".

The bill also incorporates proposals from the Lord Chancellor's Civil Justice Review, which recommended an overhaul of civil court procedure to speed up and simplify cases and make litigation cheaper.

The central plank of the proposals is to give the county court the power to deal with substantial numbers of cases, particularly injury cases, reserving the High Court for complex and specialist cases. The county court will be able to grant all the remedies now available in the High Court.

The bill's most contentious provision, which has polarised the profession's two branches, sets up a framework for solicitors to appear in the higher courts, now the barrister's preserve. Rules are to be drawn up by the Law Society, subject to approval by the Lord Chancellor and four senior judges.

Lord Mackay conceded that the judges should have a say in approving the rules for solicitors advocated after his original, more radical, green paper proposals drew unprecedented public criticism from the judiciary.

Solicitors feared the judges' veto might result in rules limiting their new rights, but the bill lays down a tight framework which will restrict the room for manoeuvre.

In approving the rules, the Lord Chancellor and the judges will have to take advice from a new lay[26]-dominated Advisory Committee on Legal Education and Conduct, chaired by a senior judge. The other members will be: two barristers, two solicitors, two law teachers and eight lay members.

Solicitors who gain rights to appear in the High Court will be eligible for High Court judgeships, as will circuit judges who were formerly solicitors.

The bill will also remove the statutory ban which prevents lawyers taking cases on a "no-win, no-fee" basis. Lawyer will not be able to take an American-style slice of the damages if successful, but they will be able to ask for an extra percentage on top of their normal costs, with a maximum to be fixed by the Lord Chancellor.

Banks, building societies, and insurance companies will be allowed to offer homebuyers a "one-stop" service including conveyancing, subject to safeguards against unfair competition and conflicts of interest.

The Lord Chancellor originally intended that lenders should be self-regulating, but since publishing the white paper he has decided to set up a new Authorised Conveyancing Practitioners' Board, with consumer representatives, to police[27] lenders offering conveyancing services. A conveyancing appeals tribunal will be set up to hear appeals against the decisions of the board.

Also new is the provision for a Conveyancing Ombudsman[28] to investigate complaints against lenders doing conveyancing.

The bill also creates a Legal Services Ombudsman to oversee complaints procedures against solicitors and barristers. The ombudsman will have power to recommend that a lawyer or professional body pay compensation, but not to compel payment.

The Law Society will have powers to suspend a solicitor convicted of a serious crime from practice before taking disciplinary proceedings, and to intervene in the practices of solicitors who are incapacitated or have abandoned their practices.

Solicitors will lose their monopoly on applying for grants of probate[29] to deal with wills.[30] Banks, building societies and insurance companies will be able to apply for probate if they have a proper complaints handling scheme.

The bill envisages that non-lawyers belonging to professional bodies may be given rights in future to appear in court and conduct litigation in some types of cases.

Magistrates will be given the same immunity from claims for cost or damages over their actions in court as judges now enjoy. Solicitors will have the same immunity as barristers from legal actions over the way they conduct cases in court. Judges will have powers to fine litigants for failing to turn up at court hearings. The Lord Chancellor will be given power to make rules allowing magistrates to disallow a solicitor's costs or order him to pay costs if he fails to act reasonably competently or expeditiously. The bill also allows the Lord Chancellor to make rules restricting the present automatic right of appeal to the Court of Appeal in some types of case. Lord Donaldson, Master of the Rolls, has suggested that family cases should require leave of the court before an appeal could be launched.

A spokesman for the Lord Chancellor's Department said there would be wide consultation before any restrictions on the right of appeal.

The statutory ban on solicitors entering into partnership with other professionals, such as accountants, is to be lifted. But the Law Society and the Bar are free to retain professional rules which prevent barristers and solicitors from practising in partnership with each other or with other professionals.

Dyer, 'Barrister's rights go in strategic reform', *The Guardian*, 8 December 1989.

Text notes:

26 not a member of the legal profession
27 i.e. to supervise
28 official investigator of complaints (from Swedish)
29 certificate granted by a court to the effect that a will has been proved and registered
30 statement of how one's money and possessions should be distributed after death

Let us now consider the answers to the pre-reading questions – these are provided in note form:

1 Will the Act increase access to legal services?
- Extended rights of audience to solicitors will increase number of advocates and increase consumer choice.
- Banks and building societies offering conveyancing will increase access to these services.
- 'No win, no fee' actions may make lawyers available to people who might otherwise be deterred by the cost of legal action.

2 Will the Act reduce charges?
- Increased number of advocates should make fees more competitive.
- Competition between solicitors, banks and building societies for conveyancing business should make fees more competitive.
- Solicitors' rights of audience in higher courts will reduce the need to employ both a barrister and a solicitor and reduce costs.

3 Will it improve the quality of legal services?
- Competition between solicitors, banks and building societies should improve conveyancing services.
- Authorised Conveyancing Practices Boards and the Conveyancing Ombudsman should ensure high quality of service from banks and building societies.
- Legal Services Ombudsman will strengthen complaints procedures against solicitors and barristers and safeguard standards.
- Magistrates' power to disallow costs to incompetent solicitors should protect clients.

The Courts and Legal Services Bill received the Royal Assent on 1 November 1990. We can see that there are many ways in which the Courts and Legal Services Act should benefit the consumer of legal services. Nevertheless there have been many critics of the Act and some doubts expressed over its efficacy. The Bar remains apprehensive over the impact that the loss of the monopoly of rights of audience in the higher courts will have on its members and the standard of advocacy; solicitors fear that the competition from banks and building societies will adversely affect small solicitors' practices. Also, concern has been expressed that senior judges who have publicly opposed the extension of rights of audience have a significant role in determining the rules which will govern its implementation. More generally, Lord Benson has stated that the Act does nothing to address the long-standing problems of the legal profession (Law Society, *Gazette*, February 1990). One thing is certainly clear – it will take some time before the impact of the Act can be accurately assessed.

Legal exercises

6 Why is a high standard of advocacy particularly important in the English legal system?

7 Contingency fee actions are very common in the United States of America. Why do you think they have been banned in England?

8 Outline the provisions of the Courts and Legal Services Act.

9 What impact could the following have on the legal profession?
 a Extended rights of audience to solicitors.
 b Banks and building societies offering conveyancing services.

10 Write a 750 word essay on the following question: 'Will the Courts and Legal Services Act provide a better legal service to the public?'

Question 10 asks you to compare the current standard of service offered by the legal profession to that which might be available after the provisions in the Courts and Legal Services Act are implemented. The analysis of the Act you completed earlier in this section will help you to answer the question. Read the following essay plan for guidance:

1 Analysis of the present system and its effect on the standard of service available.
2 The arguments for and against reform from the Benson report to the Courts and Legal Services Act; remember that the question does not ask about the fusion of the two sides of the profession but the removal of restrictive practices and monopolies.
3 Analysis of the possible good and bad effects of the Courts and Legal Services Act.

Research

11 Make a copy of the table on p.122 leaving the second and third columns blank. Complete these columns with details of the legal profession in your own country. If there is a single legal profession you will only need to complete one factual column.

6.1.2 Legal services outside the profession

The next passage looks at some alternative sources of legal services. After reading it make a list of these other sources and then find out if similar services are available in your country and, if so, which people make most use of them.

It is by no means uncommon for people to be overawed at the prospect of having to consult a solicitor. This feeling is often accompanied by the fact that solicitors have been reluctant to establish their practices in deprived urban areas because such areas do not provide them with their traditionally lucrative[31] commercial and property conveyancing work. The result of this situation is that there is an unmet need for legal services.

These shortcomings in the provision of legal services have been remedied in various ways. Citizens' Advice Bureaux provide, countrywide, publicly-funded free general legal advice and information. A large number of trades unions provide their members with legal advice and representation and newspapers, radio and television often provide help with individuals' legal problems. America provided the stimulus for the development in this country of neighbourhood law centres, which are intended to provide a legal service in poor areas of the country. In America in the 1960s a major feature of the war against poverty was the desire to make legal services more readily available to the poor. This was done largely through the setting up of Neighbourhood Law Firms in deprived areas. From this developed the idea in England of law centres, set up in areas traditionally ignored by solicitors' firms, staffed by salaried solicitors who have obtained a waiver from the Law Society of professional rules relating to such matters as advertising and the provision of services to clients free of charge. The first law centre in England was set up in North Kensington, London, in 1970.

Law centres are variously funded, some by the local authority, others by charitable foundations and some by the Lord Chancellor's Department. For the proponents[32] of law centres the inadequacy of their funding (some 2 per cent of the money spent on legal services by central and local government) and the lack of any coherent government policy is a cause for concern. Their main areas of work are housing, social security, employment, race relations, immigration and consumer problems; the kind of matters with which the poor are more likely to have to grapple than other citizens.

Benson recommended the extension of Citizens' Advice Bureaux and the improvement of legal services in deprived areas by the establishment of some Citizens' Law Centres which would be publicly funded and by the provision of interest free loans to solicitors who set up practice in such areas.

Sim and Scott, *A Level Law* (Butterworths 1984), pp. 112–13.

Text notes:
31 profitable
32 people who argue for ('pro') something

6.2 The state funding[33] of legal services

It is an important feature of a fair legal system that the law should be accessible to all and not denied to people who cannot afford to pay the costs of legal services. Consequently the state provides a system of funding which goes some way to providing access to legal services for those who could not otherwise afford it. These services are categorised as legal advice and assistance and legal aid. The former provides funding for all actions done by a solicitor short of[34] appearing in court; the latter includes court appearance. First, let us look at the legal advice and assistance scheme.

The Legal Advice and Assistance Act 1972 . . . set up a scheme whereby any person could visit a participating solicitor and, providing that the person's finances came within the limits, the solicitor could provide £25 worth of work, including the giving of advice, writing of letters and the drafting of documents. This figure has been raised to £50, or £90 for undefended divorce cases, although it can be extended with permission from the local legal aid office. The Legal Aid Act 1979 gave the Lord Chancellor power to order that the scheme could cover representation in certain cases. This 'assistance by way of representation' (ABWOR) is commonly found in domestic cases in magistrates' courts and also applies to mental health review tribunals and prison disciplinary cases. It is designed to facilitate and expedite the funding of representation in relatively simple cases. It is useful as far as it goes, but its critics say it does not go far enough and would have to be extended to far more cases to make any real impact.

The legal advice and assistance scheme – known as 'the green form scheme' because of the colour of the form – does not have a 'merits' test as required for legal aid. If the solicitor agrees to deal with the problem, the only remaining question is the client's financial state. The 'means test'[35] applies to both disposable income and disposable capital. The word 'disposable' indicates the amount remaining after deductions have been made for items like tax, national insurance, allowances for dependants (income), and house, furniture, clothes and tools of trade (capital) . . .

The Royal Commission on Legal Services considered that everyone should be entitled to half an hour's free legal advice for the purpose of diagnosing the problem. The solicitor should then be able to perform up to four hours' work without obtaining permission from the legal aid office. In fact,[36] The Law Society has operated a scheme for several years, known as 'The Fixed-Fee Scheme', whereby solicitors can agree to give half an hour's advice for a payment of £5. This scheme, which is not widely known about, is clearly designed to attract potential clients for future business.

The main problem with the green form scheme can be seen in its usage. It was envisaged on its introduction in 1973 that the scheme would bring into solicitors' offices a whole new range of work, particularly in the area of welfare law. In fact, about half the cases involve matrimonial disputes and about a further fifth involve crime. Only about two per cent of cases involve problems which would be dealt with in tribunals and about five per cent of cases concern landlord and tenant disputes. This suggests that many people with everyday problems are still not visiting solicitors. Maybe it is their image that is the problem, or maybe it is the lack of publicity about the scheme. Restrictions on solicitors' advertising are slowly being removed by The Law Society but there is still a considerable way to go.

Dugdale *et al.*, *A Level Law* (Butterworths 1988), pp. 147–8.

Text notes:
33 provision of money
34 except for
35 assessment of income and outgoings to see if financial assistance is needed
36 a signpost to introduce a contrast

Comprehension check

12 a What sort of clients did the green form scheme expect to attract?
b What sort of cases did the scheme expect to attract?
c What two reasons are suggested for the failure of **b** above?

Despite the problem referred to in the extract, the green form scheme is seen as an invaluable means of access to legal advice: 'It occupies a central position in the provision of legal services. That cannot be stressed too strongly' (*New Law Journal*, 16 September 1989, p. 655). Nevertheless the scheme is under threat. Under the provisions of the Legal Aid Act 1988 the newly created Legal Aid Board, which is responsible for administering the system of legal aid and advice, was required 'as an early task' to consider ways in which certain advice work could be transferred from solicitors to advice agencies such as Citizens' Advice Bureaux. These agencies would be contracted to provide advice in certain areas such as welfare, housing and employment, and these would then be excluded from the green form scheme. It was argued that this proposal, if implemented, would reduce the points of access to legal advice, destroy the cooperation between advice agencies and local solicitors, place an unreasonable administrative burden upon the agencies and reduce the level of service offered to the consumer.

The first official report of the Legal Aid Board moved away from contracting out services to agencies and proposed instead a system of 'franchising'. A critical analysis of this proposal is contained in the following newspaper article:

> High Street solicitors, already fearing new competition for conveyancing work, now see threats to another of their staple sources of income – legal aid. Under a new proposal from the Government-appointed Legal Aid Board, only a small number of selected firms would be 'franchised' to give advice. According to both the Law Society and the Legal Action Group, access to the law will be reduced and consumers will be restricted in their choice of solicitor.
>
> At first sight, such comments are difficult to understand. Franchised firms would be able to do more work for the client than is at present possible under the legal aid scheme without prior authority from the Board. They would also receive more frequent payments on account. In return, the quality of their work would be monitored by the Board.
>
> The proposed system will introduce a new principle into the administration of legal aid. Legal aid solicitors have not, until now, been required to meet general standards about, for instance, their specialised expertise or the location and opening hours of their offices.
>
> When the legal aid scheme was set up in 1949 by the Law Society on the Labour Government's behalf, the Society, as befitted the solicitors' trade association, did nothing to alter the existing economic and business structure of the profession. Legal aid was simply supplied through the existing network of private solicitors' firms which had been created to serve a very different property-owning and business clientele from that which was meant to be reached by the new scheme. In practice, it made little difference that legal aid fees came out of public money.
>
> Franchising could change all that. It is a step towards a system which, in the words of the Legal Aid Board, 'has quality assurance built into it'. Another attraction is that it could reduce the bureaucracy which bedevils legal aid both centrally and in the solicitor's offices.
>
> At present each case has to be scrutinised to ensure that money is properly spent. Monitoring the quality and efficiency of selected legal aid practices could allow the Legal Aid Board to save some of the cost of examining individual cases while leading to a better and quicker service for the client.
>
> In addition, scarce resources could be concentrated on the firms which are committed to doing a large amount of legal aid work. Most firms do some, but most do very little – less than would keep one solicitor in the office fully occupied. That is understandable when, compared to other work, legal aid pays very badly.
>
> Providing faster and larger payments on account would make a great deal of difference to the firm whose main income is £100,000 a year from the legal aid fund, but would do little for the firm receiving £1,000 a year or less and which is more interested in developing its commercial conveyancing.
>
> As long as the Law Society was in charge of legal aid, it refused to countenance any such discrimination between its members. The Legal Aid Board which took over on April 1 this year suffers from no such inhibitions. Franchising, like many of the proposals in the recent White Paper on changes in the legal profession, is based on ideas which were first put forward more than ten years ago by reformers who were mostly on the left. However, franchising is now proposed in circumstances which suggest that cutting

public expenditure is a higher priority than improving or even maintaining the quality of the service.

Under the Board's original proposals all firms receiving £40,000 a year or more in legal aid fees would qualify for a franchise. The rest – three quarters of the estimated 11,500 offices at present offering help under the scheme – would not.

The £40,000 limit indicates that quantity rather than quality is the main concern of the Board. The proposal received wide criticism. No research had been done to ascertain whether the firms doing most legal aid work also do it best – or whether the rest do it worse.

The original criterion did not even measure commitment to legal aid. The firm with 40 partners grossing more than £40,000 is less committed to the scheme than the sole practitioner grossing £39,000. In many parts of the country there is not enough legal aid work. Most firms outside the inner cities would not have qualified for a franchise.

Last week in a meeting with interested organisations the Board announced that it had abandoned the crude £40,000 test – but it had not yet decided what the new selection criteria would be. Whatever they are, most firms doing legal aid work are unlikely to qualify. The Board says that they would be able to carry on as at present. But its consultation paper makes clear that that is only the case until the Board decides that franchised firms provide enough geographical coverage.

As for quality, the Board is unlikely to undertake much monitoring before or after selection. It is at present making staff redundant. The aim of the current exercise is to reduce administrative costs by cutting the number of legal aid outlets.

Finally, the franchising proposals are upside down. They apply only to that part of the legal aid scheme which pays for advice, the green form scheme. They do not affect those parts of the scheme providing representation in the courts, which are economically and structurally much more important. The indirect effects will be considerable.

That defect shows that the proposals are not the fruit of endeavours to improve the effectiveness of legal aid, but rather the burgeoning offspring of a political deal made betweeen the Lord Chancellor's Department and the Treasury in the days of Lord Hailsham. In 1985 he had to agree to an efficiency scrutiny of legal aid to get Treasury acceptance of his expenditure estimates. The scrutiny could not recommend measures to control criminal legal aid – the fastest growing area of expenditure – because that would damage what Lord Hailsham has always called his 'own' profession: the Bar.

Instead, the scrutiny suggested curbs on the green form scheme. When the Legal Aid Board was set up by the new Lord Chancellor, Lord Mackay, he passed the ball to them: among their first tasks was to consider possible exclusions from the green form scheme.

Hansen, 'A limiting franchise on giving legal aid', *The Guardian*, 22 September 1989.

Comprehension check

13 a List the advantages of 'franchising' mentioned by the writer in paragraphs 2–7.
b Why was the proposed £40,000 limit criticised?
c Why is geographical coverage important?
d What does the writer think is the Legal Aid Board's main aim?

The article highlights a general criticism of the Legal Aid Act 1988, described by the Law Society as 'an unimaginative cost cutting exercise'. The fear expressed by the critics is that the purpose of the Act is to cut costs and thereby reduce the level of available services. This criticism is directed not only at the proposals for reforming the green form scheme but also at the provision of legal aid. Let us now examine how this system works.

Legal aid in civil proceedings is available in actions in the county and higher courts and in most domestic proceedings in the magistrates' courts. It is not available in defamation and undefended divorce actions, nor in most tribunals. Its administration is under the control of the Legal Aid Board and performed through local and area committees. To qualify for civil legal aid an applicant must pass both a means test and a legal merits test. The means test, as with the green form scheme, considers the applicant's disposable income and disposable capital which must be within prescribed financial limits. These financial limits on eligibility are periodically reviewed by the Lord Chancellor. An applicant may receive completely free aid or be required to make a contribution or be refused. The legal merits test considers whether the applicant has reasonable grounds for being a party to the action. If both tests are passed a legal aid certificate is granted.

Criminal legal aid also comes under the control of the Legal Aid Board but it is administered by the courts. An application will usually be made to the magistrates' court where it will be dealt with by the magistrates' clerk. Under the Legal Aid Act 1988 the clerk now has the power to refuse legal aid as well as grant it. Prior to the Act only the magistrates could refuse legal aid. The applicant is again subject to means and merits tests, the latter being assessed 'in the interests of justice'. In determining this the 'competent authority' must take into account whether the applicant's liberty is at stake,[37] whether the case involves a substantial area of law, whether the applicant is disadvantaged through an inadequate knowledge of English or mental incapacity and whether the case involves the tracing and interviewing of witnesses. The merits test is presumed to be satisfied in charges of murder, when the prosecution appeals to the House of Lords and the accused is kept in custody.

In addition to legal aid most courts also operate a duty solicitor scheme which provides for a rota[38] of local solicitors to be present in magistrates' courts to advise defendants who are unrepresented.

Legal aid was described by the former Lord Chancellor, Lord Hailsham, as the fastest growing social service in the country. The total cost in 1986/7 increased fivefold on the 1979/80 cost to a figure exceeding £400,000,000. Yet during the period 1979 to 1989 it has been estimated that 14.79 million people have come out of eligibility[39] for legal aid. This is primarily because the financial limits for eligibility have not been raised to keep pace with inflation.[40] Critics argue that this means that only the very poor or the very rich now have access to legal services – the very poor because they qualify for legal aid and the very rich because they can afford to proceed on their own financial resources. A large proportion of the population fall between the two extremes – not poor enough to qualify for legal aid but with insufficient resources of their own to pay for the high costs of legal action.

In addition to this criticism the system is also seen to be under threat by the inadequate remuneration paid to solicitors for legal aid work. As a result an increasing number of practices are giving up legal aid work, particularly in criminal cases. The Legal Aid Act 1988 abolished the principle of fair remuneration for fair work which had been contained in earlier legal aid legislation. The Lord Chancellor has the power to fix payment for legal aid work and his perceived failure to provide adequate remuneration has prompted a hostile response from the legal profession.

There is no doubt that these financial restraints have made an inroad into the provision of legal services to those who cannot afford to pay but like all other social services there is a limit to the funds the state can provide. Finding the correct balance is inevitably a political decision determined by the priorities of the government of the day.

Text notes:
37 at risk
38 list of people and when they work
39 'eligible' means 'having the right qualifications'
40 economic term for a rise in prices and incomes

Comprehension check

14 What are the two results of financial restraints which are mentioned above?

Research

15 Find out the answers to the following questions:

- **a** Is there a system of legal assistance and legal aid in your country?
- **b** If so, how is it funded and when is it available? If not, is there a need for such a system and how great is that need?

Legal exercises

16 Distinguish between legal advice and assistance and legal aid.

17 How does the green form scheme operate? What is its purpose?

18 Mrs Phillips has been involved in a car accident caused by Mr Hunt's negligence. The damage to her car will cost about £1,250 to repair. Mr Hunt has offered to pay her £1,000 but Mrs Phillips wishes to sue him for the full £1,250. Mrs Phillips is unemployed and she wishes to know how she can receive free legal advice and financial help in taking her case to court.

19 M.V. Singh is an overseas student living in England. He has been charged with theft and wishes to apply for legal aid. What factors will be taken into account when determining his eligibility?

6.3 The unmet need for legal services

Central to our discussion in this chapter has been the need for adequate and appropriate legal services to which everyone has access. Undoubtedly the present system is imperfect but there is also a broader view of the subject.

This is outlined in the next extract. Two main points can be drawn from the extract; try and identify them as you read it.

> So far, we have considered the provision of legal services by the legal profession and the extent to which this is assisted by state funding in the form of the legal aid and advice schemes. Already it will have become apparent that the situation is unsatisfactory in several respects. The financial limits of legal aid and advice schemes and the high cost of lawyers means that large areas of the population are unable to use the services of solicitors. Even those who seek help do so[41] for a fairly narrow range of subjects, in particular divorce and crime. It seems there are many people with legal problems who are not obtaining any advice at all. This[42] is what is usually referred to as 'the unmet[43] need' for legal services.
>
> The phrase is not free from controversy: some people argue that it has no meaning. Nevertheless, Richard White in 1973 offered a number of examples which would seem to fall within it:[44]
>
> (a) a person does not realise that a problem is a legal one, so does not seek legal advice;
> (b) a person realises that a problem is a legal one but is unaware of the appropriate legal service or the entitlement to use it;
> (c) a person realises that a problem is a legal one and knows that a particular legal service will give advice, but does not approach it for some reason such as fear of expense or ignorance of the legal aid scheme;
> (d) a person realises that a problem is a legal one and wants legal advice but cannot find a developed legal service available.
>
> These problems cannot be solved in the same way. Problems (b) and (c) could be alleviated, if not eradicated, by an improvement in the provision of information. Problem (d) requires that lawyers or other agencies offering legal advice should offer a wider range of services. Problem (a) involves the difficulty of defining a 'legal problem'. For some people, a problem may not be worth a legal solution or attempting to solve at all. Anyone who buys a 'single' gramophone record in London and takes it hom to Bristol is unlikely to take any action if the record turns out to be faulty. But what about a compact disc bought in the local town centre? The impoverished student may rush back to the shop whereas the wealthy businessman may not bother. Most disputes allow for a legal solution, but for some people the need to pursue it is far greater than for others.
>
> Dugdale *et al.*, *A Level Law* (Butterworths 1988), pp. 154–5.

Text notes:
41 see question **20a** below
42 see question **20b** below
43 'to meet a need' means 'to satisfy that need'
44 see question **20c** below

Comprehension check

20 a Note 41: What is meant by 'so' here?
b Note 42: To what does 'this' refer here?
c Note 44: To what does 'it' refer here?

The two main points are:

1 Many people fail to use legal services through a lack of awareness of the legal system.

2 There is a need for an extension in the type of legal services which are currently offered.

Comprehension check

21 For which of (a), (b), (c) and (d) in the extract would each of these points be a solution?

These points are examined in more detail in the concluding extract below. In particular, the author addresses the issue of suiting the type of legal service to the legal problems involved.

It seems unlikely that there will be major changes in the predominantly adversarial style of dispute resolution in the foreseeable[45] future. If this is so, advice, assistance and representation are of considerable importance in helping litigants to cope with the system. Yet we have seen that there are enormous gaps in the provision of legal services in both the criminal and the civil process. In proceedings before magistrates' courts large numbers of defendants are unrepresented and alarmingly few defendants receive any legal help prior to charge or summons. For major civil claims matters are not quite as bad, though in debt cases debtors seem all[46] too readily to submit to the claims of creditors. In the areas of small claims and of tribunal adjudication which were designed for use without representation, there is inadequate assistance available and the dramatic differences in the success rates of represented and unrepresented litigants indicates a failure in the design of the system. The solution for these difficulties is the ready availability of advice and assistance, and, in many cases, also of representation. Such representation must be of a quality and price to match the dispute. For less complex matters the use of para-legal[47] workers is a real possibility. The legal aid scheme providing,[48] albeit[49] at lowish[50] rates of remuneration, expensive lawyers for litigants may not be the best solution to the problems of lack of assistance and representation. There is a need for a broader consideration of the means of delivering legal services which encompasses both the public and the private sectors and which does not ignore the important contribution of para-legals. At present the Law Society and the Bar seem to regard the non-professionally qualified as irrelevant in considering[51] policies for the delivery of legal services. The need for a more representative[52] body to oversee such policies is urgent. More public money needs to be spent on legal services. There is much merit in the argument for increased spending on law centres, but there is also a need for a salaried public litigation service. Such a service could be split into criminal and tribunals divisions. A salaried body of solicitors, barristers and para-legal workers could then be available to represent individuals with claims before criminal courts and a wide range of tribunals. Small claims are excluded because, with increased funding, lawyers and others working with consumer groups and in consumer advice centres could take on this work. A major contribution of increased use of para-legals is that the background and social composition of the providers of legal services is likely to be dramatically widened. The issue of the competence of para-legals would need to be addressed,[53] but just as the profession of legal executive has developed within the private sector, and will probably come of age[54] with the solicitors' loss of the conveyancing monopoly, there is no reason why para-legals should not develop an organisation similar to the Institute of Legal Executives with the ability to certificate[55] its members.

The law has become too complex, even when unnecessary mystification is removed, for all members of society to act for themselves in claims which reach the stage of formal adjudication. Where help is available, for many people it unfortunately tends to be too little and too late, except for serious criminal offences and major civil claims. For this reason more resources should be devoted to education about one's legal rights in schools and to the provision of effective advice and assistance at the earliest stages of claims. The concept of access to justice for all demands greater recognition of the need to inform individuals of their rights and of the choices available to them in securing enjoyment of those rights.

White, *The Administration of Justice* (Blackwell 1985), pp. 269–70.

Text notes:
45 i.e. the near future
46 much
47 similar to lawyers but with lower qualifications
48 which provides
49 although (in formal language)
50 rather low
51 when they consider
52 see question **22a** below
53 dealt with
54 become adult, i.e. be accepted as part of the legal system
55 a verb, meaning 'to license'

Comprehension check

22 a Note 52: Than what does the body need to be 'more representative'?

b On what evidence does the writer say that small claims and tribunal adjudication are badly designed?

c Why does the writer think that the 'background and social composition of the providers of legal services is likely to be dramatically widened'?

d Para-legals are proposed for work in (where?) . . . ., just as legal executives now work with (whom?) . . . .

23 Complete the notes below on 'problems' and 'solutions' which are mentioned in the extract above.

Problems:
1. Magistrates courts:
   a) . . . .
   b) . . . .
2. Major civil claims: . . . .
3. Small claims, tribunals: . . . .

Solutions:
1. . . . .
2. . . . .
3. . . . .
4. . . . .

Research

24 Find out the following information by visiting a local firm of lawyers which handles a wide range of legal problems, both civil and criminal:

a Which area of law is the one which most people consult the firm about?

b Do all sections of society consult them equally on **a**?
c What are the areas of law which the least number of people consult them on?
d What are the reasons for the failure of people to consult them on **c**?
e Does the firm offer a different type of service for different types of legal problems?

25 Devise a simple questionnaire which will enable you to obtain information on why people decide to consult a lawyer, in what circumstances have they consulted a lawyer and what factors would deter them from doing so. Circulate the questionnaire to 20–30 people and then write a 500 word report on the conclusions.

The following questions should form the basis of your questionnaire; add any other questions which you think are appropriate and would help you complete your report. Remember that the purpose of the questionnaire is to find out if and when people use legal services.

1. Have you ever consulted a lawyer?
2. If yes, what were your reasons for doing so? How did you choose which lawyer to consult?
3. If no, is it because:

   (a) You have not needed to do so?
   (b) You needed to but could not afford to do so?
   (c) You did not know how to choose one?
   (d) You were afraid to do so?

4. Have you consulted any person or body other than a lawyer for legal advice?
5. If yes – who?
6. On which of the following problems would you consult a lawyer?

   (a) divorce
   (b) conveyancing
   (c) employment
   (d) housing
   (e) social security
   (f) noisy neighbours.

Additional reading

Many textbooks will be out of date on the subject of the legal profession because of the Courts and Legal Services Act. Nevertheless Zander's *Cases and Materials on the English Legal System* (Weidenfeld & Nicholson) provides thought-provoking reading on the debate over the legal profession as does his *A Matter of Justice* (Tauris). The subject of legal aid is also comprehensively covered in both these books. *The English Legal Process* by Ingham (Blackstone) provides the most up-to-date account of legal aid with details of the Legal Aid Act 1988. *The Administration of Justice* by White (Blackwell), extracts from which are included in this chapter, is a very readable analysis of the wider social issues involved in the provision of legal services.

Revision 2: Legal knowledge and legal skills

Test your knowledge

Answer the following questions as briefly as possible.

1 Distinguish between courts of first instance and appellate courts.

2 Which of the following courts are courts of first instance and which appellate courts: **a** Court of Appeal? **b** House of Lords? **c** county courts? **d** Crown Courts? **e** the High Court? **f** magistrates' courts?

3 Name the division of the High Courts which adjudicates on disputes over wills.

4 Give the titles of the judges who will hear an appeal in the Civil Division of the Court of Appeal.

5 Prior to the Courts and Legal Services Act what was the financial limit on contract and tort actions which could be heard in the county courts?

6 Why are financial limits an arbitrary way of distinguishing between cases?

7 What was the original purpose of the county courts?

8 Why have they been criticised for failing to fulfil this purpose?

9 What is the title of the person who will hear cases in the small claims courts?

10 What are the two major criticisms of the system of civil justice?

11 How will the Courts and Legal Services Act change the jurisdiction of the civil courts?

12 What is the burden of proof in: **a** civil actions; **b** criminal actions?

13 Can a private individual bring a prosecution?

14 Which body was responsible for prosecutions before the creation of the CPS?

15 What limitations are placed on the jurisdication of tribunals?

16 Define hierarchical.

17 Which judges have the most authority?

18 In which court do puisne judges sit?

19 Distinguish between lay magistrates and stipendiary magistrates.

20 Do judges play an active role during the course of a trial?

21 Name two ways in which judges make law.

22 Does Lord Denning 'trust the judges'?

23 Does Professor Griffiths 'trust the judges'?

24 Which civil actions may be heard before a jury?

25 Who has issued guidelines on jury vetting?

26 Does the defence have a right to peremptory challenge of a potential juror?

27 Why might jurors dislike jury service?

28 What are 'shadow juries'?

29 What is the common purpose of the two branches of the legal profession?

30 What is the name of the case which is the authority for the fact that barristers are not liable to their clients in negligence whilst appearing in court?

31 How do professional bodies reinforce the exclusivity of their professions?

32 Why is the Benson Report so named?

33 In which case did the Court of Appeal confirm the power of the senior courts to decide who has rights of audience?

34 How has this power been changed by the Courts and Legal Services Act?

35 What was the reason for the solicitors' conveyancing monopoly?

36 Which statute regulates the state funding of legal services?

37 How did Lord Hailsham describe legal aid?

38 Why is it important to increase regularly the financial limits for eligibility for legal aid?

39 Define 'para-legals'.

40 Why does White advocate the increased use of para-legals?

Test your legal skills

41 In the case of *Rylands* v. *Fletcher* (1868) the defendants built a reservoir[1] on their land. The reservoir burst and flooded the plaintiff's property. The plaintiff sued to recover his losses. Read the extracts below from the judgment of Blackburn J. in the lower court and Lord Cairns in the House of Lords and answer **in your own words** the questions which follow. You will need to read the passage several times before you can answer the questions. There are two main issues in the judgments: **i** in what circumstances will the owner of land be under a duty to protect the owners of adjoining property,[2] and **ii** what is the duty which the law imposes on the landowner in the circumstances? Think about these issues as you read the judgments.

BLACKBURN J (reading the judgment of the Court) . . . The plaintiff, though free from all blame on his part, must bear the loss, unless he can establish that it was the consequence of some default for which the defendants are responsible.

The question of law, therefore, arises: What is the liability which the law casts upon a person who, like the defendants, lawfully brings on his land something which, though harmless while it remains there, will naturally do mischief if it escape out of his land? It is agreed on all hands that he must take care to keep in that which he has brought on the land, and keep it there in order that it may not escape and damage his neighbour's, but the question arises whether the duty which the law casts upon him under such circumstances is an absolute duty to keep it in at his peril, or is, as the majority of the Court of Exchequer have thought, merely a duty to take all reasonable and prudent precautions in order to keep it in, but no more. If the first be the law, the person who has brought on his land and kept there something dangerous, and failed to keep it in, is responsible for all the natural consequences of its escape. If the second be the limit of his duty, he would not be answerable except on proof of negligence, and consequently would not be answerable for escape arising from any latent defect which ordinary prudence and skill could not detect . . .

We think that the true rule of law is that the person who, for his own purposes, brings on his land, and collects and keeps there anything likely to do mischief if it escapes, must keep it in at his peril, and, if he does not do so, he is prima facie answerable for all the damage which is the natural consequence of its escape. He can excuse himself by showing that the escape was owing to the plaintiff's default, or, perhaps, that the escape was the consequence of vis major,[3] or the act of God; but, as nothing of this sort exists here, it is unnecessary to inquire what excuse would be sufficient. The general rule, as above stated, seems on principle just. The person whose grass or corn is eaten down by the escaped cattle of his neighbour, or whose mine is flooded by the water from his neighbour's reservoir, or whose cellar is invaded by the filth of his neighbour's privy, or whose habitation is made unhealthy by the fumes and noisome vapours of his neighbour's alkali works, is damnified without any fault of his own; and it seems but reasonable and just that the neighbour who has brought something on his own property which was not naturally there, harmless to others so long as it is confined to his own property, but which he knows will be mischievous if it gets on his neighbour's, should be obliged to make good the damage which ensues if he does not succeed in confining it to his own property. But for his act in bringing it there no mischief could have accrued, and it seems but just that he should at his peril keep it there, so that no mischief may accrue, or answer for the natural and anticipated consequences. On authority this, we think, is established to be the law, whether the thing so brought be beasts or water, or filth or stenches . . .

LORD CAIRNS LC: . . . The principles on which this case must be determined appear to me to be extremely simple. The defendants, treating them as the owners or occupiers of the close on which the reservoir was constructed, might lawfully have used the close for any purpose for which it might, in the ordinary course of the enjoyment of land, be used, and if, in what I may term the natural user of that land, there had been any accumulation of water, either on the surface or underground, and if by the operation of the laws of nature that accumulation of water had passed off into the close occupied by the plaintiff, the plaintiff could not have complained that that result had taken place. If he had desired to guard himself against it, it would have lain on him to have done so by leaving or by interposing some barrier between his close and the close of the defendants in order to have prevented that operation of the laws of nature.

As an illustration of that principle, I may refer to a case which was cited in the argument before your Lordships, *Smith v. Kenrick* in the Court of Common Pleas. On the other hand, if the defendants, not stopping at the natural use of their close, had desired to use it for any purpose which I may term a non-natural use, for the purpose of introducing into the close that which, in its natural condition, was not in or upon it – for the purpose of introducing water, either above or below ground, in quantities and in a manner not the result of any work or operation on or under the land, and if in consequence of their doing so, or in consequence of any imperfection in the mode of their doing so, the water came to escape and to pass off into the close of the plaintiff, then it appears to me that that which the defendants were doing they were doing at their own peril; and if in the course of their doing it the evil arose to which I have referred – the evil, namely, of the escape of the water, and its passing away to the close of the plaintiff and injuring the plaintiff – then for the consequence of that, in my opinion, the defendants would be liable . . .

These simple principles, if they are well founded, as it appears to me they are, really dispose of this case. The same result is arrived at on the principles referred to by Blackburn J in his judgment in the Court of Exchequer Chamber . . .

In that opinion, I must say, I entirely concur. Therefore, I have to move your Lordships that the judgment of the Court of Exchequer Chamber be affirmed, and that the present appeal be dismissed with costs.

Rylands v. *Fletcher* (1866) LR 1 Ex 265; (1868) LR 3 HL 330.

Text notes:

1 storage place for water
2 do Blackburn J and Lord Cairns agree on these details?
3 an irresistible force, e.g. storm, earthquake

---

a What are the three main features of the tort according to Blackburn J.?

b What additional requirement for liability was added by Lord Cairns?

c Discuss the following situations in the light of *Rylands* v. *Fletcher.* You should examine each situation carefully, looking to see whether the necessary circumstances for liability exist.

  i Fullblast plc own a factory which is used to reprocess chemical waste. One day the factory receives a delivery of some particularly dangerous chemical waste. Whilst the waste is being unloaded an explosion occurs which destroys the tanker and seriously injures the driver. The explosion does not damage any surrounding property.

  ii Percival owns a large country estate which he has turned into a wildlife park. The park is surrounded by a five metre high metal fence and is regularly patrolled by security guards. One night one of the lions gets free by digging a hole under the fence. The lion kills a valuable horse in the adjoining field which is owned by Henry.

  iii Christine owns a large garden adjoining Michael's farm. A large number of wildflowers grow in the garden and the seeds from these are blown on to Michael's property thereby reducing the value of his crops.

42 Section 1 of the Official Secrets Act 1911 states:

1. *Penalties for spying*
   (1) If any person for any purpose prejudicial to the interests or safety of the State –
      (a) approaches . . . or is in the neighbourhood of, or enters any prohibited place within the meaning of this Act; or

(b) makes any sketch, plan, model, or note which is calculated to be or might be or is intended to be directly or indirectly useful to an enemy; or

(c) obtains, [collects, records, or publishes,] or communicates to any other person . . . any sketch, model, article, or note, or other document or information which is calculated to be or might be or is intended to be directly or indirectly useful to an enemy;

he shall be guilty of felony . . .

a Bernie lives in Archester, a quiet country village. There is an airfield two miles from the village which is owned by the Ministry of Defence and used to train fighter pilots in low flying techniques. The noise of the aircraft is very loud and disturbs the peace of the village. Bernie and other angry residents of Archester decide to march to the airfield and protest against the noise by sitting on the ground in front of the aircraft to prevent them taking off. Bernie and the other demonstrators are arrested one mile from the airfield and charged under section 1 of the Official Secrets Act.

b Phil is an investigative journalist employed by the *Daily Splurge.* He is writing an article on the training of British fighter pilots and wants some photographs to accompany the article. He hires a helicopter and flies over the airfield near Archester taking photographs. The photographs and the article are published in the *Daily Splurge.* Phil has been charged under section 1 of the Official Secrets Act.

Remember that, when answering this type of question, you must carefully identify the various terms of the Act (in this case the offences) and apply these to the situations using your knowledge of the process of statutory interpretation.

7

Introduction to the law of contract

Summary

Legal content

7.1 Introduction to contract
7.2 Offer and acceptance
7.3 Supermarket sales and ticket machines
7.4 Communication of acceptance
Additional reading

Aim

To provide an introduction to a substantive area of civil law through an examination of offer and acceptance in the law of contract. Analytical skills will be developed by means of case studies and the application of legal skills to problem questions. Extracts from articles will provide a critical analysis of the law.

Language content

Vocabulary: negative adjective forms (in-, un-)
Oral function: asking for the full form of abbreviations
Study skills: recognising arguments and counter-arguments

7.1 Introduction to contract

Many people assume that a contract is only legally enforceable if it is in writing and signed by the parties to the contract. This is a mistaken belief: most of us during our daily lives enter into unwritten contracts which are as legally enforceable as the most complex written documents. Simple transactions such as the purchase of a bus ticket or a packet of frozen peas from a supermarket are enforceable agreements and governed by the rules of the law of contract. In this chapter we will be examining two of the primary rules, **offer** and **acceptance**, but before doing this you should have an understanding of the general nature of contracts. This is provided in the following text.

A contract is simply an agreement which can be enforced through the courts. This enigmatic definition needs expansion in two ways: what is meant by an agreement? What sort of agreements will the law enforce?

Underlying the notion of agreement is the idea that different people or groups, having[1] distinct, even contradictory objectives, reconcile their differences in a mutually[2] beneficial[3] arrangement which both sides believe to be binding and will treat as binding. The law treats agreement as the essential principle around which economic and social life is based. It is the means by which exchange relationships are supported. If you want my car you might take it by stealing or by force. If this were to be the main way in which goods are transferred, then society would soon break down. If, however, you have something I want, such as money in sufficient quantities, then we can talk business, and perhaps reach a mutually satisfying resolution of our differing requirements.

Some agreements involve virtually instantaneous exchange. In a butcher's shop, you give the butcher your money with one hand and take the meat with the other. In many other contexts, though, the transaction is extended over a longer period. For example, if a builder is employed to build a house, or a manufacturer has a continuing agreement to receive components from another manufacturer, one side may receive a benefit from the other well[4] before the other receives the corresponding benefit. In that case, there must be **reliance** on the **promise** of the other to perform his side of the bargain.[5]

A promise is an act whereby one person binds him or herself to do or refrain[6] from doing something in the future. Contracts usually consist of **mutual promises.** A promise creates for the **promisor** (the person making the promise) a future **obligation**. For the **promisee** (the person to whom the promise is made) it creates an **expectation** that the promise will be fulfilled. Furthermore, the promisee will often **rely** on the promise.

Consider the following example. Arthur promises Ben £10 if Ben digs his garden. The money is to be paid on completion of the job. While Ben is performing his part of the bargain, he will be **relying** on the promise (by digging the garden) and **expecting** a benefit (the £10). If Arthur breaks his promise, then there may be two views of what Ben has lost and needs to be compensated for: his efforts in reliance on the promise or the benefit he expected to gain. In contract damages are normally assessed by considering what benefit the injured party expected to receive from the contract breaker at the time the contract was made . . .

Although there may be a moral obligation to honour one's promises, English law has never gone so far as to enforce all promises. Enforcement through the courts depends on the **circumstances** of the promise, or its **nature and contents.**

English law recognises that a promise should be enforced within the circumstances of an exchange relationship, that is, where there are mutual promises given one for another. A gratuitous promise is not legally enforceable unless it is accompanied by special formalities. Thus, if I want to bind myself to give a certain sum of money, say to Oxfam,[7] with no corresponding promise from Oxfam, then that promise can only be enforced by Oxfam if it is made in the form of a deed. A deed is a promise signed, sealed, and delivered to the promisee.

Thus, apart from the special circumstances of a deed, a promise is only legally enforceable if there is an act or promise given in return for it. This element of **reciprocity**, which is the primary criterion of promissory liability, is known as **consideration . . .**

A promise involves taking on a commitment to act in a certain way. By an act of his own will, the promisor binds himself to a future course of behaviour. The obligation is taken on **voluntarily.** If the promisor breaks his promise than he may be liable because he has assumed the obligation. This can be contrasted with liability in tort . . . where the obligation (e.g. not to injure others negligently) is imposed **objectively** regardless of the will of the person committing the tort (known as a **tort feasor**). If I agree to dig someone's garden for £10 and fail to do the job, then I am liable because I have broken an undertaking voluntarily assumed. If I negligently run someone over in my car, then I am liable because **the law** imposes a duty on me to take care. English contract law recognises the private autonomy of contracting parties to make their own legal arrangements.

Johnson, *Contract Law in Action* (Oxford Polytechnic 1986), pp. 1–3.

Text notes:
1 who have
2 each to the other, reciprocal
3 having a good effect
4 i.e. a considerable time
5 agreement to exchange
6 not to do something
7 a charitable organisation

Comprehension check

1 The following definitions and descriptions are used in the extract above. Find the items which are defined or described:

- **a** An act whereby one person binds him or herself to do or refrain from doing something in the future.
- **b** The person who does the above.
- **c** A relationship where mutual promises are given one for another.
- **d** The element of reciprocity.
- **e** The means by which exchange relationships are supported.
- **f** An agreement which can be enforced through the courts.
- **g** The person to whom a promise is made.
- **h** A promise which is signed, sealed and delivered to the promisee.
- **i** A person committing a tort.

Legal exercises

2 Which of the following agreements will be enforced by the courts?

- **a** John agrees to sell his car to Peter for £500.
- **b** John agrees, as a favour, to take Peter on holiday with him.
- **c** John agrees to give Peter a valuable painting and signs a deed to this effect which is sealed and delivered to Peter.

3 Gill agrees to sell Bryan an antique table for £250. Before the sale is completed Gill discovered that the table is worth £3,000. She refuses to deliver the table to Bryan. What damages could Bryan claim and on what basis would they be assessed?

4 Distinguish between liability in tort and liability in contract.

7.2 Offer and acceptance

We have seen that agreement between the parties is an essential ingredient of contract. This agreement takes the form of an offer made by the offeror and acceptance of the offer by the offeree. An offer has been defined as 'an expression of willingness to contract on certain terms made with the intention that it shall be binding as soon as it is accepted by the person to whom it is addressed' (Treitel, *The Law of Contract*, Stevens, 1987). An offer must be clear and contain the details of the contract; for example, if A asks B 'would you like to buy my car' and B replies 'yes', there is no contract because the offer did not include an essential detail, the price. The offeree may choose to accept or reject the offer but once it is accepted the contract is concluded and the parties are bound by its terms. An offer can be withdrawn or revoked before it has been accepted but not after that time.

The acceptance must be communicated to the offeror and exactly match the offer. Any deviation[8] from the terms of the offer is called a counter-offer which the original offeror is then free to accept or reject. This is illustrated in the case of *Hyde* v. *Wrench* (1840) 3 Beav 334. The defendant offered to sell his farm for £1,000. The plaintiff offered to buy the farm for £950. This offer was rejected and the plaintiff then agreed to pay £1,000 and sought, unsuccessfully, to enforce the sale through the courts.

> *The Master of the Rolls [Lord Langdale].* Under the circumstances stated in this bill, I think there exists no valid binding contract between the parties for the purchase of the property. The Defendant offered to sell it for £1000, and if that had been at once unconditionally accepted, there would undoubtedly have been a perfect binding contract; instead of that, the Plaintiff made an offer of his own, to purchase the property for £950, and he thereby rejected the offer previously made by the Defendant. I think that it was not afterwards competent for him to revive the proposal of the Defendant, by tendering[9] an acceptance of it; and that, therefore, there exists no obligation of any sort between the parties . . .

Text notes:
8 moving away
9 offering

Comprehension check

5 What was the counter-offer in this case?

The importance of determining which part of the transaction constitutes the offer and which the acceptance rests on the fact that once the offer has been accepted the contract is concluded. If, after this point, one of the parties fails to perform his or her obligations, the other party may apply to the courts for a legal remedy. A failure to fulfil a contractual obligation is called a **breach of contract.**

In most simple transactions the offer and acceptance can be easily defined:

Peter to John: 'Will you buy my car for £500' – the offer.

John to Peter: 'Yes' – the acceptance.

But even in some relatively simple transactions the position is not so straightforward. Look at the facts of the case of *Harvey* v. *Facey* [1893] AC 552.

a Harvey telegraphs[10] Facey: 'Will you sell us Bumper Hall Pen? Telegraph lowest cash price.'
b Facey telegraphs Harvey: 'Lowest cash price to buy Bumper Hall Pen £900.'
c Harvey telegraphs Facey: 'We agree to buy Bumper Hall Pen at £900 asked by you.'

One analysis of this exchange of telegraphs could be that **b** was an offer to sell Bumper Hall Pen for £900 and that **c** was an acceptance of that offer. However, the court held that **b** was merely a statement of the price; **c** was an offer to buy Bumper Hall Pen which Facey was free to accept or reject.

A pre-contractual statement such as **b** is called an **invitation to treat**.[11] It is very important to distinguish between an offer and invitation to treat but this becomes more difficult in prolonged and complex negotiations. Let us examine *Gibson* v. *Manchester City Council* [1979] 1 All ER 972; [1979] 1 WLR 294. In this case the courts were asked to decide, on the basis of an exchange of correspondence, whether a contract had been concluded between the plaintiff and the defendants.

G was a council house tenant[12] and in 1970 the council sent him details of a scheme for the sale of council houses to existing tenants. G responded by sending the necessary £3 administration fee and the completed application form. The council replied: *'The corporation may be prepared to sell the house to you at the purchase price of £2,725 less 20 per cent £2,180.'* The second paragraph of the letter then gave details of mortgage arrangements and stated, 'This letter should not be regarded as a firm offer of a mortgage. *If you would like to make a formal application to buy your council house, please complete the enclosed application form and return it to me as soon as possible.'* G completed and returned the form and requested that the purchase price be reduced to take account of the cost of repairs. The council replied that they would take account of these costs when setting the purchase price. G responded, 'In view of your remarks I would be obliged if you will carry on with the purchase as per my application already in your possession.'

At this stage in the transactions there was a local election and the new Labour[13] council refused to sell any more council houses except when it was legally bound to do so. G applied to the courts for an order of **specific performance** (this is an equitable remedy which requires one party to a contract to perform his or her contractual obligations). The question for determination was whether a binding contract had been concluded.

Comprehension check

6 Before reading the judgment it would be useful for you to tabulate the negotiations between the parties in the way used on p.151 for *Harvey* v. *Facey*. Given that contracts are based on agreement, do you think that there was agreement between Gibson and the council over the sale of the house? Write down your answer in note form and then compare it the judgment below.

G was successful at first instance and on appeal by the council to the Court of Appeal. Lord Denning took the view that the case could not be determined by the conventional analysis of offer and acceptance; it was necessary to 'look at the correspondence as a whole and at the conduct of the parties and see whether the parties had come to an agreement on everything that was material'.[14] On appeal, the House of Lords unanimously[15] reversed the decision. As you read Lord Diplock's judgment note the way in which he analyses the conduct of the parties in order to determine whether there is agreement between them. In particular you should be aware that he is assessing their intentions objectively, that is he is considering how their actions would be interpreted by the disinterested[16] observer and not by the subjective views of the parties involved.

Text notes:
10 sent a telegram
11 to negotiate (in this context)
12 person renting property
13 social democratic political party
14 important
15 with all agreeing
16 not influenced by personal feelings (cf. uninterested)

My Lords, there may be certain types of contract, though I think they are exceptional, which do not fit easily into the normal analysis of a contract as being constituted by offer and acceptance; but a contract alleged to have been made by an exchange of correspondence between the parties in which the successive communications other than[17] the first are in reply to one another is not one of these. I can see no reason in the instant case for departing from the conventional approach of looking at the handful of documents relied on as constituting the contract sued on and seeing whether on their true construction there is to be found in them a contractual offer by the council to sell the house to Mr. Gibson and an acceptance of that offer by Mr. Gibson. I venture to think that it was by departing from this conventional approach that the majority of the Court of Appeal was led into error . . .

My Lords, the words I have italicised, [see italicised words in statement of facts, above, p. 152] seem to me, as they seemed to Geoffrey Lane L.J.,[18] to make it quite impossible to construe[19] this letter as a contractual offer capable of being converted into a legally enforceable open contract for the sale of land by Mr. Gibson's written acceptance of it. The words "may be prepared to sell" are fatal to this; so is the invitation, not, it is to be noted, to accept the offer, but "to make formal application to buy" on the enclosed application form. It is, to quote Geoffrey Lane L.J., a letter setting out the financial terms on which it may be the council would be prepared to consider a sale and purchase in due course [20]

Both Ormrod L.J. and the county court judge, in reaching the conclusion that this letter was a firm offer to sell the freehold interest in the house for £2,180, attached importance to the fact that the second paragraph, dealing with the financial details of the mortgage of which Mr. Gibson had asked for particulars, stated expressly, "This letter should not be regarded as a firm offer of a mortgage." The necessary implication from this, it is suggested, is that the first paragraph of the letter *is* to be regarded as a firm offer to sell despite the fact that this is plainly inconsistent with the express language of that paragraph. My Lords, with great respect, this surely must be fallacious.[21] If the final sentence had been omitted the wording of the second paragraph, unlike that of the first, with its use of the indicative mood in such expressions as "the interest rate *will* change," might have been understood by council tenants to whom it was addressed as indicating a firm offer of a mortgage of the amount and on the terms for repayment stated if the Council were prepared to sell the house at the stated price. But whether or not this be[22] the explanation of the presence of the last sentence in the second paragraph, it cannot possibly affect the plain meaning of the words used in the first paragraph . . .

My Lords, the application form and letter of 18th March 1971 were relied on by Mr. Gibson as an unconditional acceptance of the council's offer to sell the house; but this cannot be so unless there was a contractual offer by the council available for acceptance, and, for the reason already given I am of opinion that there was none. It is unnecessary to consider whether the application form and Mr. Gibson's letters of the 5th and 18th March 1971 are capable of amounting to a contractual offer by him to purchase the freehold interest in the house at a price of £2,180 on the terms of an open contract, for[23] there is no suggestion that, even if it[24] were, it was ever accepted by the council.

Text notes:

17 except for
18 abbreviation for Lord Justice
19 explain
20 when the right time comes
21 based on error
22 the subjunctive (used in legal or archaic language after 'if' or 'whether')
23 because
24 see question **7e** below

Comprehension check

7 **a** Does Lord Diplock think Mr Gibson's case is an 'exceptional' one as described in lines 2–3?
b What did paragraph 1 of the council's letter deal with?
c What did paragraph 2 of the letter deal with?
d Why was the sentence 'this letter should not be regarded as a firm offer of a mortgage' included in the council's letter?
e Note 24: To what does 'it' refer?

You will see that Lord Diplock concluded that there was no contract between the parties because:

1 the council had made no contractual offer to sell the house; and
2 even if G's letter had constituted an offer to buy the property, the council had not accepted it.

In many other cases the point at issue[25] is not whether a contract exists but at what point during the transactions it was concluded. We will examine some of these situations in the following case studies but you should do the exercises below before continuing.

Text note:

25 in dispute

Legal exercises

Questions 8 and 9 are problem questions. If you need to refresh your memory as to how to answer these questions refer back to the instructions provided in section 3.1.2, legal exercise 18, on p. 53.

8 Brian hears from a friend that Greg wishes to sell a set of silver spoons. Brian writes to Greg expressing an interest in buying the spoons and asking him how much he is willing to sell them for. Greg replies that he will sell the spoons to Brian for £500. Brian responds by saying that he wishes to buy the spoons for that sum. The next day Greg sells the spoons to Gordon for £550 Advise Brian.

9 Maureen wishes to employ a manager to run her hairdressing salon. David applies for the job and Maureen offers it to him at a salary of £12,000 per year. David replies that he is willing to take the job but at a salary of £13,000. Maureen cannot afford to pay the additional £1,000 so the next day David agrees to accept her original offer. In the meantime Maureen has decided that David is not really suitable for the position and has employed Michelle instead. David is seeking to enforce the contract and Maureen seeks your advice on whether she must employ him.

10 a Why was the county court the court of first instance in the *Gibson* case?

b In *Gibson* v. *Manchester City Council* why did Lord Diplock reject the argument that the first paragraph in the council's letter was a firm offer because it did not contain an express statement to the contrary as had the second paragraph which related to the mortgage? Do you think that his decision would have been different if the first paragraph had contained the words 'the corporation is prepared to sell the house to you'?

7.3 Supermarket sales and ticket machines

Some modern selling practices have created uncertainty over the point at which the sale takes place. The courts have determined this by analysing the transactions through the traditional process of invitation to treat, offer and acceptance.

The first case we will look at involves supermarket sales. In *Pharmaceutical Society of Great Britain* v. *Boots Cash Chemists* [1952] 2 QB 795; [1953] 1 QB 401, the defendant's shop operated a self-service system. The customers selected the goods from the shelves, placed them in the shopping basket and presented them to a cashier for payment. Section 18(1) of the Pharmacy and Poisons Act 1933 required that certain drugs should only be sold under the supervision of a registered pharmacist. In the defendant's shop a registered pharmacist, who had the power to refuse to provide the drugs, was stationed by the cashier's desk. The plaintiffs argued that the display of goods on the shelves was an offer which the customers accepted by taking the goods from the shelves and placing them in the shopping basket. The sale was completed at that stage and therefore not under the supervision of the registered pharmacist.

Per Somervell LJ:

> The point taken by the plaintiffs is this: it is said that the purchase is complete if and when a customer going round the shelves takes an article and puts it in the receptacle[26] which he or she is carrying, and that therefore, if that is right, when the customer comes to the pay desk, having completed the tour of the premises, the registered pharmacist, if so minded, has no power to say: "This drug ought not to be sold to this customer." Whether and in what circumstances he would have that power we need not inquire, but one can,

of course, see that there is a difference if supervision can only be exercised at a time when the contract is completed.

I agree with the Lord Chief Justice in everything that he said, but I will put the matter shortly in my own words. Whether the view contended for by the plaintiffs is a right view depends on what are the legal implications of this layout – the invitation to the customer. Is a contract to be regarded as being completed when the article is put into the receptacle, or is this to be regarded as a more organised way of doing what is done already in many types of shops – and a bookseller is perhaps the best example – namely, enabling customers to have free access to what is in the shop, to look at the different articles, and then, ultimately, having got the ones which they wish to buy, to come up to the assistant saying "I want this"? The assistant in 999 times out of 1,000 says: "That is all right," and the money passes and the transaction is completed. I agree with what the Lord Chief Justice has said, and with the reasons which he has given for his conclusion, that in the case of an ordinary shop, although goods are displayed and it is intended that customers should go and choose what they want, the contract is not completed until, the customer having indicated the articles which he needs, the shopkeeper, or someone on his behalf, accepts that offer. Then the contract is completed. I can see no reason at all, that being clearly the normal position, for drawing any different implication as a result of this layout.

The Lord Chief Justice, I think, expressed one of the most formidable difficulties in the way of the plaintiffs' contention when he pointed out that, if the plaintiffs are right, once an article has been placed in the receptacle, the customer himself is bound and would have no right, without paying for the first article, to substitute an article which he saw later of a similar kind and which he perhaps preferred. I can see no reason for implying from this self-service arrangement any implication other than that which the Lord Chief Justice found in it, namely, that it is a convenient method of enabling customers to see what there is and choose, and possibly put back and substitute, articles which they wish to have and then to go up to the cashier and offer to buy what they have so far chosen. On that conclusion the case fails, because it is admitted that there was supervision in the sense required by the Act and at the appropriate moment of time. For these reasons, in my opinion, the appeal should be dismissed.

Text note:
26 See question **11** below

Comprehension check

11 Note 26: Can you work out from the context what 'receptacle' means?

12 According to the extract above are the following statements true or false?

- **a** In a self-service shop a customer must pay for what is in his or her basket.
- **b** If the contract were completed when a customer picked up an article then the customer would have no right to change his or her mind at the time of paying.
- **c** A customer has the right to decide not to buy at the time of paying and the shopkeeper has the right to refuse to sell because the contract has not been completed at that time.

Although it is not clear from the judgment which action constitutes acceptance in this situation it is clear that the display of goods on the shelves in a supermarket is an invitation to treat and that the customer makes an offer by presenting the goods to the cashier. The cashier is then free to accept or reject the offer. There has been some criticism of this tabulation, of the negotiations; these are discussed in the next extract:

> The general rule is that a display of price-marked goods in a shop window is not an offer to sell goods but is an invitation to a customer to make an offer to buy. The same is true of an indication of the price at which petrol is to be sold at a filling station. Similarly, the display of goods on the shelves of a self-service shop is merely an invitation to treat; the customer makes an offer to buy when he carries the goods to the cashdesk, where the shopkeeper may accept or reject it. The general rule is well established, but the reasons given for it are not entirely convincing.
>
> One reason is that "a shop is a place for bargaining, not for compulsory sales." But the modern English shop, in which goods are generally bought on the shopkeeper's terms, is scarcely a place for bargaining; and even if the display of goods were an offer, any resulting sale would not be compulsory. The shopkeeper need not display goods which he does not want to sell. Another argument is that if the display were regarded as an offer, the shopkeeper might be exposed to many actions for damages if more customers purported to accept than his stock could satisfy. But the offer could be construed as one which automatically expired when the shopkeeper's stock was exhausted: this would probably be in keeping with the common expectation of both shopkeeper and customer. It has also been said that, if a display in a self-service shop were an offer, the undesirable result would follow that the customer would be bound to buy as soon as he picked up the goods to examine them. But if the display were an offer, it could be argued that there was no acceptance until the customer did some less equivocal[27] act, such as presenting the goods at the cashdesk. Finally, it may be asked whether the general rule does not sometimes cause injustice. Customers may be induced by a window display to believe that they will be able to buy goods at exceptionally low prices and to wait outside the shop for many hours in reliance on that belief. Is it right to allow the shopkeeper to go back on such a statement at the very moment when the customer demands the goods? Perhaps in exceptional cases window or shelf displays can be offers. The special terms of a display, or the circumstances in which it is made, may be evidence of intention to be bound ousting[28] the prima facie rule that the display is not an offer. But even if this is the case, the customer may still lose his bargain, since an offer can be withdrawn at any time before acceptance.
>
> Treitel, *The Law of Contract* (Stevens 1987), pp. 9–10.

Text notes:
27 having uncertain meaning
28 'to oust' means 'to push out', 'remove'

Comprehension check

13 List under **i** the arguments put forward for the rule that a display of goods is not an offer, and under **ii** Treitel's reasons for finding these arguments unsatisfactory.

a **i** shop = place for bargaining, not compulsory sales
ii . . . .
b **i** . . . .
ii . . . .
c **i** . . . .
ii . . . .

In the *Boots* case the point at issue was whether the shopkeeper could refuse to proceed with the transaction once the customer had presented the goods to the cashier. To decide this the court had to determine at what point the offer took place. In the case of *Thornton* v. *Shoe Lane Parking Ltd* [1971] 2 QB 163; [1971] 2 WLR 585, the question for the court was whether the defendants were protected from liability to the plaintiff by an exclusion notice displayed inside their premises.[29] To determine this the court had to decide at what point the contract had been concluded.

Exclusion notices or clauses are a common feature of many contracts. They seek to limit the liability of one party to the contract, for example an exclusion clause may place a financial limit on the damages to be paid for breach of contract. To be effective they must form part of the contract and, remembering that contracts are based on agreement, must be agreed between the parties before the contract is concluded. Neither party to the contract can unilaterally[30] impose an additional contractual term or obligation after that time.

In *Thornton* v. *Shoe Lane Parking* the plaintiff was suing the defendants for personal injuries sustained by him whilst parking his car in their public car park. The car park was operated by an automatic ticket barrier which issued a ticket to the customer. This ticket made reference to a notice inside the car park which stated that the owners were not liable for any loss or damage to the vehicle or injury to the customer. The defendants relied on this exclusion notice to deny liability.

In his judgment Lord Denning reviewed several precedents which have become known as the 'ticket cases'. These involved exclusion notices which had been printed on tickets which had been issued by hand. He then continued by distinguishing these cases from the instant one.

Text notes:
29 place where business is carried out
30 by one side only

LORD DENNING M.R., having referred, *inter alia*, to *Parker* v. *South Eastern Railway* . . ., *McCutcheon* v. *MacBrayne* . . . and *Thompson* v. *L.M.S.* . . . continued:

None of those cases has any application to a ticket which is issued by an automatic machine. The customer pays his money and gets a ticket. He cannot refuse it. He cannot get his money back. He may protest to the machine, even swear at it. But it will remain unmoved. He is committed beyond recall. He was committed at the very moment when he put his money into the machine. The contract was concluded at that time. It can be translated into offer and acceptance in this way: the offer is made when the proprietor of the machine holds it out as being ready to receive the money. The acceptance takes place when the customer puts his money into the slot. The terms of the offer are contained in the notice placed on or near the machine stating what is offered for the money. The customer is bound by those terms as long as they are sufficiently brought to his notice before-hand but not otherwise. He is not bound by the terms printed on the ticket if they differ from the notice, because the ticket comes too late. The contract has already been made: see *Olley* v. *Marlborough Court, Ltd* . . . The ticket is no more than a voucher or receipt for the money that has been paid (as in the deckchair case, *Chapelton* v. *Barry Urban District Council* . . .), on terms which have been offered and accepted before the ticket is issued.

In the present case the offer was contained in the notice at the entrance giving the charges for garaging and saying "at owner's risk," *i.e.*, at the risk of the owner so far as damage to the car was concerned. The offer was accepted when Mr. Thornton drove up to the entrance and, by the movement of his car, turned the light from red to green, and the ticket was thrust[31] at him. The contract was then concluded, and it could not be altered by any words printed on the ticket itself. In particular, it could not be altered so as to exempt the company from liability for personal injury due to their negligence.

Text note:
31 pushed

Comprehension check

14 Complete the following sentence which is based on the extract above:

The exclusion clause was not part of the contract because .....
....

Sir Gordon Willmer, whilst not prepared to locate the precise time at which the contract was concluded, nevertheless agreed that the defendants could not rely on the exclusion clause:

SIR GORDON WILLMER. It seems to me that the really distinguishing feature of this case is the fact that the ticket on which reliance is placed was issued out of an automatic machine. I think it is right to say – at any rate, it is the fact so far as the cases that have been called to our attention are concerned – that in all the previous so-called "ticket cases" the ticket has been proffered by a human hand, and there has always been at least the notional opportunity for the customer to say – if he did not like the conditions – "I do not like your conditions: I will not have this ticket." But in the case of a ticket which is proffered by an automatic machine there is something quite irrevocable about the process. There can be no *locus poenitentiae*.[32] I do not propose to say any more upon the difficult question which has been raised as to the precise moment when a contract was concluded in this case; but at least it seems to me that any attempt to introduce conditions after the irrevocable[33] step has been taken of causing the machine to operate must be doomed to failure. It may be that those who operate garages of this nature, as well as those who instal other types of automatic machines, should give their attention to this problem. But it seems to me that the judge below was on the right track when he said, towards the end of his judgment, that in this sort of case, if you do desire to impose upon customers stringent[34] conditions such as these, the least you can do is to post a prominent notice at the entrance to the premises, warning your customers that there are conditions which will apply.

Text notes:
32 right to withdraw before concluding a contract
33 unalterable
34 severe

Comprehension check

15 Complete the following sentence:

Previous ticket cases differed because ....

....

Legal exercises

16 Which of the following constitutes an offer?

a A display of goods in a supermarket.
b An automatic barrier at the entrance to a car park.
c Asking to purchase a ticket from the person in the box office at the theatre.
d Booking a room from the receptionist in an hotel.

17 Ramona is shopping for a special dress to wear to her brother's wedding. She has seen nothing suitable until she notices a very nice dress, priced at £50, in the window of a small boutique. She tells the shop assistant that she wishes to buy the dress but the shop assistant refuses to sell it to her as it is for display purposes only. Can Ramona insist that the shop assistant sell her the dress?

18 Howard and Felicity are staying the night in London at the Upclass Hotel. They sign the register at the reception desk and the porter shows them to their room. In the room there is a notice on the back of the door stating 'The owners of this hotel accept no responsibility for the property of the guests.'

While Howard and Felicity are out to dinner the porter leaves the door to their room open and Felicity's diamond bracelet is stolen. She claims compensation from the owners of the hotel who claim that they are not liable because of the exclusion clause on the door of the bedroom.

a Can Felicity recover on the basis of *Thornton* v. *Shoe Lane Parking Ltd*?
b Would your answer to **a** be different if the exclusion notice had been prominently displayed at the reception desk where they signed the register?

7.4 Communication of acceptance

We have already seen that for an acceptance to be effective it must exactly match the offer and be communicated to the offeror. In face-to-face transactions the time of communication is easy to establish. However, many business transactions are conducted at a distance and offer and acceptance may be communicated by a variety of means. Different rules have therefore been established to take account of different forms of communication. A general distinction is drawn between instantaneous communication and communication by post. The rule for acceptance by post is that it is effective from the time of posting. This is illustrated by the case of *Byrne & Co.* v. *Van Tienhoven & Co.* (1880) 5 CPD 344. You will see that the case also considers the distinction between acceptance by post and revocation[35] by post. It may help you to clarify the facts of the case by making a timetable of the sequence of events as you read the passage.

LINDLEY J.,[36] having stated the facts and held that a revocation, to be effective, must be communicated, continued: I pass, therefore, to the next question, *viz.*,[37] whether posting the letter of revocation was a sufficient communication of it to the plaintiff. The offer was posted on October 1, the withdrawal was posted on the 8th, and did not reach the plaintiff until after he had posted his letter of the 11th accepting the offer. It may be taken as now settled that where an offer is made and accepted by letter sent through the post, the contract is completed the moment the letter accepting the offer is posted: *Harris' Case* (L.R. 7 Ch. 587); *Dunlop* v. *Higgins* (1 H.L. 381), even although it never reaches its destination. When, however, these authorities are looked at, it will be seen that they are based upon the principle that the writer of the offer has expressly or impliedly assented to treat an answer to him by a letter duly posted as a sufficient acceptance and notification to himself, or, in other words, he has made the Post Office his agent[38] to receive the acceptance and notification of it. But this principle appears to me to be inapplicable to the case of the withdrawal of an offer. In this particular case I can find no evidence of any authority in fact given by the plaintiffs to the defendants to notify a withdrawal of their offer by merely posting a letter, and there is no legal principle or decision which compels me to hold, contrary to the fact, that the letter of October 8 is to be treated as communicated to the plaintiff on that day or on any day before the 20th, when the letter reached them. But before that letter had reached the plaintiffs they had accepted the offer, both by telegram and by post; and they had themselves resold the tinplates at a profit. In my opinion, the withdrawal by the defendants on October 8 of their offer of the 1st was inoperative; and a complete contract binding on both parties was entered into on October 11, when the plaintiffs accepted the offer of the 1st, which they had no reason to suppose had been withdrawn. Before leaving this part of the case it may be as well to point out the extreme injustice and inconvenience which any other conclusion would produce. If the defendants' contention were to prevail no person who had received an offer by post and had accepted it would know his position until he had waited such a time as to be quite sure that a letter withdrawing the offer had not been posted before his acceptance of it. It appears to me that both legal principles, and practical convenience require that a person who has accepted an offer not known to him to have been revoked, shall be in a position safely to act upon the footing[39] that the offer and acceptance constitute a contract binding on both parties . . .

Text notes:
35 reversal or withdrawal
36 see section on abbreviations below
37 abbreviation of *videlicet* (Latin), meaning 'namely'
38 person or organisation acting on behalf of another
39 basis

Abbreviations

'Lindley J' means Mr Justice Lindley. (The American equivalent is Justice Lindley.) The plural abbreviation is 'JJ', for example 'Smith and Jones JJ' means 'Mr Justice Smith and Mr Justice Jones'. In a following extract you will see 'Denning LJ' which means Lord Justice Denning. The plural would be 'LJJ' which means 'Lords Justices'.

The judgment makes reference to the reasons for the rule that acceptance takes place at the time of posting. Lindley J considers that the alternative analysis would create injustice to the offeree.[40] This is no doubt true, but it is argued that the rule creates injustice in other ways. The arguments for and against the rule are analysed in the next article by Professor Winfield:

Arguments for the rule.

(i) The Post Office is the agent of the offerer not only to deliver the offer, but also to receive acceptance of it. This is what is really meant by the loose expression that the Post Office is 'the common agent of both parties'.

(ii) If the rule were otherwise, 'no contract could be completed by the post, for if the defendants were not bound by their offer when accepted by the plaintiffs till the answer was received, the plaintiffs ought not to be bound till after they had received the notification that the defendants had received their answer and assented to it. And so it might go on *ad infinitum*.'[41]

(iii) It is the better rule for purposes of evidence.[42]

Arguments against the rule.

(i) It is a fiction,[43] for it assumes communication of an acceptance where they may have been no communication.

(ii) It is harsh to the offeree who, having once posted his letter of acceptance, is not allowed to change his mind.

But why should he be allowed to do so when once he has taken a decision?[44]

(iii) If the letter of acceptance is lost or delayed, it may entail hardship on either party. This was certainly so in *Household Fire Insurance Co.* v. *Grant*, where the offeror applied for shares in a company, was allotted the shares by post, never received the letter and was nevertheless held liable as a contributory[45] when the company went into liquidation[46] three years later.

To this it has been replied that the reliability and general competence of the modern Post Office make the risk of loss or delay almost negligible.[47,48]

The results of this investigation may be thus[49] stated. We can start with the general proposition that contract is founded upon the agreement of the parties. But when we pass to the determination of what constitutes agreement we are faced with the intensely practical question, 'What facts will satisfy a Court of law that there has been an agreement?' In contracts by correspondence, different countries have answered this in at least five different ways. The arguments for and against each of these five are so evenly balanced that the selection of any one of them to the exclusion of the other four must in the end be a matter of what each country considers best for its own system. From the purely insular point of view, the rule adopted by English law has worked well enough here to make it inadvisable to agitate for any change. From the higher standpoint of international commerce, there is no doubt that in theory unification of the law is desirable. But it is questionable whether, in practice, the stage is yet set for another attempt to achieve it. The mere[50] fact that the five different rules are to a large extent empirical[51] might raise the inference that it is a matter of indifference[52] which of them should be selected by any conference for unifying the law. But that is a short-sighted view of the problem. We have to reckon also with the ingrained[53] habits of legal thought peculiar to[54] this or that country . . . Indeed, there is something to be said for[55] adopting different rules for different species[56] of contracts. In a purely personal contract, like that originating in a proposal of marriage, it might well be urged that until the offeror actually receives the acceptance, there ought to be no contract, however well-suited the Anglo-American rule may be to most commercial contracts.

Winfield, 'Some Aspects of Offer and Acceptance' (1939) 55 LQR 499, 508.

Text notes:
40 person receiving offer
41 Latin phrase meaning 'without end'
42 see question **19a** below
43 something imagined
44 see question **19b** below
45 a person liable to contribute (i.e. help pay) towards the loss
46 unable to pay money owed
47 can be ignored
48 see question **19c** below
49 in this way
50 only the fact
51 based on experience (cf. theoretical)
52 it is unimportant
53 deeply fixed
54 used only by
55 some advantage in
56 types

Comprehension check

19 a Note 42: Can you see why point (iii) should be so?
b Note 44: Is this an argument for or against the rule?
c Note 48: Is this an argument for or against the rule?

20 a How does the writer think a choice can be made between the five different definitions of an agreement used by different countries?
b Why does the writer think the English definition should not be changed?
c What is the writer's opinion of the English rule in relation to: **i** personal contracts; **ii** commercial contracts?

As a final point on acceptance by post you should be aware that the rule can be modified. Acceptance by post must be reasonable in the circumstances so that, for example, a postal acceptance to an offer sent by fax may be unreasonable. Equally the rule would not apply if a letter had been wrongly addressed or inadequately stamped. Also an offeror can dictate[57] the means of communication. In *Holwell Securities* v. *Hughes* [1974] 1 WLR 155, an option to purchase property was stated to be exerciseable by giving 'notice[58] in writing to the intending vendor'.[59] The letter exercising the option was sent but was not received by the defendants. It was held that the wording used implied that **actual** notice was required and that the acceptance was therefore invalid.

Text notes:
57 say with authority, specify
58 in this context means 'to inform'
59 person selling something

In *Entores Ltd* v. *Miles Far East Corporation* [1955] 2 QB 327, [1955] 2 All ER 493, the offer and acceptance were communicated by telex. The

Court of Appeal was asked to decide when the contract was concluded in order to determine in which legal jurisdiction an action for breach of contract should take place.

The plaintiffs in London made an offer by telex to the defendants' agents in Holland. The acceptance was received on the plaintiffs' telex machine in London. The defendants argued that the contract was made in Holland.

> DENNING L.J.: When a contract is made by post it is clear law throughout the common law countries that the acceptance is complete as soon as the letter is put into the post box, and that is the place where the contract is made. But there is no clear rule about contracts made by telephone or by Telex. Communications by these means are virtually[60] instantaneous and stand on a different footing.
>
> The problem can only be solved by going in stages. Let me first consider a case where two people make a contract by word of mouth in the presence of one another. Suppose, for instance, that I shout an offer to a man across a river or a courtyard but I do not hear his reply because it is drowned by an aircraft flying overhead. There is no contract at that moment. If he wishes to make a contract, he must wait till the aircraft is gone and then shout back his acceptance so that I can hear what he says. Not until I have his answer am I bound. I do not agree with the observations of Hill J. in *Newcomb* v. *De Roos.*
>
> Now take a case where two people make a contract by telephone. Suppose, for instance, that I make an offer to a man by telephone and, in the middle of his reply, the line goes "dead" so that I do not hear his words of acceptance. There is no contract at that moment. The other man may not know the precise moment when the line failed. But he will know that the telephone conversation was abruptly broken off: because people usually say something to signify the end of the conversation. If he wishes to make a contract, he must therefore get through again so as to make sure that I heard. Suppose next, that the line does not go dead, but it is nevertheless so indistinct[61] that I do not catch what he says and I ask him to repeat it. He then repeats it and I hear his acceptance. The contract is made, not on the first time when I do not hear, but only the second time when I do hear. If he does not repeat it, there is no contract. The contract is only complete when I have his answer accepting the offer.
>
> Lastly, take the Telex. Suppose a clerk in a London office taps out on the teleprinter an offer which is immediately recorded on a teleprinter in a Manchester office, and a clerk at that end taps out an acceptance. If the line goes dead in the middle of the sentence of acceptance, the teleprinter motor will stop. There is then obviously no contract. The clerk at Manchester must get through again and send his complete sentence. But it may happen that the line does not go dead, yet the message does not get through to London. Thus the clerk at Manchester may tap out his message of acceptance and it will not be recorded in London because the ink at the London end fails, or something of that kind. In that case, the Manchester clerk will not know of the failure but the London clerk will know of it and will immediately send back a message "not receiving." Then, when the fault is rectified,[62] the Manchester clerk will repeat his message. Only then is there a contract. If he does not repeat it, there is no contract. It is not until his message is received that the contract is complete.
>
> In all the instances I have taken so far, the man who sends the message of acceptance knows that it has not been received or he has reason to know it. So he must repeat it. But, suppose that he does not know that his message did not get home.[63] He thinks it has. This may happen if the listener on the telephone does not catch the words of acceptance, but nevertheless does not trouble to ask for them to be repeated: or the ink on the teleprinter fails at the receiving end, but the clerk does not ask for the message to be repeated:

so that the man who sends an acceptance reasonably believes that his message has been received. The offeror in such circumstances is clearly bound, because he will be estopped[64] from saying that he did not receive the message of acceptance. It is his own fault that he did not get it. But if there should be a case where the offeror without any fault on his part does not receive the message of acceptance – yet the sender of it reasonably believes it has got home when it has not – then I think there is no contract.

My conclusions is, that the rule about instantaneous communications between the parties is different from the rule about the post. The contract is only complete when the acceptance is received by the offeror and the contract is made at the place where the acceptance is received.

In a matter of this kind, however, it is very important that the countries of the world should have the same rule. I find that most of the European countries have substantially the same rule as that I have stated. Indeed, they apply it to contracts by post as well as instantaneous communications. But in the United States of America it appears as if instantaneous communications are treated in the same way as postal communications. In view of this divergence, I think that we must consider the matter on principle: and so considered, I have come to the view I have stated, and I am glad to see that Professor Winfield in this country (55 *Law Quarterly Review*, 514), and Professor Williston in the United States of America (*Contracts* §[65] 82, p. 239), take the same view.

Applying the principles which I have stated, I think that the contract in this case was made in London where the acceptance was received.

Text notes:
60 in fact
61 unclear
62 put right
63 arrive
64 prevented by law
65 symbol often used in USA meaning 'paragraph'

Comprehension check and notemaking

21 Complete the following note outline of example situations given in the extract above:

	Offeror	Offeree
1.	Shouts offer	Shouts acceptance
	Can't hear ∵ noise	. . . .
	. . . . → contract	
2.	Telephones offer	. . . .
	. . . .	. . . .
	. . . . →	
3.	Telephones offer	. . . .
	Can't hear	
	a) asks for repetn.	. . . .
	. . . . →	
	b) doesn't ask for repetn.	. . . .
	. . . . →	
4.	Telexes offer	. . . .
		. . . .
	→	

5. Telexes offer . . . .
   Ink runs out
   a) . . . .
   . . . . → . . . .
   b) . . . . → . . . .

22 Now complete the summary below of Lord Justice Denning's judgment by deciding whether or not a contract has been completed by telex:

a Acceptance not rec'd by offeror; offeree knows this → contract/no contract?
b Acceptance not rec'd by offeror; offeror does not inform offeree of non-receipt → contract/no contract?
c Acceptance not rec'd by offeror; offeror does not know acceptance has been sent; offeree does not know acceptance has not been rec'd → contract/no contract?

Lord Denning bases his judgment on a distinction between instantaneous communications and communications by post. An alternative analysis of the case is argued in the next extract. What is the distinction drawn by the author?

It is a principle of the English law of contract that 'acceptance means in general communicated acceptance' (Anson's *Law of Contract*, 20th ed., 1952, p. 82), and that this communication must be to the offeror himself unless he has expressly or impliedly provided for some other method of acceptance. Bowen L.J.'s dictum in *Carlill* v. *Carbolic Smoke Ball Co.* [1898] 1 Q.B. 256, 269 that: 'One cannot doubt that, as an ordinary rule of law, an acceptance of an offer made ought to be notified to the person who makes the offer, in order that the two minds may come together' has never been questioned. The 'acceptance by letter' cases are no exception to this rule, for, as Lord Herschell stated in *Henthorn* v. *Fraser* [1892] 2 Ch. 27, 33, the post is the usual means of communicating 'according to the ordinary usages of mankind.' It is important to note, however, that in these letter cases the acceptance has been delivered to an authorised third person, and is no longer under the control of the acceptor. The same is true, of course, of a telegram. It is the existence of the third person which makes the rule a rational one as it means that the acceptor must, if necessary, give evidence concerning an affirmative act which can be subjected to cross-examination; on the other hand, if an acceptance by letter were not effective until it had been received, the offeror could deny its receipt, and it is notoriosuly difficult to disprove a negative. Thus if A says to B, 'Give your acceptance to C who will telephone it to me,' then B's acceptance is effective as soon as he has communicated it to C, even though A may not receive it. On the other hand if A says to B, 'Telephone your acceptance to me,' the acceptance is almost certainly not effective under English law until A has heard it, unless, for some special reason, A is estopped from saying that he did not receive it (*per* Denning L.J. at p. 333). It has been suggested that in the United States a telephoned acceptance is effective when spoken, but this is exceedingly doubtful (*cf.* Corbin, *Contracts*, 1950, § 79).

If these principles are applied to the present case it would seem to follow that there is a clear distinction between a message sent by Telex and a message sent by telegram because in the former there is no third party between the acceptor and the offeror. A Telex acceptance is therefore not effective until it has been received. It thus becomes unnecessary to consider whether there is a distinction between communication by post and instantaneous communications to which reference is made in the judgments.

The difficulty of basing a conclusion on the rapidity of the communication is that it has been pointed out that in practice Telex messages are not always intended to be instantaneous, as it may be well known to the sender that although the office of the receiver has closed for the day the Telex machine will continue to function.
Law Quarterly Review, Vol. 72 (1956), p. 10.

Comprehension check

23 According to the writer, when is an acceptance effective in the following cases?

a A letter: . . . .
b A telegram: . . . .
c Telephone:
  i . . . .
  ii . . . .
d Telex: . . . .

Abbreviations

If you want to know the full form of an abbreviation, you can say:

'What does DPP stand for?'

or 'What is *viz.* short for?'

24 Use these questions with a partner to obtain the full form of the following abbreviations which have already been used in the book. You could also find some new ones by using a dictionary. If you are working alone, check your understanding of the abbreviations in the answer key.

a DPP
b MP
c MR
d AG
e ABWOR
f LJ
g LJJ
h J
i viz.
j e.g.
k i.e.

Language practice

25 Complete the list below with the negative form of the adjectives, all of which are used in this chapter.

a conditional
b written
c applicable
d willing
e convenient
f operative
g certain
h distinct
i adequate
j reasonable
k necessary
l advisable

Research

26 Professor Winfield's article draws attention to the different rules which apply to acceptance by post in different legal jurisdictions. Find out what the relevant rules are in your country and if they differ from acceptance by telex.

Legal exercises

27 Where is the contract concluded in the following situations?

- **a** Bob posts a letter of acceptance in London which is received two days later by Peter in Oxford.
- **b** Bob is in New York when he telephones his acceptance to Peter in London.
- **c** Bob sends his acceptance by fax from his office in Brighton to Peter's office in Newcastle.
- **d** Bob sends his acceptance by telex from his office in Reading to Peter's office in London.

28 Oilco plc write to Transhipping plc on 1 May offering to sell the company 5,000 gallons of crude oil at £1 per gallon. The letter states that 'the acceptance will be effective if it reaches our office by 5 p.m. on 10 May'. Transhipping receive the letter on 4 May and post a letter of acceptance at 3.00 p.m. on 5 May. On 3 May Oilco receives an offer for the oil of £1.50 per gallon from Industrial Shipping Ltd. Oilco posts a letter of revocation to Transhipping at 4.00 p.m. on that day. Transhipping's letter of acceptance is received by Oilco at 3.00 p.m. on 10 May. Transhipping plc receives Oilco's letter of revocation on 11 May.

Advise Transhipping plc on its legal position.

Moot

Stage a moot[66] on the problem which follows. To do this you will need to select two members of your group to present the plaintiffs' case and two members to present the defendants'. You should ask your teacher or a member of the legal profession to act as a judge. If you are working on your own, prepare written arguments for both sides of the case.

You will prepare for the moot in a similar way to a debate but also using the problem question technique:

1. Identify the areas of law on which you will need to base your arguments.
2. Reread the chapter very carefully, analysing the relevant case law.
3. Prepare an argument in favour of your client supported by case law – you may quote relevant passages from any judgment.

Text note:
66 a mock trial of a given set of facts

---

29 At 10.00 a.m. on Monday, 5 June, Mr Lloyd, the managing director of Poshcars Ltd, sends a telex to Mr Barclay, a regular customer, offering to sell him a rare vintage car for £50,000. On receiving the telex Mr Barclay immediately writes a letter of acceptance to Mr Lloyd which he posts at 1.00 p.m. Worried that the letter may be delayed in the post, Mr Barclay sends a telex accepting the offer at 9.00 a.m. on Tuesday, 6 June. Mr Lloyd is late arriving at work that day and he fails to notice the telex. During the day he receives an offer of £55,000 for the car from Ms Halifax. He telexes a revocation to Mr Barclay at 5.30 p.m. Mr Lloyd knows that Mr Barclay's office is closed between 5.00 p.m. and 9.00 a.m. Mr Barclay receives the revocation telex at 9.00 a.m. on Wednesday, 7 June. Mr Lloyd receives Mr Barclay's acceptance letter and the telex at 9.30 a.m. on the same day. He refuses to sell the car to Mr Barclay, who is now suing him for breach of contract.

Additional reading

The law of contract is a subject which can be studied satisfactorily at a variety of levels. Good introductory accounts can be found in Hogan, Seago and Bennett's *A Level law* (Sweet and Maxwell) and *A Level Law* by Dugdale *et al.* (Butterworths). There are a large number of books dealing specifically with the subject, some of which are included in this chapter. Others are *Cheshire, Fifoot and Furmston's Law of Contract* by Furmston (Butterworths), *Contract* by Davies (Sweet and Maxwell), *An Outline of the Law of Contract* by Treitel (Butterworths) and *Textbook on Contract* by Downes (Blackstone Press). Extracts from cases with commentary can be found in *Contract Cases and Materials* by Beale, Bishop and Furmston (Butterworths), and an excellent but quite complex account of the economic background to the present law is given in *The Rise and Fall of Freedom of Contract* by Atiyah (Clarendon Press).

The Observer Book of Moots by Dobson and Fitzpatrick (eds) (Sweet and Maxwell) contains a selection of hypothetical cases for moots, together with instructions on the preparation, presentation and procedure of mooting.

8
An introduction to criminal law

Summary

Legal content

8.1 The nature of crime
8.2 *Actus reus*
8.3 *Mens rea*
  8.3.1 A case study in recklessness
8.4 Coincidence of *actus reus* and *mens rea*
Additional reading

Aim

To provide an introduction to a substantive area of criminal law through an examination of the two major elements of criminal liability. Analytical skills will be developed by means of case studies and the application of legal skills to problem questions. Extracts from articles will provide a critical analysis of the law.

Language content

Grammar: 'pseudo-cleft' sentences; decoding long complex sentences by recognising parenthetical commas, conjunctions and relative clauses
Vocabulary: everyday words with specific legal meaning

8.1 The nature of crime

Criminal law is a very broad and complex subject. This complexity relates to the nature of crime. Criminal acts vary in seriousness; the same act may be a criminal offence in one country and not in another. Equally, as we have seen in Chapter 1, the same act can be both a criminal offence and a civil wrong. Some of these problems are discussed in the following extract. Comprehension questions have been inserted in the extract and should be read as you go through the text; you should answer each one after reading the paragraph following it.

> Most people have heard of the saying that "ignorance of the law is no defence" which is the result of another well-known phrase or saying that "everyone is presumed to know the law." Unlike many maxims which have no basis in reality, these do represent the very harsh rule in criminal law that it is no defence to a criminal charge that the person charged was unaware that the act he was performing was a criminal offence. Nor would it make any difference to his guilt or innocence that he had consulted a lawyer who had told him that there was no such offence.

1 In the next paragraph does the writer attempt to give a definition of a crime? If so, what is it?

This gives rise to several questions. For instance what is a crime and how do you know whether given conduct is or is not a crime? What[1] such questions are not unreasonably looking for is a definition of crime which will at the same time act as an infallible test by which to determine whether given conduct[2] is a crime. Unfortunately no such definition has ever, or is ever, likely to be found. The best that can be offered is to say that a criminal offence is conduct which may be followed by criminal proceedings and sentence. This is very little help to the man in the street[3] who wants to know whether it is a criminal offence to drive a car without properly working windscreen wipers, but given that[4] you can find out whether or not certain conduct can or cannot be followed by criminal proceedings, it is a watertight definition of a crime. Thus[5] in this country adultery[6] cannot be followed by criminal proceedings so therefore it is not a crime. Intercourse with a woman without her consent can be followed by criminal proceedings and is therefore a crime . . .

2 Is the running of a brothel[7] a civil wrong or a criminal offence?

Criminal law tends to represent society's attitude towards conduct. It is a decision that certain conduct should not be permitted and that it should not be left to the "victims" of this conduct to bring the matter to court. A good example of this is the law relating to brothels. If you find that a brothel has been opened up in the house next door, you can clearly sue its owners for a civil action in nuisance, but the law takes the view that this is a situation in which the private citizen should not be forced to make the running.[8] It is therefore made a criminal offence and the state, through the police force, can take action in the criminal courts to stop the activity.

3 Complete the sentences below with information from the next paragraph:

a Acts which are clearly not a crime: e.g. . . . .

b Acts which are crimes in some societies and not in others: e.g. . . . .

c Acts which are clearly a crime: e.g. . . . .

The question, however, of what acts can be followed by criminal proceedings can only be answered by reference to the law as laid down by Parliament in statutes and regulations, and in the decisions of the courts over the last few centuries. Of course most people know that it is a crime to kill, rape, steal, injure and equally that it is not an offence to wear bow ties. In the middle however is a great band of conduct over which various societies take differing views. Thus it is possible to take widely differing views on such matters as homosexual activity, incest,[9] drug possession and adultery. But in relation to what we can, for the moment, call real crimes such as murder, rape, assault, theft, and damage to property, most people have a reasonable idea of what activity is or is not criminal.

4 What is the difference beween 'regulations' and 'statutes'?

5 What opinion does the writer have of regulations?

However the picture has been complicated over the last 50 years by the increasing use of regulations (which have the force of statutes, but are passed without full Parliamentary debate) to control all aspects of every day life. Thus, in relation to road traffic, most citizens are aware of the major offences relating to bad, or drunken driving, which are contained in statutes passed by full Parliamentary discussion, but very few would know of the detailed regulations (not contained in the statute) concerning depth of tread[10] on the tyres. Breach of such regulations is often sanctioned[11] by fines and this makes the activity a criminal offence. There are literally hundreds of such regulations passed each year in all spheres of everyday life, and they make a mockery[12] of the notion that all people are presumed to know the law. In fact[13] some countries have taken the view that breach of such regulations should not be classified as criminal offences, with all the stigma[14] that involves; instead breaches are termed violations or contraventions to distinguish them from true crimes (see Justice Report, "Breaking The Rules," 1980). It is indeed highly questionable that any conduct should be made sanctionable with any form of penalty unless there has been the opportunity for full Parliamentary discussion.

Seago, *Criminal Law* (Sweet and Maxwell 1989), pp. 1–3.

Text notes:

1 see language point 1 below
2 behaviour
3 the average person
4 because
5 here introduces an example
6 sexual intercourse where at least one partner is married to a third person
7 premises where prostitutes sell their services
8 set the pace, take the initiative
9 sexual intercourse with close family member
10 grooves in the rubber of car tyres
11 here means punished (NB: in other contexts can also mean 'to authorise')
12 cause to look foolish
13 see language point 2 below
14 mark of shame

Language points

1 If you have difficulty understanding this sentence, consider the following sentence which is constructed in the same way but is shorter:

What he needs is a good lawyer. = He needs a good lawyer.

The sentence in the extract above can also be expressed in this way:

Such questions are, not unreasonably, looking for a definition . . .

The sentence in the extract is a fairly informal construction and tends to give more emphasis to the object of the verb, i.e. 'a definition'.

2 'In fact' can be used in two contrasting ways:

a As here, to strengthen an idea or add more supporting evidence, for example:

It would not be helpful to consult a lawyer in this matter; in fact, it would be a waste of time.

In this sense 'indeed' is more commonly used.

b To correct something stated in the previous sentence, for example:

Officially he is in charge; in fact, his assistant takes all the decisions.

The extract emphasises the distinction we drew in Chapter 1 between criminal and civil law – that the difference lies not in the nature of the act but the legal consequences which follow it. This is the descriptive model adopted by Professor Glanville Williams which defines a crime as an act which is capable of being followed by criminal proceedings and may result in punishment. An alternative to this is the prescriptive model of crime which analyses the characteristics of criminal conduct, 'Crime is crime because it consists in wrongdoing which directly and in serious degree threatens the security and well-being of society, and because it is not safe to leave it redressable only by compensation of the injured party' (Carleton, *Legal Duties and Other Essays in Jurisprudence*, Clarendon Press 1931). Given the disparate nature of criminal acts, to seek for any common, distinguishable feature and through this a single definition of crime is an impossible task.

Vocabulary revision

6 Before reading the next extract, revise some of the key vocabulary relating to civil and criminal proceedings used in Chapter 1 by completing the following sentences:

a In criminal proceedings a (**i**) . . . . prosecutes a (**ii**) . . . . If the latter is guilty, he or she will be (**iii**) . . . . and may be punished.

b In civil proceedings, a (**i**) . . . . sues a (**ii**) . . . . If the latter is found (**iii**) . . . . he or she may have to pay (**iv**) . . . .

In the next extract a practical test for distinguishing between criminal and civil acts is proposed.

From time to time the courts have found it necessary to determine whether a proceeding is criminal or not. Before the Criminal Evidence Act 1898, the defendant could not give evidence on oath on his own behalf in a criminal case whereas (since the Evidence Act 1851) he had been able to do so in a civil action. If he wished to give evidence the nature of the proceeding had to be ascertained. The same problem could arise today if it were sought to *compel* the defendant to give evidence. But much the most fruitful source of this problem has been the Judicature Act 1873 s.47, and its successor, the Judicature Act 1925, s.31 (1) (a), which, until 1968, provided that no appeal should lie to the Court of Appeal 'in any criminal cause or matter'. The question whether a particular proceeding is a criminal cause or matter has frequently come before the Court of Appeal and the House of Lords. In these cases the test which has regularly been applied is whether the proceedings may result in the punishment of the offender. If it may, then it is a criminal proceeding. As a practical test, this seems to work well enough; but it must always be remembered that it is a rule with exceptions; for[15] some actions for penalties are undoubtedly civil actions, and yet they have the punishment of the offender as their objective; for this reason the test of punishment is jurisprudentially[16] unsatisfactory.

The meaning of punishment itself is not easy to ascertain; for the defendant in a civil case, who is ordered to pay damages by way of compensation, may well feel that he has been punished. It has been suggested that:

'What distinguishes a criminal from a civil sanction[17] and all[18] that

> distinguishes it . . . is the judgment of community condemnation which accompanies and justifies its imposition.'

According to this view it is the condemnation, plus the consequences of the sentence – fine or imprisonment, etc. – which together constitute the punishment; but the condemnation is the essential feature. From this, it is argued that 'we can say readily enough what "a crime" is':

> 'It is not simply anything which the legislature chooses to call a "crime". It is not simply anti-social conduct which public officers are given a responsibility to suppress. It is not simply any conduct to which a legislature chooses to attach a "criminal" penalty. It is conduct which, if duly shown to have taken place, will incur a formal and solemn pronouncement of the moral condemnation of the community.'

But if 'the formal and solemn pronouncement' means the judgment of a criminal court (and what else can it mean?) we are driven back to ascertaining whether the proceeding is criminal or not. How is the judge to know whether to make 'solemn and formal pronouncement of condemnation' or to give judgment as in a civil action? Surely, only by ascertaining whether the legislature (or the courts in the case of a common law crime) have prescribed that the proceedings shall be criminal; and this must depend, primarily, upon whether it is intended to be punitive.[19]

Smith and Hogan, *Criminal Law* (Butterworths 1988), pp. 22–4.

Text notes:
15 because
16 according to the science of law
17 see question **7** below
18 the only thing
19 the adjective from 'to punish'

Comprehension check

7 Note 17: Which meaning of the word 'sanction' is being used here?

8 Give the date when each of the following situations began and arrange them in chronological order (i.e. order of time):

- **a** Defendant can give evidence in criminal action.
- **b** No appeal can be made to Court of Appeal in criminal cases.
- **c** Appeals can be made to Court of Appeal in criminal cases.
- **d** Defendant can give evidence in civil action.

9 According to the extract, are the following statements true or false?

- **a** Only criminal prosecutions aim to punish the offender.
- **b** The writer thinks that the condemnation of the community distinguishes a crime from a civil wrong.

Research

10 In the extract from Seago the author mentions 'a great band of conduct over which various societies take differing views'. As examples he gives homosexual activity, incest, drug possession and adultery. Find out whether these actions are criminal offences in your country.

Legal exercises

11 Using the same procedure which was suggested in question 43 of Chapter 2, organise a debate with your group on the proposition:

'The criminal law should play no part in the enforcement of morality.'

This may at first appear to be a very difficult proposition but it is a subject which you have probably thought about or discussed with your friends and family at some time. It is very much related to the issues in the research above. In some countries certain actions such as adultery are considered to be morally wrong but they are not criminal offences; in other countries they will be both morally wrong and criminal offences. The proposition is asking you to discuss the relative merits of the two approaches.

This is a subject which has been at the centre of debate amongst philosophers and jurists over many years. The nineteenth-century English philosopher J.S. Mill argued that the law should only be used to regulate individual behaviour which has an adverse effect on other people – murder is an obvious example. All other behaviour should be left to the choice of the individual. This approach was supported in the 1960s by H.L.A. Hart in his book *Law, Liberty and Morality* (OUP 1963). He also believed that the individual should have the freedom to decide how to behave without fearing the sanction of the criminal law. The debate at that time focused on the decriminalisation of homosexual acts between adult males. Those in favour of decriminalisation argued that the law should only intervene as far as it was necessary to protect vulnerable people such as children; it is not the function of the criminal law to impose the moral standards of some groups on all people. A leading proponent of the opposing view was Lord Devlin. In his book *The Enforcement of Morals* (OUP 1965) he argued that society was a 'seamless web' and that the behaviour of all individuals had an effect on its well-being; the law should be used to regulate the behaviour of individuals in order to preserve the broader good of society.

This brief summary of the arguments involved should provide some guidelines for your debate. References to these and other books on the subject are included in the additional reading section at the end of this chapter and in the Bibliography.

If you are working on your own write a 500 word essay arguing both sides of the proposition.

8.2 *Actus reus*

The *actus reus* of an offence is one of the two principal elements of criminal liability. *Actus reus* means 'the unlawful act', but the term also incorporates other factors.

The basic maxim applicable to criminal law is: *Actus non facit reum nisi mens sit rea:* An act does not make a man guilty of a crime unless his mind is also guilty.

It can be seen therefore that there are two fundamental elements to a crime – a **physical element** known as the *actus reus* and a **mental element** known as *mens rea*. This can clearly be seen in a diagrammatic form:

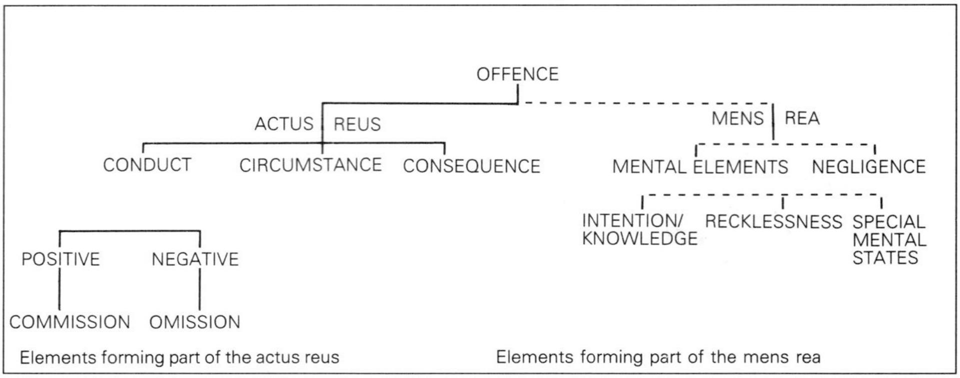

Before a person can be convicted of a crime it is necessary for the prosecution to prove both elements, i.e.:

(a) that a certain event or state of affairs which is forbidden by the criminal law has been caused by D's[20] conduct; and
(b) that D's conduct was accompanied by the necessary *mens rea* to establish the offence.

It is quite clear that the burden of proving these essential elements of any offence rests upon the prosecution who must prove the existence of both elements beyond reasonable doubt.

DEFINING ACTUS REUS

It is not enough to say that the *actus reus* is equivalent to the prohibited conduct in relation to any crime, clearly it is a wider concept than this:

Treacy v *DPP* [1971] All ER 110 (HL)

Lord Diplock at p. 120: 'Conduct which constitutes a crime consists of a person's doing or less frequently omitting to do physical acts, and the defintion of the crime also contains a description of physical acts or omissions,[21] though it may, and in English law generally does, also require that the physical acts or omissions which constitute the described conduct should be done with a particular intent, either expressly cited in the definition or to be implied from the mere fact that Parliament has made the described conduct punishable.'

Hence *actus reus* is clearly much more than simply the prohibited conduct, it is more than a physical act for it also includes an omission of act. It would seem that it means the whole definition of the crime except the *mens rea*. To this extent it is a *residual*[22] *concept*, it is that which remains once the mental element has been removed.

Professors Smith and Hogan identify two categories of crime:

(i) **Conduct crimes:** Where D's conduct is the central feature of the crime.
(ii) **Results crimes:** Where the consequence/result of D's conduct is the central feature of the crime. It should be observed that in many results crimes, such as murder, it is not just the result that is of importance, the conduct which causes the result may be of equal significance.

Conduct and result are not the only features of significance. The circumstances in which the conduct or result take place may be of equal importance. In rape, for example, the circumstance that the woman did not consent is a necessary part of both the *actus reus* and *mens rea*.

We can say therefore that the *actus reus* of an offence may include:

(i) the **CONDUCT** which is the central feature of the crime;
(ii) the surrounding material **CIRCUMSTANCES;**
(iii) the result/**CONSEQUENCES** of D's actions.

ESTABLISHING AN ACTUS REUS

An unlawful intention may exist by itself (e.g. D may intend to rob X), however this is not *per se*[23] punishable; **the criminal law does not punish for guilty mind alone.** An *actus reus* must be established in each case, if there is no *actus reus* there can be no crime.

R v *Deller* (1952) 36 Cr.App.R. 184 (CA)

D induced P to purchase D's car by representing to P that the car was free from any hire purchase[24] agreement. In fact D had previously entered into an HP agreement with a bank in relation to the car and believed this agreement to be subsisting at the time he made the representation.[25] However, the HP agreement was in fact void[26] *ab initio*[27] for technical reasons of which D was not aware. D was charged with obtaining property (purchase price) from P by deception (representing that the car was not covered by HP).

CA held: D's conviction be quashed. Despite D's dishonest state of mind, *there was no actus reus*. D's statement was, in fact, true, due to reasons unknown to him at the time, and therefore could be no deception.

VOLUNTARINESS

It is an essential element of any crime that D controlled his action, that his actions were willed. The law gives a complete defence where it can be established that D had no control over his actions, the defence is automatism . . . Voluntariness is considered to be a fundamental element of any criminal offence, if D acted **involuntarily** he may be afforded a defence . . . But consider the following case:

R v *Lipman* [1969] 3 All ER 410 (CA)

D, whilst on an LSD 'trip',[28] was subject to the illusion that his girlfriend, who was in bed with him at the time, was a snake, attacking him. D was convicted of the manslaughter of the girlfriend, by beating her and ramming some 8 inches of sheet down her throat, causing asphyxia[29] . . . D argued that since at the time, due to his self-induced[30] incapacity through drugs, he did not know what he was doing, therefore his actions were not willed (i.e. involuntary) he could not be guilty as charged.

CA held: Since this was a case of self-induced incapacity, the fact that D did not appreciate what he was doing due to the intoxication was irrelevant and no defence.

Hence in a case of self-induced incapacity, such that D no longer had control over his actions, there may still be an *actus reus*, despite the fact that D's actions were involuntary.

However, the defence of **automatism** directly recognises the need for a voluntary *actus reus*. In *Bratty* v *Attorney General for Northern Ireland* [1963] AC 386 (HL), Lord Denning took the view that:

'Automatism: means an act which is done by the muscles without any control by the mind such as a spasm, a reflex action or convulsion; or an act done by a person who is not conscious of which he is doing, such as an act done whilst suffering from concussion[31] or whilst sleepwalking.'

Automatism is a very narrow defence, which leads to complete acquittal if established. There is a further defence relating to voluntariness, this is the defence of duress.

Where D can establish **duress** D has a complete defence. The nature of the defence of duress[32] is to establish that D's actions were involuntary because his will to act was overborne by threats of immediate death or serious injury.

CAUSATION AND ACTUS REUS

When we are concerned with crimes where the result or consequence is an essential part of the *actus reus* (**result crimes**) it is essential to establish some causative link between the defendant's act or omission and the given result. This link is frequently referred to as the 'chain of causation'. The problem of establishing a 'chain of causation' is particularly difficult in relation to crimes of homicide,[33] i.e. establishing the 'chain of causation' between the defendant's actions and the death of the victim.

A good example of the problem, however, is to be found in *R* v *White* [1910] 2 KB 124 (CA). The victim was found dead, next to the body was found a glass of drink prepared by D. The drink contained a quantity of poison. However, the victim had died from heart failure due to some other cause. There was no evidence to show that the victim had taken any of the drink. D was indicted for murder and convicted of attempted murder. D appealed against his conviction, his appeal was dismissed by the Court of Appeal.

It is clear that D could not be convicted of the full offence of murder since there was no 'chain of causation' between D's placing the poison in the victim's glass and the victim's death. However, this was not an impediment[34] to D's conviction for an attempt to kill.

OMISSIONS AND ACTUS REUS

Historically *actus reus* has been taken to mean unlawful conduct, that is some positive action on the part of the defendant. Equally, however, a failure on the part of the defendant to perform some act (i.e. an omission) may form the *actus reus*, where D is under a duty to act.

Omissions are considered an *actus reus* only where the defendant is under a duty to act and has omitted to do so. The duty to act may be imposed by common law, by statute or under contract.

R v *Pittwood* (1902) 19 TLR 37

D was employed to keep guard at a railway crossing, his job was to operate the gates so as to allow pedestrians to cross the line. D left his post and went off, leaving the gates in a position enabling pedestrians to cross the line. D was charged with the manslaughter of a pedestrian hit by a train at the crossing.

Held: Since D was under a contractual duty to his employer to keep the gates shut to pedestrians and safeguard the public, D's omission to act was in breach of that contractual duty and could therefore amount to the *actus reus* of the offence.

R v *Instan* [1893] 1QB 450

D omitted to give food to P, a helpless invalid, who died in consequence from malnutrition.

Held: D was in breach of his common law duty to care for P. D had assumed the duty of looking after P, his actions thereafter by failing to feed P amounted to the *actus reus* of manslaughter.

Pannett, *Criminal Law in Action* (Oxford Polytechnic, 1986), pp. 2–4, 6–9.

Text notes:

20 i.e. the defendant
21 failure to do something
22 the meaning is contained in the next few words
23 (Latin) by itself
24 contract to pay for something in instalments
25 see question **12** below

26 of no legal effect
27 (Latin) from the beginning
28 condition resulting from taking the drug LSD
29 no air in the lungs
30 see language point 1 below
31 injury to the brain
32 the meaning is contained in the last part of the sentence
33 see language point 2 below
34 something which could prevent

Comprehension check

12 Note 25: To what does 'representation' refer here?

13 a Two types of crime are mentioned what are they?
b What are the two elements of a crime?
c What are the three components of the *actus reus* of some offences?

14 Are the following statements true or false?
a *Actus reus* refers only to the commission of an unlawful act.
b Automatism and duress are both examples of involuntariness which will lead to acquittal.
c *Actus reus* includes everything except *mens rea*.

Language points

1 'Self-induced' means 'caused by him or herself'. There are many words formed in this way, using nouns, adjectives and adverbs, for example:
self-employed (working in one's own business)
self-confidence (belief in one's own ability)
self-centred (excessively interested in oneself)

2 'Homicide' means 'killing a human being'. Other words formed with this suffix (-cide) include:
patricide (killing one's father)
fratricide (killing one's brother)
suicide (killing oneself)
infanticide (killing a baby under 12 months)

The extract above shows that the concept of the 'unlawful act' is more complex than the simplicity of the term suggests. This is perhaps particularly so in the area of omissions which amount to *actus reus*. We shall examine this in more detail through a case study of *R* v. *Miller* [1983] 2 AC 161.

The defendant was a vagrant who was squatting[35] in an unoccupied house. One night he lit a cigarette before falling asleep and later woke to find that the cigarette had set fire to the mattress. He did nothing to extinguish the fire but moved to another room where he again fell asleep. The fire caused considerable damage to the house. M was convicted of arson. His appeal was dismissed by the Court of Appeal and he appealed to the House of Lords.

LORD DIPLOCK: [T]he Court of Appeal certified that the following question of law of general public importance was involved:

'Whether the actus reus of the offence of arson is present when a defendant accidentally starts a fire and thereafter, intending to destroy or damage property belonging to another or being reckless as to whether any such property would be destroyed or damaged, fails to take any steps to extinguish the fire or prevent damage to such property by that fire?'[36]

. . In the instant case, as the argument before this House has in my view demonstrated, it is the use of the expression 'actus reus' that is liable to mislead, since it suggests that some positive act on the part of the accused is needed to make him guilty of a crime and that a failure or omission to act is insufficient to give rise to criminal liability unless some express[37] provision[38] in the statute that creates the offence so[39] provides.

The first question to be answered where a completed crime of arson is charged is: 'Did a physical act of the accused start the fire which spread and damaged property belonging to another[40] (or did his act cause an existing fire, which he had not started but which would otherwise have burnt itself out harmlessly, to spread and damage property belonging to another)?' I have added the words in brackets for completeness. They do not arise in the instant case; in cases where they[41] do, the accused, for the purposes of the analysis which follows, may be regarded as having started a fresh fire.

The first question is a pure question of causation; it is one[42] of fact to be decided by the jury in a trial upon indictment. It should be answered 'No' if, in relation to the fire during the period starting immediately before its ignition and ending with its extinction, the role of the accused was at no time more than that of a passive bystander. In such a case the subsequent questions to which I shall be turning would not arise. The conduct of the parabolical[43] priest and Levite on the road to Jericho may have been indeed deplorable, but English law has not so far developed to the stage of treating it as criminal; and if it were ever to do so there would be difficulties in defining what should be the limits of the offence.

If on the other hand the question, which I now confine to: 'Did a physical act of the accused start the fire which spread and damaged property belonging to another?' is answered 'Yes', as it was by the jury in the instant case, then for the purpose of the further questions the answers to which are determinative of his guilt of the offence of arson, the conduct of the accused, throughout the period from immediately before the moment of ignition to the completition of the damage to the property by the fire, is relevant; so is his state of mind throughout that period.

Since arson is a result-crime the period may be considerable, and during it[44] the conduct of the accused that is causative of the result may consist not only of his doing physical acts which cause the fire to start or spread but also of his failing to take measures that lie within his power to counteract the danger that he has himself created.

. . . I see no rational ground for excluding from conduct capable of giving rise to criminal liability, conduct which consists of failing to take measures that lie within one's power to counteract a danger that one has oneself created, if at the time of such conduct one's state of mind is such as constitutes a necessary ingredient of the offence. I venture to think that the habit of lawyers to talk of 'actus reus', suggestive as it is of action rather than inaction, is responsible for any erroneous[45] notion that failure to act cannot give rise to criminal liability in English law.

R v. *Miller* [1983] 2 AC 161.

Text notes:

35 occupying without permission
36 see the language point below
37 this word was discussed in Chapter 2
38 statement (legal meaning)

39 see question **15a** below
40 a pronoun meaning 'another person'
41 see question **15b** below
42 see question **15c** below
43 refers to the parable (i.e. story) in the Bible in which a priest and a Levite failed to stop to help an injured person
44 see question **15d** below
45 see question **15e** below

Comprehension check

15 a Note 39: Can you see what 'so' refers to?
b Note 41: To what does the pronoun 'they' refer here?
c Note 42: To what does 'one' refer here?
d Note 44: To what does 'it' refer here?
e Note 45: Can you guess the meaning of 'erroneous'?

Language point

Sentences in legal cases are often long and it's easy to become lost before the end. Unfortunately English uses fewer commas than some other languages so that the division of a sentence into sections (clauses) is not so easy to see. Sometimes, however, commas are used rather like brackets and then the part of the sentence between the commas may be treated separately. For example (from lines 3–7 of the extract):

'Whether the *actus reus* of the offence of arson is present when a defendant accidentally starts a fire and thereafter [, intending to destroy . . . or damaged,] fails to take any steps to extinguish the fire or prevent damage to such property by that fire?'

The following sentence (taken from lines 8–13) is also long; commas give some help but you can divide the sentence by identifying conjunctions, for example and, or, if, unless, since.

'In the instant case [,as . . . demonstrated,] it is the use of the expression "actus reus" that is liable to mislead, / since it suggests that some positive act on the part of the accused is needed to make him guilty of a crime / and that a failure or omission to act is insufficient to give rise to criminal liability / unless some express provision in the statute that creates the offence so provides.'

16 Try to use the technique described above for dividing the sentence on lines 33–40:

'If on the other hand the question, which I now confine to: "Did a physical act of the accused start the fire which spread and damaged property belonging to another?" is answered "Yes", as it was by the jury in the instant case, then for the purpose of the further questions the answers to which are determinative of his guilt of the offence of arson, the conduct of the accused, throughout the period from immediately before the moment of ignition to the completion of the damage to the property by the fire, is relevant . . .'

Writing exercise

17 Summarise the meaning of each paragraph in the judgment in your own words. The following opening words may help you:

Para 1: The important question of law involved in the case of *R* v. *Miller* was . . . .

Para 2: The term *actus reus* is misleading because . . . .

Para 3: First it is necessary to ask the question . . . .

Para 4: If the answer to the question is 'no' . . . .

Para 5: When the answer to the question is 'yes' the conduct of .

Para 6: The accused may cause the result not only by . . . .

Para 7: Although the term *actus reus* suggests . . . .

Legal exercises

18 In which of the following situations would a defence of automatism be successful?

- **a** While riding his bicycle A is hit on the head by a stone which is thrown up from the road. He loses control of the bicycle and injures B, a pedestrian.
- **b** A is a diabetic and assaults B whilst suffering from a deficiency of blood sugar.
- **c** A is holding a knife when B seizes his hand and forces the knife into C's chest.
- **d** After drinking two bottles of wine, A is involved in a fight during which he shoots and kills B.

19 Henry plans to kill Mabel. He puts some poison in a glass which Mabel subsequently drinks. Ten minutes later and before the poison has taken effect, Mabel is involved in a car accident and dies from her injuries. Is Henry guilty of murdering Mabel?

20 Keith is employed as a swimming pool attendant. His job is to maintain order on the premises and to ensure the safety of the swimmers. One evening Keith goes home early although he knows that there are some children swimming in the pool. After he leaves, one of the children gets into difficulties and subsequently drowns.

- **a** Has Keith committed a criminal act?
- **b** Would your answer to **a** be different if Keith was a bystander who saw that the child was in difficulty but failed to help?

8.3 *Mens rea*

We have seen that *actus reus* comprises a number of components. Equally the simplicity of the term *mens rea* belies[46] its complexity. Literally translated, *mens rea* means 'guilty mind' but we will see that it means more than that. In this section three categories of *mens rea* are considered: intention, recklessness and strict liability. The discussion is based on the division of offences into offences requiring fault (guilty mind) and those which do not require fault (strict liability offences). You will see from the following extract and diagrams that even this division can be further subdivided.

Text note:
46 misrepresents

It is important from the outset to distinguish . . . three forms of *mens rea*. It is sometimes said that criminal offences can be divided into offences requiring fault (i.e. guilty mind) and those which do not require fault (i.e. strict liability offences).

The category of offences requiring fault may be further subdivided:

(i) offences requiring intention/knowledge;
(ii) offences requiring reckless state of mind;
(iii) offences requiring a 'special mental state', e.g. dishonesty, in the crime of theft.

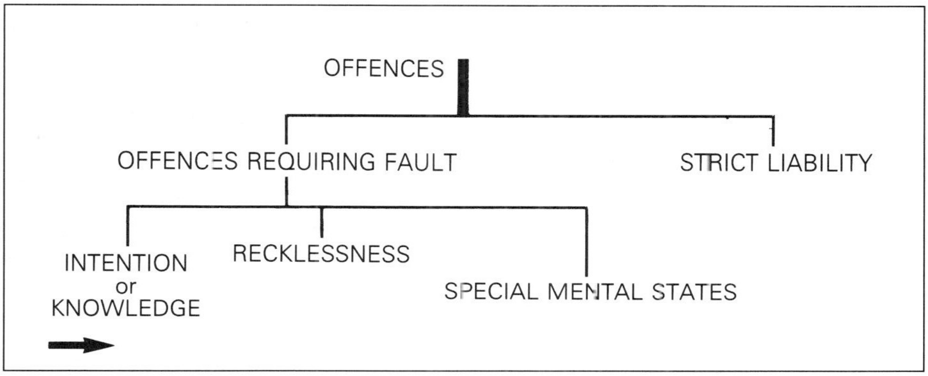

It is quite clear that some mental element is present in all crimes, even those of so-called strict liability.

Sweet v *Parsley* [1970] AC 132

The appellant sub-let[47] rooms at a farm where she was the tenant.[48] The persons to whom the rooms were let used the premises for cannabis smoking. The appellant was charged under s5(b) Dangerous Drugs Act 1965; **being concerned in the management of premises which were used for the purpose of cannabis smoking.**

She was convicted before the magistrates, albeit[49] that they accepted that she had no knowledge that the house was being used for that purpose. Her conviction was affirmed by the Divisional Court. On a further appeal to the House of Lords, the House allowing her appeal held that there was a need for knowledge on her part of the activity of cannabis smoking, otherwise she could not be said to be managing the premises for that purpose.

INTENTION

A starting point for a definition of intention is to be found in Law Commission Working Paper No 31:

'A person intends an event not only:

(a) when it is his purpose to cause that event; but also
(b) when he has no substantial doubt that the event will result from his conduct; and
(c) when he foresees that that event will probably result from his conduct.[50]

Therefore with intention there must be foresight[51] of consequences and a desire that these consequences be brought about.' This view has been confirmed by the House of Lords in the case of *Hancock* v *Shanklin* [1986] AC 455, [1986] 1 All ER 641.

RECKLESSNESS

Recklessness is a particularly intricate[52] concept to understand. It is important to understand its meaning in order to comprehend certain criminal offences, e.g. criminal damage, rape, and assault.

. . .This area of the criminal law has been the subject of significant changes in recent years and much academic debate. Professors Smith and Hogan in their textbook state that:

'A man is reckless with respect to a consequence of his act where he foresees that it may occur, but does not desire it, nor foresees it as virtually certain. Recklessness with respect to circumstances means a realisation that the circumstances may exist without knowing or hoping that they do.'

The academic debate on the subject of recklessness has centred around whether there is a need for a realisation on the part of D that the prohibited consequence may occur. Traditionally two viewpoints have been put forward:

A The Objective View

This approach has seen recklessness as simply a higher form of negligence. Negligence is an objective standard, **based upon the conduct of the reasonable man.**

Andrews v *DPP* [1937] AC 576 (HL)

Lord Atkin observed: 'Simple lack of care as will constitute civil liability is not enough. For the purpose of the criminal law there are degrees of negligence, and a very high degree of negligence is required to be proved before the crime (manslaughter) is established. Probably of all the epithets that can be applied "reckless" most nearly covers the case'.

B The Subjective View

This approach requires of the defendant some appreciation[53] of the risk of the forbidden consequence, irrespective of whether a reasonable man in the position of the accused would have appreciated the risk.

The leading case which supports this view is *R* v *Stephenson* [1979] 3 WLR 193 (CA). The court was concerned to construe s1(1) Criminal Damage Act 1971:

'A person who without lawful excuse . . . damages any property belonging to another . . . being **reckless** as to whether such property would be damaged shall be guilty of an offence'.

The facts of the case were that D, a tramp, went to a haystack for shelter. He crept into a hollow in the haystack. To keep himself warm he lit a small fire! The whole haystack was destroyed by fire, and D was charged under s1(1) with arson.

In the words of Lane L.J. . . . 'The problem is not difficult to state. Does the word "reckless" require that the defendant must be proved actually to have foreseen the risk of some damage resulting from his actions and nevertheless to have run the risk (the subjective test), or is it sufficient to prove that the risk of damage resulting would have been obvious to any reasonable person in the defendant's position (the objective test)?'

Lane L.J. went on to formulate a definition of recklessness:

'A man is reckless when he carries out the deliberate act **appreciating that there is a risk** that damage to property may result from his act. It is, however, not the taking of every risk which could properly be classed as reckless. The risk must be one which it is in all the circumstances unreasonable for him to take.

We wish to make it clear that the test remains **subjective**, that the **knowledge or appreciation of risk of some damage must have entered the defendant's mind** even though he may have suppressed it or driven it out'.

Although the subjective test is no longer generally accepted it remains the only test for some offences, e.g. statutory offences containing the word 'malicious'.

C The Middle View

The debate as to the correct approach to recklessness has been fuelled by the House of Lords decisions in *MPC* v *Caldwell* [1981] 2 WLR 509, and *R* v *Lawrence* [1981] 2 WLR 524.

The Middle View may be summarised thus: D closes his mind to an obvious risk of the consequences occurring. The risk need not be one which is obvious to D, it need only be a risk which would be obvious to a reasonable man.

MPC v *Caldwell* was concerned with the meaning of recklessness with regard to the s1(2) Criminal Damage Act 1971. The defendant, who was charged under s1(2) Criminal Damage Act 1971, bore a grudge[54] against his ex-employer. He set fire to the hotel at which he had been employed and adduced evidence that at the time of setting fire to the hotel he was so drunk as not to realise the risk of people being present in the building and of their lives being endangered by his actions. The indictment charged D with damaging the property of another, being reckless as to whether the life of another would be endangered by his actions.

D pleaded that he was so incapacitated by reason of self-induced intoxication that he was unable to realise that the life of another would be endangered by his actions and he was not reckless in this regard.

Let us now consider the respective views of their Lordships in *Caldwell.* Lord Diplock in *Caldwell* regards recklessness as 'an ordinary English word'. Put another way, that it should be given its ordinary everyday meaning and not be placed within a straightjacket of definition. Lord Diplock observes that 'recklessness covers a whole range of states of mind, from failing to give any thought at all to whether or not there is any risk of those harmful consequences, to recognising the existence of the risk and nevertheless deciding to ignore it'.

Lord Diplock's definition is broader than a purely subjective approach. He is clearly opposed to categorising recklessness by means of subjective or objective labels: 'The label solves nothing. It is a statement of the obvious; *mens rea* is by definition a state of mind of the accused himself at the time he did the physical act that constitues the *actus reus* of the offence; it cannot be the mental state of some non-existent hypothetical person'.

Hence Lord Diplock recognises the need for a mental element on the part of D, therefore a reckless state of mind cannot be notional.[55] But what state of mind is required of D? It would seem that where D has closed his mind to an obvious risk, albeit the taking of such a risk was unreasonable, both these states of mind amount to recklessness under the 1971 Act.[56] Therefore where D has closed his mind to the risk of other person's lives being endangered by his actions, this will satisfy s1(2) in the same way as if he had forseen the risk of life being endangered and determined to run it albeit that it was unreasonable for him to do so.

This view was accepted by Lords Keith and Roskill and forms the majority view of the House. The dissentients[57] were Lords Edmund Davies and Wilberforce.

Lord Edmund Davies is in 'profound disagreement' with Lord Diplock as to the meaning of recklessness. He distinguishes recklessness from

> negligence by observing that recklessness requires foresight of consequence. In that Lord Edmund Davies regards foresight of consequence as an essential element of the definition of recklessness he takes a purely subjective approach.
>
> We can therefore summarise the courts' approach to the test for recklessness in this way. Prior to *Caldwell* the test was subjective. Caldwell introduced an objective limb; the defendant is reckless when he fails to give a thought to the risk but had he (i.e. the reasonable man) done so he would have seen the risk.

STRICT LIABILITY OFFENCES

These offences form a special category. They are an exception to the normal type of offence, since they require of the defendant a more limited form of *mens rea*.

Strict liability offences are mainly prohibitory in their nature. They have arisen due to legislation which has sought to prohibit certain forms of anti-social or unconscionable commercial behaviour, i.e. Trade Descriptions Act 1968, Food and Drugs Act 1955, Misuse of Drugs Act 1971, etc.

It is important . . . to define the meaning of the terms 'strict' and 'absolute' liability . . .

> There is a clear distinction between strict and absolute offences. Following *Sweet* v *Parsley* . . . strict liability requires some degree of foresight or knowledge on the part of the defendant, whereas absolute liability has no such requirement, and will impose liability regardless of knowledge or foresight. The courts have, however, moved away from absolute liability . . . It would seem that apart from certain common law anomalies (i.e. blasphemous libel), the rationale behind most of these offences is to prohibit certain forms of anti-social conduct (e.g. pollution). The nature of these kinds of offences tends to be prohibitory or regulatory.

Pannett, *Criminal Law in Action* (Oxford Polytechnic 1986), pp. 13, 15–18.

Text notes:

47 charged money for the use of rooms
48 person paying rent to the owner
49 although (in formal use)
50 either of (a), (b) or (c) will be sufficient to establish intent
51 noun from 'to foresee'
52 complicated
53 understanding
54 felt resentment
55 abstract
56 see question **21a** below
57 see question **21b** below

Comprehension check

21 a Note 56: Which Act is referred to here?
b Note 57: Can you guess the meaning of 'dissentients' from the context?

22 Put the following subdivisions of *mens rea* in order according to the mental element: absolute liability, recklessness, intention, strict liability.

Greatest mental element: **a** . . . .
b . . . .
c . . . .
Least mental element: **d** . . . .

23 In note form state how Lords Atkin, Diplock, Edmund Davies and Lane view 'recklessness'. Say whether their view is subjective or objective as used in the extract.

8.3.1 A case study in recklessness

The majority of the House of Lords in *Caldwell* moved away from the subjective view of recklessness. In particular, Lord Diplock's words 'failing to give any thought to whether there is any such risk in circumstances where, if any thought were given to the matter, it would be obvious that there was', have been interpreted in later cases as 'obvious to the reasonable man' and therefore objective. This view of recklessness is supported by Professor Williams who argues that a subjective view is 'not a concept which is likely to secure many convictions'. Certainly the objective test catches those who may wish to plead lack of perception because of a self-induced state such as intoxication or anger, but it also catches those who fail to appreciate the risk for some other reason. This issue was addressed in *Elliot* v. *C (a Minor)* [1983] 1 WLR 939, where the *Caldwell* test was followed with reluctance.

Comprehension check

24 According to the paragraph above are the following statements true or false?

a Lord Diplock's interpretation of recklessness has since been interpreted as an objective view.

b Professor Williams thinks that a subjective interpretation is more useful.

Comprehension questions have been inserted in the following extract which you can answer by reading the paragraph which follows them.

25 a What was the verdict in the court of first instance?

C, a 14-year-old schoolgirl, in a remedial[58] class at school, who had been out all night without sleep, entered a garden shed. She found white spirit which she poured on the carpet in the shed and ignited it. The shed was destroyed by fire. The justices found C not guilty of destroying the shed and contents contrary to section 1(1) of the Criminal Damage Act 1971. The justices concluded that because of her age, limited understanding, lack of experience of white spirit and exhaustion, the risk of destroying the shed would not have been obvious to her or been appreciated by her if she had given thought to the matter. The prosecution appealed.

b Is Robert Goff LJ happy with the decision he has reached?

ROBERT GOFF L.J. I agree with the conclusion reached by Glidewell J. but I do so simply because I believe myself constrained[59] to do so by authority. I feel moreover that I would be lacking in candour if I were to conceal my unhappiness about the conclusion which I feel compelled to reach. In my opinion, although of course the courts of this country are bound by the doctrine of precedent, sensibly interpreted, nevertheless it would be irresponsible for judges to act as automatons, rigidly applying authorities without regard to consequences. Where therefore it appears at first sight that authority compels a judge to reach a conclusion which he senses to be unjust or inappropriate, he is, I consider, under a positive duty to examine the relevant authorities with scrupulous care to ascertain whether he can, within the limits imposed by the doctrine of precedent (always sensibly interpreted), legitimately interpret or qualify the principle expressed in the authorities to achieve the result which he perceives to be just or appropriate in the particular case.[60] I do not disguise the fact that I have sought to perform this[61] function in the present case . . .

c Identify the *actus reus* and *mens rea* of the offence.

[His Lordship quoted Lord Diplock's model direction in *Caldwell* and continued.] Now, if that test is applied literally in the present case, the conclusion appears inevitable that, on the facts found by the magistrates, the respondent was reckless whether the shed and contents would be destroyed; because first she did an act which created an obvious risk that the property would be destroyed, and second she had not given any thought to the possibility of there being any such risk.

d Why does Robert Goff LJ feel that C was not 'reckless', according to the ordinary interpretation of the word?

Yet if I next pause . . . and ask myself the question: would I, having regard only to the ordinary meaning of the word, consider this girl to have been, on the facts found, *reckless* whether the shed and contents would be destroyed, my answer would, I confess, be in the negative. This is not a case where there was a deliberate disregard of a known risk of damage or injury of a certain type or degree; nor is it a case where there was mindless indifference to a risk of such damage or injury, as is expressed in common speech in the context of motoring offences (though not, I think, of arson) as 'blazing on regardless'; nor is it even a case where failure to give thought to the possibility of the risk was due to some blameworthy cause, such as intoxication. This is a case where it appears that the only basis on which the accused might be held to have been reckless would be if the appropriate test to be applied was purely objective: a test which might in some circumstances be thought justifiable in relation to certain conduct (*e.g.* reckless driving), particularly where the word 'reckless' is used simply to characterise the relevant conduct. But such a test does not appear at first sight to be appropriate to a crime such as that under consideration in the present case, especially as recklessness in that crime has to be related to a particular consequence. I therefore next ask myself the question whether I can, consistently with the doctrine of precedent sensibly interpreted, legitimately construe or qualify the principle stated by Lord Diplock in *Caldwell* so as to accommodate what I conceive to by the appropriate result on the facts of the present case, bearing in mind that those facts are very different from the facts under consideration by the House of Lords in *Caldwell*, where the defendant had set fire to a hotel when in a state of intoxication.

e **i** What was C's original acquittal based on?
ii Why does Robert Goff LJ reject this qualification?
iii Is C convicted on appeal?

Here again, it would be unrealistic if I were to disguise the fact that I am well aware that the statement of principle by Lord Diplock in *Caldwell* has been the subject of comment, much of it critical, in articles written by jurists; and that I have studied certain of these articles with interest. I find it striking that the justices, in reaching their conclusion in the present case, having done so (no doubt in response to an argument advanced on the respondent's behalf) by imposing on Lord Diplock's statement of principle a qualification similar to one considered by Professor Glanville Williams in his article 'Recklessness Redefined' (1981) 40 C.L.J. 252 at 270–271. This is that a defendant should only be regarded as having acted recklessly by virtue of his failure to give any thought to an obvious risk that property would be destroyed or damaged, where such risk would have been obvious *to him*[62] if he had given any thought to the matter. However, having studied Lord Diplock's speech, I do not think it would be consistent with his reasoning to impose any such qualification. I say that not only because this qualification does not appear in terms in his conclusion which I have already quoted, but also because, when considering earlier in his speech Professor Kenny's definition of recklessness (which he rejected as being too narrow), Lord Diplock expressly adverted[63] to the fact that that definition presupposed that 'if thought were given to the matter by the doer before the act was done, it would have been apparent *to him* that there was a real risk of its having the relevant harmful consequences . . .' (see [1981] 1 All E.R. 961 at 964. [1982] A.C. 341 at 351; my emphasis). It seems to me that, having expressly considered that element in Professor Kenny's test, and having (as I think) plainly decided to omit it from his own formulation of the concept of recklessness, it would not now be legitimate for an inferior court, in a case under this particular subsection, to impose a qualification which had so been rejected by Lord Diplock himself. It follows that for that reason alone I do not feel able to uphold the reasoning of the magistrates in the present case. But I wish to add that, for my part, I doubt whether this qualification can be justified in any event. Where there is no thought of the consequences, any further inquiry necessary for the purpose of establishing guilt should prima facie be directed to the question why such thought was not given, rather than to the purely hypothetical question of what the particular person would have appreciated had he directed his mind to the matter.

From Goff LJ's judgment in *Elliott* v. *C.*

Text notes:
58 i.e. for pupils of below average intelligence
59 forced
60 see language point below
61 see question **26a** below
62 see question **26b** below
63 referred

Comprehension check

26 a Note 61: Which 'function' is referred to here?
b Note 62: Is this a subjective or objective interpretation?

27 a What was the court of first instance? (You may need to refer to Chapter 3.)
b What was the name of the appellate court?
c What procedure allowed the prosecution to appeal?

Language point

This sentence (lines 17–24) is another long, complex one. As before, sections between commas can be put to one side whilst you are trying to find the main structure. In addition to the **conjunctions** which were pointed out earlier in this chapter, relative clauses (beginning with **which, who, that, whose,** and so on) also indicate divisions in the sentence:

'Where therefore it appears at first sight that authority compels a judge to reach a conclusion / which he senses to be unjust or inappropriate, / he is [, I consider,] under a positive duty to examine the relevant authorities with scrupulous care to ascertain whether he can, [within . . .,] legitimately interpret or qualify the principle expressed in the authorities to achieve the result which he perceives to be just or appropriate in the particular case.'

Writing exercises

28 Using the paragraph questions in **25** as guidelines, write a 150-word summary of the judgment of Robert Goff LJ.

Legal exercises

29 Read section 1(1) of the Criminal Damage Act given below and answer the questions which follow:

'Destroying or damaging property:
1 (1) A person who without lawful excuse destroys or damages any property belonging to another intending to destroy or damage any property or being reckless as to whether any such property would be destroyed or damaged shall be guilty of an offence.'

a What constitutes the *actus reus* and *mens rea* of section 1(1) of the Act?

b Consider the following situation in the light of section 1(1):

Jason is employed as a computer operator by Britbank plc. One day his work is criticised by the manager of the bank. Jason feels that the criticism is unjustified and he becomes so angry that he switches the computer off without following the correct procedure. As a result the computer is damaged and its records destroyed.

30 Reread the section on strict liability offences and consider the following situation.

The Licensing Act 1964 regulates the sale of alcoholic drinks. Section 169(1) makes it a criminal offence knowingly to allow the consumption of intoxicating liquor by persons under 18 and knowingly to allow a person to sell intoxicating liquor to persons under 18.

David owns a nightclub which is frequented by many young people. It is the policy of the club to refuse admission to people under 18. David employs an attendant to assess visually the age of people coming into the club but he accepts that it is inevitable that some younger people will be admitted. Several people aged 16 and 17 are found by the police, on the premises drinking alcohol. David has been charged under section 169(1) of the Licensing Act 1964.

a Has David committed an offence under section 169(1)?
b Would your answer to **a** be different if the word 'knowingly' was deleted from the section?

8.4 The coincidence of *actus reus* and *mens rea*

We have seen that in most cases there are two elements to criminal liability – *actus reus* and *mens rea.* In addition to proving these elements the prosecution must also establish that they were concurrent. Consider this situation: X plans to kill Y on Friday night by poisoning his drink but he is unexpectedly prevented from doing so. On Saturday X and Y are both members of the same hunting party. During the hunt X accidentally shoots and kills Y who was concealed behind some bushes. Is X guilty of murder? The answer is no – the *mens rea* of the offence occurred on Friday and the *actus reus* on Saturday. However, in some cases, where the *actus reus* and the *mens rea* are separated in time but part of a continuing series of events, the defendant has been convicted. Let us first look at a situation where the *mens rea* occurred prior to *actus reus.* The case is *Thabo Meli* v. *R.* [1954] 1 All ER 373. The facts are outlined in Lord Reid's judgment:

> It is established by evidence, which was believed and which is apparently credible, that there was a preconceived[64] plot[65] on the part of the four accused to bring the deceased man to a hut and there to kill him; and then to fake an accident, so that the accused should escape the penalty for their act. The deceased man was brought to the hut. He was there treated to beer and was at least partially intoxicated; and he was then struck over the head in accordance with the plan of the accused . . .
>
> There is no evidence that the accused then believed that he was dead, but their Lordships are prepared to assume that they did; and it is only on that assumption that any statable case can be made for this appeal. The accused took out the body, rolled it over a low krantz or cliff, and dressed up the scene to make it look like an accident. Obviously they believed at that time that the man was dead, but it appears from the medical evidence that the injuries which he received in the hut were not sufficient to cause the death and that the final cause of his death was exposure[66] where he was left at the foot of the krantz.
>
> The point of law which was raised in this case can be simply stated. It is said that two acts were necessary and were separable: first, the attack in the hut; and, secondly, the placing of the body outside afterwards. It is said that, while the first act was accompanied by mens rea, it was not the cause of death; but that the second act, while it was the cause of death, was not accompanied by mens rea; and on that grounds it is said that the accused are not guilty of any crime except perhaps culpable[67] homicide.
>
> It appears to their Lordships impossible to divide up what was really one transaction in this way. There is no doubt that the accused set out to do all these acts in order to achieve their plan and as parts of their plan; and it is much too refined a ground of judgment to say that, because they were under a misapprehension at one stage and thought that their guilty purpose had been achieved before in fact it was achieved, therefore they are to escape the penalties of the law.
>
> *Thabo Meli* v. *R* [1954] 1 All ER 373 (PC).

Text notes:
64 see question **31** below
65 secret plan
66 lack of protection against the cold
67 deserving of blame

Comprehension check

31 Note 64: Can you guess the meaning of 'preconceived' from the context here?

Thabo Meli involved a charge of murder and a series of events which brought about the planned consequence albeit in a different manner. The principle in the case was subsequently applied to manslaughter in the case of *R* v. *Church* [1966] 1 QB 59 where there was no original plan to kill the deceased.

The appellant had taken a woman into his van for sexual purposes. A fight ensued[68] and Church knocked the woman unconscious. Believing her to be dead he threw her into a river where she died of drowning. He appealed against a conviction for manslaughter on the grounds that he did not have the necessary *mens rea* at the time of performing the act which caused the death. His appeal was rejected.

> . . . the jury was entitled[69] to bring in the verdict which they did on either one or both of two independent grounds. First, the jury was entitled to regard the whole course of events from the moment the defendant struck the deceased to the moment he put her living body into the river as all one transaction, so that, if at the beginning of, or indeed at any time during, this course of events he had the intention to cause bodily harm, then the fact that he may not have the intent when he put the body in the river owing to a belief that the woman was dead through his assault on her, makes no difference to his guilt in relation to a charge of manslaughter.
>
> *R* v. *Church* [1966] 1 QB 59.

Text notes:
68 happened afterwards
69 had the right

The application of *Thabo Meli* to cases of manslaughter has been criticised because there is no intention to kill. Note the comprehension questions inserted in the following extract which should be answered after reading the text below.

> In the case of *Church* [1966] 1 Q.B. 59 . . . the problem of the supposed corpse[70] arose in relation to a conviction of manslaughter. The appellant struck and attempted to strangle[71] a woman. She fell unconscious and the appellant, believing her dead following his extremely cursory[72] examination of her, threw her into a river where she drowned. He was convicted of manslaughter and on appeal that conviction was upheld. The Court of Criminal Appeal appears to have upheld the conviction on the basis of gross negligence manslaughter (now referred to as reckless manslaughter) although it also made comments on the 'series of acts' doctrine in *Thabo Meli.*
>
> The court was of opinion that the judge should have directed the jury that—

'. . . they were entitled (if they thought fit[73]) to regard the conduct of the appellant in relation to Mrs. Nott [the deceased] as constituting throughout a series of acts which *culminated*[74] *in her death*, and that, if that was how they regarded the accused's behaviour, it mattered not[75] whether he believed her to be alive or dead when he threw her in the river' (emphasis added)

32 a Whilst reading the next paragraph consider the question: 'In what way can the cases of *Thabo Meli* and *Church* be distinguished?'

The problem with this approach is that it begs a question;[76] was it such a series of acts that would have led to conviction under the *Thabo Meli* approach? In *Thabo Meli* the acts of attack and disposal were part of a concerted[77] plan to kill the accused and then dispose of the corpse. There was no such plan in *Church* (nor could there be in a case of manslaughter unless it[78] arose as a result of a plea of diminished responsibility), so were the acts of original attack and the act of disposal part of a series? In *Thabo Meli* the acts formed a series, not because the act of disposal followed sequentially on the attack, but because they were concerted acts in pursuance of a plan. In speaking of *Thabo Meli* the Court of Criminal Appeal stated that, with regard to the charge of murder against *Church* (of which he was acquitted),

'. . . the jury should have been told that it was still open to them to convict of murder, notwithstanding[79] that the appellant may have thought his blows and attempt at strangulation had actually produced death when he threw the body into the river, if they regarded the appellant's behaviour from the moment he first struck her to the moment when he threw her into the river as a series of acts designed to cause death or grievous bodily harm.'

b Which words emphasise this difference in the next paragraph?
c Why does the writer say that the disposal of the body in the river cannot be considered part of a plan to kill Mrs Nott?

This statement talks of a 'series of acts designed to cause death' whereas, in respect of manslaughter, the court talked of a 'series of acts which culminated in . . . death.' It is difficult to follow the court's reasoning when it talks of a series of acts designed to cause death as[80] the act of disposal is for the purpose of disposing of a *body*, it being the actor's belief that death had occurred already.

Where does this leave the law in respect of manslaughter? It may be that policy should dictate that 'if a killing by first act would have been manslaughter, a later destruction of the supposed corpse should also be manslaughter.' Unfortunately, the Court of Criminal Appeal baulked[81] from delivering a purely policy-based decision and attempted to wrap up its decision in legal principle. The judgment is accordingly confused and confusing.

Elliot and Allen, *Elliot and Wood's Casebook on Criminal Law* (Sweet and Maxwell 1989), pp. 52–3.

Text notes:
70 dead body
71 kill by squeezing the throat
72 hurried, not thorough
73 suitable
74 reached highest point
75 very formal (archaic) negative construction
76 assumes something has been proved
77 organised

78 refers to 'a case of manslaughter'
79 in spite of the fact
80 because
81 refused

Now let us consider the situation where the *actus reus* occurs prior to the *mens rea.* Again we are looking at situations involving a continuous series of events. The leading case is *Fagan* v. *Metropolitan Police Commissioner* [1968] 3 All ER 442 which, like *Miller,* involves omissions.

The defendant was ordered by a police constable to park his car. In doing so he inadvertently[82] drove his car onto the constable's foot. The constable said, 'Get off, you are on my foot,' to which the defendant replied, 'F . . . you, you can wait.' He switched off the car engine and only moved the car reluctantly after further requests from the police constable. He was accused of assaulting a constable in the execution of his duty. On appeal to the Queen's Bench:

> **James J** [with whom **Lord Parker CJ** concurred] . . . In our judgment, the question arising which has been argued on general principles, falls to be decided on the facts of the particular case. An assault is any act which intentionally – or possibly recklessly — causes another person to apprehend[83] immediate and unlawful personal violence. Although 'assault' is an independent crime and is to be treated as such, for practical purposes today 'assault' is generally synonymous with the term 'battery', and is a term used to mean the actual intended use of unlawful force to another person without his consent. On the facts of the present case, the 'assault' alleged involved a 'battery'. Where an assault involved a batery, it matters not, in our judgment, whether the battery is inflicted directly by the body of the offender or through the medium of some weapon or instrument controlled by the action of the offender. An assault may be committed by the laying of a hand on another, and the action does not cease to be an assault if it is a stick held in the hand and not the hand itself which is laid on the person of the victim. So, for our part, we see no difference in principle between the action of stepping on to a person's toe and maintaining that position and the action of driving a car on to a person's foot and sitting in the car while its position on the foot is maintained.
>
> To constitute this offence, some intentional act must have been performed; a *mere* omission to act cannot amount to an assault. Without going into the question whether words alone can constitute an assault, it is clear that the words spoken by the appellant could not alone amount to an assault; they can only shed a light on the appellant's action. For our part, we think that the crucial question is whether, in this case, the act of the appellant can be said to be complete and spent[84] at the moment of time when the car wheel came to rest on the foot, or whether his act is to be regarded as a continuing act operating until the wheel was removed. In our judgment, a distinction is to be drawn between acts which are complete – though results may continue to flow – and those acts which are continuing. Once the act is complete, it cannot thereafter be said to be a threat to inflict unlawful force on the victim. If the act, as distinct from the results thereof, is a continuing act, there is a continuing threat to inflict unlawful force. If the assault involves a battery and that battery continues, there is a continuing act of assault. For an assault to be committed, both the elements of actus reus and mens rea must be present at the same time. The 'actus reus' is the action causing the effect on the victim's mind: see the observations of Parke B, in *R* v. *St George* [(1840) 9 C & P 483 at pp 490, 493]. The 'mens rea' is the intention to cause that effect. It is not necessary that mens rea should be present at the inception of

the actus reus; it can be superimposed on an existing act. On the other hand, the subsequent inception[85] of mens rea cannot convert an act which has been completed without mens rea into an assault.

In our judgment, the justices at Willesden and quarter sessions were right in law. On the facts found, the action of the appellant may have been initially unintentional, but the time came when, knowing that the wheel was on the officer's foot, the appellant (i) remained seated in the car so that his body through the medium of the car was in contact with the officer, (ii) switched off the ignition of the car, (iii) maintained the wheel of the car on the foot, and (iv) used words indicating the intention of keeping the wheel in that position. For our part, we cannot regard such conduct as mere omission or inactivity. There was an act constituting a battery which at its inception was not criminal because there was no element of intention, but which became criminal from the moment the intention was formed to produce the apprehension[86] which was flowing from the continuing act. The fallacy of the appellant's argument is that it seeks to equate the facts of this case with such a case as where a motorist has accidentally run over a person and, that action having been completed, fails to assist the victim with the intent that the victim should suffer.

We would dismiss this appeal.

Fagan v. *MPC* [1968] 3 All ER 442.

Text notes:
82 carelessly, unintentionally
83 here means 'to anticipate with fear'
84 see question **33** below
85 beginning
86 noun from 'to apprehend' – see note **83** above

Comprehension check

33 Note 84: Can you work out the **legal** meaning of 'spent' in this context?

34 When 'assault' and 'battery' are distinguished, what is the difference?

35 In which paragraph are the following topics mentioned? Which topics are the **main** topic of the paragraph?

- **a** The difference between battery and assault.
- **b** The means used to inflict injury.
- **c** Did Fagan's words constitute an assault?
- **d** How long can Fagan's action be said to continue?
- **e** Did *actus reus* and *mens rea* occur at the same time?
- **f** The plea of omission by the appellant is fallacious.

36 Below is a diagram representing the situation where *actus reus* and *mens rea* are clearly concurrent:

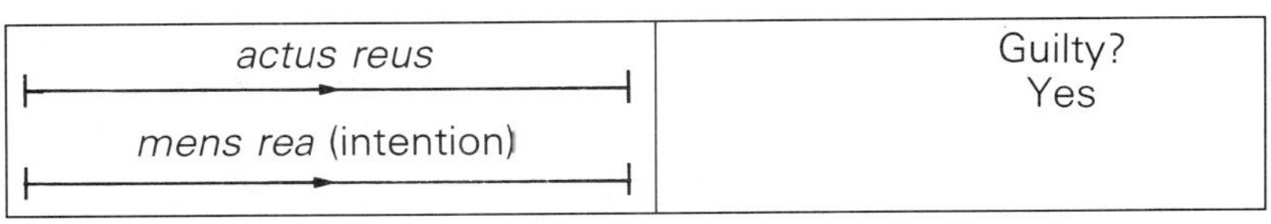

Two other situations are mentioned in the extract. Draw similar diagrams to represent them and say whether a criminal offence has been committed. Which diagram represents the basis of the appellant's argument in *Fagan* v. *MPC?*

In conclusion we can say that although in most cases the rule is that the prosecution must prove that *actus reus* and *mens rea* occurred concurrently, a further rule emerges that a complete offence is committed when the *actus reus* and *mens rea* occur at different points in time providing that they are both part of a continuing sequence of events.

Vocabulary

37 Many words which are used in everyday language can have a different meaning when they are used in legal contexts. Use the items in italics in sentences **i** to **ix** below (where they are used in their everyday context) to fill the gaps in sentences **a** to **i** which follow:

- **i** Most citizens *prefer* to live peacefully.
- **ii** The hotel *provides* only bed and breakfast.
- **iii** The barrister stood up and *addressed* the jury.
- **iv** The letter was sent by *express* mail.
- **v** The police *found* new evidence.
- **vi** I am afraid we only have *instant* coffee.
- **vii** It was a great *relief* to the parents when their daughter returned home safely.
- **viii** He *held* his knife in his left hand.
- **ix** The trousers are alright but the jacket does not *fit*.

- **a** The problem of long delays will have to be . . . .
- **b** The CPS was asked to . . . . charges against the suspected thief.
- **c** The House of Lords . . . . that the defendant was liable.
- **d** The magistrates saw . . . . to punish the defendant with imprisonment.
- **e** The House of Lords held that the precedent did not apply in the . . . . case.
- **f** The statute . . . . for the compulsory wearing of seat belts.
- **g** The prisoner gave . . . . instructions to his solicitor.
- **h** A majority of the Court of Appeal . . . . for the appellant.
- **i** The judge refused to grant . . . . to the plaintiff.

38 Complete the vocabulary table below, using your dictionary if necessary. At least one form of all the words has appeared in this chapter.

Nouns	*Verbs*	*Adjectives*
a	sanction	**b** . . . .
c	offend	**d** . . . .
e		**f** . . . .
g	condemn	×
h	punish	**i** . . . .
j	omit	×
error	**k**	**l** . . . .
provision	**m**	×
n	concur	**o** . . . .

Legal exercises

39 Discuss the following situation on the basis of *R* v. *Miller*:

Cyril goes to his local shop to buy a packet of cigarettes. As he leaves the shop he meets a friend and stops to talk to her. While doing so he lights a cigarette and throws the match away. After his friend leaves, Cyril notices that the match has set light to some papers in the doorway of the shop. The shop is now closed so Cyril walks away. The fire spreads and causes considerable damage to the shop. Cyril has been charged under the Criminal Damage Act for 'damaging by fire a house . . . intending to do damage to such property or recklessly as to whether such property was damaged'.

40 While driving his car in bad weather David skids on an icy patch of road and crashes into a pedestrian. David stops his car and sees that the pedestrian, who is badly injured, is his neighbour Gladys. David has recently had an argument with Gladys so he decides to drive away without helping her. What factors will be taken into account in determining whether David has committed the offence of battery?

Moot

41 Stage a moot on the following case, following the instructions given at the end of Chapter 7. Reread the sections on automatism and coincidence of *actus reus* and *mens rea*, with particular attention to *Thabo Meli* and *Church*. If you are working on your own prepare written arguments for both sides of the case.

Caroline and her friend Cynthia decide to spend the day in a boat on the river. During the course of the afternoon they drink several bottles of wine and begin to argue. Cynthia becomes increasingly angry and hits Caroline with an empty wine bottle. Caroline falls back and hits her head on the side of the boat. Cynthia thinks that Caroline is dead and she pushes her body into the water. When the body is discovered two days later an examination shows that Caroline died of drowning. Cynthia has been charged with murder.

Additional reading

The subject of law and morality is discussed in most books on jurisprudence but a clear introduction to the subject is contained in *Introduction to Law* by Harris (Weidenfeld & Nicholson).

As with the law of contract, there are many books published on the subject of criminal law. The A level texts mentioned in the additional reading section in Chapter 7 are also relevant to criminal law. In addition, *Introduction to Criminal Law* by Cross, Jones and Card (Butterworths) provides useful reading whilst case extracts and thoughtful commentary can be found in *Criminal Law Cases and Materials* by Smith and Hogan (Butterworths).

9
Law reform

Summary

Legal content

Aim

To consider the progressive nature of law and the legal system through a critical examination of the existing machinery of law reform and possible alternatives. Awareness of the practical problems of reforming the law will be increased through a case study of a substantive area of law and its application to theoretical problems.

Language content

Grammar: use of the subjunctive after verbs of recommendation, demand, etc.; cohesion in a paragraph

9.1 The nature of law reform

Throughout the book we have considered many proposals for reform of individual aspects of the English legal system. In this chapter we will look at the subject of law reform in general in relation to both substantive and procedural law. To do this you must first understand why there is a need for law reform.

The law cannot remain static because it must reflect the social, economic and moral values and needs of the society it regulates. As these develop and change, so must the law. There are many examples which can be cited – the law relating to the motor car, homosexuality and education have all changed in reaction to different social attitudes. The current debate on the criminalisation of rape within marriage reflects the changed perspective of a woman's marital role. Effective law reform, therefore, requires more than the technical expertise of lawyers. Mr Justice Scarman (now Lord Scarman) addressed this model of law reform in the Lindsay Memorial Lectures delivered at the University of Keele in November 1967. He began his first lecture, 'The New Pattern', this way:

> Law reform is not exclusively a legal topic: it is also a social and moral problem. It is no longer possible to think of the law as an esoteric[1] and

technical discipline, whose values are safe in the hands of the Judges and the profession. Contemporary society requires that it be[2] given the opportunity to test its laws by its own criteria; it insists that laws are either to serve the needs of society or to be rejected. In other words, our fellows in society require first to understand, and then to evaluate the laws that govern them. We demand, not only that the tables[3] be[4] brought down from the mountain and their meaning made clear, but that we have the liberty to smash and replace them. And so, to meet and overcome the challenge of law reform, we must call not only for the technical learning of the lawyer, but for a full understanding of, and sympathy with, the habits, feelings and values of ordinary men. Unless this challenge is met, law reform will be, in very truth, a barren[5] exercise. A difficulty presents itself at the outset:[6] it is that none of our existing institutions possesses, in itself, the blend of technical learning, social awareness, and power to get things done that are required. The courts have the technical learning most assuredly; the social awareness perhaps; but neither the opportunity nor the power to tackle the job systematically. The government,[7] by its control of Parliament,[8] has the power and the opportunity, but lacks the learning and, sometimes, the will. Parliament has the social awareness but, if one has to face realities, neither the learning nor the opportunity – though in theory sovereign, it is controlled not by itself but by the government. And the government is, more often than not, overwhelmed by the tide of its own business.

If therefore law reform, in any worth-while sense, is to have a future in England, the ultimate problem can be seen to be one of the machinery of government. A revolution in our law making procedures is required. The revolution must ensure that those who have the power, that is to say, the government and Parliament, create for themselves the opportunity to use it; and recruit to their service the experience, learning and knowledge to enable them to use it wisely. In a consititutional context, this means that our legislative processes must be reformed: in a legal context, this means that use must be made of a far greater variety of disciplines and skills, legal and otherwise, than have so far been harnessed to the direct service of the law.

Scarman, *Law Reform* (Routledge & Kegan Paul 1968), pp. 7–8.

Text notes:

1 only for specialists
2 see language point 1 below
3 refers to the flat pieces of stone on which were written the Ten Commandments (Laws) as told in the Bible
4 see language point 1 below
5 empty, opposite of 'fertile'
6 beginning
7 see language point 2 and question **2a** below
8 see question **2b** below

Language point

1 This form of the verb 'to be' is an example of the subjunctive which is used in 'that' clauses following verbs of recommendation, demand, and so on. For example:

Society requires that . . .
We demand that . . .

The subjunctive is the infinitive form for all subjects, for example:

. . . that it be given . . .
. . . that the tables be brought down . . .

This construction is found in formal style; in speech an alternative would be used, for example:

Formal: We ask that every member arrive on time.
Spoken/informal: We ask every member to arrive on time.

2 You will recall from Chapter 2 that 'government' can mean either the system of governing a country (e.g. a democratic government) or those Members of Parliament who belong to the ruling political party.

Comprehension check

1 'None of our existing institutions possesses, in itself, the blend of technical learning, social awareness and power to get things done'. Complete the following table using information from the extract:

	Courts	*Government*	*Parliament*
Technical learning	✓		
Social awareness		×?	
Power to get things done			

2 **a** Note 7: Which meaning of 'government' is relevant here?
b Note 8: From Chapter 2 can you remember the constituent parts of Parliament?

In this passage Lord Scarman argued that effective law reform can only be achieved through reformed legislative procedures. This argument is based on his recognition that, as a source of law, common law now takes second place to statute law, '. . . the bulk of English law that matters has found its way to the statute book' (Scarman, *Law Reform*, Routledge & Kegan Paul 1968). This focus on Parliament as the central actor in law reform will be debated further in later sections.

Of course, changes in the law are not always merely a reaction to changes in social attitudes; the law also has an important role in changing public behaviour. Legislation preventing discrimination against people on the grounds of race and sex are good examples of this dynamic[9] function of the law. Equally attempts by governments to persuade people to wear seat belts and to refrain from drinking alcohol whilst driving have had limited success without the force of law to support them.

As well as changes in substantive law the legal system must also accommodate the need for change in procedural law. Unfair procedure can cause injustice as much as unfair law; as an example you will remember the criticisms of cost and delay which we examined in Chapter 4 on the civil courts. The juxtaposition between these two areas of law reform are discussed in the next extract.

Text note:
9 see question **3** below

Comprehension check

3 Note 9: What word is used in contrast to 'dynamic' earlier in the paragraph?

Pre-reading question

4 What are the main topics of the following extract?

There are several aspects of law reform. At the most obvious level, the law may need reforming because it produces results which are contrary to common sense or unfair. This may arise from defects[10] in the substantive law, or defects in procedural law, or both. Substantive law is concerned with rights and wrongs and with the remedies for their violation.[11] Procedural law is concerned with the process by which remedies are made available. Sometimes there is no very clear distinguishing line between substantive and procedural law: thus[12] the definition of a criminal offence, including the maximum punishment prescribed, is substantive law, but whether it is triable summarily or on indictment is procedural. Further, if we consider legal aid, the part of the law that governs eligibility is substantive, yet since the whole purpose is ancillary[13] to bringing or defending cases we think of it as being procedural. However, we must continue to make a distinction because when a part of the law is working badly, different authorities may be responsible depending on whether substantive law or procedure is identified as the source of the trouble. If, for example, some regulations concerning motor vehicles do not seem to be enforced, inquiry may show that the regulations need amending, which is a matter for the Minister of Transport. If the trouble lies in procedure in magistrates' courts, that is nominally[14] for the Lord Chancellor and practically for the Home Office; or enforcement may be tied up with the respective roles of ministry inspectors, police and traffic wardens, which is administrative and not a matter for law reform except insofar as the organisation and procedure of courts is concerned.

At a less obvious level part of the law may be in need of reform because it is in an inconvenient shape rather than because it produces unfair results. Reformers have said over the years that the law ought to be simple, intelligible, certain, well arranged, adequately indexed and put into a physical form that will allow copies to be made available in public libraries as well as in courts and offices. At present the law is to be found in several hundred volumes of law reports and a less number of volumes of statutes and subordinate legislation, and lawyers need many textbooks and a considerable apparatus of periodicals, digests and so forth to find their way through so much material and to keep themselves up-to-date. To take a simple example, in this country we have no Penal Code. Thus there is no official book which the citizen may consult to discover even in the vaguest outline what behaviour is and is not a criminal offence, and even for the trained expert the task will sometimes be a difficult one. It is too much to expect that all the law that is required to regulate all the activities and relationships in a complex society could be made simple, but there is a great deal that can be done to improve the form of the law.

Spencer (ed.), *Jackson's Machinery of Justice* (Cambridge University Press 1989), pp. 493–4.

Text notes:

10 imperfections
11 'to violate' means 'to break'
12 see question **5a** below
13 secondary, helping
14 see question **5b** below

Comprehension check

5 **a** Note 12: What do you expect to follow 'thus' in this context, a consequence or an example?

b Note 14: Here 'nominally' is contrasted with 'practically' later in the sentence. Can you work out what it means?

6 **a** Is there always a clear distinction between substantive and procedural law?

b Why is it necessary to maintain a distinction?

Writing

7 Based on the information given so far in this chapter, use the topic headings below to write a short essay, entitled: 'Discuss the statement that "the process of law reform requires more than the technical expertise of lawyers".' Add any other information or examples of your own.

Introduction: Why is law reform needed?

Para. 1: Changing laws to promote change in public behaviour.

Para. 2: Changes in substantive law, procedural law and in the 'physical shape' of the law.

Para. 3: Three requirements of changing law: technical learning, social awareness, power to change laws.

Research

8 Transplant surgery is now an accepted form of medical treatment although it remains an emotive[15] issue. Many people carry a donor card which gives permission for their organs to be used for this purpose in the event of unexpected death, for example in a car accident. The law presumes that persons not carrying a donor card do not wish their organs to be used. Because of the shortage of organs for transplant many people argue that the law should be changed to reflect the presumption that the organs of a deceased person can be used unless that person is carrying a card witholding permission to do so.

a What is the law regulating the use of donor organs in your country?

b Prepare a questionnaire which will enable you to assess the attitudes of a sample of 30 people on this issue. It should include questions on people's knowledge of the existing law, whether they have any moral objections to transplant surgery and whether they would prefer the law to be dynamic or passive in this area.

c Write a 750-word report on the present law and suggest reforms based on the results of your survey.

Text note:
15 from the word 'emotion'

9.2 The process of law reform

In this section we will look at the existing machinery of law reform, its strengths and its weaknesses. First, the role of the judiciary.

9.2.1 Judges as law reformers

In the next extract the authors refer to the retrospective[16] effect of judicial law reform. This is related to the declaratory theory of law, that the judges state what the law is and always has been. Examples of the problems this can cause are given in the following extract:

Text note:
16 applying to the past

The judges play a relatively minor role in promoting the kind of legal change we have just discussed. To an extent[17] both they and the legal profession as a whole may function as a pressure group, particularly influential when their work is likely to be affected by any change . . . The Law Lords may also exert a direct influence on the details of changes through their Parliamentary position in the legislative House of Lords. But by and large, the judges would adhere to the view of Lord Reid that such matters are not properly within their province. However, when it comes to "lawyers' law," to reform of legal rules and principles developed over many years largely through the case law decisions of the judges, there seems to be little constitutional objection to judges changing or reforming that law. In recent years the judges have displayed an increasing willingness to overturn old case law and develop new principles more appropriate to modern conditions. The development of liability for economic loss . . . is but[18] an example of this continuing process. Nevertheless, there are limitations to judicial decision making as a method of law reform . . .

Apart from the doctrines of precedent and *stare decisis* . . . there are three further considerations which limit the potential of judicial law reform. First, any judicial change of the law will have a restrospective effect for the parties – this could only be avoided if English Courts adopt the American practice of prospective[19] overruling. As a consequence, judicial change may produce injustice for those who have organised their affairs, *e.g.* by effecting[20] insurance policies or settling claims on the basis of the old law. Secondly, the lack of information presented to the judge may inhibit change. It may be easy for the judge to realise that the present law is wrong, less easy on the basis of the limited information relating to the particular case before him, to know what general principles applicable to all cases should replace the existing law. A third related problem arises where the proposed reform requires not simply the replacement of one general principle with another but rather with more detailed provisions. The court can explain how a reform applies to the particular case before it and leave future cases to work out the details of the reform in other factual contexts, but the resulting uncertainty may produce more injustice than leaving the law unreformed. Where law reform demands a wide ranging investigation of available information and detailed reforming provisions with no retrospective effect, the courts are clearly not the most appropriate medium. Rather the task is better left to the permanent law reform agencies.

Farrar and Dugdale, *Introduction to Legal Method* (Sweet and Maxwell 1984), pp. 209–10.

Text notes:
17 the more usual phrase is 'to a certain extent'
18 only
19 'looking forward', contrasted with 'retrospective' earlier in the sentence
20 bringing into effect

In addition to the limitations mentioned by the authors above, the role of the judge as law reformer is further restricted by the fact that a case involving an area of law which is in need of reform may not come before the courts at a suitable time. As Professor Jackson states, 'litigants and appellants cannot be relied upon to produce precedent-fodder when it is needed'. He then proceeds to provide a case study to illustrate the inadequacy of judicial law reform:

> An example may be taken which is now a little dated, but is still of interest because it shows the influence of a member of the judiciary who was undoubtedly a reforming influence. *Ghani* v. *Jones* dealt with police searches. The main point was whether documents seized as the result of a search could be retained or should be returned forthwith,[21] but wider issues came to be considered. There was a tiresome precedent in an earlier case which said that if the police had lawful authority to search premises where someone was arrested, material relevant for *any* crime committed by *any* person could be seized. In *Ghani* v. *Jones* Lord Denning made an attempt to put the law into better shape: after making an admirable summary of the problem he formulated five requisites for police taking articles for use as evidence. The third requisite was that: 'The police officers must have reasonable grounds to believe that the person in possession of it has himself committed the crime, or is implicated in it, or is accessory to it'. But that did not cover the case of the innocent possessor. Suppose your car is driven away without your permission and the police have now recovered it and want to examine it for finger-prints, bloodstains and so on: can you insist on having you car back at once? Another tiresome earlier case suggested that an innocent owner could refuse to allow his car to be inspected. In his original oral judgment Lord Denning expressed 'some misgiving'[22] over that decision, but did not deal with the point further, then in the later written version of his judgment he added a suggestion that the police could inspect the car against the innocent owner's wishes if the owner's refusal was 'quite unreasonable'. This is hardly a tolerable way to reform the law. The first point about the case was that it showed up a shocking gap in the law in that there was no provision allowing a search warrant[23] to be obtained to look for evidence of murder or other serious offences, however obvious it was that relevant evidence was likely to be found on the premises: but it was beyond the competence of the Court of Appeal to deal with that, because the power to issue search warrants is regulated by statute, and it was a case for legislation. As things stood, all the court could do was to lay down rules about what the police could and could not do once[24] they had managed to get access. The second point is that no judge, not even one so well equipped as Lord Denning, can formulate principles or rules to govern police action simply as a result of hearing submissions in court. The higher courts in the USA have the practice of *amicus* briefs filed by persons who are not actual parties to the litigation, and the European Court at Luxembourg invariably has a report from an Advocate General representing the public interest. We have no such system and the court hears no more than what the parties see fit to put forward: there may be many points and considerations that are relevant but which are not put before the court. It is almost inevitable that

rulings arrived at through the courts operating in this way will be insufficient and they may be positively detrimental[25] to the public interest. But in the case of something as important as the scope of police powers it is not realistic to expect the courts to do a satisfactory job even with this kind of help, and the only process that ought to be acceptable to a civilised system is that a draft[26] of any proposed change in the law should be available for examination and discussion.

Spencer (ed.), *Jackson's Machinery of Justice* (Cambridge University Press 1989), pp. 494–5.

Text notes:
21 at once
22 feelings of doubt
23 written authority
24 as soon as
25 harmful
26 outline

This analysis highlights the third and fourth problems discussed in the extract from Farrar and Dugdale. The law relating to police powers of search is too complex to be resolved by judicial decisions. Such matters can only be fairly regulated by statute. The relevant police powers are now laid out in the Police and Criminal Evidence Act 1984.

So we can see that the role of the judge as law reformer is limited. Nevertheless, the limitations should be weighed against one important strength – judicial law reform does not rely upon political priorities, government goodwill and the availability of parliamentary time. This is a very significant advantage.

Writing

9 The two previous extracts (from Farrar and Dugdale, and Spencer) discuss the problems relating to law reform by the judiciary. The first extract mentions four limitations and the second illustrates two of these. A fifth limiting factor is raised by Professor Jackson's comment following the first of these extracts.

Use these five points in a short essay discussing the role of the judiciary in law reform. Do not lift material directly from the extracts; first make notes, then use your notes to write the essay.

9.2.2 Law reform agencies

The most effective part of the machinery of law reform exists in the form of government agencies with the specific function of examining possible areas of reform. These agencies may be *ad hoc*[27] or permanent.

Ad hoc *commissions*

Royal Commissions are *ad hoc* agencies which are set up by the government to review a specific issue. A good example of these is the Royal Commission on Legal Services which produced the Benson Report in 1979. These commissions undertake a wide-ranging investigation of the area involved.

The members are eminent people in their field of expertise. However, Royal Commissions are not permanent bodies and they have no permanent administrative framework; the members are very busy people who have many other commitments.

Text note:
27 organised when the need arises, not permanent

Permanent standing committees
A better solution is seen in the setting up of permanent standing committees to which problem areas can be referred. The **Law Reform Committee** examines reforms in the civil law whilst the **Criminal Law Revision Committee** deals with the criminal law. These agencies have been effective in recommending reforms which have resulted in legislation. For example, the work of the Law Reform Committee led to the passing of the Occupiers Liability Act 1957; the Suicide Act 1961 and the Theft Act 1968 resulted from reports of the Criminal Law Revision Committee.

Both agencies – although permanent – are, however, limited in their effectiveness. Their members are part-time and they are restricted by a lack of financial and research facilities. Of particular importance is the fact that they are not self-motivated; they can only consider problems which have been referred to them by the relevant Minister. Moreover, they can only make proposals whilst the actual implementation of them is left to Parliament. The effectiveness of their work is therefore determined by political priorities and the availability of parliamentary time.

The Law Commission
In an attempt to overcome some of these weaknesses a permanent, full-time agency, the Law Commission, was established in 1965. Its first chairman was Lord Scarman – then Mr Justice Scarman, a High Court judge. The Law Commission comprises four other Law Commissioners and a supporting staff of 50. The Commissioners are appointed for five years from the legal profession, the judiciary and academic lawyers.

The Law Commission Act 1965 specifies a comprehensive range of responsibilities of the Commission. First, the codification of the law. This involves reducing the case law and statute law on a particular subject into a single statute. An example of this is the Sale of Goods Act 1979 which brought together the principles of the Sale of Goods Act 1893 and the cases which evolved from it. The second function is the revision of the statute book by proposing the repeal of obsolete laws. The third is that of consolidation which involves bringing together all the relevant statutes on one topic into a single piece of legislation. Finally, it has the responsibility of simplification and modernisation of the law.

Law Commission reforms
The Commission has established a procedure for carrying out its proposals. It first publishes a working paper on the relevant subject and receives comments and opinions on it. It then issues a final report which contains a draft bill for the government to enact if the proposals are accepted.

Many of the Law Commission's proposals have resulted in legislation. In the period 1965–76 it produced 41 reports, 85 per cent of which were implemented. However, this figure dropped to less than 50 per cent in the following period to 1982. This reduction again highlights the essentially political nature of law reform. Spencer argues that the Law Commission is 'tied hand and foot to the Lord Chancellor and the Lord Chancellor's department' (*Jackson's Machinery of Justice*, CUP 1989). This view can be compared to that of Mr Justice Scarman who saw the nature of the Law Commission as essentially apolitical. Let us examine these two views in more detail.

First, Mr Justice Scarman speaking in 1967 as the first chairman of the Law Commission:

> The Commission is an advisory body; Parliament is to be the source of any new law that may arise from proposals of the Commission. The Commission has been called into being to advise the government and Parliament, first in the planning of law reform; secondly, in the formulation of detailed proposals for the reform of the law. The theory that underlies the Act is that law reform should be the province of the legislature; that the legislature requires specialist advice in the planning and formulation of law reform; and that this advice should be provided by a body independent of the executive and of Parliament. It is significant that members of the Commission are disqualified from sitting in the House of Commons. It is equally significant that it is possible to appoint to the Commission one who holds judicial office, without the need of relinquishing his office.[28] It is clearly contemplated by the Act that, once the Lord Chancellor has approved a programme prepared by the Commission for the purpose of law reform, both the programme, and any proposals made by the Commission in the light of the programme, shall become public property. There is therefore a significant difference between government legislation and legislation based upon proposals by the Commission. It is the practice of governments to keep secret their detailed legislative proposals until the appropriate Bill is introduced. Law Reform Bills introduced pursuant[29] to a Commission proposal are likely, however, to follow the draft of a Bill already published with the Commission's proposal.
>
> A plain implication of these provisions of the Act is that proposals for the reform of the law, though made to the legislature, ought to be kept outside the field of political controversy. They are to be carefully considered by an expert body before the introduction of legislation. The public is to be given an opportunity of debating them – also before the introduction of legislation. And, finally, when Parliament itself has to consider them, it should have the benefit of expert advice and prior public discussion.
>
> Two further features of the Commission should be mentioned. It holds an initiative in the reform process, and it is more than a mere committee, whose existence may be terminated by the stroke of a Minister's pen. It is an institution, having a statutory existence. Neither the anger of a Minister nor the rebellion and resignation of Commissioners can destroy it. It exists until Parliament by enactment delivers the coup de grâce[30] . . . Equally important, . . . is its right and duty to originate proposals in the field of reform. These proposals are embodied into a programme which, once it survives the veto of the Lord Chancellor, must be published, and confers upon the Commission independence of action within its limits.
>
> The new pattern of law reform has, I hope, emerged from this outline. The government and Parliament have recognised reform as a responsibility of the legislature. They have established an advisory legal body, institutional in character, to plan the course of reform, and to formulate detailed reform proposals for their consideration and, also, for the consideration of the

public. Nevertheless, it is intended to keep law reform out of politics. In this endeavour reliance will be placed both upon the character of the Commission, divorced as it is from the executive and Parliament, and upon the very process it is called upon to operate, i.e. the independent planning and formulation of proposals – both to be carried out in the full glare of publicity before submission to the government or Parliament. The idea is that this independent specialist body should engage in a process which is itself designed to produce proposals that, by the time they are submitted to Parliament, will enjoy a substantial consensus of opinion, both in the legal profession and amongst the lay interests affected.

Yet[31] the Commission does not enjoy the independence of the courts. The government can refuse to approve its programme. If the Minister imposes his veto upon the programme, or any part of it, the Commission is powerless. Furthermore, the members of the Commission have not the security of tenure[32] enjoyed by the judicary. They hold office as Commissioners, 'subject to such conditions as may be determined by the Lord Chancellor'. And, finally, there is no compulsion, other than the force of public opinion, upon the government to introduce, or even to provide Parliamentary time for, the Commission's legislative proposals.

Notwithstanding this degree of government control, the Law Commission does represent an attempt to introduce into the law-making process the independent thought and technical learning which one expects to find in the courts. It is an attempt to make available to government and Parliament this independence and learning, without involving either in political controversy. It is too early yet to decide whether this subtle experiment will work. The Law Commission has the delicate task of keeping clear of political controversy. The government and Parliament must impose upon themselves a discipline strict enough to provide time and opportunity for the Law Commission's proposals. Perhaps the real ground[33] for optimism is the belief that Parliament would not have created this body if it did not intend to use it, and that its very existence, if accompanied by a flow of published legislative proposals, should build up a public pressure for action which could lead to results.

Scarman, *Law Reform* (Routledge & Kegan Paul 1968), pp. 11–16.

Text notes:

28 see question **10a** below
29 in accordance with
30 finishing stroke which kills someone (French)
31 note the importance of this 'signpost' word as it marks a turn to contrasting issues
32 holding a post for an assured period of time
33 reason

Comprehension check

10 a Note 28: Why is this point significant?
b How is the political independence of Commission members encouraged?
c What are the two tasks of the Commission?
d What is the important difference between government legislation and legislation resulting from Commission proposals?
e What two aids will the Commission provide when Parliament comes to consider legal reform proposals?
f What strengths and weaknesses of the Commission does Mr Justice Scarman point out?

Mr Justice Scarman was speaking only two years after the creation of the Law Commission. His optimism over its future role may now be judged by some to have been misplaced; whilst recognising the dependence of the Commission on the goodwill of government and the potential for control by the Lord Chancellor, he was confident that this would not significantly limit its effectiveness. Spencer analyses these problems and over twenty years later reaches a different conclusion:

> The Law Commission's functions as laid down in the Law Commissions Act 1965 look impressive – but close attention should be given to the phrases which are printed in italic type in the quotation that follows:
>
> 3(1) It shall be the duty of each of the Commissions to take and keep under review all the law *with which they are respectively concerned* with a view to its systematic development and reform, and including in particular the codification of such law, the elimination of anomalies,[34] the repeal[35] of obsolete[36] and unnecessary enactments, the reduction of the number of separate enactments and generally the simplification and modernisation of the law, and for that purpose –
>
> (a) to receive and consider any proposals for the reform of the law *which may be made or referred to them*;
>
> (b) to prepare *and submit to the Minister* [i.e. the Lord Chancellor] from time to time programmes for the examination of different branches of the law with a view to reform, including *recommendations* as to the agency (whether the Commission or another body) by which any such examination should be carried out;
>
> (c) to undertake, *pursuant to any such recommendations approved by the Minister*, the examination of particular branches of the law and the formulation, by means of draft Bills or otherwise, of proposals for reform therein;[37]
>
> (d) to prepare from time to time *at the request of the Minister* comprehensive programmes of consolidation and statute law revision, and to undertake the preparation of draft Bills pursuant to any such programme *approved by the Minister*,
>
> (e) to provide advice and information to government departments and other authorities *concerned at the instance*[38] *of the Government* with proposals for the reform or amendment of any branch of the law;
>
> (f) to obtain such[39] information as to[40] the legal system of other countries as[41] appears to the Commissioners likely to facilitate[42] *the performance of any of their functions*.
>
> (2) The Minister shall lay before Parliament any programmes prepared by the Commission *and approved by him* and any proposals for reform formulated by the Commission pursuant to such programmes.
>
> (3) Each of the Commissions shall make an annual report to the Minister on their proceedings, and the Minister shall lay the report before Parliament *with such comments (if any) as he thinks fit*.
>
> What this means is that the Law Commission looks at nothing except what the Lord Chancellor tells it to look at, and that nothing happens in response to one of its Reports except what the Lord Chancellor is prepared to allow. The Law Commission is independent only in the very limited sense that nobody can tell it what to say about a problem if it is permitted to say anything at all . . .
>
> . . . The Law Commission was conceived on a grand scale as a body that would take its own panoramic view of the law, identify the parts that are working badly, and propose sensible reforms. Now it looks increasingly as if it is being reduced to a kind of government research institute existing to provide specific answers to narrow legal problems as and when a minister desires one – or wishes to forget a problem whilst appearing to do something

about it. Instead of being the architect of the new law it could become the jobbing-builder[43] of the old.

Spencer (ed.), *Jackson's Machinery of Justice* (Cambridge University Press 1989), pp. 504–6.

Text notes:
34 deviations from established order
35 annulment, cancellation
36 out of date
37 (formal) in that place, i.e. in this context in particular branches of law
38 suggestion
39 see note **41**
40 relating to
41 see language point below
42 make easier
43 person specialising in small repairs

Language point

Note the construction indicated by notes 39 and 41 in the extract:

'such information . . . as appears . . .'

meaning:

'any information which appears'

Legal exercises

11 How does the doctrine of *stare decisis* limit the ability of the judiciary to reform the law?

12 What is the main advantage of judicial law reform?

13 List the permanent law reform agencies and their functions.

14 In what circumstances would the government set up a Royal Commission?

15 Why is the reactive nature of most reform agencies a limit on their effectiveness?

16 Is the Law Commission reactive or self-motivating?

17 Distinguish between codification and consolidation.

18 Why is Spencer so critical of the Law Commission Act 1965?

19 How could the Law Commission Act be amended to take account of these criticisms?

9.3 A case study in law reform: liability for defective premises

This case study provides an interesting example of law which was changed over a period of time by both the legislature and the judiciary. The resulting confusion is made apparent in the text.

Liability for defective premises

An owner of premises was for long regarded as owing no duty of care to anyone to whom he sold them. The owner might have negligently built a house or indeed a housing estate with the result that many years later the premises suffered from subsidence[44] but under the old rule he would not have been liable to the purchasers. However, if the builder was not also the owner/seller he would have been liable to the purchasers under the general *Donoghue* v. *Stevenson* principle. Thus a house purchaser's rights against a negligent builder depended entirely upon whether the builder was also the owner, a result which was capricious,[45] unjust and in the light of the steadily widening *Donoghue* duty principle, increasingly anomalous.[46]

As with the assessment of damages, this problem was also included in the Law Commission's first programme of reform. The Commission reported in 1970 recommending that the owner's immunity from negligence liability should be abolished. The Commission went further and recommended that all those who undertake work in connection with dwellings should owe a duty of care to anyone acquiring an interest in the property to see that their work was done in a proper manner. This duty would obviously be broken by a negligent buider but also by one who simply provided work of a defective quality. Finally, the Commission recommended that the limitation period for bringing a claim for breach of this proposed duty should be six years from the date of completion of the work. These recommendations were enacted in the Defective Premises Act 1972, section 1 of which established the new statutory duty and section 3 abolished the owners' immunity.[47]

By an unfortunate coincidence,[48] just after the Defective Premises Bill was introduced into Parliament in December 1971, the Court of Appeal itself decided upon reform in their decision in *Dutton* v. *Bognor Regis Urban District Council* There the majority stated that the owner immunity principle was wrong and that a builder/owner owed a duty of care like anyone else. Subsequent cases have clearly established this to be the new common law.[49] Thus, with the decision in *Dutton*, section 3 of the Act became redundant.[50] It is in the words of one commentator, 'an unparalleled instance of legislation being otiose[50] before it has even been passed.'

Worse was to follow. In *Dutton*, Lord Denning had stated that the six-year limitation period for common law claims against the builder should run from the date of his negligent work as that was the date of the damage and limitation periods for the sort of negligence run from the date of damage. At least on this basis, a plaintiff would not be disadvantaged by suing under the statute rather than under common law and section 1 would still offer the advantage of imposing a stricter duty on the builder. But in a case called *Sparham-Souter* v. *Town & Country Developments* in 1976, Lord Denning and the Court of Appeal changed their view as to the date from which the common law limitation period should run. Now they decided that the period should run only from the date on which the damage might reasonably have been discovered by the plaintiff. Take the common case where the evidence of the builder's negligent work, the subsidence, etc., does not appear until more than six years from the completion of work: the plaintiff could not sue the builder under section 1 of the Act as the statutory limitation period has expired but he could sue at common law following the *Sparham-Souter* decision. The court in *Sparham-Souter* recognised that their decision effectively out-reformed[51] the reform legislation but they saw the problem in terms of a lack of co-ordination. Roskill L.J. said, 'in the (early 1970s) law reform was being pursued through two different channels, the Law Commission and Parliament on the one hand, and the court on the other . . . without either apparently appreciating what developments the other was seeking to make.'

Sparham-Souter upset the neat pattern of law reform recommended by the Law Commission, but worse still[52] was to follow. What it did was to open up the possibility of claims against the builder and others being brought many years after the completion of the work. In *Dennis* v. *Charnwood Borough Council* in 1982, the house owners brought a claim over 25 years after the house was completed. They succeeded because the damage that occurred could not reasonably have been discovered until 21 years from completion and they claimed within six years from that date. In fact the owners in this case sued the local authority for negligently approving the builder's poor foundations. They did not sue the building firm probably because they were no longer in existence. Many claims of this nature have been made against local authorities. The long periods between completion and claim puts them in a very difficult position. Many will not have any records relating to what they did 30 years ago. In his concluding remarks in *Dennis*, Lawton L.J. suggested that a compulsory insurance scheme for builders might solve the problem, but this type of reform is certainly beyond the scope of the judiciary and most likely the Law Commission as well.

In the event[53] the House of Lords moved[54] to provide at least a temporary half-solution. In late 1982 the case of *Pirelli General Cable Works Ltd.* v. *Oscar Faber & Partners*, they decided that both the views of limitation periods taken in *Sparham-Souter* and that originally taken in *Dutton* were wrong. The period should run from the date when the damage actually occurred. This might be years before it could have been reasonably discovered but equally it might be years after completion. The new rule may give a plaintiff some advantage as a result of suing under the common law rather than under the Defective Premises Act but the advantage will be nothing like as great as was the case under the *Sparham-Souter* rule. The new rule does, however, present a very difficult factual problem; how do you tell when hidden damage first occurred? The *Pirelli* decision is likely to mark the last judicial attempt to reform this particular area of law. The Law Lords all looked forward to the results of a new review of the problem by the Law Reform Committee. As Lord Scarman said, 'the reform needed is not the substitution of a new principle or rule of law for an existing one but a detailed set of provisions to replace existing statute law. The true way forward is not departure from precedent but by amending legislation.'[55]

Farrar and Dugdale, *An Introduction to Legal Method* (Sweet and Maxwell 1984), pp. 215–17.

Text notes:

44 sinking lower into the ground
45 often changing, unreliable
46 see note **34** above
47 exemption, safety
48 happening at the same time
49 *Dutton* was overruled by HL in *Murphy* v. *Brentwood District Council* [1990] 2 All ER 908
50 both words mean 'superfluous', 'unnecessary'
51 see language point below
52 even worse
53 what actually happened
54 took action
55 these situations are now covered by the Latent Damage Act 1986

Language point

Note the construction of the verb 'to outreform', meaning 'to surpass in reforming'. This is not a usual word but is formed on the pattern of:

to outdo = to surpass, do better than
to outlive = live longer than

Comprehension check

20 Using note form, list in chronological order the changes made to statutes and the common law in relation to liability for defective premises:

Pre-1971 Builders owed duty of care only if . . . .
1971 . . . .
etc.

Whilst acknowledging that this example may give an unfair impression of the process of law reform, the authors justify its use to counteract any impression 'that legal change can be fitted into neat analytical compartments'. They conclude:

> . . . that although it is useful to analyse the different types of legal change and the different methods of achieving it, real life does not fit neatly into the categories. Reform of 'lawyers law'[56] may indirectly raise issues of social policy and vice versa. Judges, reform agencies and politicans all have their own interest in promoting change. Rather than holding back to leave the matter to the most appropriate body, they may plunge in with the feeling that it is better to do something when the opportunity arises rather than to wait for the perfect time and approach. All this is part of the 'internal dynamic' of the law. It is this dynamic – the ever-changing nature of law which makes its study both stimulating and challenging.
>
> Farrar and Dugdale, *Introduction to Legal Method* (Sweet and Maxwell 1984), pp. 220–1.

Text note:
56 i.e. as decribed in the extract from Farrar and Dugdale on p. 203

Legal exercises

21 Botchitt Construction plc build an estate of houses in 1969. The foundations are negligently laid and this causes structural damage to the houses. Reginald buys one of the houses from Botchitt in 1970. In 1975 cracks begin to appear in the walls of the loft. Reginald does not notice the cracks until 1979. He is advised that it will cost £20,000 to rectify the fault. He wishes to sue Botchitt Construction plc to recover this cost. Advise him if he could recover under:

a the law prior to 1972;
b the Defective Premises Act 1972;
c *Dutton* v. *Bognor Regis Urban District Council*;
d *Sparham-Souter* v. *Town & Country Developments*;
e *Pirelli General Cable Works Ltd* v. *Oscar Faber & Partners*.

9.4 The need for a Ministry of Justice?

We have seen that political considerations and the mechanics of the legislative process are significant factors in the implementation of proposals for reform.(1) Success is dependent upon the priorities of government and the availability of parliamentary time to enact the proposals.(2) These problems are further compounded by the way in which responsibility for the different aspects of the legal system is divided between different government departments.(3) Gifford, in *Where's the Justice*, argues that this is not only inefficient but also leads to injustice and partiality.(4)

Language point

What is a paragraph?

The above text is a good illustration of how a paragraph differs from a series of disconnected sentences. In a paragraph the sentences are bound together in various ways:

Sentence (1) introduces the concepts of 'political considerations' and the 'mechanics of the legislative process'.

Sentence (2) gives examples of these concepts.[57]

Sentence (3) refers back to 'these problems' in sentence (2).

Sentence (4) uses 'this' to refer back.[58]

Text notes:
57 see question **22a** below
58 see question **22b** below

Comprehension check

22 a Note 57: What are the examples given in sentence (2)?
b Note 58: What does 'this' refer back to?

Some of the present divisions of responsibility between the Lord Chancellor and other ministers make no sense at all. The Lord Chancellor is responsible for the administration and procedures of the civil courts, and of the Crown Court, but not of the magistrates' courts, which are the preserve of the Home Office. But the Home Secretary has major responsibilities for the police, and should be removed from any control of the magistrates' courts, in which the police have a partisan interest.[59] For the same reason it is wrong that the reform of the criminal law is a matter for the Home Secretary, though civil law reform is for the Lord Chancellor.

The Lord Chancellor is involved, either directly or through recommendation to the Prime Minister, in the appointment of most of the people who sit in courts and tribunals – but not all. A glaring[60] exception concerns immigration adjudicators, who hear appeals of crucial importance about people's rights to enter or stay in Britain. They are appointed by the Home Secretary, whose department is responsible for the very decisions which are being appealed against. Many of them have a background in the colonial service or the civil service. It is not surprising that there are bitter complaints about their anti-immigrant bias.

The position with regard to the funding of law centres[61] has become chaotic. The majority have received grants from the Department of the Environment under the Urban Programme. That department has determined that it will only fund law centres over their starting years, and it expects local authorities to take over the funding. Local authorities, however, are often the other party[62] to actions brought by law centres' clients. Many refuse to fund an agency which will sue them when they neglect their legal duties, and some law centres have had to close down after a change in the political control of a local authority. Seven law centres were rescued from closure by

Lord Elwyn-Jones when he was Lord Chancellor, but Lord Hailsham, while keeping this funding going, has refused to extend it to any others. The Lord Chancellor's Advisory Committee on Legal Aid in its January 1985 report complained that 'lack of clear ministerial responsibility and direction for legal services is a chronic problem'.

This confusion causes injustice, above all to those whose rights need greater protection. What is needed is a clear and sensible division of responsibilities. On the one hand those agencies of the State which are designed to control and order people, such as the police, the prison service and the immigration service, should stay with the Home Office. On the other hand those agencies which are designed to provide justice, which includes the control of the abuses and errors of the controlling agencies, are the proper concern of a Ministry of Justice.

Gifford, *Where's the Justice* (Penguin 1986), pp. 19–21.

Text notes

59 lacking objectivity (before the establishment of the Crown Prosecution Service the police brought prosecutions in the magistrates' courts and also collected the evidence)
60 obvious
61 places where free legal advice is available
62 the opposing side

Comprehension check

23 a Draw a diagram to show the present divisions of responsibilities described in paragraphs 1 and 2.
b Draw a diagram to show Gifford's proposed division of responsibilities.
c Why does Gifford think that immigration adjudicators should not be appointed by the Home Secretary?
d Why does Gifford think that local authorities are unwilling to fund law centres?

The argument for the creation of a Ministry of Justice is that in addition to increasing efficiency and fairness it would make one minister accountable to Parliament for the provision of legal services and the progress of law reform. Gifford proposes that the minister's duties should be defined as follows: 'It shall be the duty of the Minister of Justice to promote the establishment in England and Wales of comprehensive legal services to secure that the people of England and Wales receive such advice and assistance as may be effective and necessary for them to obtain justice under the law for the redress of their grievances.'[63] Such a declaration he argues 'would fix the accountability of the Minister to Parliament and set the goal to be achieved'.

The idea of a Ministry of Justice is not new. It was first proposed by the Haldane Committee in 1918 and more recently by the Alliance[64] and Labour Parties. It is, however, an idea with many opponents. The arguments for and against are considered in the next extract.

Text note:

63 injustice
64 one of the major opposition parties in the 1980s

It is often said that the course of law reform would be much smoother if there was a single Ministry of Justice which was responsible for all legal matters, as in many other countries. When nobody is responsible for a thing, the usual result is that there is consistent neglect and therefore there should be a single minister who is definitely responsible . . .

The Machinery of Government Committee, under the chairmanship of Lord Haldane, reviewed the whole position of the administrative side of the legal system. This Committee broke fresh ground in pointing out 'the difficulty of getting the attention of the Government to law reform', and added this argument to that[65] of 'the total inadequacy of the organisation which controls the general administration of the very large staffs' to produce a most impressive case for the establishment of a Minister of Justice. The Committee proposed that the Home Secretary should become Minister of Justice, by the process of transferring some of the work of the Home Office to other departments, leaving the Home Office with its present duties connected with legal administration, and transferring to the Home Office the general work of administration in connection with justice that is now vested in the Lord Chancellor. This would leave the Lord Chancellor free to devote his energies to judicial work and to his position as principal legal adviser to the government. The proposals were not limited to a mere shuffle of existing duties. 'The Minister of Justice would probably sit in the House of Commons and he ought to be accessible to those who have suggestions to make. Besides his administration of the staffs of the various Courts in England, his Department should contain experts charged with the duty of watching over the necessities of law reform, and of studying the development of the subject at home and abroad.'

It is unfortunate that the name Minister of Justice has a sinister sound to many English ears, despite the fact that such a minister is commonly found in most respectable countries. The fear is that 'justice' would then come under his 'control'. In 1986, when the idea was again put forward by the Liberal-SDP Alliance, Lord Hailsham told the bar that it would be 'a menace to the independence of the courts and the judiciary'.

This argument is difficult to dispel because no critic ever explains exactly what it is that he thinks would happen. In some countries with a Ministry of Justice, the appointment and promotion of judges is in the hands of the Minister of Justice. In England the question of a Ministry of Justice need not be complicated by this problem, for there is no reason why this power has to be given to the Minister of Justice, and it could be retained by the Lord Chancellor: indeed, this is what the Machinery of Government Committee of 1918 recommended. It is difficult to see how giving a Minister of Justice control over the administrative arrangements of all the law courts, and the appointment of all the supporting staff, could interfere with the independence of the judges or the integrity of the process of trial. Over many years the Lord Chancellor's Department has been taking over the administrative side of the law courts by a piecemeal process,[66] and nowadays it is only the magistrates' courts which remain largely outside his control. It has not been suggested that any judge has a scrap[67] less independence as a result of this (although it has meant that judges have lost their power to appoint relatives to jobs as court officials without there being any opportunity for public criticism). If the anticipated evil is a Minister of Justice who might sit in the House of Commons and so be an ordinary political minister, without the legal standing and conventional aloofness[68] of the Lord Chancellor, it must be remembered that the Home Secretary already performs many of the duties of a Minister of Justice, and that he no more controls or seeks to control criminal courts than the Lord Chancellor controls or seeks to control civil courts. . .

. . . Professor Jackson was originally a strong supporter of the idea of a Minister of Justice when he wrote the first edition of this book in 1940, but in his latest edition he said this:

Many people who are anxious for law reform have continued to regard a Ministry of Justice as being most desirable, and think that such a ministry would resolve their difficulties. I was of that opinion when I first wrote this book, but I have since come to the conclusion that a ministry is not a matter of such great importance. There is often some gain in rearranging departments. In the last few years the ministries responsible for health and housing have been rearranged, but that does not of itself ensure better health or more houses. I do not know of any project for law reform that has failed to progress for lack of a minister. The fact that some suggested reform has not been taken up either by the Lord Chancellor or the Home Secretary does not show that a sound project has fallen between two stools,[69] for who can say that a Minister of Justice would have been more receptive? The original proposal in *Law Reform Now* was that a Law Commission should have a Vice-Chancellor as its head and that he should sit in the House of Commons. That would have made him a minister and a politician. The course actually followed was to create an independent Law Commission and the fact that the Commission's proposals appear to find their way to the statute book without undue difficulty or delay weakens the case for having a Minister of Justice.

Since this was written we have been through a period dominated by an increasingly idiosyncratic[70] Lord Chancellor who was plainly little interested in the Law Commission. When anxious to reform civil procedure, as he was, he set up his own Civil Justice Review . . . – which he managed to do with such little tact that he seems to have antagonised[71] many of those whose cooperation would be needed if any of the reforms were actually to be carried out. Meanwhile a number of careful and sensible reports from the Law Commission have been permitted to languish unattended to, not because there were any real objections of principle to what they contained, but because other departments besides the Lord Chancellor's Department were involved and could not be bothered with them, and the Lord Chancellor's Department lacked either the muscle or the interest to conquer their[72] apathy.[73] Speaking of the influence of the Department of the Environment on various reports on the law of landlord and tenant, Oerton[74] writes 'it was not that any of our Reports was itself political or biased: no one suggested that. It was simply that any Bill dealing with landlord and tenant law might (so it was said) be made a bone of political contention and so be difficult to pilot through Parliament. And the Department was not prepared to make the necessary sacrifice of time and energy for Bills designed, not to win votes for the Government of the day nor to further Government polices, but merely to improve the law'.

A former Law Commissioner, Stephen Cretney, is less bitter and more optimistic about what has been happening to the Law Commission's proposals than is Oerton; but concludes a review by saying 'I personally doubt whether much more can be achieved short of a major restructuring of departmental responsibilities – involving, for example, a transfer of responsibility for reform of the criminal law from the Home Office to the Lord Chancellor/Minister of Justice.'[75] If Professor Jackson were still alive he might now be returning to his original views on the subject.

Spencer (ed.), *Jackson's Machinery of Justice* (Cambridge University Press 1989), pp. 506–8.

Text notes:

65 i.e. the argument
66 one part at a time
67 a small amount
68 being apart
69 here means having failed because neither of two people feels responsible
70 possessing characteristics peculiar to himself

71 aroused hostility
72 see question **24** below
73 lack of interest
74 *A Lament for the Law Commission* (1987).
75 'The politics of law reform' (1985) 48 MLR 493, 513.

Comprehension check

24 Note 72: Who is being referred to by 'their'?

It is suggested by some that law reform has such a low priority on the political agenda because it is not an issue which concerns the electorate and therefore is not likely to attract many votes. If this is true it only serves to highlight the fact that, as with the effectiveness of the present system of law reform, any change in the system will be determined by political priorities and attitudes.

Comprehension check

25 According to the proposals of the Haldane Committee how would the following areas of responsibility be allocated:

- **a** administration of court staff in England?
- **b** general administrative work related to justice?
- **c** judicial work?
- **d** study of need for law reform?
- **e** principal legal adviser to government?
- **f** study of law reform in England and overseas?

26 Working with a partner, and with reference to paragraphs 1–4 of the extract above, one of you should list the arguments and counter-arguments (arguments which reply to previous arguments) **for** the proposal for a Minister of Justice, and other should list the arguments **against** the proposal. Then, present these arguments orally. If you are working alone, list arguments both **for** and **against**.

27 What reason(s) does Professor Jackson give in paragraph 5 for changing his mind?

28 What factors are mentioned in paragraph 6 which could explain the last sentence in the extract?

Research

29 Does the government in your country include a Ministry of Justice? If so:

- **a** What are its responsibilties?
- **b** To whom is the minister accountable?

If not:

- **a** Who is responsible for the administration of justice?
- **b** What agencies exist for the purpose of law reform?

Additional reading

Law reform is not a subject which is usually covered in very much depth in general textbooks on the English legal system, although most will contain some information about it. *The Law-Making Process* by Zander (Weidenfeld & Nicholson) contains a very stimulating chapter on the process of law reform which includes materials and commentary. *Introduction to Legal Method* by Farrar and Dugdale (Sweet and Maxwell) takes a wider perspective by setting law reform in its social and cultural perspective. *The Law Commission and Law Reform* by Zellick (Sweet and Maxwell) provides a list of Law Commission reports and publications and the resulting legislation.

10
The European dimension

Summary

Legal content

Aim

To provide an introduction to the nature of the European Convention on Human Rights and the institutions and law of the European Community (EC). Particular emphasis will be placed on the impact of these institutions on the English legal system and English law. Case studies will increase awareness of the issues involved.

Language content

Grammar: possessive adjectives + gerund; 'neither' + verb inversion; subjunctive in 'be it . . . or . . .'; subject–verb inversion in unreal conditionals

Vocabulary: verb + noun collocations

10.1 The European Convention on Human Rights

The European Convention on Human Rights (ECHR) is based on the Universal Declaration of Human Rights (UDHR) which was adopted by the General Assembly of the United Nations in 1948. This Declaration sought to define a set of individual rights which were considered to be fundamental to the well-being of citizens of all countries. They included the right to an adequate standard of living, the right to work, the right to a fair trial and the right to own property. The ECHR is not as broad as the UDHR but is nevertheless an important document. Its aims are discussed in the following extract.

Pre-reading question

1 What were the aims of the ECHR when it was founded?

The Convention was drafted under the auspices[1] of the Council of Europe, an international organisation composed of 21 West European states which was formed in 1949 as the result of the first post-war attempt at unifying Europe. The impetus[2] for the Convention came from the need to define more closely the obligations of members of the Council concerning 'human rights', and, more generally, from the wish to provide a bulwark[3] against communism and to prevent a recurrence[4] of conditions which Europe had then recently witnessed. It was believed that the Convention would serve as an alarm that would bring violations of human rights to the attention of the international community in time for it[5] to take action to suppress them.[6] In practice, this function of the Convention, which imagines large-scale violations of human rights, has largely remained dormant.[7] The Convention has instead been used primarily to raise questions of isolated weaknesses in legal systems that basically conform to its requirements and which are representative of the 'common hertitage of political traditions, ideals, freedom and the rule of law' to which the Preamble to the Convention refers. Most commonly such questions have concerned the administration of criminal justice, although the impact of the Convention in other areas is increasingly being explored. The Convention is concerned mainly with civil and political rights.

Bailey, Harris and Jones, *Civil Liberties Cases and Materials* (Butterworths 1980), p. 17.

Text notes:

1 helped by
2 see question **2a** below
3 see question **2b** below
4 noun from 'to recur'
5 see question **2c** below
6 see question **2d** below
7 inactive

Comprehension check

2 **a** Note 2: Use the context to guess the meaning of 'impetus'.
b Note 3: Use the context to guess the meaning of 'bulwark'.
c Note 5: To what does 'it' refer here?
d Note 6: To what does 'them' refer here?

The rights included in the Convention include the right to life, the right to liberty and security of person, the right not to be subjected to inhuman or degrading treatment, not to be required to perform forced or compulsory labour, the right to a fair hearing,[8] to respect for private life, to freedom of thought, conscience and religion, to freedom of expression and assembly and free elections. These, and the other provisions of the ECHR are called Articles.

The parties to the Convention are Austria, Belgium, Cyprus, Denmark, France, the Federal Republic of Germany, Greece, Ireland, Italy, Luxemburg, Malta, the Netherlands, Norway, Portugal, Spain, Sweden, Switzerland, Turkey and the United Kindgom. Liechtenstein is a member of the Council of Europe but not a party to the Convention.

The Treaty provides for individual states to bring a complaint against a member state for breach of the terms of the Convention. Article 25 also allows for complaints to be received from individuals but only if the country against which the complaint is being made has recognised the jurisdiction of the individual to do so. It was not until 1966 that the United Kingdom government ratified[9] the individual right to petition but only on a five-yearly renewable basis. Individuals must comply with the local remedies rule under Article 26 which requires that all domestic remedies of the state's legal system first be[10] exhausted and that a petition be brought within six months from the date on which the final national decision was taken.

Let us now look at the procedure for bringing a petition for breach of the Convention.

Text notes:
8 trial
9 confirmed
10 subjunctive after 'require that . . .'

The machinery for enforcing the Convention consists of a Committee of Foreign Ministers of member states, a body of Commissioners elected by the Committee, and a court composed of judges nominated by the member states. To set the machinery in motion, an individual makes a written application to the Commission, setting out his complaint. This is examined by a single Commissioner, called the *rapporteur*,[11] and on the strength of his *rapport* the Commission decides whether or not to investigate further. Most applications are ruled inadmissible as falling outside the scope of the Convention altogether, either on the basis of the preliminary *rapport*, or, where the *rapporteur* suggests there is a *prima facie* case, as soon as arguments against admissibility have been submitted by the state against which the complaint has been made. If after this the Commission still finds the complaint to be admissible, it holds an investigation of the facts *in camera*,[12] with the aim of procuring a friendly settlement to the dispute. If no friendly settlement is reached, the Commission then reports on the case to the Committee of Ministers, stating whether or not it considers the facts found disclose a breach of the Convention. In addition, the Commission may refer the matter to the court – as may the state complained about (although not the individual complainant). The number of cases which thus eventually get heard by the court is small, rarely exceeding half-a-dozen each year.

The European Court of Human Rights is composed of twenty-one judges, one for each member state. Occasionally all judges sit on a case, but usually cases are heard by a panel of no more than seven. The hearings are oral, and the court has funds available to provide legal aid for individual complainants to be legally represented. In due course the court pronounces in public on whether or not it finds the Convention has been violated.

Spencer (ed.), *Jackson's Machinery of Justice* (Cambridge University Press 1989), pp. 429–30.

Text notes:
11 often used word from French for which there is no single English equivalent to convey the same meaning, roughly the person responsible for investigating and reporting to a higher committee
12 (Latin) in private

You will notice that the author refers to the machinery for **enforcing** the Convention. The word 'enforce' in this context does not bear its usual meaning. Although under Article 53 the 'High Contracting Parties' agree to abide by the decisions of the European Court, the Court does not have the power to compel member states to comply with the terms of the Convention. An adverse judgment does not have any automatic effect on national law nor is the decision of the national court reversed. The Court is not a court of appeal; its decisions can do no more than apply moral pressure on the government involved.

Equally the Commission does not specify what action is required and the lack of supervision of any reforming measures by the Committee of Ministers is a serious weakness. Friendly settlements are more satisfactory as the offending state must satisfy the Commission of the adequacy of any reforms.

The *Golder* case (1975) exemplifies the inadequacy of enforcement procedures. The European Court held that the Home Secretary's refusal to permit the applicant, a prisoner in Parkhurst prison, access to his solicitor was a violation of his rights under Articles 6 and 8. The decision was complied with by a change in the Prison Rules, but with an important limitation that inmates must first ventilate[13] their complaints through the normal internal channels. Six years later, in the case of *Reed* v. *United Kingdom* (1981), this was held to be a restriction on the right of access to the courts; in a friendly settlement a simultaneous ventilation procedure was introduced. The judgment from the case report provides an interesting illustration of the machinery of friendly settlements.

Text note:
13 to publicise for discussion

Comprehension check

3 Why is a friendly settlement more satisfactory than a judgment by the European court?

On 6 December 1979, following the decision on the admissibility of the application and its deliberations on the merits, the Commission placed itself at the disposal of the parties with a view to seeking a friendly settlement in accordance with Article 28 *b.* of the Convention and invited the parties to submit any proposals they wished to make.

On 24 September 1980 the respondent Government made certain proposals for the settlement of part of the application. As a result, on 27 October 1980 a meeting was held in London between representatives of the Commission, assisted by the Secretary, first with the applicant's solicitor and subsequently with representatives of both parties at which proposals for a settlement of the whole application were considered. These proposals comprised two elements, namely[14] the offer of an ex gratia[15] payment to the applicant and an undertaking to implement certain changes in the Prison Rules relating to the internal ventilation of complaints and the restrictions on correspondence relating to prison conditions. These changes had been referred to by the respondent Government in their observations on the merits of the application as already in view. The Government have specified that these proposals were made without admission of liability under the Convention or otherwise.

On 24 February 1981 the Commission asked the applicant's lawyer to state his client's response to these proposals and to indicate the total amount of his fees and disbursements[16] incurred on his client's behalf. This was received on 9 March 1981. After further correspondence the Commission considered the proposals for the settlement on 16 July 1981 and on 23 July 1981 the Secretary wrote to the parties suggesting that a settlement of the whole application might be secured on certain terms.

The applicant's solicitor confirmed by telex of 16 October 1981 that:

"The applicant, Mr Reed, is prepared to declare this application as settled on the basis of the proposals set out in the Secretary's letter of 23 July 1981."

By letter of 11 November 1981 the respondent Government confirmed their agreement to the settlement in the following terms:

"The Government, therefore, without implying any admission of a violation of the Convention, undertakes to do the following in order to bring about a friendly settlement of the whole of this application:

(i) to make an ex gratia payment to Mr Reed of £2000;

(ii) to implement the changes in the restrictions on previous correspondence referred to in paragraph 14 *a* and *b* of the Government's observations on the merits of 1 December 1981. With regard to the change referred to in sub-paragraph *c* of paragraph 14, the Government has subsequently decided that the prior ventilation rule, whereby a prisoner may not raise a complaint about his prison treatment externally until it has been raised through the appropriate internal channel and the investigation has been completed, should be replaced by simultaneous ventilation rule. Prisoners will continue to be required to raise complaints about prison treatment through the appropriate internal channel so that the prison authorities may know about the complaint, investigate it and take any action which may be necessary. However, the prisoner will not have to await the outcome of the investigation before being able to raise the complaint externally. This change, which goes further than the change proposed in paragraph 14 *c* of the Government's observations on the merits will also be implemented on 1 December 1981; and

(iii) to pay Mr Reed 6247.30FF in respect of his lawyer's fees and disbursements."

On 19 November 1981 the Secretary wrote to the applicant and his solicitor pointing out the further change proposed by the replacement of the internal ventilation rule by a simultaneous ventilation rule and requesting them to notify the Commission before 7 December 1981 if these amended proposals were unacceptable to the applicant.

The Commission at its session on 12 December 1981, found that, since no such notification had been received, the parties had come to an agreement regarding the terms of a settlement. It further found, having regard to Article 28 *b* of the Convention, that a friendly settlement of the present application has been secured on the basis of respect for human rights as defined in the Convention. For these reasons, the Commission adopts this Report.

Report of the European Commission of Human Rights, Application No. 7630/76, John Michael REED against United Kingdom, adopted on 12 December 1981, Part 11.

Text notes:

14 that is, i.e.
15 as a favour, without admitting liability
16 payments

Vocabulary

4 From the followng list of words choose 11 wh ch could replace words used in paragraphs 1 and 2 in the extract above:

a after that
b under consideration
c with the intention of
d discussions
e a promise
f airing
g to carry out
h consisted of
i consequently
j to put forward
k made itself available

Despite the lack of enforcement procedures the moral pressure to comply with the rulings of the ECHR is considerable as few countries wish to be seen by the international community to be in breach of their Treaty obligations. Up to September 1985 the Court had determined[17] fourteen cases involving the United Kingdom. In twelve of these it found that there had been a violation of the Treaty. As a result there have been a number of changes in United Kingdom law. For example, in *Dudgeon* v. *United Kingdom* (1981) the law in Northern Ireland which made homosexual acts between adult males a crime was held to be a violation of the individual's right to privacy contained in Article 8. The law in Northern Ireland was changed to reflect the decision. Similarly legislation was passed forbidding the use of corporal punishment in schools after the case of *Campbell and Cosans* v. *United Kingdom (1982)*. Perhaps the most publicised case brought before the Court was *The Sunday Times* case. It involved the important issues of freedom of expression and the administration of justice and provides a useful model for assessing the nature of the Convention and its impact on United Kingdom law.

Text note:
17 passed judgment in

10.2 Article 10: A case study on the Convention

Before we look at the facts and judgment in *The Sunday Times* case you will need to understand the concepts of *sub judice*[18] and contempt of court.[19] Under the *sub judice* rule it is a contempt of court to publish comments which could be prejudicial[20] to the outcome of a case. It is designed to secure a fair trial in both civil and criminal proceedings. The law is now governed by the Contempt of Court Act 1981 but at the time of *The Sunday*

Times case contempt of court was a common law offence. *R* v. *Bolam (ex parte*[21] *Haigh)* (1949) illustrates that the penalties attached to the offence can be very severe; in that case the *Daily Mirror* newspaper was fined £10,000 and its editors jailed for three months for publishing material which suggested that John Haigh was responsible for more than the one murder with which he had been charged.

Undoubtedly the *sub judice* rule is a restriction on the freedom of the press to publish whatever it wishes but this freedom must be balanced against the proper administration of justice and the right to a fair trial. The point at issue in *The Sunday Times* case was whether the existing law struck the correct balance. Let us now look at the background to the case.

In the late 1950s Distillers Co. Ltd manufactured a sedative which contained the drug thalidomide. Up to 1961 the drug was prescribed to a number of pregnant women who later gave birth to seriously deformed babies. These deformities were traced to the drug which was subsequently withdrawn from the market. Although writs[22] were issued against Distillers for damages in negligence, no legal proceedings had begun ten years after the births of the children. Distillers had settled 70 actions out of court but negotiations continued on the remaining 389 claims. Several newspapers published articles on the subject and in 1972 *The Sunday Times* began a campaign to heighten public awareness of the plight[23] of the children and to persuade Distillers to settle the outstanding claims quickly and generously. The tone of the first article can be gauged from the following extract.

Text notes:

18 (Latin) under consideration by a court (see also note **30**, Chapter 5)
19 breaking the rules of court
20 damaging
21 on behalf of
22 court order commencing legal proceedings
23 serious condition

> [The] thalidomide children shame Distillers. It is appreciated that Distillers have always denied negligence and that if the cases were pursued, the children might end up with nothing. It is appreciated that Distillers' lawyers have a professional duty to secure the best terms for their clients. But at the end of the day what is to be paid in settlement is the decision of Distillers, and they should offer much, much more to every one of the thalidomide victims. It may be argued that Distillers have a duty to their shareholders[24] and that, having taken account of skilled legal advice, the terms are just. But the law is not always the same as justice. There are times when to insist on the letter of the law is as exposed to criticism as infringement[25] of another's legal rights. The figure in the proposed settlement is to be £3.25 million, spread over 10 years. This does not shine as a beacon[26] against pre-tax profits last year of £64.8 million and company assets worth £421 million. Without in any way surrendering on negligence, Distillers could and should think again.
>
> *The Sunday Times*, 24 September 1972, pp. 67–8.

Text notes:

24 people who own part of the company's capital
25 going against
26 bright light

Comprehension check

5 Which of the following opinions is/are expressed in *The Sunday Times* extract?

- **a** Distillers should accept liability for the thalidomide children.
- **b** Distillers should pay more money to the thalidomide children.
- **c** Distillers could increase the settlement to the children without accepting the charge of negligence.
- **d** If the case were taken to court the victims might lose.

Under the common law of contempt of court the *sub judice* rule applied in civil actions from the time that a writ was issued. Despite complaints from Distillers the Attorney-General decided to take no action after the publication of the first article. The editor of *The Sunday Times* then sent a draft copy of the second article to the Attorney-General for his comment on whether its publication would be a contempt of court. This article gave details of Distillers' production and safety practices which suggested that the drug had been put onto the market without sufficient care. It also summarised the arguments on behalf of Distillers. The Attorney-General applied to the High court for an injunction to restrain publication of the article. This was granted on the grounds that 'publication of the article complained of[27] would create a serious risk of interference with Distillers' freedom of action in the litigation'.

Text note:
27 this is a past participle, i.e. 'which was complained of'

It suffices, we think to say that the article is clearly the product of many years of work, and that it traces the history of the development, marketing and testing of thalidomide from the very earliest times and in very considerable detail.

The article does not purport[28] to express any views as to the legal responsibility of Distillers for the sufferings of the children concerned, but it is quite clear that it is in many respects critical of Distillers and charges them with neglect in regard to their own failure to test the product, or their failure to react sufficiently sharply to warning signs obtained from the tests by others. No one reading the article could, we think, fail to gain the impression that the case against Distillers on a footing[29] of negligence was a substantial one.

AG v. *Times Newspapers Ltd* [1972] 3 All ER 1136.

Text notes:
28 claim
29 basis

The Sunday Times' appeal to the Court of Appeal was successful; Lord Denning emphasised the public interest in freedom of expression: 'It must always be remembered that, besides the interests of the parties in a fair trial or a fair settlement of the case, there is another important interest to be considered. It is the interest of the public in matters of national concern and the freedom of the press to make fair comment on these matters. The one interest must be balanced against the other. There may be cases where the subject-matter is such that the public interest counter-balances the private interest of the parties' (*AG* v. *Times Newspapers Ltd* [1973] 1 QB 710).

In addition the Court of Appeal unanimously agreed that a publication was only capable of being in contempt if it presented a substantial danger of prejudicing pending[30] litigation. In this case the litigation had been dormant for a number of years and was unlikely to come to court. The Attorney-General appealed to the House of Lords. Although not in agreement on all the issues involved the five Law Lords unanimously reversed the decision of the Court of Appeal and reimposed a ban on publication of the article. The case was not dormant; active negotiations for a settlement were continuing and any improper pressure to force a litigant to settle on terms with which he did not agree was a contempt.[31] But their main concern was over the issue of prejudgment.

Text notes:
30 waiting to be decided
31 see question **6** below

Comprehension check

6 Note 31: Does this sentence express fact or opinion?

But, to my mind, there is another consideration even more important than the effect of publication on the mind of the litigant. The controversy about the tragedy of the thalidomide children has ranged widely but as yet there seems to have been little, if any, detailed discussion of the issues which the court may have to determine if the outstanding claims are not settled. The question whether Distillers were negligent has been frequently referred to but, so far as I am aware, there has been no attempt to assess the evidence. If this material were released now, it appears to me to be almost inevitable that detailed answers would be published and there would be expressed various public prejudgments of this issue. That I would regard as very much against the public interest.

There has long been and there still is in this country a strong and generally held feeling that trial by newspaper[32] is wrong and should be prevented . . . What I think is regarded as most objectionable[33] is that a newspaper or television programme should seek to persuade the public, by discussing the issues and evidence in a case before the court, whether civil or criminal, that one side is right and the other wrong . . .

I think that anything in the nature of prejudgment of a case or of specific issues in it is objectionable, not only because of its possible effect on that particular case but also because of its side effects[34] which may be far reaching. Responsible "mass media" will do their best to be fair, but there will also be ill-informed, slapdash[35] or prejudiced attempts to influence the public. If people are led to think that it is easy to find the truth, disrespect for the processes of the law could follow, and, if mass media are allowed to judge, unpopular people and unpopular cases will fare[36] very badly. Most cases of prejudging of issues fall within the existing authorities on contempt. I do not think that the freedom of the press would suffer, and I think that the law would be clearer and easier to apply in practice if it is made a general rule that it is not permissible to prejudge issues in pending cases.

Attorney-General v. *Times Newspapers Ltd* [1974] AC 273; [1973] 3 All ER 54; [1973] 3 WLR 298; House of Lords (Lord Reid).

Text notes:
32 see question **7a** below
33 'to object' means in this context 'to oppose'
34 see question **7b** below
35 careless
36 progress, get on

Comprehension check

7 **a** Note 32: What do you think is meant by 'trial by newspaper'?
b Note 34: What examples are given of the 'side effects' mentioned here?

This decision in effect placed a blanket ban on publications which prejudged[37] a specific case regardless of any risk of prejudice[38] to the proceedings. This absolute rule would undoubtedly achieve the certainty desired by the House of Lords but it was severely criticised as a barrier to investigative journalism and the public's right to know, a factor which weighed so heavily with the Court of Appeal. Whilst acknowledging the need to balance this interest with the proper administration of justice Lord Morris stated that 'there can be no such thing as a justifiable contempt of court'.

Language note

Notice in notes 37 and 38 the important distinction made between these two words with similar roots. In everyday language 'prejudice' will usually mean an opinion which is based on incomplete knowledge, for example racial prejudice. In legal contexts 'prejudice' means damage or injury. 'To prejudge' has a similar meaning in both everyday and legal contexts, that is to judge before all the facts are known.

The Sunday Times took the case to the ECHR for breach of Article 10 which states:

> 1. Everyone has the right to freedom of expression. This right shall include freedom to hold opinions and to receive and impart information and ideas without interference by public authority and regardless of frontiers. This Article shall not prevent States from requiring the licensing of broadcasting, television or cinema enterprises.
> 2. The exercise of these freedoms, since it carries with it duties and responsibilities, may be subject to such formalities, conditions, restrictions or penalties as are prescribed by law and are necessary in a democratic society, in the interests of national security, territorial integrity or public safety, for the prevention of disorder or crime, for the protection of health or morals, for the protection of the reputation or rights of others, for preventing the disclosure of information received in confidence, or for maintaining the authority and impartiality of the judiciary.

You will see that whilst Article 10 gives the right to freedom of expression it also allows the restriction of that right to protect certain interests. The question for the Court in *The Sunday Times* case was whether the injunction was 'necessary for maintaining the authority and impartiality of the judiciary'. The meaning of this phrase is discussed in the following extract from the judgment of the Court:

> None of the Law Lords concerned based his decisions on the ground that the proposed article might have an influence on the 'impartiality' of the judiciary. This ground was also not pleaded before the Court and can be left out of account.
>
> The reasons why the draft article was regarded as objectionable by the House of Lords may be briefly summarised as follows:
>
> by 'prejudging' the issue of negligence, it would have led to disrespect for the processes of the law or interfered with the administration of justice; it was of a kind that would expose Distillers to public and prejudicial discussion of the merits of their case, such exposure being objectionable as it inhibits[39] suitors[40] generally from having recourse to the courts;
>
> it would subject Distillers to pressure and to the prejudices of prejudgment of the issues in the litigation, and the law of contempt was designed to prevent interference with recourse[41] to the courts;
>
> prejudgment by the press would have led inevitably in this case to replies by the parties,[42] thereby creating the danger of a 'trial by newspaper' incompatible with the proper administration of justice;
>
> the courts owe it to the parties to protect them from the prejudices of prejudgment which involves their[43] having to participate in the flurries[44] of pre-trial publicity.
>
> The Court regards all these various reasons as falling within the aim of maintaining the 'authority . . . of the judiciary' as interpreted by the Court in the second sub-paragraph of paragraph 55 above.
>
> Accordingly, the interference with the applicant's freedom of expression had an aim that is legitimate under Article 10 (2).
>
> C *Was the interference 'necessary in a democratic society' for maintaining the authority of the judiciary?*
>
> 58. The applicants submit and the majority of the Commission are of the opinion that the said interference was not 'necessary' within the meaning of Article 10(2). The Government contend that the minority of the Commission was correct in reading a contrary conclusion and rely, in particular, on the margin of appreciation enjoyed by the House of Lords in the matter.
>
> 59. The Court has already had the occasion in its above-mentioned HANDYSIDE judgment to state its understanding of the phrase 'necessary in a democratic society', the nature of its functions in the examination of issues turning on that phrase and the manner in which it will perform those functions.
>
> The Court has noted that, whilst the adjective 'necessary', within the meaning of Article 10 (2), is not synonymous with 'indispensable', neither[45] has it the flexibility of such expressions as 'admissible', 'ordinary', 'useful', 'reasonable', or 'desirable' and that it implies the existence of a 'pressing social need' . . .
>
> *The Sunday Times* v. *UK* [1979] 2 EHRR 245.

Text notes:
39 stops
40 parties to a suit
41 seeking help
42 see question **8a** below
43 see language point 1 below
44 nervous hurry
45 see language point 2 below

Language points

1 Notice this use of the possessive 'their'. In less formal writing 'them' could be used. (This construction would not usually be possible with inanimate nouns.) For example:

> She objected to his/him publishing the photograph of her.
>
> She objected to the newspaper (**not** the newspaper's) publishing the photograph).

2 'not . . . neither' is more formal than the usual 'neither . . . nor' construction:

> . . . is **neither** synonymous with 'indispensable', **nor** has it the flexibility . . .

Notice that in both constructions, where the second verb is different from the first (here, first verb = is, second verb = has), the second verb comes before the subject. (NB: In the 'not . . . neither' construction the second verb is always different from the first.)

Comprehension check

8 **a** Note 42: Who are the 'parties' referred to here?
b On what legitimate ground did the ECHR decide that the Law Lords had tried to restrict *The Sunday Times*' draft article?
c What words did the court use to interpret 'necessary' in this case?

The Court then analysed the respective roles of the contracting states and the ECHR in determining the level of restriction which is acceptable under Article 10. Then, after considering the reasoning of the House of Lords, the judgment concludes:

> As the Court remarked in its HANDYSIDE judgment, freedom of expression constitutes one of the essential foundations of a democratic society; subject to paragraph 2 of Article 10, it is applicable not only to information or ideas that are favourably received or regarded as inoffensive or as a matter of indifference, but also to those that offend, shock or disturb the State or any sector of the population.
>
> These principles are of particular importance as far as the press is concerned. They are equally applicable to the field of the administration of justice, which serves the interests of the community at large and requires the co-operation of an enlighted public. There is general recognition of the fact that the courts cannot operate in a vacuum. Whilst[46] they are the forum for the settlement of disputes, this does not mean that there can be no prior discussion of disputes elsewhere, be[47] it in specialised journals, in the general press or amongst the public at large. Furthermore, whilst the mass media must not overstep the bounds imposed in the interests of the proper administration of justice, it is incumbent on them[48] to impart information and ideas concerning matters that come before the courts just as in other areas of public interest. Not only do the media have the task of imparting such information and ideas: the public also has a right to receive them.
>
> To assess whether the interference complained of was based on 'sufficient' reasons which rendered it 'necessary in a democratic society', account must thus be taken of any public interest aspect of the case . . .
>
> 66. The thalidomide disaster was a matter of undisputed public concern. It posed the question whether the powerful company which had marketed the

drug bore legal or moral responsibility towards hundreds of individuals experiencing an appalling personal tragedy or whether the victims could demand or hope for indemnification[49] only from the community as a whole; fundamental issues concerning protection against and compensation for injuries resulting from scientific developments were raised and many facets[50] of the existing law on these subjects were called in question.

As the Court has already observed, Article 10 guarantees not only the freedom of the press to inform the public but also the right of the public to be properly informed . . .

In the present case, the families of numerous victims of the tragedy, who were unaware of the legal difficulties involved, had a vital interest in knowing all the underlying facts and the various possible solutions. They could be deprived of this information, which was crucially important for them, only if it appeared absolutely certain that its diffusion would have presented a threat to the 'authority of the judiciary'.

Being called upon to weigh the interests involved and assess their respective force, the Court makes the following observations:

In September 1972, the case had, in the words of the applicants, been in a 'legal cocoon'[51] for several years and it was, at the very least, far from certain that the parents' actions would have come on for trial. There had also been no public enquiry . . .

The Government and the minority of the Commission point out that there was no prohibition on discussion of the 'wider issues', such as the principles of the English law of negligence, and indeed it is true that there had been extensive discussion in various circles especially after, but also before, the Divisional Court's initial decision . . . However, the Court considers it rather artificial to attempt to divide the 'wider issues' and the negligence issue. The question of where responsibility for a tragedy of this kind actually lies is also a matter of public interest.

It is true that, if *The Sunday Times* article had appeared at the intended time, Distillers might have felt obliged to develop in public, and in advance of any trial, their arguments on the facts of the case . . . however, those facts did not cease to be a matter of public interest merely because they formed the background to pending litigation. By bringing to light certain facts, the article might have served as a brake on speculative and unenlightened discussion.

67. Having regard[52] to all the circumstances of the case and on the basis of the approach described in paragraph 65 above, the Court concludes that the interference complained of did not correspond to a social need sufficiently pressing to outweight the public interest in freedom of expression within the meaning of the Convention. The Court therefore finds the reasons for the restraint imposed on the applicants not to be sufficient under Article 10 (2). That restraint proves not to be proportionate to the legitimate aim pursued; it was not necessary in a democratic society for maintaining the authority of the judiciary.

68. There has accordingly been a violation of Article 10.

The Sunday Times v. *UK* [1979] 2 EHRR 245.

Text notes:

46 see question **9** below
47 see language point below
48 it is their duty
49 compensation for damage or loss
50 sides
51 here means a protective covering (like those made by some insects)
52 taking into consideration

Language point:

This is another example of the subjunctive, found only with 'to be', in formal language. Compare:

Neutral	. . . whether it is in specialised journals or . . .
More formal	. . . whether it be in specialised journals or . . .
	. . . be it in specialised journals or . . .

Comprehension check

9 Note 46: What word other than 'whilst' could be used here?

In 1981 the Contempt of Court Act was passed to 'harmonise the law of England and Wales with the majority judgment of the Strasbourg Court in *The Sunday Times* case'. Although the Act covers many aspects of contempt of court it is sections 2 and 5 which are relevant to that case. The former replaces the prejudgment rule imposed by the House of Lords by providing a clearer test of what constitutes a contempt of court. It is necessary to establish a 'substantial risk' that the proceedings will be 'severely prejudiced'. The latter[53] provides a defence of any prejudice being 'incidental'[54] to a bona fide[55] discussion of general public interest. For example, an article discussing the plight of handicapped children in general would have been relevant to the victims of thalidomide but would have been 'incidental' to their specific circumstances.

It is clear from later cases brought under the Contempt of Court Act that a substantial risk of prejudice or a risk of severe prejudice will not satisfy the section 2 test. The result is that the law is less certain as what amounts to a substantial risk of severe prejudice will be determined by the courts in each individual case; the level of public concern, the importance of the issue and the interests of those involved may be relevant considerations. There is no guarantee, however, that section 2 will be interpreted as narrowly as the ECHR judgment would suggest that it should.

Text notes:
53 see question **10a** below
54 not deliberately done
55 (Latin) genuine

Comprehension check

10 a Note 53: What is being referred to here?
b Under the 1981 Contempt of Court Act what must be established to constitute a contempt?
c What defence is allowed under the 1981 Act?
d Give examples of what will be taken into account by courts when deciding whether a contempt has occurred.

11 The case study on the ECHR is quite long. It will help you to see the pattern of events if you list the stages in the proceedings. Do this in note form, starting as follows:

a *Sunday Times* (ST) article, 24 Sept. 1972
b Complaint by Distillers (D)
c A.G. . . . .
d . . . .
e . . . .
f . . . .
g . . . .
h . . . .

Research

12 Find out whether there is a law of contempt of court in your country and whether this law relates to pre-trial publications. If there is no *sub judice* rule how does the legal system ensure that legal proceedings are not prejudiced by such publications?

Legal exercises

13 List three ways in which you think a pre-trial publication could prejudice the outcome of a case.

14 Do you think that the *sub judice* rule should be applied differently when a case is to be heard **a** before a jury, **b** before a single judge?

15 Why did the Court of Appeal reverse the decision of the High Court in *The Sunday Times* case?

16 What was the primary concern of the House of Lords over pre-trial publications?

17 How did the House of Lords judgment create certainty in the law of contempt of court?

18 Would the following parties be guilty under sections 2 and 5 of the Contempt of Court Act 1981?

a Dr Loveday works as a consultant in a maternity hospital. On one occasion he delivers a baby which is seriously mentally and physically deformed. He decides not to treat the baby and, after administering a mild sedative, leaves the baby to sleep in a cot. The baby dies twenty-four hours later and Dr Loveday is charged with its murder. A week before his trial commences Margaret Spock, a well-known anti-abortion campaigner, publishes a pamphlet calling for the repeal of the law on abortion which allows the termination of a pregnancy when the foetus is physically or mentally deformed. Margaret distributes this pamphlet to the 1,200 members of the Anti-Abortion Society.

b Crank, a homeless alcoholic, is found sitting in the office of a Member of Parliament in the House of Commons. He is drinking some wine taken from a cupboard in the office. Crank is charged with stealing the wine. The following week *The Daily Sludge* publishes an article giving details of Crank's medical history and previous criminal convictions. *The Sunday Investigator* also publishes an article criticising the security system at the House of Commons because it failed to prevent Crank from gaining access to the MP's office.

10.3 The Convention as a Bill of Rights?

In Chapter 2 we discussed the debate over the need for a Bill of Rights in the United Kingdom. Many supporters of this proposition argue that this should be achieved by incorporating the ECHR into the British constitution. The constitutions of some of the High Contracting Parties[56] provide for automatic incorporation of the Treaty into domestic law. In Britain the process requires legislation. Without this its provisions are merely persuasive. Reference to the Treaty in many cases demonstrates that it is relevant to English law but the arguments for and against its incorporation are more complex.

Text note
56 member states

The arguments for and against doing this are worth examining. Besides the argument that incorporating the European Convention into British law would save us international embarrassment, the main reason advanced for doing this is that the human rights which it guarantees are immensely valuable and would be better protected here if the Convention was incorporated into British law than is the case at present. This would give us fairer laws and a legal system which worked more fairly, and everyone would be happier and better.[57] This sort of argument does not usually appeal to those in government, who see and resent the prospect of a greater amount of judicial review, which means more interference from the lawyers and judges in the day-to-day doings of government servants and in the implementation of the government's favourite plans. But there are more respectable arguments against the scheme than the mere reluctance of those who have power to submit to legal controls. The first is that it would necessarily give the judges wider powers, and this would politicise them. This means more than that the judges would find themselves making decisions which pleased one political party and offended another – which they sometimes have to do already. It means that the judges would start making decisions that are 'political' in the broad sense that they are big decisions about how society is to be run, and thus the sort of decisions which we are accustomed to have made by Parliament as part of the democratic process. The rights which the European Convention contains are vague, and in various ways they conflict with one another; and where there is a conflict it is largely a matter of personal choice how the conflict is to be resolved. For example, the Convention protects both freedom of speech and freedom of religion: so we must resolve the question of where, by what means and how loudly one person is to be permitted to speak freely against another person's religion. One might think the obvious answer would be 'as loudly as he likes, as long as this does not interfere with another person actually practising his religion', but it is possible to hold other views on where the line should be drawn. In an English court case on the ambit[58] of the crime of blasphemy,[59] Lord Scarman – who is one of the public supporters of legislation to incorporate the European Convention into British law – referred in his judgment to the European Convention in terms which suggest he thought that if it were in force in Britain, it would justify a ban on publishing in a newspaper intended for homosexuals a poem which offended Christians who happened to read it because it rather crudely ascribed homosexuality to Christ.

In that case, the House of Lords was dealing with the existing crime of blasphemy, which they decided made this publication potentially illegal. As things stand[60] they could not have so decided if there had been no crime of blasphemy to hang this decision upon. But if the European Convention had been directly incorporated into British law, the courts could presumably have decided in favour of some sort of ban on this publication simply on the basis of the Convention even if there had been no existing criminal offence, had they agreed[61] with Lord Scarman's interpretation of it. Indeed, Lord Scarman has publicly stated that if the Convention is incorporated by statute 'it will fill the gaps in our law. Our courts, for example, will be in a position to develop a modern and effective law of privacy. They will be able to protect victimised members of minority groups.'

Whether books are banned because they offend a group of religious believers is surely a matter to be decided by Parliament, not by the courts, and so too are such matters as discrimination against minority groups and how far newspapers should be restrained from publishing matters which invade other people's privacy.

The second[62] objection to making the Convention part of British law is that it would unsettle all sorts of rules which the process of litigation has satisfactorily settled. For example, over the years the powers of the police to make demonstrators move on have been worked out as the courts have construed the criminal offences of obstructing the highway, and assaulting and obstructing the police in the execution of their duty. The result does not please everyone, of course, but it is a reasonably satisfactory compromise, and it is unlikely that the courts would wish to alter the present rules. If the European Convention was brought directly into force then probably all the rules which have been developed would be relitigated by hopeful defendants to see if the courts would strike them down as inconsistent with the 'right to freedom of peaceful assembly', which the Convention expressly protects. It is unlikely that the end result would be any different from the present law, and the only people who would gain would be the lawyers who would have a field-day[63] with it first. Despite these objections, the idea of incorporating the European Convention into British law has attracted quite a lot of support from influential lawyers, and there was considerable press support when the Bill which attempted to do this came before Parliament in 1987. It is therefore quite possible that at some future date it may be done.

Spencer (ed.), *Jackson's Machinery of Justice* (Cambridge University Press 1989), pp. 431–2.

Text notes:

57 see question **19a** below
58 scope
59 irreverent reference to God or sacred things (see example which follows in the extract)
60 are at present
61 see language point below
62 see question **19b** below
63 take pleasure in taking advantage

Language note

This inversion of subject and verb can be used (in rather formal language) in unreal conditionals in the past instead of an 'if . . .' clause, for example:

'had they agreed . . .' instead of

'if they had agreed . . .'

Quite common, even in speech, is the expression:

'had I known . . .' (instead of 'if I had known . . .')

Comprehension check

19 a Note 57: Is this the writer's opinion or fact?
b Note 62: Where is the 'first' objection?

20 Identify the main arguments mentioned by Spencer and list them **briefly** (50–70 words) in note form:

'Less respectable arguments':
For: . . . .
Against: . . . .

'More respectable arguments':
Against: . . . .

The author appears to favour the arguments against the ECHR as a statutory Bill of Rights. Many of those who are in favour of its enactment are nevertheless pessimistic as to its effectiveness; the problem, they argue, lies with the judges. The necessary broadness of the Articles and their exceptions would leave a large area of judicial discretion; it is argued that British judges are too cautious in their protection of human rights and that they are too prepared to uphold the status quo. Let us, for example, consider whether the House of Lords would have reached a different decision in *The Sunday Times* case if the Convention had been incorporated into United Kingdom law. Given that the broad considerations of the ECHR and the House of Lords were similar but led to different conclusions, it is possible to argue that they would not. The blanket ban on pre-publications imposed by the House of Lords suggests a conservative approach to the right to freedom of expression.

Research

21 In the extract on pages 235–6 Professor Spencer uses the crime of blasphemy to illustrate the problems which could arise by incorporating the ECHR into the British constitution. In the United Kingdom, the crime of blasphemy relates only to actions which offend against the principles of the Christian religion, which is the official religion of the state. Find out the following information about the law in your country.

a Is there an official state religion? If so, what is it?
b Is there a law which prohibits actions which offend against its principles? If so is it part of the criminal or civil law?
c Does this law also relate to other religions?
d What are the penalties attached to a breach of this law?
e If your country does not have an official state religion, are there any laws, similar to the law of blasphemy, which relate to all religions?
f If there are no such laws in your country, what are the reasons for this?

10.4 The institutions of the European Community

By the passing of the European Communities Act 1972 the United Kingdom became a member of what was then called the European Economic Community. This Community grew out of the post-war rejection of nationalism and the perceived need for pan-European economic and political cooperation.

> If we cast our minds back to the early post-war days we will realise that a Community approach was the practical answer to many problems. Europe was in ruins politically and economically; the European colonial empires faced liquidation; the importance of the single European states which dominated the League of Nations was diminished; the 'dollar-gap' resulted in great influence of the United States of America not only as a benevolent saviour but also as a potential master; an 'iron curtain' was drawn across Europe and the world cowered[64] in the shadows of great powers: the United States of America and Soviet Russia facing each other menacingly across Europe. Only rapid recovery in concert[65] could restore Europe's self-respect. What is more it became only too obvious that economic reconstruction had to match political aspirations. Thus the idea of a European Community was forced upon Europeans as an economic and political necessity. As for grand designs, the architects of the Community soon realised that great ideologies and elaborate blueprints[66] were of little practical use and that nothing could be achieved at one stroke. Robert Schuman, the great French European, said: 'L'Europe ne se fera pas d'un coup dans une construction d'ensemble, elle se fera par des réalisations concrètes créant d'abord une solidarité de fait . . .'[67]
>
> This factual solidarity can be traced to events of great importance to Europe and the world at large, as the work of world recovery and reconstruction began to create a fabric of international economic co-operation.
>
> Lasok and Bridge, *Law and Institutions of the European Communities* (Butterworths 1988), pp. 183–4.

Text notes:
64 (literally) lowered the body in fear
65 see question **22** below
66 building plans
67 trans.: 'A United Europe will not arise overnight nor by means of an all-embracing constitution: it will only arise through specific projects providing a solid foundation of fact . . .'

Comprehension check

22 Note 65: Can you guess the meaning of 'in concert' from the context?

The aim therefore of the European Community was to remove economic and political barriers between the member states to ensure, amongst other things, the free movement of services and capital and the integration of national agricultural and transport policies. The present twelve member states are Belgium, France, Germany, Italy, Luxembourg, Netherlands, Denmark, the Republic of Ireland, Greece, Spain, Portugal and the United Kingdom.

There are four principal institutions of the European Community: the Parliament, the Council, the Commission and the Court of Justice. Their respective functions are outlined in the next series of extracts.

10.4.1 The Parliament

As created by the Treaty of Rome in 1957, the European Parliament, called in that Treaty the Assembly (but now required by the SEA[68] to be called the Parliament), was not a democratic body, although the Treaty provided for the eventual[69] introduction of direct elections. It consisted of representatives of member States who were required to be members of a national parliament. The introduction of direct elections which occurred in 1979 has now resulted in increased democracy (although no uniform voting procedure has yet been agreed) and increased concentration and expertise, since members are responsible to their electorate, and as anyone is now eligible to stand, many are no longer subject to the rigorous demands of the 'dual mandate'[69] at home and in Europe. It has also, not unexpectedly, resulted in demands for increased powers.

As befitted a non-elected body the original Parliament had few powers. Its functions were advisory and supervisory. It was not intended as a legislative body. This is still the case, although since direct elections Parliament has played an increasingly important part in the legislative process and now has the final say over certain aspects of the budget . . .

Text notes:
68 Single European Act
69 coming at last
70 authority given to MPs by voters

10.4.2 The Council

The Council consists of representatives of the member States, each State delegating to it one of its members (Article 147). Although it is a political body, its task is 'to ensure that the objectives set out in this Treaty are attained' (Article 145). To this end[71] it 'shall[72] . . . ensure coordination of the general economic policies of the member states; [and] have power to take decisions'.

Since the Council has the final power of decision on most secondary legislation[73] some control by the member States is thus assured. However, in most cases it can only act on the basis of a proposal from the Commission, and in an increasing number of circumstances it must consult Parliament and the Economic and Social Committee. Under the procedures introduced by the SEA, if it wishes to override Parliament's opposition to a measure it must do so by unanimous vote. Similarly it may amend the Commission's proposals provided it does so unanimously (Article 149).

The Council is not a fixed body. Although it is limited to one voting delegate from each State, membership may fluctuate depending on the topic under discussion. For example, where matters of agriculture are at stake, the Ministers of Agriculture will normally participate; if the matters relate to general economic policy the Chancellors may be present; where high-level policy matters are to be discussed, the Council may consist of Heads of State . . .

Text notes:
71 for this purpose
72 see language point below
73 see the extract from Ingham on p. 243.

Language point

Note that 'shall' in legal contexts is not just a substitute for the future 'will'; it implies the force and obligation of a legal requirement.

10.4.3 The Commission

The Commission has been described as the 'guardian of the Treaties'. The present Commission consists of 17 members (two from each of the big four[74] and Spain, and one from each of the other States), chosen on the grounds of their general competence and 'whose independence is beyond doubt' (Merger Treaty, Article 10). Appointed by 'common accord of the governments of the member States' (Merger Treaty, Article 11), they must, in the performance of their duties, 'neither seek nor take instructions from any government or from any other body' (Merger Treaty, Article 10).

The functions of the Commission are threefold. First, it acts as initiator or 'motor' of Community action. All important decisions made by the Council must be made on the basis of proposals from the Commission (subject to the Council's power to 'request the Commission to undertake any studies which the Council considers desirable for the attainment of the common objectives, and to submit to it any appropriate proposals') . . .

Secondly, the Commission acts as the Community watchdog. Member States are obliged under Article 5 to: 'take all appropriate measures . . . to ensure fulfilment of the obligations arising out of this Treaty or resulting from action taken by the institutions of the Community . . . They shall abstain from any measure which could jeopardise the attainment of the objectives of this Treaty.' It is the Commission's task to seek out and bring to an end any infringements of EEC law by member States, if necessary by proceedings under Article 169 . . . before the European Court . . .

Thirdly, the Commission functions as the executive of the Community. Once a policy decision has been taken by the Council, the detailed implementation of that policy, often requiring further legislation, falls to the Commission. Much of this legislation will again require a final decision by the Council . . .

Finally, in pursuit of the Community's external policies, the Commission is required to act as negotiator, leaving agreements to be 'concluded by the Council, after consulting the Assembly where required by this Treaty' (Article 228).

10.4.4 The European Court of Justice (ECJ)

The task of the European Court is to 'ensure that in the interpretation and application of this Treaty the law is observed' (Article 164). It is the supreme authority on all matters of Community law, and in this capacity may be required to decide matters of constitutional law . . . administrative law . . . social law . . . and economic law . . . in matters brought directly before it or on application from national courts. In its practices and procedures it draws on Continental models, in developing the substantive law it draws on principles and traditions from all the member States.

Since the EEC Treaty is a framework treaty the Court has been extremely influential in 'filling the gaps', and in doing so has created law in bold, and, to those accustomed to English methods of interpretation often surprising ways.

As Lord Diplock pointed out in *R* v. *Henn* [1981] AC 850:

> The European Court, in contrast to English courts, applies teleological[75] rather than historical methods to the interpretation of the Treaties and other Community legislation. It seeks to give effect to what it conceives to be the spirit rather than the letter of the Treaties; sometimes, indeed, to an English judge, it may seem to the exclusion of the letter. It views the Communities as living and expanding organisms and the interpretation of the provisions of the Treaties as changing to match their growth.

The Court consists of 13 judges, one from each member State and a President of the Court, assisted by five advocates-general. They must be 'chosen from persons whose independence is beyond doubt' (Article 167). An advocate-general's function is to assist the Court by presenting his 'submissions' – a detailed analysis of all the relevant issues of fact and law together with his recommendations to the court. Although his recommendations are not always followed, where they are they are useful as a means of ascertaining the reasoning behind the Court's decision. The judgment itself, which is a single collegiate[76] decision, is to English eyes, terse,[77] cryptic,[78] with little indication of the reasoning on which it is based. Even where the advocate-general's recommendations are not followed they may still be invoked as persuasive authority in a subsequent case. Although the European Court seeks to achieve consistency in its judgments, its precedents are not binding in the English sense; it always remains free to depart from previous decisions in the light of new facts.

Under the SEA, the Council now has power to create a new court of first instance (Article 11, 12 SEA (EEC)). When implemented this will undoubtedly ease the burden of the Court, whose work-load and consequent backlog[79] has been increasing from year to year. It is intended that the new court will deal principally with trade and competition law.

These four institutions, Parliament, Council, the Commission and the Court are subject to the principle of legality. Each must act 'within the limits of the powers conferred upon it by this Treaty' (Article 4).

Any illegal act or failure to act on the part of the first three is subject to proceedings before the Court under Article 173 or Article 175.

. . . The only institution whose decisions are not subject to legal challenge is the Court itself.

Steiner, *Textbook on EEC Law* (Blackstone Press 1988), pp. 8, 10–15.

Text notes:

74 i.e. France, Germany, Italy and the UK
75 based on doctrine of final results
76 collective, i.e. speaking for all judges
77 very brief
78 with hidden meaning
79 business waiting to be dealt with

You will see from these outlines that the institutions of the EC cannot be equated with the traditional institutions of national governments; for example, the Parliament has no legislative powers, and the Commission has the role of both executive and civil service. The institutions are also different in another significant way:

The uniqueness of the Communities[80] stems from the deep involvement of their institutions in matters traditionally within the exclusive control of each individual state and their capacity to make rules directly and automatically binding not only on the member states themselves but also on individuals and corporate bodies within those states. Thus the unique character of the Communities lies in the degree of their penetration into the internal legal relations of the member states, whereas classical international organisations tend to be involved merely with the external legal relations of their members.

Lasok and Bridge, *Institutions and Law of the European Community* (Butterworths 1988), pp. 183–4.

Text note:
80 there are three Community treaties – see the second paragraph of the next extract

---

Comprehension check: notemaking

23 Complete the following summary of the previous extracts:

European Parliament:
1. 1957: ....
2. 1979: ....
3. Functions: ....

Council:
1. Consists of ....
   but ....
2. Function: ....
3. If voting unanimous ....

Commission:
1. Consists of ....
2. Members chosen on basis of ....
3. Functions:
   – ....
   – ....
   – ....
   – ....

ECJ:
1. Function: to decide on ....
2. Consists of ....
3. Interprets Treaties using diff. methods from English law i.e. . Its judgments are ....
4. Basic diff. between EC & other inernational organisational organisations =

....

10.5 The law of the European Community

In this section we will first look at the sources of Community law and then at their impact on national law.

10.5.1 Sources of European Community law

The different forms of Community law are contained in Article 189 of the EEC Treaty. The varying ways in which they are incorporated into national law are outlined in the next extract:

> Most of English domestic law, such as contract, tort, land law, family law and criminal law, is not affected by United Kingdom membership of the European Community. European Community law is concerned mainly with restrictive trade practices, agriculture, coal, steel, nuclear energy, and the free movement of labour, capital and services.
>
> The *primary* European Community legislation consists of the three treaties that established the Communities, namely, the European Coal and Steel Community Treaty, the Euratom Treaty and the European Economic Community Treaty. The provisions of these treaties are directly applicable in the United Kingdom, without the need for further legislation by the UK Parliament, by virtue of the European Communities Act 1972, s. 2(1).
>
> The *secondary* European Community legislation consists of regulations, decisions, directives, recommendations and opinions made or given by the Council of Ministers or the Commission. Recommendations and opinions are not directly applicable in the United Kingdom but can be given legal effect in the UK by statute or by delegated legislation made under the European Communities Act 1972, s. 2(2). In general, the same applies to directives, although they can sometimes produce direct legal effects and create rights without having been implemented by domestic legislation if they fulfil certain criteria, notably a criterion of clarity (see, e.g., *Van Duyn* v. *Home Office* [1975] Ch 358, CJEC).
>
> Decisions *may* be, and regulations *are*, directly applicable in the United Kingdom by virtue of the European Communities Act 1972, s. 2(1). Moreover, they are published in the *Official Journal* of the Communities of which[81] judicial notice[82] . . . is taken in the United Kingdom. Judicial notice is also taken of the treaties and of decisions and opinions of the European Court of Justice or any court attached thereto (European Communities Act 1972, s. 3(2), as amended by the European Communities (Amendment) Act 1986 . . . The *validity* of the *primary* European Community legislation (the treaties) is not subject to review either in national courts or in the European Court of Justice. The power of the courts in relation to the treaties is limited to *interpretation* (EEC Treaty, art. 177 . . .)
>
> . . . But the *validity*, as well as the meaning or effect, of *secondary* Community legislation can be challenged both in national courts and in the European Court of Justice (EEC Treaty, art. 177) *and* on grounds wider than those on which United Kingdom delegated legislation may be impugned. Secondary Community legislation may be attacked on the basis of substantive *ultra vires*, infringement of the treaties, misuse of powers, or failure to observe some procedural requirement (. . . art. 173). A court in the United Kingdom, instead of determining the point itself, may decide to refer any question of the validity of secondary Community legislation to the European Court of Justice (ibid.,[83] art. 177).
>
> Ingham, *The English Legal Process* (Blackstone Press 1990), pp. 187–8.

Text note:

81 see question **24** below

82 published Acts of Parliament of which a judge is presumed to have knowledge

83 (Latin) means 'in the same place', i.e. EEC Treaty

Comprehension check and notemaking

24 Note 81: To what does 'which' refer here?

25 Complete the following note outline:

Applicability of EC law in the UK

1. **Primary EC legislation** = a) . . . .
b) . . . .
c) . . . .
Directly applicable? . . . .
Can validity be challenged? . . . .

2. **Secondary EC legislation:**

	Directly applicable?
a)	. . . .
b)	. . . .
c)	. . . .
d)	. . . .
e)	. . . .

Can validity be challenged? . . . .

You will see that some EC law is incorporated into English law without the need for legislation by the British Parliament whilst other forms of EC law require such additional legislation. The distinction lies in the need to obtain uniformity within the EC whilst taking account of the different cultures of the Community states. Regulations seek strict uniformity whilst directives usually only seek harmonisation on their aims leaving the means of achieving the aims to the national governments. However, the ECJ has taken the view that national governments should not benefit from any failure to implement a directive and has ruled that directives involving individual rights will have direct effect.

> These provisions impose on Member States a precise obligation which does not require the adoption of any further measures on the part either of the Community institutions or of the Member States and which leaves them, in relation to its[84] implementation, no discretionary power . . . In particular where the Community authorities, by directive, imposed on member states the obligation to pursue a particular course of conduct, the useful effect of such an act would be weakened if individuals were prevented from relying on it before their national courts and if the latter were prevented from taking it into consideration as an element of Community law.
>
> *Van Duyn* v. *Home Office* [1974] ECR 1337; [1975] 1 CMLR 1.

Comprehension check

26 Note 84: To what does 'its' refer here?

The full impact of the direct effect of Community law which protects individual rights will be examined in the following section.

10.5.2 The impact of European Community law

At the heart of any discussion on the impact of Community law is the question of parliamentary sovereignty: to what extent does Britain's membership of the EC limit Parliament's freedom to legislate?

Section 2(1) of the European Communities Act states:

> All such rights, powers, liabilities, obligations and restrictions from time to time created or arising by or under the Treaties, and all such remedies and procedures from time to time provided for by or under the Treaties, as in accordance with the Treaties are **without further enactment** to be given legal effect or used in the United Kingdom shall be recognised and available in law, and be enforced, allowed and followed accordingly.[85] (Emphasis added.)

Text note:
85 see the language point below if you have difficulty with this paragraph

---

Language point

Section 2(1) of the EC Act consists of one sentence with little help from punctuation to divide it into manageable sections. Even for a native speaker it is not easy but the following points may help:

1 The original text has no comma between 'United Kingdom' and 'shall' but a comma would make comprehension easier.
2 As usual, it helps to read the sentence as quickly as possible.
3 The relative clauses are not introduced by 'which'; instead past or present participles are used alone ('created', 'arising', 'provided for').

The effect of section 2(1) is that all EC law, past or future, which has direct effect will become part of the law of the United Kingdom without further enactment by Parliament. In addition section 2(4) states that **any** law passed by Parliament should reflect Britain's Community obligations: '. . . any enactment passed or to be passed, other than one contained in this part of the Act, will be construed and have effect subject to the foregoing provisions of this section'.

The European Communities Act therefore established the primacy of EC law over national law; where there is a conflict between the two the former, if directly applicable, will prevail. There is no doubt that this limits the freedom of Parliament to legislate and derogates[86] from its supremacy. The issue has arisen in many cases. In *McCarthys* v. *Smith* [1979] 3 All ER 325, CA, Lord Denning approached the subject by distinguishing between unintentional and intentional conflict.

Text note:
86 lessens the effect of

> In construing our statute, we are entitled to look to the Treaty as an aid to its construction;[87] but not only as an aid but as an overriding force. If on close investigation it should appear that our legislation is deficient or is inconsistent with Community law by some oversight of our draftsmen then it is our bounden duty to give priority to Community law. Such is the result of s 2(1) and (4) of the European Communities Act 1972.

I pause here, however, to make one observation on a constitutional point. Thus far I have assumed that our Parliament, whenever it passes legislation, intends to fulfil its obligations under the Treaty. If the time should come when our Parliament deliberately passes an Act with the intention of repudiating[88] the Treaty or any provision in it or intentionally of acting inconsistently with it and says so in express terms then I should have thought that it would be the duty of our courts to follow the statute of our Parliament. I do not however envisage[89] any such situation. As I said in *Blackburn* v *Attorney-General*: 'But if Parliament should do so, then I say we will consider that event when it happens.' Unless there is such an intentional and express repudiation of the Treaty, it is our duty to give priority to the Treaty.

McCarthys v. *Smith* [1979] 3 All ER 325, CA.

Text notes:
87 noun from the verb 'to construe'
88 refusing to recognise
89 foresee

So Lord Denning recognised the continuing sovereignty of Parliament in two ways:

1 Community law is given supremacy by an Act of Parliament which, by its sovereignty, Parliament was free to enact; and
2 Parliament remains free to pass legislation which expressly conflicts with Community law.

Lord Justice Lawton goes further: 'Parliament's recognition of European Community law and the jurisdiction of the European Court of Justice by one enactment can be withdrawn by another.'

So it is Parliament's freedom to repeal the European Communities Act 1972 which maintains its sovereignty.

Such an extreme solution does not satisfy critics of Britain's membership of the European Community. The controversy has been brought into sharp focus recently by the decision of the ECJ in *R* v. *Secretary of State for Transport ex parte Factortame Ltd and others*, case no. C-213/89, 19 June 1990. We will need to look at the background to the case before examining the ECJ's judgment.

The Common Market fishing policy fixes national quotas[90] for fishing fleets, its purpose being to prevent the over-fishing of some species of fish. A number of Spanish fishing companies registered their ships in Britain in order to take advantage of Britain's fishing quota, although the companies continued to be owned and controlled by Spanish nationals, a practice known as 'quota-hopping'. In order to prevent the practice Parliament passed the Merchant Shipping Act 1988 which required that vessels registered in the United Kingdom be owned by companies whose directors or shareholders were British citizens and domiciled in Britain. Factortame Ltd and the other companies failed to satisfy these requirements. They applied to the High Court for judicial review of the Merchant Shipping Act on the grounds that it contravened European Community law. The Divisional Court referred the case to the ECJ for a ruling on whether the statute conflicted with Community law. This process would take at least two years so the Divisional Court granted the applicants interim relief by an order (injunction) restraining the Secretary of State from enforcing the relevant provisions of the Merchant Shipping Act during that time. This would have the effect of setting aside the legislation and allowing the applicants to continue to operate their fishing vessels until the ECJ decided the issue.

The Court of Appeal reversed the decision of the High Court on the grounds that the courts have no power to suspend the application of legislation or to grant an injunction against the government. The companies appealed to the House of Lords. The details of the judgment are contained in the headnotes[91] of the law report of the case:

> **Held** – (1) The court had no power to make an order postponing the
> *c* coming into force of a statute pending a reference to the European Court
> to determine it validity. Accordingly, the Divisional Court had had no
> power to make the interim[92] order disapplying the provisions of Pt II of
> the 1988 Act until some uncertain future date, since those provisions
> required no assistance from the court for their enforcement and were
> unambiguous[93] in their terms. Moreover, if the applicants failed to
> establish the rights they claimed before the European Court, the grant of
> *d* the interim relief would have had the effect of conferring on them rights
> directly contrary to Parliament's sovereign will and of depriving British
> fishing vessels, as defined by Parliament, of a substantial proportion of
> the United Kingdom quota of fish stocks protected by the common
> fisheries policy (see p 702 *j* to p 703 *c* and p 710 *h* to p 711 *b*, post); *F*
> *Hoffmann-La Roche & Co AG v Secretary of State for Trade and Industry*
> [1974] 2 All ER 1128 distinguished.
> (2) Moreover, the court had no power to grant an interim injunction
> *e* against the Crown in judicial review proceedings because injunctions had
> never been available at common law in proceedings on the Crown side
> and that position had been effectively preserved by ss 21(2)[b] and
> 23(2)(*b*)[c] of the Crown Proceedings Act 1947. Furthermore, s 31(2)[d] of
> the Supreme Court Act 1981 had not conferred a new jurisdiction on the
> court to grant interim injunctions against the Crown in judicial review
> proceedings and RSC[94] Ord 53, r 1(2)[e], which was in identical terms,
> *f* could not extend the jurisdiction of the court in that respect (see p 705 *g*,
> p 706 *b* to *d*, p 708 *b* to *d f g*, p 709 *a b* and p 710 *h* to p 711 *b*, post); dicta
> in *IRC v Rossminster* [1980] 1 All ER 80 disapproved; *R v Secretary of*
> *State for the Home Dept, ex p Herbage* [1986] 3 All ER 209 and *R v*
> *Licensing Authority, ex p Smith Kline & French Laboratories Ltd*
> *(Generics (UK) Ltd intervening) (No 2)* [1989] 2 All ER 113 overruled.
> (3) However, the question whether, irrespective of the position under
> *g* national law, there was an overriding principle of Community law that
> national court was under an obligation to provide an effective
> interlocutory[95] remedy to protect rights having direct effect under
> Community law where a seriously arguable claim of entitlement to such
> rights was advanced and the party claiming those rights would suffer
> irremediable damage if he was not effectively protected during the
> interim period pending determination of the existence of those rights
> *h* would be referred to the European Court for a preliminary ruling under
> art 177 of the EEC Treaty (see p 710 *c* to *f h* to p 711 *b*, post); *Srl CILFIT*
> *v Ministry of Health* Case 283/81 [1982] ECR 3415 applied.[96]
>
> *Factortame Ltd and Others* v. *Secretary of State for Transport* [1989] 2 All ER 692, 693.

Text notes:
90 limited number or amount which is allowed
91 see legal note below
92 provisional, temporary
93 'ambiguous' means 'of uncertain meaning', 'having two meanings'
94 Rules of the Supreme Court
95 (legal) intermediate
96 see language point below

Language point

If you find paragraph 3 above difficult to understand, the main subject ('the question') and the main verb ('would be referred') are separated by a large number of subsidiary clauses. These can be divided where there are commas and where there are relative clauses (introduced by 'that' (line 31), a present participle 'having' (line 33), 'where' (line 34) and a conjunction 'and' (line 35):

However, *the question* whether / , . . ., / there was an overriding principle of Community law / that . . . / having . . . where . . . / and . . . *would be referred to the European Court for a preliminary ruling under art. 177 of the EEC Treaty.*

Legal note

The headnotes in a law report provide a summary of the judgment in the case. They are a very useful source of quick information. There is one feature which you should note: the letters of the alphabet at the side are a means of reference. Note how they are used in the headnotes to refer you to the relevant part of the judgment (e.g. 'see p 702 *j* to p 703 *c* and p 710 *h* to p 711 *b*'). Also included are the names of cases which have been overruled, disapproved, distinguished and applied.

The crucial question to be determined by the ECJ was whether the British courts, in protecting the rights of individuals under Community law, have the power to suspend an Act of Parliament. Not surprisingly, the ECJ ruled that they do. It had reached a similar decision in 1978 in the *Simmenthal* case and in the 1987 *Kloppenburg* case.

Reaction to the judgment was explosive; anti-marketeers were outraged claiming that the ruling destroyed the sovereignty of Parliament. Richard Sheppard, a Conservative MP, said, 'It sets aside our constitution as we have understood it for several hundred years. We have had, for the first time in our national history, the imposition of a ruling that overrides the sovereignty of the British people.' In contrast others argued that the fact that Parliament is no longer sovereign should not come as such a shock. By passing the European Communities Act Parliament agreed to accept the supremacy of Community law. It is free to repeal that Act at any time but until it should wish to do so Parliament must comply with its provisions. It was also argued that if the Merchant Shipping Act had contained a clause expressly derogating from the European Communities Act, then the courts would have been obliged to give it[97] precedence. This was based on Lord Denning's judgment in *McCarthys* v. *Smith*.

Text note:
97 see question **27** below

Comprehension check

27 Note 97: To what does 'it' refer here?

Perhaps it is possible to summarise the arguments by concluding that, although the fact that Community law has supremacy over national law is not new, the power given to the courts to review and suspend an Act of Parliament pending a ruling by the ECJ is a change to their traditional constitutional role. It places the judges in a similar position to those who operate in countries with a written constitution

Legal exercises

28 What are the main sources of European Community law?

29 Distinguish between primary and secondary law.

30 What do you understand by the term 'direct effect'?

31 In what circumstances will a directive have direct effect?

32 Summarise the provisions of sections 2(1) and 2(4) of the European Communities Act 1972.

33 Why did the High Court consider that it was necessary to grant interim relief to the applicants in the *Factortame* case?

34 What was the effect of granting the interim relief?

35 Does the ECJ decision in *Factortame* diminish the sovereignty of the British Parliament?

10.5.3 Article 177 of the EEC Treaty

The process of referring to the ECJ for a preliminary ruling on the meaning of Community law is contained in Article 177 of the EEC Treaty. It provides:

> The Court of Justice shall have jurisdiction to give preliminary rulings concerning:
>
> (a) the interpretation of the Treaty;
> (b) the validity and interpretation of acts of the institutions of the Community;
> (c) the interpretation of the statutes of bodies established by an act of the Council, where those statutes so provide.
>
> Where such a question is raised before any court or Tribunal of a Member State that court or tribunal may, if it considers that a decision on the question is necessary to enable it to give judgment, request the Court of Justice to give a ruling thereon.
>
> Where any such question is raised in a case pending before a court or tribunal of a Member State, against whose decision there is no judicial remedy under national law, that court or tribunal shall bring the matter before the Court of Justice.

The purpose of Article 177 is, again, to achieve uniformity. Community law is stated in terms of broad principles and lends itself to a multiplicity of interpretations. Article 177 seeks to eliminate these potential differences. As we saw in the *Factortame* case, the hearing in the national court is suspended whilst the question is referred to the ECJ. After the ruling the case recommences in the national court.

You will observe that Article 177 specifies that 'a court or tribunal against whose decision there is no judicial remedy under national law **shall** make a referral'. So, for example, the House of Lords as the highest court in the United Kingdom is under an obligation to do so when it considers it necessary; other courts have a discretion whether or not to refer. The procedure is expensive and causes considerable delay. In *H. P. Bulmer Ltd & another* v. *J. Bollinger SA & others* (1974) Lord Denning addressed the question of when it was 'necessary' to make a referral under Article 177. A referral should not be made where the point was free from doubt, where the point was not conclusive of the case, where the facts had not been decided and where there had been a previous ruling on the same point.

Before ending this section, mention should be made of the different approach to statutory interpretation required by Community law. As mentioned earlier, it is stated in broad principles which cannot be interpreted literally. The ECJ has made it clear that it prefers the purposive[98] approach to interpretation and this has been adopted by many English judges, in particular by Lord Denning.

> 'Beyond doubt the English courts must follow the same principles as the European court. Otherwise there would be differences between the countries of the nine. That would never do.[99] All the courts of all nine countries should interpret the [EEC Treaty] in the same way . . .
>
> 'Likewise the regulations and directives . . .
>
> '[The English courts] must follow the European pattern. No longer must they examine the words in meticulous detail. No longer must they argue about the precise grammatical sense. They must look to the purpose or intent . . . They must divine the spirit of the treaty and gain inspiration from it. If they find a gap, they must fill it as best they can. They must do what the framers[100] of the instrument[101] would have done if they had thought about it.'
>
> *H.P. Bulmer Ltd* v. *J. Bollinger SA* [1974] Ch 401, 426.

Text notes:

98 see third paragraph of the next extract
99 (idiomatic) never be acceptable
100 'to frame' in this context means 'to construct'
101 document containing the statute

Legal exercise

36 Articles 9 and 13 of the EEC Treaty prohibit the imposition of any charges having an equivalent effect to custom duty on imports. As a result of an outbreak of 'mad cow' disease in some countries of the European Community the British Parliament passes the Public Health (Meat Inspection) Act 1992. This provides that all beef imported from the affected areas will be subjected to public health inspection on entry into Britain and that the cost of this inspection will be paid by the local importer.

International Importers (UK) Ltd imports beef from the relevant countries. The company applies to the High Court for judicial review of the Act on the grounds that it contraveres Articles 9 and 13 of the EEC Treaty in that the cost of the inspection fee has an equivalent effect to a custom duty on the imported meat. The High Court refers the case to the ECJ for a preliminary ruling. International Importers (UK) Ltd requests interim interim relief in the form of an injunction suspending the implementation of the Act. It argues that the cost of paying the inspection fees pending of judgment from the ECJ will seriously damage its financial position.

a Under which procedure will the referral be made?

b What factors will be considered when deciding whether a referral should be made?

c Consider the possible outcome of the case in the light of *Factorame*.

10.6 Article 119: A case study on the EEC Treaty

The case of *McCarthys* v. *Smith* [1979] 3 All ER 325; [1979] 1 WLR 1189, provides a useful basis for study as it involves a number of the issues we have already discussed: conflict between national law and Community law and referral under Article 177. The action was concerned with Article 119 of the EEC Treaty:

> Each Member State shall during the first stage ensure and subsequently maintain[102] the application of the principle that men and women should receive equal pay for equal work.
>
> For the purpose of this Article, 'pay' means the ordinary basic or minimum wage or salary and any other consideration, whether in cash or in kind, which the worker receives, directly or indirectly, in respect of his employment from his employer.
>
> Equal pay without discrimination[103] based on sex means:
>
> (a) that pay for the same work at piece rates shall be calculated on the basis of the same unit of measurement;
>
> (b) that pay for work at time rates shall be the same for the same job.

Text notes:

102 i.e. shall ensure and maintain

103 unfair treatment

Vocabulary

37 Which words are used in Article 119 which are similar in meaning to the explanations below?

a weekly pay for (manual) work

b monthly pay for non-manual work

c in proportion to the amount produced

d in commodities, i.e. not in cash

e recompense, something given in return

Mrs Smith was employed by McCarthys Ltd as a warehouse manageress. Her position had previously been held by a man who had left the company four months earlier. Her predecessor had been paid a wage of £60 a week whilst Mrs Smith was paid £50. She brought proceedings before an industrial tribunal under the terms of the Equal Pay Act 1970 as amended by the Sex Discrimination Act 1975. She was successful at first instance and on appeal by her employer to the Employment Appeal Tribunal. The employers appealed to the Court of Appeal. The issues for the court were the interpretation of section 1(2)(a)(i) of the Act and whether it conflicted with Article 119. Section 1(2)(a)(i) requires that a woman shall be paid the same salary as a man 'where the woman is employed on like[104] work with a man in the same employment'. Did this provision apply only to men and women employed at the same time or was it applicable to consecutive employment? The majority decided on the former.

Text note:
104 an adjective, meaning 'similar'

Per Lawton LJ:

> In my judgment the grammatical construction of s 1(2) is consistent only with a comparison between a woman and a man in the same employment at the same time. The words, by the tenses used,[105] look to the present and the future but not to the past. They are inconsistent with a comparison between a woman and a man, no longer in the same employment, who was doing her job before she got it.

Comprehension check

38 Note 105: Find an example of these tenses in the quote from section 1(2) given in the text above the extract.

Lord Denning disagreed:

> The relevant part of this Act was passed not in 1970 but in 1975 by s 8 of the Sex Discrimination Act 1975.
>
> Section 1(2)(*a*)(i) of the Equal Pay Act 1970 introduces an 'equality clause' so as to put a woman on an equality with a man 'where the woman is employed on like work with a man in the same employment'. The question is whether the words 'at the same time' are to be read into that subsection so that it is confined to cases where the woman and the man are employed *at the same time* in the same employment.
>
> Reading that subsection as it stands, it would appear that the draftsman had only in mind cases where the woman was employed *at the same time* as a man. The use of the present tense 'is' and of the phrase 'in the same employment' carry the connotation that the woman and the man are employed on like work *at the same time* . . .
>
> Some light is thrown on the problem by reference to the Sex Discrimination Act 1975. It applies to all cases of discrimination against a woman in the employment field: see ss 1 and 6(1) and (2) except where she is paid less money than the man: see s 6(6). Now take a case where a man leaves his job and the employer discriminates against an incoming woman by offering her (not less money) but less benefits than he would offer a man for the same job: for instance, less holidays or less travelling facilities or the like. And she accepts them. That would be discrimination against her on the

ground of her sex. It would be unlawful under ss 1 and 6(1) and (2). In such a case you would think that there should be an 'equality clause' introduced under s 1(2) of the Equal Pay Act: so that, in regard to her holidays or her travel facilities, she would be put on equal terms with the man. But in order to achieve that just result, it is necessary to extend s 1(2)(*a*), so that it extends not only to employment 'at the same time' as the man but also to employment in succession to a man.

Now stand back and look at the statutes as a single code intended to eliminate discrimination against women. They should be a harmonious whole. To achieve this harmony s 1(2)(*a*)(i) of the Equal Pay Act should *not* be read as if it included the words 'at the same time'. It should be interpreted so as to apply to cases where a woman is employed at the same job doing the same work 'in succession' to a man.

Comprehension check: notemaking

39 Complete the following summary:

1. Lord J. Lawton looks at section . . . . of . . . .
2. L. Denning looks both at . . . .
3. L.D. agrees that Section 1(2) had in mind . . . .
4. Under the 1975 Act it is unlawful to . . . .
5. L.D. looks at both statutes together; in order that they sh'd harmonise to eliminate discrimination against women, ...

Lord Denning argued that this construction of the wording of the Act was in accordance with Article 119, the terms in which could be used to aid interpretation of the Equal Pay Act.

Again Lord Denning was in a minority. Lord Justice Lawton and Lord Justice Cummings-Bruce were unclear on the meaning of Article 119 but were sure that it could not be used to subvert[106] the natural and ordinary meaning of the words of the statute. Nevertheless, given their uncertainty over its meaning there may be a conflict between European law and national law and in those circumstances the Court was under an obligation to refer the matter to the ECJ under Article 177.

Text note:
106 to overturn

Per Lawton LJ:

Being in doubt as to the ambit of art 119 and being under an obligation arising both from the decisions of the European Court of Justice in the two cases to which I have referred and s 2 of the European Communities Act 1972 to apply that article in our courts, it seems to me that this is a situation to which art 177 of the EEC Treaty applies. I consider that a decision is necessary as to the construction of art 119 and I would request the European Court of Justice to give a ruling on it. The question which I suggest tentatively should be answered is this: whether art 119 applies to a case in which a woman has claimed that, because of discrimination based on sex, she was paid less than a man whose job she took over 4½ months after he had left it, her work in that job being broadly similar in nature to what he had done.

Before saying au revoir, if not adieu, to this appeal, I would like to set out my reasons for deciding as I have that there should be a reference to the European Court of Justice. First, counsel on both sides persuaded me that it would be more convenient and less expensive to the parties for this court to request the European Court of Justice to give a ruling on the application of art 119 than for the House of Lords to do so. The issue in the appeal is clear, even if by English concepts the construction of art 119 is not. The ruling when given may decide the case; and when the ruling is given, there can be no appeal from it. There seems to be nothing else which would justify an appeal to the House of Lords. Further, I can see nothing in this case which infringes the sovereignty of Parliament. If I thought there were, I should not presume to take any judicial step which it would be more appropriate for the House of Lords, as part of Parliament, to take. Parliament by its own act in the exercise of its sovereign powers has enacted that European Community law shall 'be enforced, allowed and followed' in the United Kingdom of Great Britain and Northern Ireland (see s 2(1) of the European Communities Act 1972) and that 'any enactment passed or to be passed . . . shall be construed and have effect subject to [s 2]' (see s 2(4) of that Act). Parliament's recognition of European Community law and of the jurisdiction of the European Court of Justice by one enactment can be withdrawn by another. There is nothing in the Equal Pay Act 1970 as amended by the Sex Discrimination Act 1975, to indicate that Parliament intended to amend the European Communities Act 1972, or to limit its application. Secondly, as I am in doubt as to what is the right construction of art 119 when our canons of construction are applied and in ignorance as to how the European Court of Justice would construe that article when it applies its own rules of construction, I consider myself under a judicial duty not to guess how that court would construe it but to find out how it does.

Comprehension check

40 What are Lord Justice Lawton's reasons for referring the *McCarthys* v. *Smith* case to the ECJ?

McCarthys v. *Smith* was the first case to be referred by a British court to the ECJ under Article 177. The decision of the ECJ was in agreement with Lord Denning's minority judgment.

According to the first paragraph of Article 119 the Member States are obliged to ensure and maintain 'the application of the principle that men and women should receive equal pay for equal work'.

As the Court indicated in the *Defrenne* judgment of 8 April 1976, that provision applies directly, and without the need for more detailed implementing measures on the part of the Community or the Member States, to all forms of direct and overt discrimination which may be identified solely with the aid of the criteria of equal work and equal pay referred to by the article in question. Among the forms of discrimination which may be thus judicially identified, the Court mentioned in particular cases where men and women receive unequal pay for equal work carried out in the same establishment or service.

In such a situation the decisive test lies in establishing whether there is a difference in treatment between a man and a woman performing 'equal work' within the meaning of Article 119. The scope of that concept, which is entirely qualitative in character in that it is exclusively concerned with the nature of the services in question, may not be restricted by the introduction of a requirement of contemporaneity.

It must be acknowledged, however, that, as the Employment Appeal Tribunal properly recognised, it cannot be ruled out that a difference in pay between two workers occupying the same post but at different periods in time may be explained by the operation of factors which are unconnected with any discrimination on grounds of sex. That is a question of fact which it is for the court or tribunal to decide.

Thus the answer to the . . . question should be that the principle that men and women should receive equal pay for equal work, enshrined in Article 119 of the EEC Treaty, is not confined to situations in which men and women are contemporaneously doing equal work for the same employer.

Case 129/79 McCarthys Ltd v. *Wendy Smith* [1980] ECR 1275; [1980] 2 CMLR 205.

Comprehension check

41 a Paragraph 3 contains two key words in relation to interpreting Article 119. Can you identify them and explain what they mean in the context of the extract?

b 'Contemporaneous' means 'at the same time'. Which contrasting word was used earlier to mean 'in succession'?

c Must a man and a woman in a similar job at a different time always receive the same pay and benefits?

Legal exercises

42 What rule of interpretation was used by the majority of the Court of Appeal in determining the meaning of the words in section 1(2) (a) (i) of the Equal Pay Act 1970?

43 What analogy did Lord Denning draw with the provisions of the Sex Discrimination Act 1975 in order to justify his decision in favour of Mrs Smith?

44 Was the Court of Appeal under a legal obligation to make a referral to the ECJ?

45 Did Article 119 have direct effect in English law?

46 Article 119 refers only to 'equal work'. Directive 75/117 defines this as 'work to which equal value is attributed'. Section 1(5) of the Equal Pay Act, as amended by the Sex Discrimination Act 1975, complies with this directive in the following terms:

'A woman is regarded as employed in work rated as equivalent with that of any man if, but only if, her job and their job have been given equal value in terms of demand made on the worker under various headings (for instance effort, skill, decision) . . .'

Consider the following situation in the light of this definition:

Alice is employed by Poshcars Ltd as a chef in the staff canteen. Her responsibilities include planning the menus, cooking the food, ordering the provisions and overall control of a kitchen staff of five. She underwent a three-year training programme to qualify for the position. She works a 45 hour week and is paid a monthly salary of £600.

Ted is also employed by Poshcar Ltd. His job is to supervise the manufacture of the cars and to ensure a high standard of production. He trained for three years to qualify. He works 40 hours a week which includes some night work and is paid a monthly salary of £800.

Alice is claiming discrimination on the basis of the Equal Pay Act and Directive 75/117.

a Before which 'court' will her case be heard at first instance?
b If she is not satisfied with the outcome of the hearing to which 'court(s)' can she appeal?
c What factors will be taken into account in deciding whether Poshcars Ltd are in breach of the law?

Vocabulary

47 There are many phrases of verb plus noun which commonly occur together. By matching the nouns below with the appropriate verbs you will form phrases which are used in Chapter 10.

rights, the bounds, a conflict, a convention, changes, the gap, a decision, the correct balance, certain criteria, priority, someone's privacy, someone's rights, a writ for damages.

a to violate
b to implement
c to comply with
d to strike
e to issue
f to infringe
g to overstep
h to resolve
i to fill
j to invade
k to fulfil
l to give
m to confer

Additional reading

Most books on the English legal system will contain sections on the topics in this chapter. The books from which the extracts are taken all deal with them in more detail, although you should refer to those addressed specifically to the EC for the most comprehensive coverage of the subject. You will find a comprehensive selection of case studies in *Plender and Usher's Cases and Materials on the Law of the European Communities* by Plender (Butterworths) and a thought-provoking discussion on the legal order of the European Community by a former judge of the ECJ, Lord McKenzie, in *The European Communities and the Rule of Law* (Stevens). *Guide to Case Law* by Ercman (Wilhelm Braumuller) provides an examination of the Articles of the ECHR through an analysis of cases and judgments.

Answers to questions

Chapter 1

1 **a** F; **b** T; **c** F; **d** T; **e** F; **f** T; **g** F; **h** F.

3 A codified system makes the law more certain in that it brings together in one place all the legal rules of a country in an accessible and understandable form. In England the law on any one subject may be found in different cases and statutes.

4 It is important for judges to be independent so that they can act impartially in any case and reach a fair decision. They must not be biased in favour of any party to a legal action nor must they be subject to pressure from government.

5 In the adversarial system of justice the case is decided on the evidence presented to the court by the parties to the action. This evidence is subjective in that it is in favour of the party presenting it; there is no independent body to investigate the case objectively. This can result in important evidence being ignored and not being heard by the court.

7 **a** the legal system; **b** no, they did not ('could have' indicates this); **c** to run the court in their region; **d** a permanent Royal Court; **e** in the regions; **f** the region concerned.

8 **a** one of the common law courts; **b** the Court of Chancery.

9 **a** petition; **b** historical; **c** equitable; **d** inequitable; **e** specification; **f** to specify; **g** abolition; **h** to litigate.

11

apply	4	systems	15	appellant	1		
unitary	17	union	16	committee	9		
federation	13	endure	12	application	3		
ascend	5	appellor	2	commit	8		
united	18	commission	7	criminal	11		
separate	14	crime	10	ascertain	6		
resolution	16	licence	6	liable	4		
procedural	7	appoint	1	repeal	14		
discharge	2	profitable	13	procedure	8		
proceeds	10	process	11	respondent	18		
libel	5	profit	12	represent	15		
liability	3	proceed	9	resolve	17		

12 **a** Middle Ages; **b** common law; **c** redress; **d** relief; **e** remedy; **f** common law court; **g** Court of Chancery; **h** Judicature Act; **i** Supreme Court of Judicature; **j** conflict; **k** the laws of equity; **l** prevail.

13 **a** Reported in the year 1970 in Appeal Cases at page 467.
b Reported in the year 1917 in volume 2 of King's Bench at page 822.
c Reported in the year 1966 in volume 1 of Chancery at page 276.
d Reported in the year 1987 in volume 3 of the All England Law Reports at page 678, in Queen's Bench at page 972, and in volume 3 of the Weekly Law Reports at page 537.
e Reported in the year 1980 in the Criminal Law Reports at page 107.

14 Background: lines 1–3; complaint: lines 3–4; action: lines 4–7; defence: lines 7–9; judgment: lines 10–12; reasons: lines 13–end.

16 **a** to; **b** of; **c** to; **d** by; **e** to; **f** for; **g** for; **h** in; **i** to; **j** from.

17 **a** decentralised; **b** barons; **c** permanent; **d** King's Bench; **e** judges; **f** civil; **g** criminal; **h** decided; **i** facts; **j** judge-made; **k** common; **l** Chancery; **m** remedies; **n** redress; **o** separate; **p** Judicature; **q** Supreme; **r** common; **s** equity; **t** maxims; **u** justice; **v** fairness.

18 *D. & C. Builders v. Rees*
The relevant maxim in this case is he who comes to equity must come with clean hands. The defendants could not be protected by an equitable doctrine as they had acted inequitably by withholding payment until the plaintiffs were in financial difficulty. The plaintiffs were not held to their promise to settle the debt for the lesser sum and the defendants were ordered to pay the outstanding amount. The two other maxims mentioned in the text are also relevant: that there is no legal right to equitable remedies which are granted at the discretion of the courts, and that equity recognises legal rights, in this case the plaintiffs' legal right at common law to recover the full debt

19 *Civil:* civil wrong, County Court, liable, to sue, judgment for the plaintiff, plaintiff, defendant, damages.
Criminal: crime, offence, Crown Court, guilty, to prosecute, conviction, prosecutor, defendant, punishment, to punish, to convict, life imprisonment.

20 **a** prosecutor; **b** defendant; **c** plaintiff; **d** defendant; **e** injunction; **f** sued; **g** conviction; **h** liable; **i** legal consequences.

21 **a** prosecutes; **b** punished; **c** released on probation; **d** discharged without punishment; **e** plaintiff; **f** sues; **g** pay damages; **h** injunction; **i** specific performance.

22 Murder is a criminal offence so that Bob will be prosecuted not sued. The case will not be heard in the county court as this is a court of civil jurisdiction only. Bob will be prosecuted by a prosecutor not a plaintiff, and after a successful prosecution he will be found guilty, not liable. Damages are a civil remedy not a criminal punishment although in some cases the courts do have the power to punish the defendant and also order him to pay compensation to the victim of his crime.

23 **a** civil; **b** civil; **c** criminal; **d** criminal.

24 **a** Procedure was important in the past because it was easier to understand than the abstract principles of substantive law.
b Procedure is still important today but it is more flexible and does not take precedence over substantive law.

25 **a** procedural rules; **b** rules of procedure; **c** Rules of the Supreme Court; **d** the Judicature Acts; **e** the rules of criminal procedure.

26 **a** F; **b** F; **c** F; **d** F; **e** T.

27 Substantive law: subject matter, abstract principles, substance.

Adjectival law: machinery, formal requirements, form

28 The rules of evidence play a very important part in achieving a fair trial. Statements made by witnesses can be questioned by the opposing party to make sure that they are true and correct. As Thomas's lawyer was not allowed to cross-examine PC Boot, the latter's statement that he saw Thomas running away from the scene of the crime has gone unchallenged. Equally, as the prosecuting lawyer was allowed to cross-examine Thomas, the prosecution has been given an advantage over Thomas. Both parties to the case should be given the same rights if the trial is to be a fair one. Thomas is further disadvantaged when the court is told of his previous criminal convictions. The fact that he has been found guilty of a criminal offence in the past may prejudice those deciding on his guilt or innocence in the present case. In criminal cases the court is not told if the defendant has a criminal record until after a verdict has been reached. If the defendant is found guilty previous convictions will be taken into account when deciding on the appropriate punishment.

Chapter 2

3 **a** 1787.
b Yes, but by a complex predetermined procedure.
c No, although certain elements of the constitution are contained in a number of different documents.
d Parliament.

4 **a** the constitution of the USA; **b** a constitutional amendment; **c** the constitution of England; **d** Parliament; **e** law; **f** the subject.

5 sovereign = the highest (power).

6 **a** T; **b** F; **c** F; **d** F; **e** F; **f** T.

7 **a** the American Courts; **b** the power to enforce the provisions of the constitution; **c** the reason why the UK courts do not have the power to enforce the provisions of the constitution; **d** see section 2.1 of this chapter.

8 Your answer should include six from the following, although this is not a complete list:

A right to: freedom of speech, freedom of assembly, privacy, freedom from unlawful detention, religious freedom, education, freedom from racial discrimination, freedom from sexual discrimination, freedom to work and adequate housing.

10 **a** express; **b** convention; **c** the monarch, Queen (King), sovereign; **d** the House of Commons; **e** Prime Minister.

11 **a** The Cabinet was created by convention not by statute.
b The monarch's practice of not attending cabinet meetings.
c The monarch invites the majority party leader to form a new government.
d The leader of the majority party first became Prime Minister by convention (this is now covered by statute).
e The Queen never refuses her assent to an Act of Parliament (though legally she could do so).
f By convention a Ministry which is defeated on a major issue in the House of Commons should resign or advise a dissolution of Parliament.
g If, after a dissolution, it is defeated at the next election, the party should resign.
h By convention Parliament must meet at least once a year.
i The courts are bound only by convention to apply Acts of Parliament.
j The doctrine of judicial precedent is conventional.

12 **a** **i** A government defeated on a major issue will resign and call a general election.
ii The Queen should then invite the

leader of the majority party to form the next government.

b **i** The Prime Minister should resign or ask the Queen to dissolve Parliament after a major defeat in the House of Commons.

ii Conventions are not laws in the ordinary sense and are therefore not enforceable in the courts.

c The Queen may legally withold her consent from an Act of Parliament but by convention she does not.

13 **a** Conventions are obeyed for the practical reason of political convenience; political difficulties and public disfavour could result from a failure to observe a convention. But conventions also have a certain moral force and adherence to them is seen to uphold the constitutional values of the country.

b Conventions do vary in importance; a breach of one may have very little constitutional effect whilst the breach of another may have serious results. For example, the convention of ministerial responsibility is frequently broken; it is now only used in very serious situations. A breach of this convention can cause some disapproval but it would not have the same constitutional effect as the Queen refusing to give the Royal Assent to an Act of Parliament.

c The consequences of a breach of a convention would be determined by the seriousness of the breach. Conventions are frequently breached with very little consequence. A serious breach would result in a constitutional crisis which could need to be resolved by legislation. For example, the convention that the House of Lords should not reject bills passed by the House of Commons dealing with taxation and public expenditure (money bills) was breached by the House of Lords in 1909. As a result the Parliament Act 1911 was passed. This allows a money bill to be presented for the Royal Assent without the approval of the House of Lords if it has not been approved by that House after one month.

d The main advantage of unwritten conventions is their flexibility. They evolve gradually to adapt to changing political circumstances and values without the need for the formal procedure required under many written constitutions. Indeed, even in countries with written constitutions, informal conventions have evolved to meet the practical needs of government.

14 'Parliament' here refers to the House of Commons + House of Lords + Royal Assent.

15 The relationship between the legislature and the judiciary.

16 'The Queen in Parliament', that is that legislation has passed through the stages of approval by a majority in the House of Commons and the House of Lords and has received the Royal Assent.

17 There is no legislative authority for this rule; it is a constitutional fact which is accepted by the judiciary and the legislature.

18 The Supreme Court has the power to strike down legislation which it judges to be unconstitutional because there is a written constitution which all legislation must comply with.

19 **a** The British courts will be obliged to enforce this law, even though it is unfair and discriminatory, because it satisfies the 'Queen in Parliament' test.

b The courts would not enforce the law as it would be contrary to the rights contained in the written constitution.

20 **a** three; **b** executive; **c** legislative; **d** judicial; **e** different; **f** conform; **g** executive; **h** legislature; **i** administrative; **j** United States; **k** different; **l** prescriptive; **m** descriptive; **n** judiciary; **o** independent; **p** legislature; **q** executive

21 **a** unlawful
b unfamiliar
c impractical
d illegal
e unfair
f invalid
g independence
h unmake
i injustice
j impartiality
k inequitable
l unwritten
m impracticable
n unconstitutional
o illicit

23 Your essay would begin with the details of Montesquieu's theory by identifying the three functions of government – executive, legislature and judiciary – and the principle that these should be performed by separate bodies with no one person or body having control of all three functions. In particular the judiciary should be independent from the other two organs of government so that it can pass judgment on their actions and control any abuse of power. This is considered to be very important in liberal democratic countries

You should then discuss the extent to which the British constitution conforms to this theory; the executive as part of the legislature and the role of the Lord Chancellor are particularly relevant here. Make comparisons with other countries, including the United States of America and your own country.

You could conclude by discussing the prescriptive nature of the theory – that it is a statement about the control of political power rather than a realistic description of most governments.

24 **a** internee = someone who is forced to stay in a special camp or prison.

b detainee = person who is detained.

26 As the rule of law requires all people to act within the law it is important that the judiciary is independent from the executive and legislature so that it is free to judge the legality or illegality of their actions.

27 a Are the provisions of the Prohibition of Dogs Act 1993 right or wrong? People who do not like dogs may applaud the provisions of the Act whilst those who are fond of dogs would not, but the merits of the Act are not a matter for the courts to decide – they are concerned only with its legality.

b Is the police action legal or illegal? There are two issues here:
i charging William with keeping a dog as a domestic pet, and
ii locking him in a cell for twenty-four hours.
Providing that the Act satisfies the 'Queen in Parliament' test the police action in charging William is legal as he has contravened the provisions of the Act by keeping a dog as a household pet. But the Act does not give the police the power to detain people who have been charged under it, so the action of locking William in the cell is illegal.

28 a Vice-Chancellor Megarry is saying that actions are only illegal if there is a law forbidding them, anything else is legal. The statement is saying that anything which is not authorised by law is illegal.
b The comparison can be criticised because cigarette smoking, whilst offensive to many people, does not affect what are considered to be basic human rights, in this case the right to privacy. Certainly it is not possible for the law to give authority to all human actions but some acts can be so oppressive that they should only be permitted when authorised by law. In particular, given the potential power of governments to affect the rights of individuals, their actions should be controlled by law.
c If Britain had a written constitution which protected the individual's right to privacy then the actions of the Metropolitan Police Commissioner would have been judged against this.

29 Legal: lawful, authorised by law, authorisation of law, authority given by the law, permitted.
Illegal: unlawful, breach of the law, infringing the law, forbidden.

30 a assumption; **b** contention; **c** contentious; **d** validity; **e** to validate; **f** prescription; **g** prescriptive; **h** to describe; **i** descriptive; **j** legality; **k** to legalise; **l** comparison; **m** comparative; **n** enforcement; **o** to enforce.

31 a F; **b** T; **c** T; **d** F.

32 a The question of whether the local authority have taken into account matters which they ought to have taken into account or whether they have refused to take into account or neglected to take into account matters which they ought to take into account.
b Yes.

33 a The council ought not to have changed it.
b The Secretary of State ought not to have issued it.
c The police ought not to have detained him.
d They ought not to have used them.
e The police ought not to have been there.

34 The rule of law requires that all people, including those who control the functions of government, act within the law. Judicial review is the process by which the courts ensure that this requirement is adhered to.

35 *Ultra vires* means in excess of power, that is, acting without legal authority.

36 Judicial review can prevent administrative bodies taking action which will adversely effect the lives of individual citizens unless they are authorised to do so by law.

37 The local education authority has the power to cease providing education to blue-eyed female children after they are ten years old. As Alison has grey eyes she is not affected by the provisions of the Female Education Act 1995 and the action of the education authority in ceasing to provide her with full-time education after her tenth birthday is directed against the wrong person and therefore beyond its powers (*ultra vires*).

38 The power given to the local authority under the Town Redevelopment Act 1994 is to purchase land compulsorily for the purpose of building new houses. Newtown Council's plan to purchase the houses, including Mr Stormy's, to build a new housing estate is within its powers. However, the plan also to build new council offices on the land is not included in the Act and therefore outside its powers. In addition the Act imposes a duty to consult those affected by the purchase of the land. The council has not complied with this procedural requirement which is a condition precedent to the exercise of its powers. Its action in immediately demolishing the houses is therefore *ultra vires*.

39 a The conditional indicates that a Bill of Rights has not yet been enacted; the writer is looking at a hypothetical situation which does not exist at the moment.
b An example of English laws which conflict with the European Convention on Human Rights.
c 'Little' stresses the smallness of size or amount; here the writer is saying that the

amount of headway or progress is small. 'A little' reflects a more positive outlook, e.g. 'we have made a little progress' shows that the speaker is pleased with the result; 'we have made little progress' shows that the speaker is not pleased.

40 **a** basic – fundamental (line 1).
b fixed – entrenched (line 2).
c most of the time – more often than not (line 6).
d caused – brought about (line 7).
e strengthens – reinforces (line 8).
f in spite of – despite (line 19).
g damage – prejudice (line 27).
h alone – of itself (line 37).

41 These notes are only for guidance; there are many different possibilities.

1. Nature of proposed B. of R.
   a) would contain fundamental rights, e.g. freedom of speech
   b) w'd be entrenched
   c) w'd be enforced by judiciary.
2. L.S. sees need for B. of R.
   a) imbalance in present system
   b) England's poor record + ECHR e.g. laws on contempt of court; *Sunday Times* case.
3. *But* little progress; strong opposition to Bill.
4. Arguments vs. B. of R.:
   a) w'd politicise judges
   b) w'd entrench one set of values & exclude another
   c) US experience not encouraging, e.g. legalised slavery & racial discrimination.
5. Conclusion: Bill alone can't guarantee rights – needs support of public attitudes + judiciary.

42 **a** Parliament would not be free to enact any legislation it wishes to as all legislation would be required to comply with the provisions of the Bill of Rights. Equally there would be some outside body, presumably the judiciary, which would have the authority to declare an Act of Parliament invalid.
b The courts would have the power to assess the merits of legislation and administrative action in relation to the provisions of the Bill of Rights.

43 The particular features of the British constitution which are relevant to this debate are its unwritten nature and the doctrine of parliamentary sovereignty – what effect do these have on the protection of human rights compared, for example, with the United States?

Your debate should include a consideration of whether the doctrine of parliamentary sovereignty gives the executive and legislature too much power which could be used to infringe human rights and whether a constitution based only on unenforceable conventions and social democratic traditions is sufficient protection against the possibility of abuse. How effective is judicial review in controlling abuse of power by those in authority?

What effect would a Bill of Rights have on the role of the judges and parliamentary sovereignty? Does the record of the judges of the Supreme Court in the United States demonstrate that judges are more likely to protect human rights than governments? Consider Lord McCluskey's arguments against a Bill of Rights and also Chancellor Megarry's reasoning in the *Malone* case and compare it to the argument that any action which does not have legal authority is illegal – which approach is more likely to protect human rights?

44 One of Lord McCluskey's fears over the enactment of a Bill of Rights is that it would entrench one set of rights at the expense of other, equally valid rights. In this situation the right to privacy and freedom from unwanted intrusion into an individual's private life could limit legitimate investigation by the press into a matter of public interest, for example the close association of a senior police officer with a suspected criminal.

Chapter 3

1 **a** Judge must consider precedent as part of material.
b Judge must decide present case in same way as previous case unless he or she can give a good reason not to do so.
c Judge must decide present case in same way as previous case (even if he or she has a good reason not to do so).

In **a** and **b** the precedent is persuasive; in **c** it is coercive or binding.

2 'Instant' here means present, current.

3 **a** House of Lords; **b** Court of Appeal; **c** High Court of Justice; **d** Crown Court; **e** county court; **f** magistrates' court; **g** European Court of Justice.

4 **a** F (see paragraph 2, line 4 above); **b** F (not since 1966); **c** T **d** T (except for EC law).

5 To stand by previous decisions, that is to follow the legal rules in earlier cases.

6 Prior to the 1966 Practice Statement the House of Lords was bound by its own previous decisions. This made the law very inflexible. By the 1966 Practice Statement the House of Lords may overrule a previous decision when it feels it is right to do so. This allows for more flexibility in the law.

7 The Court of Appeal may depart from its own previous decisions under the rules of

Young v. *Bristol Aeroplane Co.* These are: **a** when a decision of the Court of Appeal conflicts with a decision of the House of Lords, **b** when there are two conflicting Court of Appeal decisions, and **c** when a decision is taken *per incuriam*.

8 The European Court of Justice is not a court of appeal within the English legal system but a court of referral. Its decisions are only binding on the English courts in relation to European Community law.

9 **a** Refers to 'decision'.
b The reason for the decision.
c '. . . what his decision *would* or *might have been if* the facts of the case *had been different.*' The judge is *speculating,* forming a hypothesis regarding something which did not happen. Some grammar books call this an unreal or hypothetical conditional in the past.

The judge's words were perhaps: '*If* the facts *had been* different, I *would/might have made* a different decision.' (He is looking back at his actual decision which he made earlier.) If he is still making his decision or still presenting it, his actual words might be: 'If the facts *were* different, I *would/might make* a different decision.'

10 **e** = 1; **d** = 2; **a** = 3; **c** = 4; **b** = 5.

11 **a** The manufacturer *intends* his products *to reach the ultimate consumer in the form in which they left* the manufacturer.
b There is *no reasonable possibility of intermediate examination.*
c The manufacturer knows *that the absence of reasonable care . . . will result in injury to the consumer's life or property.*

12 'Former' in this instance refers to 'dangers'.

13 **a** responsible – accountable
b careless – negligent
c clearly stated – expressly
d wrong reports – misstatements

14 **a** The bankers inquired into the financial situation.
b He had dealings with a large company.
c They relied on his advice.
d She sued him for his negligence.
e A newspaper is not financially accountable to its readers.
f The bank was not responsible for the loss.

15 The *ratio decidendi* of a judgment is the principle of law on which a case is decided; *obiter dicta* are other statements made by the judge or said 'by the way'. It is important to distinguish the two as it is the *ratio decidendi* only which is binding on future courts in cases involving the same legal principle. The *obita dicta* is merely persuasive.

16 Reversing occurs when the same case is taken on appeal to a higher court and a judgment is reached in favour of the appellant. A judgment is overruled when, in a later case, the court refuses to confirm the legal principle contained in an earlier case.

17 It is usually possible to foresee which people will be affected by negligent acts; in the case of negligent words, on the other hand, it is not always possible to foresee at the time which people will be affected by them. For example, if a car is driven negligently it is possible to foresee that the people who may be injured are those in the immediate vicinity of the road – other drivers, pedestrians. If negligent advice on investments, for example, is broadcast on the radio or television or published in a newspaper it is not possible to foresee how many people may lose money as a result of following that advice – the number could be many thousands. The courts have always been anxious to avoid creating liability to an indeterminate number of people; the 'special relationship' requirement in *Hedley Byrne* seeks to do this.

18 **a** **Area of law involved:** Mrs Gamble has lost money as a result of following the advice of Miss Nugget and the article in the newspaper. The area of law is therefore economic loss as result of negligent words.
b **Analysis of the law:** The relevant case law is *Donoghue* v. *Stevenson* and *Hedley Byrne* v. *Heller.* Your analysis of these cases should include the factors discussed in the answer to question 17 and the definition of a 'special relationship': it must be reasonable for the plaintiff to rely on the advice and the defendant must have accepted responsibility for the accuracy of the statement.
c **Applying the law to the facts of the problem:** It would seem that there is a special relationship between Mrs Gamble and Miss Nugget; the advice was given in a formal situation where Miss Nugget should accept the responsibility for the accuracy of her advice and where it was reasonable for Mrs Gamble to rely on it. However, the loss resulting from reading the article in the newspaper raises the problem of liability to an indeterminate number of people. There is no special relationship between Mrs Gamble and the newspaper as there is no undertaking of responsibility to all its readers and it would not be reasonable for Mrs Gamble to rely on the information in the article to invest her money without taking further advice on Kwikbuild's financial position.

We can therefore conclude that Mrs Gamble would have a reasonable chance of recovering the £5,000 she has lost as a result of Miss Nugget's advice but not the £5,000 invested as a result of reading the article in the newspaper.

19 **a** justice; **b** general principles; **c** discard; **d** modify; **e** discard.

20 **a** Certainty in the law achieves justice by enabling people to know what the law is so that they may arrange their lives accordingly. Justice also requires that like cases are treated alike and that decisions on the meaning of the law are not reached in an arbitrary manner.
b Injustice can be caused if the law is too inflexible because mistakes of the past cannot be altered. Also the law must adapt to changing circumstances and social attitudes.
c Judicial precedent prevents judges reaching decisions based on a subjective view of the law and the cases before them by requiring them to follow the decisions in previous cases.
d Distinguishing provides a small degree of flexibility by allowing a judge to reach a different decision when the facts of a later case are materially different.
e 'Bad decisions' can only be overruled by the House of Lords under the 1966 Practice Statement or by the Court of Appeal if they come within the rules of *Young* v. *Bristol Aeroplane Co.*
f Lord Denning in particular has argued that justice would be more easily achieved if the Court of Appeal was able to overrule its own previous decisions because litigants would not have to suffer the delay and cost of taking a case first to the Court of Appeal and then to the House of Lords. However, you will learn in Chapter 5 that there is a procedure for some cases to bypass the Court of Appeal and go straight to the House of Lords.

21 **a** Refers to the situation where there are too many cases or they are too confusing.
b The amount of detail provided by case law.
c see lines 9–10.
d See lines 33–4; the judge is not free to make and change laws.
e By the fact that he must follow precedent unless the case can be distinguished.

22

Advantages	*Disadvantages*
a Certainty: **i** may prevent mistakes by judge; **ii** people can order their lives knowing what the law is.	**a** Too many cases; cases may be confusing.
b Justice: diff. people will be treated similarly in similar cases.	**b** Diff. to find the law $\because$ so many cases.
c Impartiality: judge is bound by prec. unless good reason not to follow it.	**c** Rigidity: mistakes of past perpetuated.
d Law can develop: courts can lay down new p.'s or extend old ones.	
e Flexibility.	

23 **a** F; **b** F; **c** T; **d** T; **e** F.

24 Continental law is usually codified and the code is all-important.

25 Refers to the fact that 'that which seems to have been clearly explained . . .'

26 **a** Writer assumed reader knew more than he or she actually did → made the document too brief or too difficult.
b Subject of document not easily expressed in words.
c Idea very complex → complex writing.
d Writer omits an aspect of the topic.

27 The four interpretations are:

a John met Peter and John raised his own hat.
b John met Peter and Peter raised his own hat.
c John met Peter and John raised Peter's hat.
d John met Peter and Peter raised John's hat.

28 'Vehicle' is a very common word but a literal interpretation of its everyday meaning is not simple. It may be defined as 'any means of conveyance' in which case all of our four items would be considered to be a vehicle as they are all used for transporting people or things. However, a sign stating 'No Vehicles in This Park' would not commonly be expected to exclude prams from the park and perhaps not bicycles. The context in which the word is used is obviously important.

29 Again this is a very common word but its meaning will change according to its context. All four items have the common characteristic of being a structure used to house people or things but there are also many differences between them; for example, a house is a permanent structure whilst the other three items are not. Legislation using such words as 'vehicle' and 'building' will usually contain an interpretation section to assist the courts.

30 **Note outline**
Para. 1:
1. Presumptions: (a) Act applies only to UK
(b) Crown not bound

(c) statute not retrospective
(d) common law not altered

Paras 2–5:
2. Aids:
(a) internal e.g. title and preamble of Act
(b) external e.g. (i) OED
(ii) Interpretn. Act
(iii) (if int'l treaties involved) *travaux préparatoires*

Paras 6–8:
3. Canons of construction: (a) Literal Rule
(b) Golden Rule
(c) Mischief Rule

31 because the particular words (house, office) were examples of places with roofs.

32 Judges seek to find the intention of Parliament because of the doctrine of the sovereignty of Parliament. The wishes of Parliament are expressed in its legislation and the judges must not alter these.

33 There is a need for statutory interpretation because of the complex nature of words which are often imprecise and may convey many different meanings. It is also not possible to foresee every situation which may arise under a particular piece of legislation.

34 Internal aids are those contained in the legislation itself. Examples are the title, preamble, headings to sections and Schedules. External aids are not contained in the legislation. They include the Interpretation Act, the *Oxford English Dictionary* and, with legislation involving international treaties, *travaux préparatoires* may be used.

35 It is possible to argue that Parliament's intention in passing the legislation which was at issue in the *Berriman* case was to protect all people who worked in dangerous circumstances on railway lines. If this was so the decision of the majority of the House of Lords did not reflect that intention.

36 **a** **i** The words which require interpretation in this situation are 'gun, pistol, knife or any other offensive weapon'.

ii As this is a list of particular words followed by general words the *ejusdem generis* rule will apply. The common feature of the particular words is that the articles mentioned are made for the purpose of causing injury.

iii The piece of broken glass which James was found to be carrying may be capable of causing injury but it was not specifically made for the purpose of doing so. Therefore the words of the Act are not applicable to this situation and James will not be guilty of the offence.

b **i** The words which require interpretation in this situation are:
– 'equipment', and
– 'in the course of his employment'.

ii – In the Act 'equipment' is stated to include 'plant or machinery, vehicle, aircraft and clothing'. The question is whether 'ships' were purposely left out of the definition by the draftsman. In reading section 1(3) the word 'includes' would suggest that the list supplied was not meant to be complete and that those items listed were merely examples of equipment. As the list includes items of transportation the statute could be interpreted to cover defective ships. It could also be argued that the purpose of the legislation was to protect employees who suffered as a result of defective equipment provided by their employers and should therefore be interpreted broadly, but remember that this argument could also be applied to the *Berriman* case where the plaintiff was unsuccessful.
– 'In the course of his employment' is quite clear – the Act will only apply to employees during the periods they are actually working for their employers.

iii – **Bert:** If the legislation is interpreted to include ships in the definition of 'equipment' he should be successful in an action against Transpo plc as his injuries occurred as a result of a defect in the ship and during the course of his employment.
– **Rose:** Under the Interpretation Act the word 'he' in an Act of Parliament also includes 'she' when this is relevant. Section 1(1) would therefore not exclude Rose because she is a female. However, although Rose is an employee of Transpo plc she is on board the *Morning Star* for a free ride and is therefore not acting in the course of her employment. Her death as a result of the defect in the ship cannot be compensated for under the Act.

37 **a** F; **b** F; **c** T; **d** T.

38 **Adjectives from nouns:** defective, reasonable, legal, descriptive, continental, statutory, conventional, excessive, equitable, hierarchical, discretionary.
Adjectives from verbs: elusive, negligent, foreseeable, coercive, preceding, attributable, speculative, reconcilable, distinguishing/distinguishable.

39 The emphasis in this question is on the amount of freedom judges have when they interpret statutes. Your essay should therefore include a discussion of the following:

- **a** The intention of Parliament – is this what the judges are seeking and is it possible for them to do so?
- **b** Are words a perfect way of communicating Parliament's intention?
- **c** The aids to interpretation demonstrating that a strict interpretation can give rise to absurdity and injustice which may not have been the intention of Parliament at the time of enactment. You must use cases here to illustrate your arguments.
- **d** The purposive approach to interpretation is central to this quotation from Lord Denning; you must explain this approach and its relationship to parliamentary sovereignty, with particular emphasis on the debate between Lord Denning and Lord Simmonds.

Revision (1)

1 **i** National law, cf. local law.
ii Case law, cf. statute law.
iii Legal systems based on precedent, cf. legal systems based on a civil code.
iv Common law rules, cf. rules of equity.

2 The countries of Western Europe, e.g. France, Denmark, Norway, Sweden, Italy and Belgium, the countries of Latin America, and Thailand, Turkey and Japan.

3 Criminal law regulates the relationships between the state and its citizens, e.g. murder, rape, driving offences. Civil law regulates the relationships between individuals, e.g. contract, tort, property.

4 The beginnings of a common legal system were established under the Norman kings with the setting up of the court of King's Bench in London which ruled on the meaning of the law in regional disputes. These rulings were communicated to the local courts or Assizes by travelling judges.

5 The common law had become very rigid and inflexible in its procedures and remedies, leaving many people without a remedy for their grievances. These people petitioned the King for redress.

6 The Court of Chancery which was headed by the King's religious and legal adviser, the Lord Chancellor.

7 Justice and fairness.

8 Equity.

9 **i** Equity follows the law. **ii** Equitable remedies are discretionary. **iii** He who comes to equity must come with clean hands.

10 The Judicature Acts brought together the courts of equity and the common law courts by establishing the Supreme Court of Judicature which could administer both the common law and equity.

11 **i** Civil law and criminal law; **ii** substantive and procedural law.

12 The executive, the legislature and the judiciary.

13 **i** Parliament may enact any law it wishes; **ii** no authority may question the validity of an Act of Parliament.

14 The three organs of government should be sufficiently separate so that no one person or group has control of all three. In particular the judiciary should be independent of the executive and legislature.

15 The judiciary can control the actions of the executive only to the extent of ensuring that it acts within its legal powers. This process is called judicial review; it reviews only the legality of executive action not the merits.

16 The role of the judiciary would change with a Bill of Rights by allowing it to question the validity of legislation in relation to the provisions of the Bill of Rights.

17 Words are an imperfect form of communication as they can mean different things in different contexts and at different times in history. It is also not possible to anticipate every situation which may arise under the legislation.

18 They have no legal status and have not been enshrined in any legislation; they are merely rules of practice.

19 The expression reflects the doctrine of parliamentary sovereignty by describing the role of the judiciary when interpreting statutes. Judges should seek to perform this task in accordance with the wishes of Parliament and not the subjective opinion of any individual judge.

20 *London & North Eastern Railway Co.* v. *Berriman*. In this case the plaintiff's husband was killed whilst carrying out maintenance of a railway line. The House of Lords was required to decide whether the words in the statute – relaying and repairing – should be interpreted to include maintaining. Applying the literal rule, a majority concluded that they did not.

21 Strict adherence to the literal rule can lead to absurdity and injustice and therefore defeat the intention of Parliament.

22 The Law Commission recommended a more flexible approach to statutory interpretation in order to achieve the purpose of the legislation.

23 Two of: an Act does not bind the Crown, legislation applies only to the United Kingdom, the common law is not altered, legislation is not retrospective.

24 a A case is distinguished when its material facts are sufficiently different from those of an earlier case to justify the judge reaching a different decision.

b A decision of a court which has not taken all the relevant law into account.

25 The factors which make up the crimes in section 1(a) are entering a building as a trespasser with the intention to commit one of the crimes in subsection (2). In section 1(b) they are committing one of the named offences after entering a building as a trespasser.

a Reg is a trespasser as he has entered Dave's house without Dave's permission. However, he did not enter with the intention of committing one of the offences in subsection (2) so is not guilty under section 1(a), nor after entering the building did he commit any of the offences in section 1(b). He is therefore not guilty of burglary.

b Peter has inflicted grievous bodily harm on Charles under section 1(b) but he has not entered the building as a trespasser so is not guilty of burglary.

c Bert is a trespasser but we must first determine whether the garden shed is a 'building'. If the courts decide that it is not, the case will go no further. For the sake of considering the other issues let us presume that the shed is a 'building'. By breaking the ladder Bert has done unlawful damage to something within the building under subsection (2), but this subsection must be read together with section 1(a) and as he did not enter the shed with the intention of causing unlawful damage he will not be guilty under section 1(a). Under section 1(b) Bert has stolen the apples but as these are in the garden and not in the building he is not guilty of burglary.

26 a The defendant relied on *Hay (Bourhill)* v. *Young* because in that case the plaintiff had not witnessed the accident but only the result of it. The plaintiff in *Boardman* v. *Sanderson* had also not witnessed his son's accident but the results of it.

b Because of the infinite variety of facts which can arise in cases involving nervous shock. Any arbitrary rule which sought to determine which cases should be successful and which not would not take sufficient account of the many possible differences between individual cases.

c There are some common features between Mary's situation and that of the plaintiff in *Boardman* v. *Sanderson*: both were parents who did not witness the incident but heard their children's screams. However, if we look at Lord Justice Ormerod's reasoning we will see that there are significant differences. The defendant in *Boardman* knew that the child was in the vicinity of his car, he knew that the father was nearby and that he would respond to the child's screams. Bob was not aware of the presence of Mark, and in particular he was unaware that Mary would hear the screams of her son. Unlike the plaintiff in *Boardman* she was not in the immediate vicinity of the incident but 50 metres away.

The material facts of Mary's case can therefore be distinguished from those in *Boardman* v. *Sanderson*. It is therefore very unlikely that she would recover damages for her injury.

Crossword answers

Across

3. *habeas corpus*; 8 and 6. *stare decisis*; 11. Act; 14. nor; 15. cases; 16. tort; 19 and 25. *per incuriam*; 22 and 21. *id est*; 29. sues; 30. *ratio*; 32. intelligence.

Down

1 and 9. op. cit.; 2. code; 3. hierarchy; 4 and 23. *obiter dicta*; 5 and 20. *ultra vires*; 7. scan; 10. just; 13 and 12. *inter alia*; 17. or; 18. legal; 24. partly; 26. Crown; 27. assent; 28. hence; 31. High.

Chapter 4

1 It refers to 'their functions' in the previous sentence.

2 a According to their functions (i.e. civil and criminal).

b Courts of original and appellate jurisdiction.

3 Because there is an overlap in both function and jurisdiction.

4 a Queen's Bench; **b** common law; **c** admiralty affairs; **d** 'wrecks'; **e** Chancery Division; **f** equity; **g** 'wills'; **h** Family Division; **i** divorce; **j** 'wives'.

5 a The High Court, the county courts and, in some family matters, the magistrates' courts.

b A single judge.

c The appellant.

d The High Court.

e The High Court, the Divisional Courts and the county courts.

f The Divisional Court.

g The House of Lords.

h The 'leap-frogging' procedure which in some instances allows an appeal to go straight from the High Court to the House of Lords, thus 'leap-frogging' the Court of Appeal.

6 **a** K; **b** J; **c** I; **d** O; **e** D; **f** N; **g** C; **h** H; **i** M; **j** B.

7 **a** because; **b** access; **c** informal; **d** formality; **e** must; **f** may; **g** agree; **h** may; **i** discouraged; **j** less; **k** nevertheless.

9 **a** As this is a civil action involving a claim for less than £500 it will be heard by the Registrar in the small claims court of the county court. The Registrar will undertake a preliminary consideration of the case agreeing on the facts with George and Nigel and advising them how to prepare for the hearing. The dispute may be settled at this stage. If not, a full hearing will take place during which the Registrar may call witnesses. The hearing will be less formal than in the normal courts. George and Nigel may have legal representation if they wish but the costs for this will not be recoverable. After hearing all the evidence the Registrar will give judgment.

b There is no right of appeal from the decision of the Registrar although his decision may be challenged in the High Court on the grounds of an error of law or unjust procedure.

10 **a** As this is a civil action involving a claim for more than £5,000 it will take place in the Queen's Bench Division of the High Court. It will be a formal hearing before a single judge who will reach a decision on the evidence presented by the lawyers appearing for Angela and Percy.

b If she is unsuccessful Angela may appeal to the Court of Appeal (Civil Division) and then to the House of Lords. If the case involves an important point of law and both parties agree, an appeal may go straight to the House of Lords under the 'leap-frogging' procedure introduced by the Administration of Justice Act 1969.

11 'Incentive' means encouragement (in the form of promised reward); 'penalties' refer to money to be paid, for example for the slow resolution of a case.

12 **a** 'a system of entry through one court'
c 'entitlements to leave'
d 'a new system of arbitration in courts'

13 **a** The procurators-fiscal.
b The CPS.
c Difficulties experienced when a system is still young and growing.
d Because there were arguments about salaries ('consequential').

14 **a** 1985
b after investigating & bringing case to court, police have strong interest to be successful in court.
c might be unwilling to reveal to defence all info. obtained in investigation.
d independent prosecution service
e Scotland
f RCCP
g CPS
h police
i CPS
j weak or unnecessary prosecutions are weeded out → easing pressure on system.

15 **a** to bring a prosecution
b to instigate action
c to institute proceedings
d to give evidence
e to conduct the prosecution
f to prefer charges
g to remedy a wrong
h to punish a criminal
i to commit an offence

16 **a** A less serious offence.
b Minor motoring offences.
c More serious offences.
d Murder
e Offences which may be serious or minor.
f Burglary.

17 **a** to try an offence
b to hear the evidence
c to reach a verdict
d to pass sentence
e to impose a fine
f to conduct an enquiry
g to assess the facts

20 The three types of criminal offences are indictable, summary and triable either way. Indictable offences are the more serious offences such as murder and rape. Summary offences are less serious offences such as minor motoring offences, and offences triable either way are offences which are capable of being committed in a serious or less serious manner such as theft.

21 **a** **Indictable offences:** The magistrates will hear the committal proceedings to establish whether or not there is sufficient evidence against the defendant for a full trial to take place in the Crown Court. If not, the magistrates will discharge the defendant.

b **Summary offences:** The magistrates will try the case, hearing the evidence and passing sentence if the defendant is found guilty. During the trial lay magistrates are advised on the law by the magistrates' clerk. The sentencing jurisdiction of the magistrates is limited to imposing a maximum fine of £1,000 or a maximum prison sentence of six months. The defendant must be referred to the Crown Court for sentencing if the appropriate sentence exceeds these limits.

c **Offences triable either way:** The magistrates will decide whether the case should be tried summarily or on indictment although the defendant can insist on being tried on indictment. The role of the magistrates will then be determined by which form of trial is chosen.

22 The judge decides on points of law and the jury decides on the facts and reaches a verdict. When the verdict is 'guilty' the judge will pass sentence.

23 The CPS is a more objective prosecuting authority than the police who also investigate the crime and have a strong interest in the outcome of the case. Also, as a national service, the CPS can establish a uniform prosecuting policy throughout the country. In addition, it relieves the pressure on the system by 'weeding out' weak cases.

24 A defendant is **discharged** after committal proceedings if there is insufficient evidence to proceed with a full trial. However, the prosecution authority may bring the case back to court if new evidence against the defendant becomes available.

A defendant is **acquitted** following a 'not guilty' verdict after a full trial. The defendant cannot then be retried for the same offence even if new evidence becomes available or even if the defendant subsequently admits to committing the offence.

25 **a** The CPS will consider whether there is a realistic prospect of conviction and whether the public interest will be best served by proceeding with the case, taking into account such factors as the staleness of the offence and the physical and mental characteristics of Mr Smith. It is unlikely with such a serious crime as murder that the latter factors would deter a prosecution although they would be relevant to the defence. The alternative action of a formal warning would certainly not be appropriate.

b A murder is an indictable offence, committal proceedings will take place in the magistrates' court to determine whether there is a prima facie case against Mr Smith. If so, the magistrates will send the case for full trial in the Crown Court before a judge and jury.

c Mr Smith may appeal to the Court of Appeal (Criminal Division) and then to the House of Lords. The prosecution cannot appeal against a verdict but it can apply to the Court of Appeal under the Criminal Justice Act 1988 for the sentence to be increased.

26 **a** As theft is an offence triable either way Mrs Brown will be tried either summarily in the magistrates' court or on indictment in the Crown Court. She may insist on trial by jury in the Crown Court but cannot insist on summary trial in the magistrates' court if the magistrates decide that her offence should be tried on indictment. The factors which the magistrate will take into account in reaching a decision are the seriousness of her offence and the possible sentence, which may be outside their jurisdiction.

b If tried summarily by the magistrates Mrs Brown may appeal to the High Court 'by way of case stated' and then to the House of Lords, or first to the Court of Appeal (Criminal Division) and then to the House of Lords. If tried on indictment in the Crown Court she may appeal to the Court of Appeal (Criminal Division) and then to the House of Lords.

27 **a** Tribunals were established to adjudicate on disputes arising out of social legislation which regulates such areas as employment, housing and social security benefits.

b There has been a rapid growth in the use of tribunals because of the interventionist policies of governments which sought to regulate the relationships between various groups in society and to provide support for people who were in a disadvantaged position.

c Tribunals deal with disputes which arise out of the everyday relationships of the ordinary citizen; disputes involving, for example, employment, housing, health and welfare benefits are of great importance because they can have such a harmful effect on the lives and standard of living of ordinary people.

28 **A** **a** lack of expertise; **b** too formal; **c** too slow; **d** too expensive.

C **a** tribunals; **b** commissions; **c** committees; **d** courts.

D the reasons for decisions.

E check that tribunals' procedures are open, fair and impartial, but has no power and can only advise the government of problems.

F **a** claims are 'trivial'; **b** lack of legal aid for tribunal work; **c** attitude that law and lawyers have little role in tribunal system.

29 **a** arbitrator; **b** arbitration; **c** claim; **d** claim; **e** adjudicate; **f** adjudicator; **g** administer; **h** administration; **i** administrative; **j** intimidate; **k** intimidation; **l** timid.

30 **a** useless; **b** misconduct; **c** discourage; **d** disagree; **e** colourless; **f** dissuade.

31 **a** exceeded; **b** appellant; **c** a debt **d** mandatory; **e** litigant; **f** stipendiary, lay; **g** summary, an indictable.

33 The points you will need to consider in your debate are:

a What are the purpose and aims of the civil justice system? Look at the variety of civil disputes and clarify the differences. Note that the statement refers to the majority of disputes; you will need to determine what these are.

b What is the existing machinery for resolving disputes? This should be a factual account of the court system.

c To what extent does the present system match its aims? You will need to analyse this question with reference to point **a.**

d What reforms would help to improve the present system? Consider the proposals of the civil justice review and the provisions of the Courts and Legal Services Act.

Chapter 5

1 **a** **i** must be a lawyer of 'considerable' experience; **ii** must be 'chosen'.
b because he is head of the judiciary and a Minister of the Crown.
c separation of legislative, executive and judicial powers.
d the Attorney-General.
e the Director of Public Prosecutions.
f by being promoted from the High Court.
g to advise lay magistrates on the law.

2 **a** 3; **b** 5; **c** 1; **d** 20; **e** 400; **f** approx. 500; **g** approx. 100; **h** approx. 25,000; **i** more than 90 per cent; **j** 1; **k** 3.

3 **a** House of Lords; **b** House of Lords; **c** Lord Chancellor; **d** the Queen; **e** High Court; **f** High Court; **g** the Queen; **h** Crown Court; **i** the Queen; **j** magistrates; **k** magistrates; **l** Lord Chancellor; **m** magistrates; **n** magistrates.

5 **a** bulwark = protection; **b** to redress = to set straight, to rectify; **c** ill-equipped = poorly prepared or qualified.

6 **a** **i** use evidence presented to them to find facts; **ii** apply the law to these facts; **iii** to make a decision.
b **i** imperfect evidence; **ii** withholding of evidence.

7 **a** where legislation is ambiguous;
b in cases which have no precedent;
c when a judge decides to extend or restrict an existing principle.

8 Under the adversarial system of justice the judges do not participate in the investigation of the cases they are trying. They must reach a decision only on the evidence presented to them in court by the legal representatives of the parties. Their role is therefore limited to ensuring that there is a fair trial, reaching a decision on the facts as presented to them and applying this to the law.

9 The traditional view is that judges do not make law: they discover what the law is and apply it to the case in question. This is known as the declaratory theory of law.

10 **Before:** There is no liability for economic loss suffered as a result of negligent words. **After:** There is liability for economic loss suffered as a result of negligent words providing there is a 'special relationship' between the giver and the receiver of the negligent advice

11 The law would have required employers to provide a warning system for employees who were 'relaying, repairing **and** maintaining' a railway line.

12 **a** The plaintiff in *Boardman* v. *Sanderson* did not witness the accident which happened to his son but he heard his screams and rushed to the scene of the accident. The plaintiff in *McLoughlin* v. *O'Brian* did not witness the accident involving her family nor did she hear it happen or go to the scene of the accident. She did not witness the results of the accident until two hours later at the hospital.
b The House of Lords changed the law on nervous shock by extending liability to the members of the family of the victims of an accident who are not present at the scene of the accident but who witness the horrific consequences or aftermath of it and suffer nervous shock as a result. Prior to this case the law did not allow recovery for nervous shock unless the plaintiff had been at or close to, the scene of the accident.

13 1. . . . both Houses of Parliament request it.
2. . . . are paid from a special fund & are not examined every year or subject to control by Parliament.
3. . . . may not be casually criticised in H. of P. Cases which are still being considered may not be discussed by Parliament.
4. Judges may not be M.P.s

5. (Examples of judges' behaviour):
a) conviction of a crime
b) bad behavior when conducting a case
c) biased public remarks

14 Here 'so' refers back to 'divert or depart from'.

16 The majority of people who do not express their opinions.

17 1. Judges 'discard all politics & all prejudices'.
2. Common conservative and Conservative background of judiciary → identify public interest + interests of authority.
3. Data indicates strong homogeneity of judiciary.
4. Accepts homogeneity & conservatism of judiciary but sees this as positive influence.

18 **a** A person who has the power to dismiss another from his/her job can have a powerful influence over that other person. Likewise if the government, or any individual member of it, had the power to dismiss the members of the judiciary there would be a risk that the judges may be influenced by this and would not make decisions which went against the government for fear of losing their jobs.

b Likewise, if the government or a member of it had control over the level of salaries paid to judges this could exert an influence over their decisions in favour of the government.

c Judges must be seen to be free of any political bias. Public criticism of an individual judge by Members of Parliament would suggest to the public that the judge was politically biased. Also the fear of criticism could influence a judge to reach a decision which would be favourable to the politicians.

d Members of Parliament inevitably hold partisan political views which are known to the public. This is contrary to the apolitical nature of the judiciary whose members must be seen by the public to be non-partisan in their views. Public confidence in the judiciary is essential to the system of justice and this would be severely undermined if it was believed that judges made decisions on the basis of their political views.

e The same arguments in **d** apply to all controversial areas of public debate.

19 Professor J.G. Griffiths argues that the common background of most judges will automatically influence their decisions. Most share the same social and educational background with those in authority and this leads them to accept certain presumptions about society which are essentially conservative. For this reason they do not act impartially and they are not truly independent.

21 60% of the 3% of criminal cases which go to the Crown Court.

22 *Civil cases*

1. Pre-1854: most civil cases tried by jury.
2. By 1933: ± ½ civil cases tried by jury.
3. Now: only
   a) mal. pros.
   b) false impris.
   c) fraud
   d) libel and slander
   } tried by jy.

   In all other cases court may decide jury trial:
   a) High Court < 1% civil cases use jury.
   b) County Court ± 20 out of 34,000 use jy.

Criminal cases
85% all cr. cases = summary.
12% all cr. cases = summary trial chosen.
3% → Crown Court → 60% plead guilty → < 1% by jury.

23 **a** eligible; **b** ineligible; **c** ineligible; **d** eligible.

24 A nurse may; a secretary in a police station may not; a woman of 65 years must; a man of 70 years may not.

25 **a** False – by the police for the DPP.
b False – 100 are chosen at random; the 12 are those who are acceptable to both prosecution and defence.
c False.
d True.

26 **a** For cause; available to both prosecution and defence.
b Stand by for Crown; available to prosecution only.

27 Jury vetting involves investigating the personal backgrounds of potential jurors to find out if there is anything in them which might influence the decision they will reach in a particular case. For example, someone who belongs to an extreme left-wing political party may be more sympathetic to a defendant charged with an offence involving the disclosure of state secrets. The randomness of the jury is undermined if people considered by those in authority to be unsuitable are excluded. Also it is argued that the influence of people holding strong views on a jury is exaggerated. The verdict of a jury is a collective decision with which all members must agree – although there is provision for a majority verdict of 10–2 in some cases – therefore the strongly held views of one member will be balanced by the views of the others.

Jury vetting is related to jury challenge in that it provides the prosecution with details of individual jurors who can be asked to stand by for the Crown if they are considered to be unsuitable.

28 **a** It is very likely that this juror will be biased in favour of the defendant because he is a family relative.

b Trial by jury is trial by one's peers, i.e. a cross-section of people, some of whom will share some common characteristics with the defendant. In this situation there are no common characteristics in relation to age, gender and race. As well as the increased risk of racial and sexual prejudice this could also limit the jury's understanding of the defendant's situation and increase willingness to accept the prosecution's arguments.

c The juror may be prejudiced against the defendant and be more willing to accept the case against him because of her sympathy for the allegedly molested child.

d The fact that the juror has been convicted of several motoring offences suggests that he or she considers these offences to be trivial and could result in prejudice in favour of the defendant.

29 **a** Never have I heard such a thing before.
b Rarely does the situation arise.
c Never will this be seen again.
d Seldom does such an opportunity present itself.

30 **a** 2; **b** 6; **c** 5; **d** 1; **e** 3; **f** 4.

31 **a** by, on; **b** for, in; **c** of or with, to; **d** on; **e** for; **f** on; **g** on; **h** in; **i** over, for; **j** from.

33 This question is asking you to consider whether you believe that trial by jury is more likely to result in a correct verdict than summary trial by magistrates. Would you have more confidence in a jury or the magistrates?

34 Section 8(1) of the Contempt of Court Act 1981 prevents disclosure of the way in which juries reach their verdicts. Although the need to prevent jury nobbling is important it is argued that the provisions of the Act are too wide because they also prevent legitimate research into the jury. If trial by jury is 'the bulwark of our liberties' then it is important that it is maintained. It is not possible to argue effectively against the critics of the system without factual evidence to support its maintenance. Whether juries are, for example, too strongly influenced by the rhetoric of lawyers can only be proved or disproved by analysis of actual cases. Without this, many of the arguments are based on speculation. Equally, it is important to be able to identify clearly any weakness in the system and provide adequate reforms. It should be possible to legislate to prevent jury nobbling whilst allowing legitimate research to be carried out.

35 One argument against the alternatives to trial by jury is that judges and other professional adjudicators become 'case-hardened'; that is, through trying so many cases they lose the ability to see each defendant as an individual and become too harsh in their application of the law. It is also argued that the presence of a jury is 'an antidote to excessive technicality'; it reduces the complexity of court procedure which must be capable of being understood by ordinary people. Nevertheless there are some cases which involve very complex legal and technical issues such as serious fraud. It is accepted by many people that these cases should be heard by a panel of judges and lay experts.

36 The first point to discuss in your essay is the extent of the decline in jury trials. You should examine civil and criminal cases separately; for civil cases you should look at the provisions of the Administration of Justice (Miscellaneous Provisions) Act 1933 and the case of *Ward* v. *James*, and for criminal cases you should consider the increase in the number of offences which are tried summarily in the magistrates courts. Support your discussion with the relevant statistics.

Then you must look at the reasons for the decline by examining the weaknesses of the system – lack of ability, unrepresentative of the community, jury nobbling, compulsory jury service and susceptibility to rhetoric. You should include details of any research into the jury and the provisions of the Contempt of Court Act 1981. Also consider the effect of the rules of eligibility and exemption – do these exclude the more educated members of society? The issues of jury vetting and jury challenge are also relevant – they have reduced public confidence in the jury as a random group of people.

These arguments must be balanced with the reasons for limiting any further decline in jury trial – public confidence, the effect of lay participation in the legal system, and its function as a protector of liberty.

Chapter 6

1 **a** usually law degree; **b** usually law degree; **c** Bar exam; **d** Final exam; **e** Inns of Court School of Law; **f** Law Society; **g** pupillage + experienced barrister; **h** articles + experienced solicitor.

2 **a** True; **b** False ('limited advertising'); **c** False (only sometimes); **d** True; **e** False (solicitors do not wear them in magistrates' courts).

3 disinterested – disinterestedness
exclusive – exclusivity
independent – independence
objective – objectivity
restrictive

4 **Declaration of Bath**
Arguments for fusion
1. . . . work could be done as efficiently and more cheaply by one person
e.g. . . . undefended divorce could be presented by solicitors
2. Overheads reduced, more machinery bought → cheaper for client

Arguments against fusion:
1. . . . if barristers are taken into a firm they aren't available to other firms
2. . . . barristers are more detached from case than a solicitor working on it

Benson report
Arguments against separation:
1. inefficiency
2. delay

3. lack of time for preparation if change of barrister
4. clients find barristers 'detached'
5. higher cost: ∵ 2 pp.

Arguments against fusion:
1. → fall in quality of justice
2. large firms w'd concentrate in richer areas → poorer areas fewer legal services
3. w'd disperse specialists
4. w'd not be cheaper

Arguments for separation:
1. spec. barristers will deal with important matters
2. sol. will collect relevant facts → barristers can concentrate on court work

6 A high standard of advocacy is particularly important because of the adversarial nature of the English legal system under which judges reach a decision only on the basis of the evidence presented in court. They are therefore dependent on the skills of the people presenting the evidence and legal arguments. A low standard of advocacy would reduce the standard of justice because the judges would have inadequate evidence and argument on which to base their decisions.

7 Contingency fees have been banned in England because it has been considered inappropriate and unprofessional for lawyers to have a financial interest in the outcome of a case; their duty is to the court and the quality of justice.

8 **a** Reallocation of business between the High Court and the county courts.
b Extension of rights of audience in higher courts to solicitors qualified under the Law Society rules and approved by the Lord Chancellor and four senior judges.
c These solicitors will be eligible for High Court judgeships.
d Banks, building societies and insurance companies to offer conveyancing services and to apply for probate.
e Conveyancing Ombudsman to investigate complaints over conveyancing services.
f Legal Services Ombudsman to supervise complaints procedures against barristers and solicitors.
g Statutory ban on contingency fees lifted.
h Non-legal professionals will be able to appear in court where appropriate.
i Judicial immunity from litigation extended to magistrates.
j Barristers' immunity from litigation extended to solicitors.

9 **a** Extended rights of audience to solicitors will further reduce the practical differences between the two sides of the profession. Although there will always be a need for a body of specialist lawyers, this role may increasingly be filled by those solicitors who qualify for rights of audience. The rules regulating the professional practices of members of the Bar could be altered to compensate for the loss of exclusive rights of audience. Vocational training for solicitors will be changed to include advocacy skills training making it more like the present vocational training for barristers. The reduction in the important differences between the two sides of the profession could lead to a common training programme and even, eventually, a fused profession.
b Conveyancing makes up a significant part of the business of most solicitors' practices. These solicitors will need to be more competitive with prices and services if they are to retain their business. A significant loss of business could lead to a reduction in the number of small firms of solicitors. Also, in many practices the lucrative conveyancing business subsidises the less profitable business relating to housing, welfare, etc. There may be a reduction in the number of practices offering advice in these areas if the conveyancing business is greatly reduced.

You should be aware that many of the points in **a** and **b** are purely speculative. It is only when the changed conditions have been in operation for some time that it will be possible to give accurate answers to these questions.

10 You should use the first part of your essay to provide a critical evaluation of the present structure of the legal profession and the standard of service it provides to the public. You will need to show your knowledge of the differences between the two sides of the profession but this information must be related to the effect these have on the standard of service currently provided. Discuss the reasons for the restrictive practices operated by the profession and whether they are still relevant. Although the question does not ask about the fusion of the profession, the arguments presented in favour of fusion are relevant to the question – duplication of work, cost, inefficiency, etc.

You should then trace the arguments for change from Benson, the Green Paper, to the Courts and Legal Services Act. As the question concentrates on the Act, so should you. Outline the major provisions which should affect the service offered to the public – extended rights of audience, conveyancing rights to banks and building societies, the Conveyancing Ombudsman, the Legal Services Ombudsman – and then analyse the ways in which they could improve the service by increasing access, reducing costs, etc. These arguments must then be balanced against those which suggest that the changes will reduce the service – reduced standards of advocacy, threat to small firms, possible conflict of interest through banks and building societies undertaking conveyancing.

12 **a** Poor clients, unable to afford to pay a solicitor.
b Particularly welfare law cases.
c Solicitors' image; lack of publicity.

13 **a** **i** Paragraph 2 (lines 8–9): Franchised firms would be able to do more work for the client.
ii Paragraph 2 (line 11): Franchised firms would receive more frequent payments on account.
iii Paragraph 2 (line 12): Franchised firms' work would be monitored by the Board.
iv Paragraph 5 (line 27): Franchising could reduce the bureaucracy normally associated with legal aid.
v Paragraph 6 (lines 30–2): Monitoring selected legal aid practices could save money and increase service to the client.
vi Paragraph 7 (lines 33–4): Resources could be concentrated on firms doing most work.
b **i** Because there was no evidence that more legal aid work by practices meant better work.
ii There is no measure of commitment, e.g. many partners earning £40,000 means less commitment than one solicitor earning £39,000.
iii Very few firms outside inner cities would qualify.
c Geographical coverage is important to ensure there are firms of solicitors providing a legally aided service in all parts of the country.
d Cutting public expenditure on legal aid.

14 **a** Not enough money to help the poor who cannot pay for legal services.
b Lawyers are not paid enough for legal aid cases so many are giving up the work.

16 Legal advice and assistance in the state-funding of all work undertaken by a solicitor short of appearing in court although there is some provision for representation under the ABWOR scheme. Legal aid includes court appearance.

17 The green form scheme is a state-funded scheme to provide preliminary legal advice and assistance up to a cost of £50, or £90 for undefended divorce. It is means tested. Its purpose is to encourage people of limited financial means to seek legal advice on a wide range of legal problems at an early stage.

18 Mrs Phillips will be able to obtain legal advice up to a value of £50 under the green form scheme. She will first have to pass the means test which will look at her disposable income and disposable capital to see whether they are below the financial limits set by the Lord Chancellor. As she is unemployed it is likely that she will qualify under the scheme. Alternatively she could seek advice under the 'fixed-fee' scheme where she will receive half an hour of legal advice from a solicitor for £5, or from a Citizens' Advice Bureau or a local law centre.

As she wishes to take her case to court Mrs Phillips must apply for legal aid. As this is a civil matter the rules relating to civil legal aid will apply. To qualify she must pass a means test and the legal merits test. The means test is the same as under the green form scheme and Mrs Phillips will probably qualify. However, the legal merits test considers whether the applicant has a good reason for being a party to the proposed legal action. Mr Hunt has offered to pay £1,000 towards the cost of repairing her car; the cost of recovering the additional £250 may be greater than the amount involved in taking her case to court and would not really justify taking the action. Mrs Philips is therefore unlikely to pass the legal merits test but, under the green form scheme, her solicitor may be able to negotiate with Mr Hunt to pay the full cost of repair.

19 As theft is a criminal offence the rules relating to criminal legal aid will apply. The court authorities will decide on his eligibility; this will most likely be the clerk to the magistrates' court. Mr Singh must pass a means test which is the same as for civil legal aid, and a merits test which is determined by 'the interests of justice'. Relevant factors are whether the applicant is disadvantaged through some incapacity, the likelihood of the applicant being sent to prison, the need to trace and interview witnesses and the complexity of the law involved.

Mr Singh's financial circumstances will determine whether he passes the means test – the fact that he is a student suggests that he may have limited financial means. With reference to the merits test, the fact that he is an overseas student suggests that his command of the English language may be limited and that he will be unfamiliar with the legal system; he may therefore qualify on the grounds of incapacity.

20 **a** Seek help.
b The previous sentence ('The fact that there are many people . . .).
c The phrase 'the unmet need'.

21 Point 1 would be a solution to (a), (b) and (c) in the extract.
Point 2 would be a solution to (d) in the extract.

22 **a** More representative than the Law Society and the Bar.
b The fact that represented litigants are much more successful than unrepresented ones.
c Because people from a variety of backgrounds will be able to become para-legal workers.
d Para-legals are proposed for work in court just as legal executives now work with solicitors.

23 **Problems:**
1. a) Large no. defendants unrepresented.
   b) Few receive legal help.
2. Debtors give in easily to creditors.
3. Represented litigants much more successful than unrepresented.

Solutions:
1. Ready availability of advice, assistance + represenation.
2. Representation at *appropriate* level & cost – e.g. use para-legal workers in less complex cases.
3. Spend more public money on legal services – e.g. law centres & public litigation service.
4. More money sh'd be spent in schools on education about legal rights.

Revision (2)

1 Courts of first instance are the courts in which a case will be heard for the first time; an appeal from the decision of a court of first instance will be heard by an appellate court.

2 **a** Appellate: civil and criminal. **b** Appellate: civil and criminal. **c** First instance: civil. **d** First instance and appellate: criminal. **e** First instance and appellate: criminal and civil. **f** First instance: criminal and civil.

3 The Chancery Division.

4 The Master of the Rolls and Lord Justices of Appeal.

5 £5,000.

6 Because a case involving a small financial claim may involve a complex area of law.

7 To provide a cheap and efficient way for ordinary people to pursue a legal action.

8 Cost, delay and the fact that the ordinary person is more likely to be the defendant in an action for recovery of a debt than the plaintiff.

9 The Registrar renamed a 'district judge' under the Courts and Legal Services Act 1990.

10 Cost and delay.

11 The financial limits on jurisdiction will be removed and cases will be heard in the country court or High Court according to their legal complexity.

12 **a** On the balance of probabilities; **b** beyond reasonable doubt.

13 Yes, they are called private prosecutions.

14 The police.

15 Their jurisdiction is limited to adjudicating on disputes which arise out of the legislation which created the individual tribunal, e.g. industrial tribunals may only hear disputes arising out of employment legislation.

16 According to increasing grades of importance or authority.

17 Lords of Appeal in Ordinary (Law Lords) who sit in the House of Lords.

18 The High Court.

19 Lay magistrates are part-time, unpaid and are not legally qualified; stipendiary magistrates are full-time, salaried and legally qualified.

20 Judges do not investigate cases but they do not play a completely passive role; they may question witnesses and they must ensure that the trial is conducted according to the rules of procedure and evidence.

21 **a** By interpreting statutes when the words are unclear or ambiguous; **b** by extending or restricting the legal principle of an earlier case.

22 Most certainly, yes.

23 Distrust is probably too strong a word but he is not confident that judges always act impartially.

24 **a** Defamation; **b** malicious prosecution; **c** false imprisonment; **d** fraud.

25 The Attorney-General.

26 The right of the defence to three peremptory challenges was removed by the Criminal Justice Act 1988.

27 Because the trial may be long and the expenses paid do not compensate for any loss of wages.

28 'Shadow juries' are sometimes used to research the adequacy of the jury system; a random group of twelve people sits in the court and hears a case and reaches a verdict which is then compared to the verdict of the real jury.

29 To provide professional service and advice on legal matters.

30 *Rondel* v. *Worsley* (1969).

31 By imposing restrictive practices and regulating entry and training.

32 The Royal Commission which published the report was chaired by Lord Benson.

33 *Abse* v. *Smith* (1985).

34 Under the Courts and Legal Services Act the rules on rights of audience will be determined by the Lord Chancellor and four senior judges on the advice of the lay-dominated Advisory Committee on Legal Education and Conduct.

35 The consequences of a negligent transfer of property could be so serious that it was considered that conveyancing is best carried out by professionally qualified people who are covered by mandatory insurance which would compensate a client if the conveyancing was performed negligently.

36 The Legal Aid Act 1988.

37 Lord Hailsham described legal aid as 'the fastest growing social service'.

38 The financial limits for eligibility for legal aid need to be increased regularly to take account of inflation and increases in people's incomes.

39 Para-legals are people who are legally trained in a specific area of law but not fully qualified lawyers.

40 White argues that many legal problems do not require the wide expertise of fully qualified lawyers and could be resolved by people who have been trained only in the relevant area of law.

41 **a** **i** lawfully brings onto the land, **ii** likely to do mischief, and **iii** escapes.

b Lord Cairns added the requirement of non-natural use, that is something which brings increased danger to others.

c **i** Applying the tests in *Rylands* v. *Fletcher* we can see that the chemical waste has been brought on to the land by Fullblast plc, it is a non-natural use of the land as it increases the danger to others. It is also something which is likely to do mischief if it escapes. However, although the driver has been seriously injured and the tanker destroyed there has been no damage to the surrounding property, that is there has been no escape. There is therefore no liability under the rule in *Rylands* v. *Fletcher*.

ii The lion has been brought onto the land by Percival, it is a non-natural use of the land, it is something which is likely to do mischief if it escapes and it *has* escaped and caused damage to the horse in the adjoining property. Percival could argue that he has done everything which could be reasonably expected of him to prevent the lion escaping by building a very high fence and providing security guards. This, however, will be no defence according to the standard of care laid down by Blackburn J. Liability is established even though there is no lack of reasonable care.

iii Although the seeds from the wildflowers have escaped from Christine's land to Michael's they are not a non-natural use of the land and there will be no liability for the damage to the crops.

42 **a** You will need to look to section 1(a) to assess Bernie's situation. He and the other residents were marching to the airfield with the intention of preventing the aircraft taking off. Such an intention could be prejudicial to the interests of the state as it would stop the pilots training. However, Bernie and the other residents have been arrested one mile from the airfield – is this too far away to be 'approaching' or 'in the neighbourhood' of the prohibited place? How would these words be interpreted literally? Also you should consider that the Act specifies the penalties for 'spying': how relevant is the purpose of the Act?

b The first words to consider in this situation are those in section 1(b) – 'makes any sketch, plan, model or note': will these words apply to photographs? Although this is a list of words they are not followed by general words so the *ejusdem generis* rule will not be relevant. This may be a situation where the words do not cover every possible situation which is likely to arise. Also look at the date of the Act: in 1911 photography was not as common as it is now. Perhaps Parliament could not have foreseen this development. You could argue that the words in the statute are all means of recording information and that a photograph will serve the same purpose.

Under section 1(c) Phil has published the photographs. The publication was not 'calculated' or 'intended' to be helpful to an enemy although they 'might' 'directly or indirectly' be so and this could be prejudicial to the interests of the state. Again you will need to consider the purpose of the Act.

Chapter 7

1 **a** promise (line 22); **b** promisor (line 25); **c** exchange relationship (line 43); **d** consideration (line 53); **e** agreement (line 8); **f** contract (line 1); **g** promisee (line 26); **h** deed (line 48); **i** tort feasor (lilne 60).

2 **a** There is a reciprocal agreement between John and Peter in that John has agreed to sell his car and Peter to pay £500; both have therefore provided consideration. The agreement is enforceable.

b There is no reciprocity in the agreement between John and Peter because Peter has given nothing in exchange for John's promise to take him on holiday. This is a gratuitous promise and not legally enforceable.

c John's promise to give Peter the valuable painting is not matched by a promise from Peter and is therefore a gratuitous promise. However, John signed a deed which has been sealed and delivered to Peter and this has made the promise legally enforceable.

3 Bryan's damages would be assessed on the basis of the benefit he expected to receive under the contract with Gill. This was an antique table which he thought was worth £250; this sum will therefore be the amount of damages he can claim.

4 Liability in tort is imposed by law on the tort feasor whereas liability in contract arises from the voluntary assumption of the obligations. Under the law of contract the parties may choose whether or not to enter into the agreement; having done so they volunteer to accept liability for any failure to perform their obligations. In tort the law imposes a duty on people to take care, they do not volunteer to do so, and likewise liability for a failure to take care will be imposed by the law.

5 The counter-offer was to buy the farm for £950.

7 **a** No.

b Paragraph 1 dealt with the financial terms on which they may be prepared to sell.

c Paragraph 2 dealt with the financial details of a council mortgage.

d To avoid misunderstanding of expressions such as 'the interest rate will change'.

e Refers to 'a contractual offer'.

8 Brian may wish to take legal action against Greg for breach of contract. It will therefore be necessary to determine whether there is a legally enforceable agreement between the parties by looking to see if there has been an offer and a clear acceptance of the terms of the offer. You will first need to distinguish between an offer and an invitation to treat using the cases of *Harvey* v. *Facey* and *Gibson* v. *Manchester City Council* as authority. You must then analyse the exchange of correspondence between Greg and Brian in the light of these cases.

On the basis of *Harvey* v. *Facey* Brian's original letter could be seen as an enquiry about the price of the spoons and Greg's reply as a statement of the price; both would therefore be invitations to treat with Brian's second letter being his offer to buy the spoons which Greg was free to accept or reject. On this analysis there is no contract between the parties and no legal remedy available to Brian. However, there is a feature of Greg's letter which distinguishes it from Facey's telegraph to Harvey; he has stated that he **will** sell the spoons to Brian. Remember that the words '**may** be prepared to sell' in *Gibson* were fatal to the plaintiff's claim that there was a binding contract with the council. The use of the definite word 'will' would suggest that Greg was making an offer to Brian which Brian accepted before Greg withdrew the offer by selling the spoons to Gordon. If this analysis was accepted by the courts, Brian could recover damages for breach of contract.

9 Again you will need to decide if there is a binding contract between Maureen and David. Maureen has certainly made a definite offer to David but has David accepted it? An acceptance must exactly match the offer – any deviation from the original offer will be a counter-offer which the original offeror is free to accept or reject. The case of *Hyde* v. *Wrench* is authority for this principle. By asking for a higher salary than was offered by Maureen, David has rejected her offer and made a counter-offer which Maureen has subsequently rejected. There is no contract between them and Maureen will not be required to employ David.

You also should know that a court order requiring a party to a contract to fulfil the obligations under the contract is called an order of specific performance. As a final note to this question you should be aware that specific performance will not be granted by the courts to enforce a contract of employment, so that even if there had been a contract between Maureen and David his only remedy woud have been damages.

10 **a** The county court was the court of first instance in the *Gibson* case because it was a contract action involving less than £5,000.

b The express statement in the second paragraph was used to counteract the positive language used in the rest of the paragraph, e.g. 'the interest rate **will** change'. Without the statement the words would read as a firm offer. Lord Diplock's reason for rejecting the argument that the first paragraph was a firm offer to sell becase it did not contain a similar statement was that the words used in the first paragraph were different – '**may** be prepared to sell' – and could not be read as a firm offer. His decision may well have been different if the first paragraph had contained the words 'the corporation is prepared to sell the house to you' because they express a clear intention to sell.

11 'Receptacle' means 'a container', e.g. a basket.

12 **a** False; **b** True; **c** True.

13 **a** **ii** Modern Eng. shop not for bargaining & even if goods offered, sale is not compulsory.
b **i** If displayed goods = offer, customer c'd sue shopkeeper if not enough goods.
ii Offer c'd be interpreted as expiring when goods finished.
c **i** If displayed goods = offer, customer w'd be bound to buy if s/he picked up goods.
ii Acceptance of offer c'd be later e.g when customer presents goods at cashdesk.

14 . . . it was communicated to Mr Thornton after the contract had been concluded.

15 . . . the ticket was given by hand and the customer could refuse to conclude the contract by refusing the ticket.

16 **a** An invitation to treat.
b An offer.
c An offer; the display of prices etc. at the box office would be the invitation to treat. Distinguish from **b** as you are dealing with a person.
d An offer as in **c**.

17 Ramona can only insist on the shop assistant selling the dress to her if the display of the dress in the window is an offer which she has accepted by telling the shop assistant that she wishes to purchase it. The law is that the display of goods in a shop window is an invitation to treat; the customers make an offer when they indicate that they wish to purchase the goods. The shop assistant may then accept or reject the offer. Ramona cannot therefore insist on the sale of the dress.

18 **a** This problem involves the validity of exclusion clauses. The owners of the Upclass Hotel have sought to exclude their liability for responsibility for the property of their guests. An exclusion clause will only be valid if it is brought to the notice of the other party before the contract is entered into. You should refer to Lord Denning's statement in *Thornton* v. *Shoe Lane Parking* as authority. Some discussion on the reciprocal nature of contracts would also be relevant here. You must then decide when the contract between Felicity and the Upclass Hotel was concluded. This was at the time of registering at the reception desk. The owners of the hotel cannot unilaterally impose another term after that time. As the exclusion notice was in the bedroom it was not brought to Felicity's attention before the contract was concluded and is therefore invalid. The owners will be responsible for the loss of Felicity's necklace.
b If the exclusion notice had been prominently displayed at the reception desk it would arguably be valid provided that it was sufficiently prominent for a reasonable person to have taken notice of it before registering at the hotel and therefore before the contract was concluded.

19 **a** Because it is easier to establish that a letter has been sent than that it has been received.
b This is an argument for.
c This is an argument for.

20 **a** Each country must choose the one which best suits its own system.
b Because it has worked well enough so far.
c **i** Not suitable; better if a contract is made only when the offeror actually receives the acceptance. **ii** Suited.

21

	Offeror	***Offeree***
1.	Shouts offer	Shouts acceptance
	Can't hear ∵ noise	Must repeat
	Hears → contract	
2.	Telephones offer	Starts acceptance but line goes dead
	Does not hear	Must reestab. contact
	Hears → contract	
3.	Telephones offer	Indistinct acceptance
	Can't hear	
	a) Asks for repet.	Repeats
	Hears → contract	
	b) Doesn't ask for repet. → no contract	
4.	Telexes offer	Telexes acceptance
		Line goes dead
	→ no contract	
5.	Telexes offer	Telexes acceptance
	Ink runs out	
	a) Asks for repetn	Repeats acceptance
	receives telex → contract	
	b) Does not ask for reptn. → contract	

22 **a** No contract
b Contract
c No contract

23 **a** When given to the postal authorities.
b When given to the postal authorities.
c **i** When acceptance received by third person nominated by offeror.
ii When acceptance received by offeror.
d When telex received by offeror.

24 **a** Director of Public Prosecutions
b Member of Parliament
c Master of the Rolls
d Attorney-General
e assistance by way of representation
f Lord Justice
g Lords Justices

h Mr/Mrs Justice
i *videlicet* = namely
j *exempli gratia* = for example
k *id est* = that is (to say)

25 **a** unconditional; **b** unwritten; **c** inapplicable; **d** unwilling; **e** inconvenient; **f** inoperative; **g** uncertain; **h** indistinct; **i** inadequate; **j** unreasonable; **k** unnecessary; **l** inadvisable.

27 **a** London: acceptance by post at the time of posting.
b London: acceptance by telephone (instantaneous communication) at the time of receipt.
c Newcastle: as in **b**.
d London: as in **b** and **c**.

28 The legal position of Transhipping plc will be assessed by determining whether there is a binding contract between them and Oilco plc. Oilco plc have made an offer to Transhipping which they accepted. However, Oilco have revoked their offer, but this revocation will only be valid if it was communicated to Transhipping before their acceptance. To determine this you will need to analyse the rules relating to the communication of acceptance and revocation.

The general rule is that acceptance must be communicated to the offeror. However, this rule does not apply to acceptance by post where acceptance takes place at the time of posting. Use *Byrne* v. *Tienhoven* as authority. Some discussion on the reasons for this would be relevant. Contrast this rule to the law on communication of revocation of an offer which is effective only from the time of receipt.

Applying these rules to the problem it would appear that Transhipping have accepted Oilco's offer at 3.00 p.m. on 5 May, several days before they receive Oilco's letter of revocation. However, there are some exceptions to the postal rule, one of which is that the offeror may require actual receipt of the acceptance. This can be expressly stated or implied from the words used – *Holwell Securities* v. *Hughes*. Oilco's offer contained the words 'acceptance will be effective if it reaches our office by 5.00 p.m. on 10 May'. This is an express statement that the normal rules of posting will not apply. As their letter of revocation was received by Transhipping before the letter of acceptance reached Oilco's office, it will be effective and there is no contract between Oilco plc and Transhipping plc.

29 Follow the same analytical procedure which was used in question 28. The points which should be argued in the Moot are:

a The law relating to communication by telex.
b The law relating to acceptance by post – was postal acceptance reasonable in this situation?
c The significance of Mr Lloyd's failure to notice the telex from Mr Barclay.
d The significance of Mr Lloyd knowing that Mr Barclay's office is closed between 5.00 p.m. and 9.00 a.m.

Chapter 8

1 Yes; a criminal offence is conduct which may be followed by criminal proceedings and sentence.

2 It is both a civil wrong and a criminal offence.

3 **a** e.g. to wear bow ties.
b e.g. homosexual activity, incest, drug possession and adultery.
c e.g. to kill, rape, steal, injure.

4 Statutes are passed by Parliament, regulations are not.

5 He thinks it is 'highly questionable' (i.e. he is not in agreement with the fact) that a person can be punished for behaviour which has not been discussed by Parliament.

6 **a** **i** prosecutor; **ii** defendant; **iii** convicted.
b **i** plaintiff; **ii** defendant; **iii** liable; **iv** damages.

7 Here 'sanction' is being used to mean 'punishment'.

8 **a** 1: 1851; **d** 2: 1898; **b** 3: 1873, 1925; **c** 4: 1969.

9 **a** False. Civil actions sometimes do (see lines 17–18).
b False. He thinks they are distinguished by whether they can be punished or not (see lines 43–4).

12 'Representation' here refers to the statement to P that the car was free from any HP agreement.

13 **a** Conduct crimes, results crimes.
b *Actus reus* (physical element) and *mens rea* (mental element).
c Conduct, circumstances, consequences.

14 **a** False. It refers also to an omission to perform some act and to a 'state of affairs'.
b True.
c True.

15 **a** 'So' refers to the fact that he is criminally liable.
b The words in brackets.
c A question.
d The period.
e Means incorrect (from 'error').

16 The main structure of the sentence is given in italics:

'*If on the other hand the question* [, which I

now confine to: "Did a physical act of the accused start the fire which spread and damaged property belonging to another?"] *is answered "Yes"* [, as it was by the jury in the instant case,] *then for the purpose of the further questions* / the answers to which are determinative of his guilt of the offence of arson, / *the conduct of the accused* [, throughout the period from immediately before the moment of ignition to the completion of the damage to the property by the fire,] *is relevant . . .*'

18 **a** A has acted completely involuntarily; he has no control over his actions. A defence of automatism would be successful.
b Although it could be argued that A's condition is to some extent self-induced, the defence of automatism has been successful in a number of cases involving similar facts.
c B has forced the knife into C's chest so A has not acted voluntarily.
d Although A may have been too intoxicated to know what he was doing his condition is self-induced and this does not amount to automatism.

19 This situation involves the question of causation. There must be a causal link between D's action and the result. Henry attempted to kill Mabel but her death is not a result of his action. There is no chain of causation between the two events.

20 **a** An omission, or failure to act, can amount to *actus reus* in certain situations, one of which is when D fails to perform a contractual duty. Keith is under a contractual duty to ensure the safety of the swimmers. By leaving the swimming pool early he has failed to perform his duty and this omission is a criminal act.
b A failure to act when there is no legal duty to do so is not *actus reus*. Although it may be morally wrong not to help a child in these circumstances, the law does not treat it as criminal.

21 **a** Criminal Damage Act 1971.
b To dissent = to disagree → dissentients = people who disagree.

22 **a** intention
b recklessness
c strict liability
d absolute liability

23 Lord Atkin = v. high degree of negligence; objective.
Lord Diplock = either foresight of risk **or** closing mind to unreasonable risk; subjective +
Lord Ed. Davies = negligence + foresight of consequence; subjective.
Lord Lane = unreasonable risk + knowledge of risk of damage; subjective.

24 **a** True.
b False.

25 **a** C was not guilty.
b No.
c '. . . did an act which created an obvious risk that the property would be destroyed' = *actus reus*.
'. . . had not given any thought to the possibility of there being any such risk' = *mens rea*.
d **i** No deliberate disregard of known risk.
ii No mindless indifference to known risk
iii Failure to give thought not due to blameworthy cause.
e **i** A subjective qualification to Lord Diplock's principle that a defendant should only be regarded as reckless if he failed to give thought to a risk which would have been obvious to him, if he had given it thought.
ii Because Lord Diplock had rejected a definition of recklessness by Professor Kenny, which implied this qualification.
iii Yes.

26 **a** The function described in the previous sentence, i.e. to achieve the appropriate result within the limits of precedent.
b Subjective.

27 **a** Magistrates' court – you know this because of reference to 'justices' and because the only time a prosecution can appeal against a not guilty verdict is from a magistrates' court.
b Queen's Bench Division of the High Court.
c By way of 'case stated'.

29 **a** The *actus reus* of the offence is destroying or damaging property belonging to another without lawful excuse; the *mens rea* is the intention to destroy or damage the property or being reckless as to whether it is destroyed or damaged.
b Section 1(1) is the one under which Jason may be charged. You will need to consider **i** whether he acted without lawful excuse, **ii** whether he acted with intention, **iii** whether he acted recklessly, **iv** are the computer and the records 'property', and **v** does he have a defence which would be accepted by the courts?
i There would appear to be no lawful excuse for Jason's actions.
ii Jason may have acted intentionally if it was his purpose to cause the damage or if he had no substantial doubt that it would occur or if he foresaw that the damage was probable.
iii Even if he has not acted with intention Jason has been reckless in that it was foreseeable that the damage could result from his action but he closed his mind to the risk. Under Lord Diplock's objective test in *Caldwell* it is not

necessary to prove that the risk was obvious to Jason but that it would have been to the ordinary person.

iv This question will be decided by the court's interpretation of the word 'property' and whether it would include the computer records. Given that computers are a very common feature of modern life it is likely that the ordinary, literal meaning of the word would include them.

v Jason could argue that he was so angry that he did not know what he was doing, i.e. that he did not act voluntarily. The defence of automatism is a very narrow one; you will need to examine the definition given in *Bratty* and the case of *Lipman* and conclude that anger would not amount to automatism.

30 **a** The case of *Sweet* v. *Parsley* illustrates the principle that there is *mens rea* requirement in strict liability offences. David has a policy of refusing admission to people under 18 and he has made reasonable efforts to enforce that policy and so comply with the law.

b If the word 'knowingly' was deleted from the section the offence would become one of absolute liability under which the law imposes liability without *mens rea.* David would therefore be guilty if intoxicating liquor was sold to people under the age of 18.

31 Means 'thought of before/earlier'.

32 **a** *Church*: a series of acts without plan. *Thabo Meli*: a planned series of acts.

b 'series of acts designed to cause death'; 'series of acts which culminated . . . in death'.

c Because the body is already dead.

33 The legal meaning of 'spent' is 'finished'.

34 Assault is causing fear of violence. Battery is actual, intended violence.

35 **a** para. 1;
b para. 1, main topic;
c para. 2;
d para. 2;
e para. 2, main topic;
f para. 3, main topic.

36 **a**

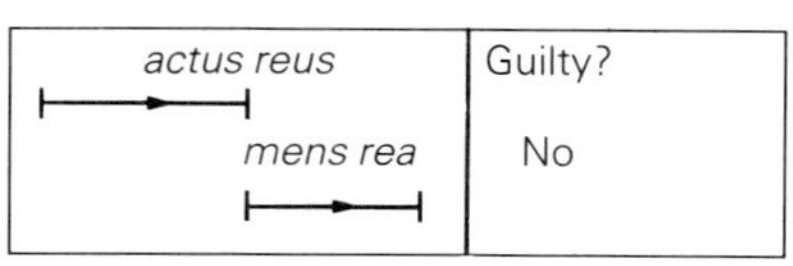

b

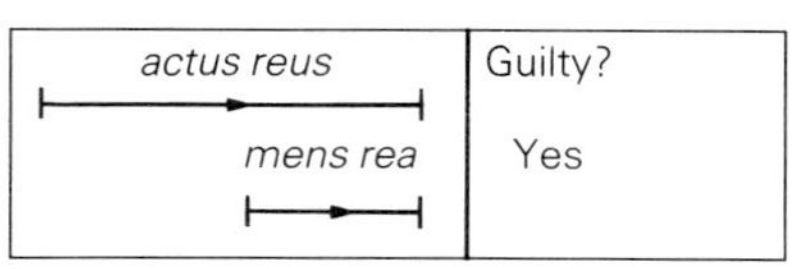

Diagram **a** represents the basis of the appellant's argument in *Fagan* v. *MPC.*

37 **a** addressed; **b** prefer; **c** held; **d** fit; **e** instant; **f** provides; **g** express; **h** found; **i** relief.

38 **a** sanction; **b** sanctionable; **c** offence; **d** offensive; **e** offender; **f** offending; **g** condemnation; **h** punishment; **i** punitive; **j** omission; **k** err; **l** erroneous; **m** provide; **n** concurrence; **o** concurrent.

39 There are three points of law to be considered in this situation: **a** omissions as *actus reas*, **b** coincidence of *actus reus* and *mens rea*, and **c** the *mens rea* of the offence.

a The term '*actus reus*' suggests the necessity for some positive act by the defendant. Although this is generally true, the law recognises that some omissions will amount to the *actus reus* of an offence. This is usually when the law imposes an obligation to act, e.g. under a contract. The principle of omission as *actus reus* was addressed by Lord Diplock in *R* v. *Miller.* Here you will need to summarise the facts of the case. Lord Diplock drew a distinction between the failure of a bystander to act and the failure to prevent or reduce a risk which has been created by the defendant. An examination of Lord Diplock's analysis should be included leading to his conclusion that the latter will constitute *actus reus.*

b The law normally requires the *actus reus* and *mens rea* of the offence to occur concurrently. However, when there is a continuing series of events the conduct of the accused will be seen as a continuous act, and if at any stage of the events the accused possesses the necessary state of mind for *mens rea*, the offence will be complete. Provide some analysis of this principle using *Miller*, *Thabo Meli* and *Fagan* as authorities.

c The *mens rea* requirement under the Criminal Damage Act is intention or recklessness. Provide some explanation of these states of mind, including Lord Diplock's approach in *Caldwell* which is the accepted test.

In applying the law to facts in the problem you can draw an analogy with the facts of *Miller* – a chain of events begins accidentally but which Cyril fails to remedy. Did Cyril possess the necessary state of mind at any time during the course of events and if so what was that state of mind, intention or recklessness?

40 You should begin your answer with a definition of the offence of battery. Do this by referring to the extract from *Fagan*; include the issues of indirect force and unintentional acts. An analysis of the facts and judgment in *Fagan* would be relevant to allow you to distinguish between that case and the problem. Note the common facts of the two situations: indirect and unintentional force. Note that there was no *mens rea* at the time of the original act in *Fagan* or in the problem as there was no intention to injure. The important distinction is that in *Fagan* there was a continuing act; the defendant refused to move his car from the policeman's foot and this was the *mens rea* of the offence which was then concurrent with the continuing intentional act. In the problem there is a complete unintentional act so there is no *actus reus* of the offence of battery. David's intention to allow Gladys to suffer does not arise until after the unintentional act is complete.

41 The points of law you are required to argue in this moot are **a** coincidence of *actus reus* and *mens rea* and **b** the defence of automatism due to intoxication. The authorities for **a** are *Thabo Meli* and *Church*, with particular emphasis on the latter as the facts of the moot case are very similar. You should refer to *R* v. *Lipman* and the section on voluntariness in relation to **b**. Cynthia's defence will argue that as she thought that Caroline was dead when she put her body in the water she had no intention to kill her at that time and therefore the *actus reus* of the offence does not coincide with the *mens rea*. The prosecution will base its arguments on the 'continuing series of events' principle in *Thabo Meli* and *Church*. Although self-induced intoxication is not sufficent for a defence of automatism, you should nevertheless present the arguments for and against it.

Chapter 9

1

	Courts	*Government*	*Parliament*
Technical learning	✓	×	×
Social awareness	perhaps	×?	✓
Power to get things done	×	✓	×

2 **a** Government: MPs from the ruling party.
b Parliament: House of Lords, House of Commons and the sovereign.

3 'a reaction'

4 Law needs reforming if:
a it produces unfair results;
b it is in an inconvenient form.
Notice the topics are contained in the second sentence of paragraph 1 and the first sentence of paragraph 2.

5 **a** An example.
b Theoretically, in name only.

6 **a** Not always.
b Because it is necessary to decide which authorities are responsible when part of the law is working badly.

10 **a** The judiciary is apolitical so political independence of the Commission is not affected.
b They are not allowed to be Members of Parliament (see lines 9–10).
c To advise government and Parliament on planning law reform; formulating detailed proposals for law reform.
d Commission proposals are published before the bill is introduced to Parliament, whereas details of government legislation are kept secret (see lines 18–21).
e Expert advice and prior public discussion (see lines 27–9).
f **Strengths:**
i The Commission is politically independent.
ii It has statutory existence.
iii It can originate proposals for reform and has independence of action after the Chancellor has agreed to its programme.
iv Its members possess a high level of technical learning about law-making.

Weaknesses:
i Government can refuse to approve its programme.
ii No security of tenure for members.
iii Government not obliged to provide parliamentary time for Commission's proposals.

11 The doctrine of *stare decisis* limits judicial law reform by requiring that judges follow the legal rules in previous cases. Unless a case reaches the House of Lords or comes within the rule in *Young* v. *Bristol Aeroplane Co.* in the Court of Appeal an unjust or outdated law cannot be reformed.

12 Judicial law reform is not dependent on political priorities and the availability of parliamentary time.

13 **a** The Law Reform Committee: the civil law; **b** The Criminal Law Revision Committee: the criminal law; **c** The Law Commission: codification and consolidation of the law, revision of the statute book and the simplification and modernisation of the law.

14 A Royal Commission will be set up by the government when there is a specific area which requires detailed investigation.

15 Most law reform agencies may only investigate those areas of law which are referred to them by the relevant minister. These referrals may be made on the basis of political expediency rather than practical necessity.

16 The Law Commission is self-motivating in that it may investigate areas requiring reform without a referral from an outside party.

17 **Codification:** the restatement and reforming of all the case law and statute law on a particular subject.

Consolidation: bringing together all the existing statutes on one area of law into a single statute without changing the law.

18 Spencer is critical of the Law Commission Act 1965 because he believes that it gives the Lord Chancellor and the government too much control over the actions of the Law Commission and the implementation of its proposals.

19 An unelected body such as the Law Commission must be subject to some control by the elected government, but an amendment which required the Lord Chancellor to submit the Law Commission's proposals to the scrutiny of Parliament or a parliamentary committee would provide for them to be more widely debated and limit the control of the Lord Chancellor and the government.

20 **Pre-1971** Builders owed duty of care to purchasers only if they were not the owner/seller.

1971 Defective Premises Bill introduced into Parliament.

Dutton v. *B. Regis:* builders and owners responsible. Limitation period = 6 yrs. from date of negligent work.

1972 Defective Premises Act: following Law Commission recommendations, builders and owners responsible; limitation period = 6 yrs. from completion of work.

1976 *Sparham-Souter* v. *Town and Country Developments:* limitation period = 6 yrs. after date when plaintiff might reasonably have discovered damage.

1982 *Dennis v. Charwood Borough Council:* claim made >25 yrs. after completion but 4 yrs. after date when could reasonably have discovered damage.

Pirelli General Cable Works Ltd v. *Oscar Faber and Partners*, H. of Lords: limitation = 6 yrs. from date when damage occurred.

21 **a** Reginald could not recover his costs under the law prior to 1972 because the owner of a house was not liable to the purchaser of the property. Botchitt Construction plc was the original builder/ owner of Reginald's house and is therefore not liable to him.

b Section 3 of the Defective Premises Act 1972 made builders and owners liable to the purchasers of their property for negligence and work of defective quality. The limitation period was six years from the completion of the work. Botchitt Construction plc are prima facie liable to Reginald under the Act but as it is over six years since the building was completed the limitation period will prevent him from recovering his costs.

c The common law and limitation period under *Dutton* are the same as those under the Defective Premises Act 1972; Reginald will be unable to recover.

d The common law limitation period under *Spraham-Souter* was extended to six years from the date on which the damage might reasonably have been discovered. Although the cracks began to appear in 1975, Reginald did not discover them until 1979. Given that the cracks appeared in the loft it may be reasonable that Reginald did not discover them until four years later in which case the limitation period will run from 1979 allowing Reginald to commence his action in 1982.

e In *Pirelli General* the common law limitation period was held to run from the date on which the damage actually occurred. The date of 1975 in this situation is seven years from the time at which Reginald decides to sue Botchitt Construction plc and is therefore one year outside the limitation period.

22 **a** Examples: 'political considerations' (meaning the priorities of government) and 'mechanism of the legislative process' (meaning availability of parliamentary time).

b To 'the way in which responsibility . . . departments' in sentence (3).

23 **a**

Lord Chancellor
- Civil courts
- Crown Court
- Appoints people who sit in courts & tribunals

Home Office
- Magistrates' courts
- Police
- Appoints, e.g. immigration adj.'s

b Home Office

Agencies for controlling and ordering, e.g. police, prison service, immigration

Minister of Justice

Agencies to provide justice, e.g. to control abuses & errors of controlling agencies (under the Home Office)

c i Because immigrants are appealing against decisions made by the Home Office.

ii Because many adjudicators come from the Colonial Service or Civil Service and (he says) may be anti-immigrant.

d Because local authorities are often being sued by law centres' clients.

24 Refers back to 'other departments besides the Lord Chancellor's Department'.

25 Minister of Justice:
a administration of court staff in England;
d study of need for law reform;
f study of law reform in England and overseas.

Home Office:
b general administration work related to justice.

Lord Chancellor:
c judicial work;
e principal legal adviser to government.

26 Arguments for Minister of Justice:
a Haldane committee:
i difficult to get government's attention to law reform (see lines 8–9);
ii total inadequacy of organisation which controls general administration of very large staffs (see lines 10–11).

Arguments against Minister of Justice:
a Lord Hailsham: 'menace to independence of courts and judiciary'.

Counter-arguments:
i No need for the power to appoint and promote judges to be removed from Lord Chancellor.
ii Control of administrative arrangements by Lord Chancellor's department has been increasing and no one suggests that judges are less independent as a result.

b Possible argument: Minister of Justice might be a political minister in House of Commons and lose his independence.

Counter-argument: Home Secretary already does many of the duties of a Minister of Justice and he does not try and control the criminal courts.

27 Proposals for law reform have not failed just because there is no Minister of Justice; in fact the Law Commission's proposals have been made law without 'undue difficulty or delay'. Also, having one responsible Minister would not ensure that he or she was more receptive than two or more separate ministers. (See lines 67–8 and 76.)

28 a Since Professor Jackson changed his mind, the Lord Chancellor has shown very little interest in the Law Commission.

b Law Commission reports have not received attention because the Lord Chancellor's department has not succeeded in interesting other departments which were involved. For example, the Department of the Environment would not spend time on bills which were not politically useful.

Chapter 10

1 a To define 'human rights' in the 21 West European states.
b To provide a defence against communism.
c To prevent war between member states.

2 a Means 'driving force'.
b Means 'defence'.
c The international community.
d Violations of human rights.

3 Because in a settlement the state which was complained about agrees to act and must therefore satisfy the Commission that it has done so; an adverse judgment can only apply moral pressure on a state.

4 a subsequently (line 10)
b in view (line 17)
c with a view to (line 3)
d deliberations (line 2)
e an undertaking (line 13)
f ventilation (line 14)
g to implement (line 13)
h comprised (line 12)
i as a result (line 7)
j to submit (lines 4–5)
k placed itself at the disposal of (lines 2–3)

5 a No
b Yes
c Yes
d Yes

6 It expresses the opinion of the Law Lords.

7 a It refers to the situation where newspaper writers make judgments about cases which are still being dealt with in the courts, with the possible outcome that decisions made in the courts are influenced by the resulting public opinion.

b **i** People may think that it is easy to find the truth of a case if newspapers appear to be doing so and they may therefore not respect the legal process.

ii If the media judge, then unpopular people and causes will do badly.

8 **a** Distillers and *The Sunday Times*.

b 'Maintaining the authority and impartiality of the judiciary'.

c 'It implies the existence of a "pressing social need"'.

9 Although

10 **a** Section 5 of the Contempt of Court Act.

b A substantial risk of severe prejudice to proceedings.

c That the prejudice is only 'incidental' to a wider discussion of public interest.

d **i** level of public concern; **ii** importance of the issue; **iii** interests of those involved.

11 **c** . . . took no action.

d ST sent draft of 2nd article to A.G. Presented both sides of argument.

e A.G. granted injunction by HC because article implied negligence of D and w'd create a serious risk of interference with D's freedom of action in the litigation.

f ST appealed to CA. Successful (1973). Denning:

1. 'Public interest counter-balances private interest of the parties'.
2. Litigation not pending but dormant.

g A.G. appealed to HL. Successful (1974):

1. Case not dormant.
2. Not permissible to prejudge in pending cases regardless of risk of prejudicing proceedings.

h ST took case to ECHR. Successful. Public interest in freedom of expression outweighed social need to maintain authority of judiciary. Article 10 violated by HL decision.

13 **a** By influencing the members of a future jury which might hear the case.

b By putting pressure on either party to the dispute to reach a settlement on terms with which they do not agree.

c By discouraging a potential litigant from pursuing legal action.

14 It can be argued that judges, by reason of their training and professional background are less likely to be influenced by pre-trial publicity than potential jurors and that the *sub judice* rule should be applied less strictly when a case is to be heard before a single judge or bench of judges.

15 The Court of Appeal decided that freedom of expression and the interest of the public in being informed of the details of the thalidomide tragedy outweighed the interests of Distillers in obtaining a settlement.

16 The House of Lords was primarily concerned over the threat of trial by newspaper, that is the case would be decided in the mind of the public without the formality of a proper trial.

17 Under the blanket ban imposed by the House of Lords the media knew that it could not publish anything which was relevant to an individual case. Section 2 of the Contempt of Court Act permits relevant material to be published providing it does not create a substantial risk of severely prejudicing a case. This test is less certain than a blanket ban on all pre-trial publicity.

18 **a** Margaret will be guilty of contempt of court under section 2 if her pamphlet creates a substantial risk of severely prejudicing Dr Loveday's trial. This situation illustrates the need, under section 2, to judge each case individually. Abortion is a very sensitive issue and Margaret's pamphlet could prejudice a potential juror against Dr Loveday, but remember that the test is one of severe prejudice. This could be determined by the tone of the pamphlet: if it is written in emotive language it is more likely to be severely prejudicial than a reasoned statement of facts. Its publication a week before Dr Loveday's trial does create a risk of prejudice – any publication will do so – but the pamphlet has not been widely distributed. It was only sent to people who, by reason of their membership of the Anti-Abortion Society, would already hold strong views on the subject. You will also need to consider the defence under section 5 of the pamphlet being incidental to the trial, that is it does not refer to the facts of Dr Loveday's trial but is about the general issue of abortion.

b *The Daily Sludge*: The publication of Crank's medical records and previous convictions certainly has the potential to create a substantial risk of severely prejudicing his case. Relevant factors would be whether he is to be tried by a jury and whether the newspaper was published nationally or locally, and, if the latter, whether it was in the locality in which the trial was to take place. There is no defence available under section 5 as the article was directly about Crank and not incidental to his case.

The Sunday Investigator: Although this article has been written as a response to Crank's actions its central focus is on the security system at the House of Commons which is incidental to Crank's case.

19 **a** Neither. It is the opinion of those (unnamed) people who favour incorporating the Convention into British law.

b '. . . it would necessarily give the judges wider powers' (see lines 14–15).

20 **'Less respectable arguments':**

For: 1. W'd save Britain international embarrassment.
2. Human rights w'd be better protected.

Against: 1. Govt. resents increased interference by lawyers & judges in govt. activity & plans.

'More respectable arguments':

Against: 1. Politicising of judges: they w'd make decisions about society which Parliament usually makes.
2. W'd lead to relitigation of settled rules with only lawyers benefiting from increased work.

22 Means 'acting together'.

23 **European Parliament:**

1. . . . created.
2. . . . 1st direct elections.
3. . . . advisory, supervisory; now plays part in legislation & budgetary control.

Council:

1. Consists of one voting delegate from each member State but other relevant officials may attend.
2. Function: coordinates general econ. policies & has power to take decisions.
3. If voting is unanimous it can override Parliament's opposition or amend Commission's proposals.

Commission:

1. Consists of 2 members from France, Germany, Italy, the UK & Spain and 1 from each of the other countries.
2. Members chosen on basis of their competence & independence.
3. Functions:
   - initiates action
   - acts as Community watchdog
   - acts as executive
   - acts as negotiator with external bodies

ECJ:

1. Function: to decide on matters of constitutional, admin., social & econ. law brought directly to it or from national courts.
2. Consists of 13 judges & President + 5 advocates-general; a-g's present analysis of facts & law & make recommendations.
3. Interprets Treaties using diff. methods from English law i.e. tries to interpret spirit of law rather than using historical precedent. Its judgments are much briefer than Eng. ones & give little background to the decision.
4. Basic diff. between EC & other international organisations = EC is involved in member states' **internal** legal relations, int'l org. usually involved in **external** relations.

24 The *Official Journal* of the Communities.

25 1. a) E.Coal & Steel Community Treaty
b) Euratom Treaty
c) EEC Treaty

Directly applicable? Yes.
Can validity be challenged? No.

2.

a)	regulations	directly appl.
b)	decisions	may be directly appl.
c)	directives	not directly appl. (unless they fulfil certain criteria)
d)	recommendations	not directly appl.
e)	opinions	not directly appl.

Can validity be challenged? Yes.

26 Refers to 'obligation'.

27 Refers to 'a clause'.

28 The three original Treaties, regulations, directives and decisions, and the recommendations and opinions of the Council of Ministers and the European Commission.

29 Primary European Community law is contained in the original Treaties; that found in the other sources of law is secondary.

30 European Community law which has direct effect becomes part of British law without the need for further enactment by the British Parliament. The original Treaties and regulations are directly effective; decisions and directives may be directly effective in some circumstances.

31 A directive will have direct effect when it involves individual rights.

32 Under section 2(1) all European Community law having direct effect will become part of British law without further enactment, and under section 2(4) all other legislation passed by the British Parliament will take account of Britain's Community obligations.

33 The High Court referred the Merchant Shipping Act 1988 to the ECJ under Article 177 for a decision as to whether it conflicted with European law. This procedure can take up to two years, and if the ECJ decided that the Act did conflict with European law the applicants would have lost considerable business during the referral period because of legislation which was invalid.

34 The effect of granting interim relief was to suspend legislation which had been approved by Parliament.

35 The sovereignty of the British Parliament was diminished by the passing of the European Communities Act 1972. The decision of the ECJ in *Factortame* was a logical consequence of that legislation and did not further diminish Parliament's sovereignty.

36 **a** The referral will be made under Article 177 of the EEC Treaty which seeks to ensure uniformity of European Community law in all the member states.
b Under the guidelines established by Lord Denning in *Bulmer* v. *Bollinger* a referral will be made to the ECJ under Article 177 where there is uncertainty over the meaning of the law, where the legal point in question is necessary to decide the case, where the facts are clear and where there has been no previous ruling on the same legal point.
c As a result of the ECJ ruling in the *Factortame* case, the High Court has the power to suspend the enforcement of the Public Health (Meat Inspection) Act until the ECJ judgment on its validity under European law. The financial hardship which will be suffered by International Importers (UK) Ltd during the period of referral would result in injustice if the legislation was held to be invalid.

37 **a** wages
b salary
c at piece rates
d in kind
e consideration

38 . . . 'where the woman **is employed** on like work with a man in the same employment'.

39 1. . . . 1(2) of the Equal Pay Act 1970.
2. . . . section 1(2) of the Equal Pay Act 1970 and also at sections 1 & 6(1) & (2) of the Sex Discrimination Act 1975.
3. . . . that Section 1(2) had in mind men and women employed at the same time.
4. . . . to offer less benefits to a woman who succeeds a man in the same job.
5. . . . the 1970 Act sh'd be interpreted to apply also to a woman who succeeds a man.

40 Notice his signpost words: **a first** (line 14), **b further** (line 21) and **c secondly** (line 34):
a more convenient and cheaper than the HL;
b Parliament's sovereignty is not infringed;
c considers himself legally bound not to guess how the ECJ w'd construe art. 119 but to ask them.

41 **a** **i** Qualitative – the type of work being done.
ii Contemporaneity – the fact of a man and woman working at the same time on a similar job.
b Consecutively.
c No, not if there are factors which are unconnected with sexual discrimination.

42 The literal rule: the use of the word 'is' could only be interpreted to mean that the Act only applied to men and women employed at the same time.

43 The Sex Discrimination Act disallows discrimination between men and women in all matters of employment except wages which are covered by the Equal Pay Act 1970. It would be contrary to the provisions of the Sex Discrimination Act to discriminate unfairly between women and men in consecutive employment. By reading the two Acts as a 'harmonious whole' Lord Denning applies the same principle to section 1(2)(a)(i) of the Equal Pay Act.

44 Article 177 states that a national court from which there is no appeal must make a referral to the ECJ when there is uncertainty over the interpretation of Community law. A referral is discretionary in other courts. As a further appeal was available to the House of Lords there was no obligation on the Court of Appeal to make the referral.

45 As an Article of one of the original Treaties, Article 199 has direct effect in English law.

46 **a** Alice's case will first be heard before an industrial tribunal.
b She may appeal to the Employment Appeals Tribunal then further to the Court of Appeal and the House of Lords.
c The relevant factors in deciding the case will be **i** the level of skill: Alice has undergone a training programme for the same length of time as Ted – this would suggest that the level of skill required for their respective jobs is the same; **ii** the level of responsibility: both have a high level of responsibility in that they are required to supervise staff and control the standards of the products they produce. They are both required to take decisions which could affect those standards; **iii** effort: Ted's responsibilities include some night work but he works less hours each week than Alice and this could be seen as equal effort.

47 **a** to violate a convention
b to implement changes
c to comply with a decision
d to strike the correct balance
e to issue a writ for damages
f to infringe someone's rights
g to overstep the bounds
h to resolve a conflict
i to fill the gap
j to invade someone's privacy
k to fulfil certain criteria
l to give priority
m to confer rights

Appendix A
The Courts and Legal Services Act 1990

Since the Courts and Legal Services Act received the Royal Assent in November 1990, the Lord Chancellor, Lord Mackay has issued a number of orders implementing some of its provisions. This appendix provides a summary of these orders; you should take them into account when reading the relevant chapters in the book and in answering the questions. Cross references are are provided to the relevant sections in the book.

1 The financial limit on the jurisdiction of the county courts will be removed on 1 July 1991. After that date all personal injuries cases involving a claim less than £50,000 will be heard in the county court. (See 4.2, 4.2.2.)

2 County court registrars have been renamed 'district judges'. (See 4.2.1.)

3 The small claims arbitration limit will be increased to £5,000 with a provision for personal injury cases to be assessed by a district judge in order to determine whether a full trial would be more appropriate. (See 4.2.1, 4.2.2.)

4 New rules of procedure will be introduced in the small claims court to allow the district judge to take a more interventionist role. (See 4.2.1.)

5 Lay representation will be allowed in some cases in the small claims court. (See 4.2.1.)

6 Compulsory pre-trial exchange of witness statements will be introduced. (See 4.2.2.)

7 The progress of cases will be monitored although this will not be implemented in the immediate future. (See 4.2.2.)

8 The first Legal Services Ombudsman took up his position in January 1991. (See 6.1.1.)

9 Lord Griffiths, a Law Lord, has been appointed to chair the Advisory Committee on Legal Education and Conduct; it is expected that this Committee will begin its work by mid-1991. (See 6.1.1.)

10 Appointments to the Authorised Conveyancing Practitioners Board will be made by mid-1991 and should be in a position to receive applications by the autumn of that year. (See 6.1.1.)

11 The first ex-solicitors have been appointed as judges in the High Court under the new rules of eligibility. (See 5.1.3.)

Appendix B
The Criminal Justice Act 1990

In February 1991, the Court of Appeal heard a further appeal in the case of the 'Birmingham Six'. Evidence was presented to show that the two main elements of the prosecution's case in the original trial were seriously flawed. First, the forensic tests which had been used to show that the defendants had handled explosives were not scientifically accurate; a positive reaction had been achieved from people who had handled playing cards and adhesive tape. Secondly, modern scientific tests proved that the police records of interviews with the defendants after their arrest had been fabricated and the police officers involved had lied about the interviews at the original trial. In March 1991 the Court of Appeal quashed the conviction of the six men and they were released from prison. At the same time the government announced the setting up of a Royal Commission on criminal justice. It will be the task of the Commission to investigate all aspects of the criminal justice system and to make recommendations for its reform.

In May 1991 the Court of Appeal also began to hear a fresh appeal in the case of the 'MacGuire Seven'. As with the Birmingham Six, the appeal has been based on the unreliability of the forensic evidence which led to the original convictions. It is expected that the Court of Appeal will allow the appeal and quash the convictions. (See 4.3.3.)

Appendix C
The European Community

On 25 July 1991 the European Court of Justice delivered its judgment in the case of *Factortame Ltd and ors* v. *Secretary of State for Transport (No 3)*. The Court acknowledged that whilst individual Member States had the power to determine the conditions for the registration of vessels which had the right to fly their flag, this power must be exercised in accordance with Community law. Article 52 of the EEC Treaty provides for freedom of establishment ('the right to take up and pursue activities as self-employed persons') and prohibits discrimination on the grounds of nationality. The requirement under the Merchant Shipping Act 1988 that owners and operators of vessels and directors and shareholders of fishing companies should be resident and domiciled in the United Kingdom was contrary to these provisions of Article 52.

Reaction to the judgment was predictable; some argued that the sovereignty of parliament had been seriously undermined and parliament was no longer free to pass any legislation which it chose to. Perhaps more realistically others pointed to section 2(4) of the European Communities Act 1972 and concluded that the ECJ judgment was only a practical and predictable illustration of the meaning of its provisions. (See 10.5.2.)

Bibliography

* Indicates books which are not extracted but given as additional reading references.

Allen, M., Thompson, B. and Walsh, B., *Cases and Materials on Constitutional and Administrative Law* (London: Blackstone Press, 1990)

* Atiyah, P.S., *The Rise and Fall of Freedom of Contract* (Oxford: Clarendon Press, 1979)

* Baldwin, J. and McConville, M., *Jury Trials* (Oxford: Clarendon Press, 1979)

Bailey, S.H., Harris, D.J, and Jones, B.L., *Civil Liberties: Cases and Materials* (London: Butterworths, 1980)

Beale, H.G., Bishop, W.D. and Furmston, M.P., *Contract Cases and Materials* (London: Butterworths, 1990)

* Bird, R., *Osborn's Concise Law Dictionary,* 7th edn (London: Sweet and Maxwell, 1983)

Birks, M. *Small claims in the county court – how to sue and defend actions without a solicitor,* Form EX 50C (London: Lord Chancellor's Department, 1981)

Bradney, A., Fisher, V., Masson, J., Neal, A. and Newell, D., *How to Study Law* (London: Sweet and Maxwell, 1986)

Brazier, M. (ed.), *Street on Torts,* 8th edn (London: Butterworths, 1988)

* Card, R. (ed.), *Cross, Jones and Card, Introduction to Criminal Law,* 11th edn (London and Edinburgh: Butterworths, 1988)

Carleton, Sir A., *Legal Duties and Other Essays in Jurisprudence* (Oxford: Clarendon Press, 1931)

Cretney, S., 'The politics of law reform' (1985) 48 *MLR* 493 (Oxford: Blackwell)

Cross, R., *Precedent in English Law,* 3rd edn (Oxford: Clarendon Press, 1977)

* Davies, F.R., *Contract,* 5th edn (London: Sweet and Maxwell, 1986)

* Denning, Lord, *The Discipline of the Law* (London: Butterworths, 1979)

* Denning, Lord, *What Next in the Law* (London: Butterworths, 1982)

* Denning, Lord, *The Closing Chapter* (London: Butterworths, 1983)

* Denning, Lord, 'The independence of the judiciary', in *The Lawyer and Justice* (London: Sweet and Maxwell, 1978)

* Denning, Lord, 'Misuse of power', in *What Next in the Law* (London: Butterworths, 1982)

* Devlin, P., *The Enforcement of Morals* (Oxford and New York: Oxford University Press, 1965)

* Devlin, P., *The Judge* (Oxford: Oxford University Press, 1979)

* Devlin, P., 'Judges, governments and politics', (1978) 41 *MLR* 501

* Dobson, P. and Fitzpatrick, B. (eds), *The Observer Book of Moots* (London: Sweet and Maxwell, 1986)

* Downes, A., *Textbook on Contract* (London: Blackstone Press, 1987)

Dugdale, A.M., Furmston, M.P., Jones, S.P., Sharin, C.H. and Stanton, K.M., *A Level Law* (London and Edinburgh: Butterworths, 1983)

Dyer, C., 'Barristers' rights go in strategic reforms', *The Guardian,* 8 December 1989

Elliot, D.W. and Allen, M.J., *Elliot and Wood's Casebook on Criminal Law,* 5th edn (London: Sweet and Maxwell, 1989)

* Ercman, S., *Guide to Case Law* (Vienna: Wilhelm Braumuller, 1981)

Farrar, J.H. and Dugdale, A.M., *Introduction to Legal Method,* 2nd edn (London: Sweet and Maxwell, 1984)

Furmston, M.P., *Cheshire, Fifoot and Furmston's Law of Contract,* 11th edn (London: Butterworths, 1986)

* Ganz, G., *Understanding Public Law* (London: Fontana, 1987)

Griffiths, J.G., *The Politics of the Judiciary,* 3rd edn (London: Fontana, 1985)

Gifford, T. *Where's the Justice: A Manifesto of Law Reform* (Harmondsworth: Penguin, 1986)

Hailsham, Lord, *Hamlyn Revisited* (London: Stevens, 1983)

Hansen, O., 'A limiting franchise on giving legal aid', *The Guardian,* 22 September 1989

* Hardy Ivamy, E.R., *Mozley and Whiteley's Law Dictionary,* 10th edn (London, Sydney and Toronto: Butterworths, 1988)

* Harris, P., *Introduction to Law*, 2nd edn (London: Weidenfeld & Nicholson, 1984)
* Hart, H.L.A., *Law, Liberty and Morality* (Oxford and New York: Oxford University Press, 1963)
Hogan, B., Seago, P. and Bennett, G., *A Level Law*, 2nd edn (London: Sweet and Maxwell, 1988)
* Holland, J. A. and Webb, J. S., *Learning Legal Rules* (London: Blackstone Press, 1991)
* Hood Phillips, P., *Leading Cases in Constitutional and Administrative Law*, 6th edn (London: Sweet and Maxwell, 1988)
Ingham, T., *The English Legal Process*, 3rd edn (London: Blackstone Press, 1990)
James, P.S., *Introduction to English Law*, 11th edn (London: Butterworths, 1985)
Johnson, N., *Contract Law in Action* (Oxford: Oxford Polytechnic, 1986)
Johnson, N. and Pannett, A., *SWOT A Level Law* (London: Blackstone Press, 1988)
Lasok, D. and Bridge, J.W., *Law and Institutions of the European Communities*, 4th edn (London: Butterworths, 1988)
Law Society, *Law Society Gazette*, No. 6, 14 February 1990
* McCluskey, Lord, *Law, Justice and Democracy* (London: BBC, 1987)
* McKenzie Stuart, Lord, *The European Communities and the Rule of Law* (London: Stevens, 1977)
* Martin, E.A. (ed.), *The Concise Dictionary of Law*, 2nd edn (Oxford and New York: Oxford University Press, 1990)
* Montesquieu, Charles de Secondat, baron de, *De L'Esprit des Lois* (Paris: Klincksieck, 1982)
Moxon, D., *Managing Criminal Justice* (London: HMSO, 1985)
Pannett, A., *Criminal Law in Action* (Oxford: Oxford Polytechnic, 1986)
Pearce, D.C., *Statutory Interpretation in Australia* (Melbourne, Sydney and Brisbane: Butterworths, 1974)
* Plender, R., *Plender and Ushers's Cases and Materials on the Law of the European Communities*, 2nd edn (London: Butterworths, 1989)
* Raistrick, D., *Index to Legal Citations and Abbreviations* (Abingdon: Professional Books, 1981)
Scarman, L., *Law Reform: The New Pattern* (London: Routledge & Kegan Paul, 1968)
Seago, P., *Criminal Law*, 3rd edn (London and Edinburgh: Sweet and Maxwell, 1989)
Sim, R.S. and Scott, D.M.M., *A Level English Law*, 6th edn (London: Butterworths, 1984)
Smith, J.C. and Hogan, B., *Criminal Law*, 6th edn (London and Edinburgh: Butterworths, 1988)
* Smith, P.F. and Bailey, S.H., *The Modern English Legal System* (London: Sweet and Maxwell, 1984)
Spencer, J.R. (ed.), *Jackson's Machinery of Justice*, 8th edn (Cambridge: Cambridge University Press, 1989)
Stein, P., *Legal Institutions: The Development of Dispute Settlement* (London: Butterworths, 1984)
Steiner, J., *Textbook on EEC Law* (London: Blackstone Press, 1988)
* Street, H. and Brazier, R. (eds), *de Smith, Constitutional and Administrative Law*, 4th edn (Harmondsworth: Penguin, 1981)
Treitel, G.H., *The Law of Contract*, 7th edn (London: Stevens, 1987)
* Treitel, G.H., *An Outline of the Law of Contract*, 4th edn (London: Butterworths, 1989)
* Twining, W. and Miers, D., *How to Do Things with Rules*, 2nd edn (London: Weidenfeld & Nicholson, 1982)
Wade, E.C.S. and Bradley, A.W., *Constitutional and Administrative Law*, 10th edn (London and New York: Longman, 1985)
Walker, R.J., *Walker and Walker, The English Legal System*, 6th edn (London: Butterworths, 1985)
White, R.C.A., *The Administration of Justice* (Oxford: Blackwell, 1985)
Williams, G., *Learning the Law*, 11th edn (London: Stevens, 1982)
Wilson, G., *Cases and Materials on the English Legal System* (London: Sweet and Maxwell, 1973)
Winfield, P.H., 'Some aspects of offer and acceptance', (1939) 55 *LQR* 499 (London: Sweet and Maxwell)

* Yardley, D.C.M., *Introduction to British Constitutional Law*, 7th edn (London, Dublin and Edinburgh: Butterworths, 1990)

Yardley, D.C.M., *Principles of Administrative Law*, 2nd edn (London: Butterworths, 1981)

Zander, M., *Cases and Materials on the English Legal System*, 5th edn (London: Weidenfeld & Nicholson, 1988)

Zander, M. *The Law-Making Process*, 2nd edn (London: Weidenfeld & Nicholson, 1985)

* Zander, M., *A Matter of Justice* (London: Tauris, 1987)

Glossary of legal terms

The words, pronunciations and definitions listed below refer to words used in the book and reflect meaning in a legal context only. For other, more general meanings, you are advised to consult a good monolingual dictionary.

ab initio (Latin) [æb ɪn'ɪʃɪəʊ] from the beginning
to abuse [ə'bju:z] to make a wrong use of
abuse (noun) [ə'bju:s] wrong use
accountable [ə'kaʊntəbl] responsible
accusatorial [əkju:zə'tɔ:rɪəl] (= adversarial) system of justice where judges do not investigate a case but reach a decision based on evidence presented by both sides
acquittal [ə'kwɪtl] judgment of not guilty
to address [ə'dres] to deal with (e.g. a problem)
to adhere to [əd'hɪə] to follow, obey
ad hoc (Latin) [ˌæd 'hɒk] organised when the need arises, not permanent
ad infinitum (Latin) [ˌæd ɪnfə'naɪtəm] without end
adjectival (law) [ædʒɪk'taɪvl] rules governing procedure
to adjudicate [ə'dʒu:dɪkeɪt] to give judgment
adultery [ə'dʌltərɪ] sexual intercourse where at least one partner is married to a third person
adversarial [ædvə'seərɪəl] see accusatorial
aegis (Latin) ['i:dʒɪs] under the aegis of = organised by
agent ['eɪdʒənt] person or organisation acting on behalf of someone
albeit [ɔ:l'bi:ɪt] although
to amalgamate [ə'mælgəmeɪt] to combine, unite
ambiguous [æm'bɪgjuəs] having more than one meaning, of uncertain meaning
ambit ['æmbɪt] scope
anomalous [ə'nɒmələs] differing from the normal
anomaly [ə'nɒməlɪ] something which is different from the normal type
to antagonise [æn'tægənaɪz] to make an enemy of someone; to irritate
apolitical [ˌeɪpə'lɪtɪkl] without political connections
to appeal [ə'pɪəl] to take a case to a higher court in the hope of a new decision
to apprehend [æprɪ'hend] to fear
arbitration [ɑ:bɪ'treɪʃn] settlement of a dispute
arson ['ɑ:sn] act of starting a fire intentionally and unlawfully
assent [ə'sent] agreement (by the Crown to a Bill in Parliament)
to attribute [ə'trɪbju:t] to consider to result from
audience (rights of) ['ɔ:dɪəns] the right to prosecute or defend in court

backlog ['bæklɒg] business still to be attended to
Bar [bɑ:] barristers
bargain ['bɑ:gən] an agreement to exchange
baron ['bærən] a noble
Bench [bentʃ] the judges
blasphemy ['blæsfəmɪ] irreverent reference to God or religious matters
on board ['ɒn 'bɔ:d] on a ship
bona fide (Latin) [ˌbəʊnə 'faɪdɪ] genuine
bound to ['baʊnd tu:] compelled to
to breach [bri:tʃ] to break
brief [bri:f] background and instructions for a case
to bring to bear ['brɪŋ tə ˌbeə] to apply
burglary ['bɜ:glərɪ] breaking into premises, intending to steal something or harm someone

in camera (Latin) [ɪn 'kæmrə] in private
circuit (judges) ['sɜ:kɪt] judges who travel to provincial courts
civil (law) ['sɪvl] law which regulates the relationships between individuals or bodies
to codify ['kəʊdɪfaɪ] to collect and set down systematically
to coerce [kəʊ'ɜ:s] to force
coercive [kəʊ'ɜ:sɪv] compulsory
coincidence [kəʊ'ɪnsɪdəns] happening at the same time
collegiate [kə'li:dʒɪət] collective, i.e. speaking for all judges
common law [ˌkɒmən 'lɔ:] law based on decisions made by judges in previous cases
common to ['kɒmən] shared by
competence ['kɒmpɪtəns] legal capacity
to comprise [kəm'praɪz] to be composed of
in concert [ɪn 'kɒnsət] acting together

to confer [kən'fɜ:] to grant
consideration [kənsɪdə'reɪʃn] a payment or benefit, given or received under a contract
to constrain [kən'streɪn] to force
to construe [kən'stru:] to interpret, explain
contempt of court [kənˌtemt əv 'kɔ:t] disobedience of the orders of the court; behaviour likely to interfere with the administration of justice
contention [kən'tenʃn] argument
contentious [kən'tenʃəs] likely to cause an argument
continental [kɒntɪ'nentl] relating to the mainland part of Europe
to contravene ['kɒntrəvi:n] to go against
contributory (noun) [kən'trɪbjʊtrɪ] person liable to contribute towards the cost
convention [kən'venʃn] custom based on general agreement
to convict [kən'vɪkt] to declare in a law court that a person is guilty
corpse [kɔ:ps] dead body
culpable ['kʌlpəbl] deserving punishment

damages ['dæmɪdʒɪz] money paid in compensation in a civil action
to deem [di:m] to consider as
defect (noun) ['di:fekt] imperfection, fault
defendant [dɪ'fendənt] person against whom legal action is brought
demise [dɪ'maɪz] death
detrimental [detrɪ'mentl] harmful
disbursement [dɪs'bɜ:smənt] payment
discrete [dɪs'kri:t] separate, distinct
discretionary (remedy) [dɪs'kreʃnrɪ] not available as of right
discrimination [dɪskrɪmɪ'neɪʃn] unfair treatment of an individual or group of people on grounds of race, sex, etc.
disinterested [dɪs'ɪntrestɪd] not influenced by personal feelings
disparate ['dɪspərət] dissimilar
dispassionate [dɪs'pæʃənət] impartial, calm
in dispute [ɪn dɪs'pju:t] in opposition to each other
to dissent [dɪ'sent] to disagree with
to distinguish [dɪs'tɪŋgwɪʃ] to point out differences of fact between two separate cases
dormant ['dɔ:mənt] inactive
draft [drɑ:ft] outline or rough copy
in due course [ɪn 'dju: 'kɔ:s] when the right time comes

ejusdem generis (Latin) [eɪ'jʊsdəm 'dʒenərɪs] of the same type
eligibility [elɪdʒə'bɪlətɪ] suitability to be chosen
to this end [tə 'ðɪs 'end] for this purpose
to ensue[ɪn'sju:] to happen as a result
entrenched [ɪn'trentʃt] firmly established
to envisage [ɪn'vɪzɪdʒ] to expect
equitable ['ekwɪtəbl] just, fair
equity ['ekwɪtɪ] 1. the application of principles of justice; 2. body of law developed by the Court of Chancery
equivocal [ɪ'kwɪvəkl] having a doubtful meaning
estopped [ɪ'stɒpt] prevented by law
eventual [ɪ'ventʃʊəl] finally resulting
evidence ['evɪdəns] information given in court
to evolve [ɪ'vɒlv] to develop gradually
ex gratia (Latin) [eks 'greɪʃə] as a favour
ex parte (Latin) [eks 'pɑ:teɪ] on behalf of
expedience [ɪk'spɪ:dɪəns] an advantageous way
to expound [ɪk'spaʊnd] to explain, interpret
express (adj.) [ɪk'spres] explicit
extra-court [ekstrə'kɔ:t] outside the court

fallacious [fə'leɪʃəs] based on error, misleading
to find for ['faɪnd fɔ:] to decide in favour of
fit [fɪt] suitable
flexible ['fleksɪbl] adaptable
forthwith [fɔ:θ'wɪð] at once
to frame [freɪm] to construct
to fuse [fju:z] to join

grievance ['gri:vəns] (sense of) injustice
on the grounds that [ɒn ðə 'graʊndʒ dət] for the reason that
guidelines ['gaɪdlaɪnz] a statement of policy
guilty ['gɪltɪ] having committed a crime

habeas corpus (Latin) [heɪbjəs 'kɔ:pəs] order requiring a person who detains another to justify that detention to the courts
to hamper ['hæmpə] to make difficult, obstruct
hardly ['hɑ:dlɪ] almost not
headnote ['hednəʊt] summary of judgment at the beginning of a law report
hearing ['hɪərɪŋ] trial
held [held] used to introduce the judgment in a case
hence [hens] as a result, therefore
hierarchy ['haɪərɑ:kɪ] organisation with levels of authority from highest to lowest
hire purchase (H.P.) [haɪə 'pɜ:tʃɪs] system of buying something by paying in instalments
homicide ['hɒmɪsaɪd] killing a human being
homogeneous [hɒmə'dʒi:nɪəs] of the same kind

ibid. (Latin) ['ɪbɪd] in the same book, article, which was already quoted
idiosyncratic [ˌɪdɪəʊsɪŋ'krætɪk] possessing characteristics which belong only to him/herself
immunity [ɪ'mju:nɪtɪ] exemption, safety
impartial [ɪm'pɑ:ʃl] just, fair; not favouring one side more than the other
impediment [ɪm'pedɪmənt] something which obstructs
inadvertent [ɪnəd'vɜ:tənt] careless, unintentional
inception [ɪn'sepʃn] beginning
incidental [ɪnsɪ'dentl] not deliberately done
incompatible [ɪnkəm'pætɪbl] cannot coexist
indemnification [ɪndemnɪfɪ'keɪʃn] compensation for damage
indeterminate [ɪndɪ'tɜ:mɪnət] not fixed, vague
indictable [ɪn'daɪtəbl] an offence that must be dealt with in the Crown Court
indistinct [ɪndɪ'stɪŋkt] not clear
infringement [ɪn'frɪndʒmənt] breaking of a law
injunction [ɪn'dʒʌŋkʃn] court order to do or not to do something
inquisitorial [ɪnkwɪzɪ'tɔ:rɪəl] system of justice where the judge investigates the case and produces evidence
(at the) **instance** (of) ['ɪnstəns] suggestion
(first) **instance** ['ɪnstəns] first place (court where a case is heard for the first time)
instant ['ɪnstənt] present
instrument ['ɪnstrʊmənt] legal document containing statute
interest ['ɪntrəst] advantage, benefit
interim ['ɪntərɪm] temporary
interlocutory [ɪntə'lɒkju:trɪ] intermediate
to intervene [ɪntə'vi:n] to come between; interfere
interventionist [ɪntə'venʃənɪst] having the characteristic of intervening
invalid (adj.) [ɪn'vælɪd] not valid, having no weight or force, e.g. in law
to investigate [ɪn'vestɪgeɪt] to examine
irrational [ɪ'ræʃənl] not based on reason
irreconcilable [ɪrekən'saɪləbl] incapable of being reconciled, incompatible, cannot be made to agree with each other
irrelevant [ɪ'relɪvənt] not applicable to the point
irrespective [ɪrɪ'spektɪv] not taking into account
irrevocable [ɪ'revəkəbl] cannot be altered
(at) **issue** ['ɪʃu:] in dispute

judiciary [dʒu:'dɪʃərɪ] the judges
jurisdiction [dʒʊərɪs'dɪkʃn] extent of legal authority
just (adj.) [dʒʌst] fair, right
just (adv.) [dʒʌst] precisely

(in) **kind** [kaɪnd] payments or benefit not in money

Law Society ['lɔ: sə'saɪətɪ] regulatory body for solicitors
lay (adj.) [leɪ] non-professional, unpaid
legitimate [lɪ'dʒɪtɪmət] lawful, justifiable
to lend itself [lend] to be suited to
liable ['laɪəbl] obliged in law; responsible for
licit ['lɪsɪt] permitted in law
like (adj.) [laɪk] similar
literal (meaning) ['lɪtərəl] usual
litigant ['lɪtɪgənt] someone involved in a lawsuit
locus poenitentiae (Latin) [ˌləʊkəs pəʊnɪ'tensɪeɪ] the right to draw back before concluding a bargain

mandate ['mændeɪt] authority given to a higher power, e.g. by voters to MP
manslaughter ['mænslɔ:tə] the unlawful killing of a person but without malice
marked (difference) [mɑ:kt] clear
material (adj.) [mə'tɪərɪəl] important
mischief ['mɪstʃɪf] wrong
misgiving [mɪs'gɪvɪŋ] doubt
misstatement [mɪs'steɪtmənt] wrong statement

namely ['neɪmlɪ] that is to say
negligent ['neglɪdʒənt] failing to take proper care
negligible ['neglɪdʒəbl] can be ignored; insignificant
nomenclature [nə'menklətʃə] system of naming
notice (to give) ['nəʊtɪs] to give a warning of what will happen
notional ['nəʊʃənl] abstract
notwithstanding [nɒtwɪð'stændɪŋ] nevertheless; in spite of
nuisance ['nju:sns] wrongful interference with another person's enjoyment of normal rights, e.g. use of property

obiter dictum (Latin) [ˌɒbɪtə 'dɪktəm] one of two parts of a judge's judgment, literally 'something said by the way'
to object [əb'dʒekt] to oppose
obsolete ['ɒbsəli:t] out-of-date, no longer used
offeree [ɒfə'ri:] person receiving an offer
ombudsman ['ɒmbʊdzmən] official investigator of complaints by citizens against the executive branch of government
to omit [ə'mɪt] to leave out

op. cit. (Latin) [ˌɒp 'sɪt] in the work already mentioned
to oust [aʊst] to push out
to override [aʊvə'raɪd] to refuse to accept
to overrule [aʊvə'ru:l] to reject, set aside

partial ['pɑ:ʃl] biased in favour of one side
party (the other) ['pɑ:tɪ] the opposing side
pending ['pendɪŋ] waiting to be decided
per incuriam (Latin) [pɜ: rɪn'kjʊərɪəm] through lack of care
per se (Latin) [ˌpɜ: 'seɪ] in itself
piecemeal ['pi:smi:l] one part at a time
piece rates ['pi:s reɪts] (pay) in proportion to the amount produced
plaintiff ['pleɪntɪf] person who brings a civil action in law
potential [pə'tenʃl] possible
preamble [pri:'æmbl] the introductory portion of a statute
to precede [prɪ'si:d] to go before
precedent ['presɪdənt] earlier decision or event which is used as an example to be followed in a later case
to prefer (charges) [prɪ'fɜ:] to bring a matter before a court
prejudicial [predʒʊ'dɪʃl] damaging
prescriptive [prɪ'skrɪptɪv] laying down rules
to prevail [prɪ'veɪl] to win
prima facie (Latin) case [ˌpraɪmə 'feɪʃi:] a case supported by evidence
prior to ['praɪə tʊ] before
probate ['prəʊbeɪt] official proving of a will
procedural (law) [prə'si:dʒərəl] rules governing the conduct of a case
promissory estoppel ['prɒmɪsrɪ ɪ'stɒpl] rule which may prevent a person going back on a promise
propriety [prə'praɪətɪ] correctness of behaviour or morals
to prosecute ['prɒsɪkju:t] to start criminal legal proceedings against someone
providing [prə'vaɪdɪŋ] if, on condition that
puisne (Old French) judge ['pju:nɪ] High Court judge
to purport [pɜ:'pɔ:t] to claim
purposive ['pɜ:pəsɪv] paying attention to the purpose or intention
pursuant [pə'sjʊənt] in accordance with

to quash [kwɒʃ] to set aside, e.g. a wrongful conviction
(not) **quite** [kwaɪt] (not) exactly
quota ['kwəʊtə] a prescribed number or amount

rape [reɪp] forced sexual intercourse without consent
rapporteur (French) [ræpɔ:'tɜ:] person responsible for investigating and reporting to higher committees
to ratify ['rætɪfaɪ] to confirm
ratio (Latin) ['ræsɪəʊ] reason
rational ['ræʃənl] based on reason
recurrence [rɪ'kʌrəns] a repeated happening
to redress [rɪ'dres] to correct
redundant [rɪ'dʌndənt] superfluous, unnecessary
to refrain [rɪ'freɪn] not to do something
Regina (Latin) [rɪ'dʒaɪnə] The Queen
to relegate ['relɪgeɪt] to place in a lower position
relief [rɪ'li:f] the redress of a wrong
remedy ['remɪdɪ] compensation for a wrong
to repudiate [rɪ'pju:dɪeɪt] to refuse to recognise
retrospective [retrə'spektɪv] applying to the past
to reverse [rɪ'vɜ:s] to annul the decision of a lower court

salary ['sælərɪ] payment for work, usually made every month
to sanction ['sænkʃn] 1. to authorise; 2. to punish
sentence ['sentəns] awarding a punishment in a criminal court
shareholder ['ʃeəhəʊldə] person who owns part of a company's capital
to solicit [sə'lɪsɪt] to make a sexual offer for payment
sovereign (adj.) ['sɒvrɪn] possessing supreme power
sovereign (noun) ['sɒvrɪn] king or queen
Speaker ['spi:kə] chairperson of House of Commons or Lords
to speculate ['spekjʊleɪt] to form opinions without complete knowledge
to squat [skwɒt] to occupy (a building) without permission
standing ['stændɪŋ] experience; status
stare decisis (Latin) ['stɑ:rɪ dɪ'saɪsɪs] following precedent
status quo (Latin) [ˌsteɪtəs 'kwəʊ] the existing state of affairs
stigma ['stɪgmə] mark of shame
stipendiary [staɪ'pendərɪ] paid
to strangle ['stræŋgl] to kill by squeezing the throat
stringent ['strɪndʒənt] strict, binding
subjective [səb'dʒektɪv] giving a personal point of view
sub judice (Latin) [ˌsʌb 'dʒu:dɪsɪ] under consideration by a judge
to sublet [sʌb'let] to charge rent to someone else for property which one has rented
subsequent ['sʌbsɪkwənt] later, following
substantive (law) [sʌb'stæntɪv] referring to

the substance of the law rather than to procedure
to subvert [sʌb'vɜ:t] to weaken
to sue [su:] to take civil legal proceedings against someone
to suffice [sə'faɪs] to be sufficient
sui generis (Latin) [su:ɪ 'dʒenərɪs] unique, of its own kind
summary ['sʌmərɪ] less serious offence tried in the magistrates' court
to summon ['sʌmən] to tell someone to appear in court
to supersede [su:pə'si:d] to replace with something else
to suspect [sə'spekt] to be inclined to believe that someone may be guilty

tacit ['tæsɪt] implied, understood though not directly stated
to tap (a telephone) [tæp] to listen to telephone conversations without the permission of the speakers
teleological [ti:lɪə'lɒdʒɪkl] based on doctrine of final results
tenant ['tenənt] person paying rent for use of property
tenure ['tenjʊə] holding a post for an assured period of time
theft [θeft] the act of stealing
thereby [ðeə'baɪ] by that means; in consequence of that
therein [ðeə'rɪn] in that place etc.
thus [ðʌs] in this way; for example
tier [tɪə] level
tort [tɔ:t] civil wrong
travaux préparatoires (French) ['trævəʊ prepærə'twɑ:] preparatory work and discussions
trivial ['trɪvɪəl] small and unimportant

ultra vires (Latin) ['ʌltrə 'vaɪrɪz] beyond the powers of
unanimous [ju:'nænɪməs] in complete agreement
unilaterally [ju:nɪ'lætrəlɪ] done by one side or party only
to usurp [ju:'sɜ:p] to take possession without right

vendor ['vendə] person selling something
to vet [vet] to examine closely
to violate ['vaɪəleɪt] to break
virtually ['vɜ:tʃəlɪ] in fact
viz. (Latin) [vɪz] namely
vocational [və'keɪʃənl] (training) for a specific career
void [vɔɪd] of no legal effect

wages ['weɪdʒɪz] payment for work, usually made weekly
warrant ['wɒrənt] written authority
will [wɪl] legal declaration of how one's property is to be owned after one's death
to withhold [wɪð'həʊld] to keep back
witness ['wɪtnɪs] person who gives evidence in court
writ [rɪt] written order from court ordering someone to do or not to do something; court order commencing legal proceedings

Index